AF342708

AMERICAN PAINTERS ON TECHNIQUE
ON TECHNIQUE
THE COLONIAL PERIOD TO 1860

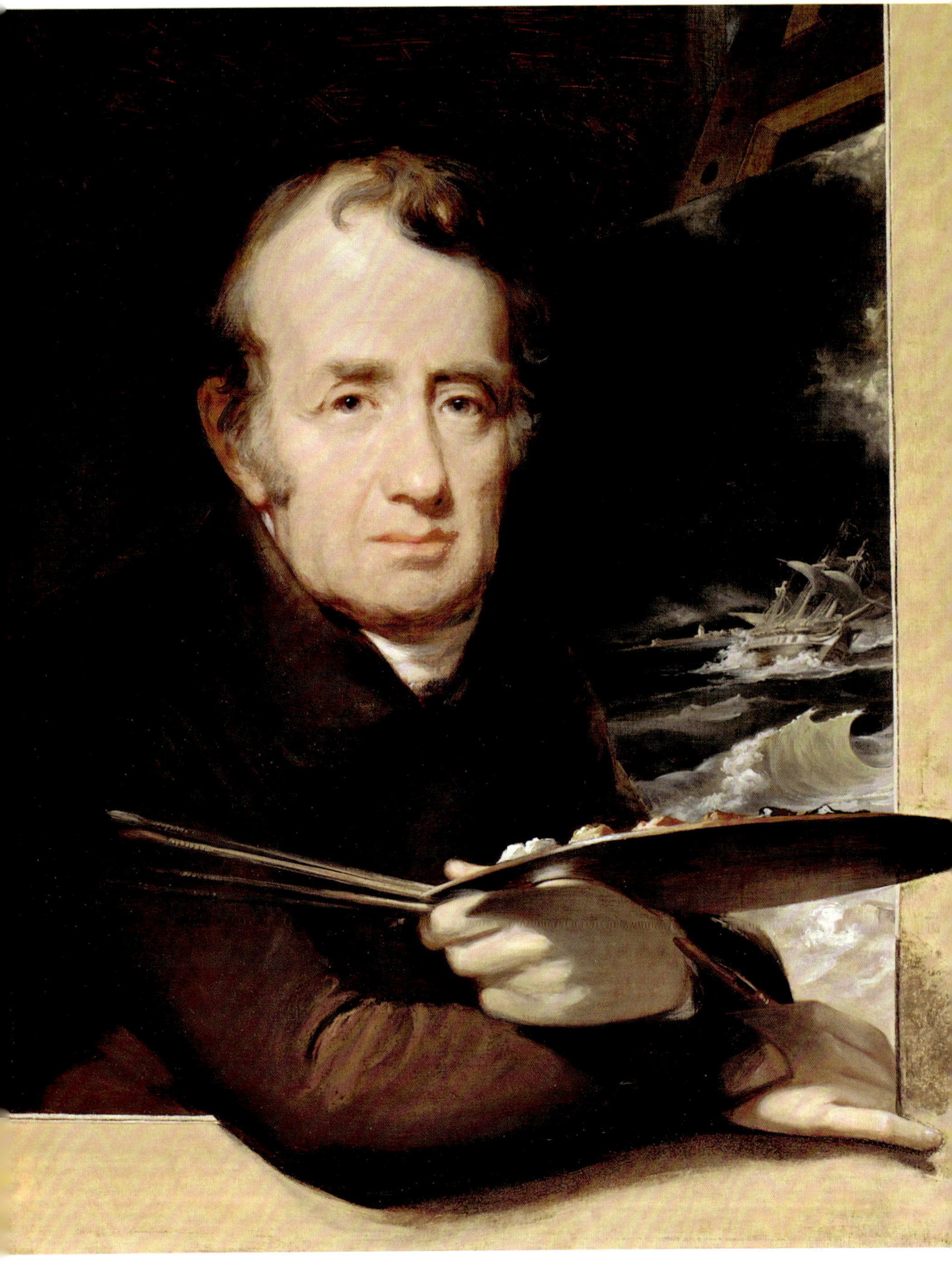

AMERICAN PAINTERS ON TECHNIQUE
THE COLONIAL PERIOD TO 1860

LANCE MAYER AND GAY MYERS

Published by the J. Paul Getty Museum, Los Angeles
Getty Publications
1200 Getty Center Drive, Suite 500
Los Angeles, CA 90049-1682
www.getty.edu/publications

Ann Lucke, *Managing Editor*
Cynthia Newman Edwards, *Manuscript Editor*
Catherine Lorenz, *Designer*
Stacy Miyagawa, *Production Coordinator*

Typesetting by Diane Franco
Printed in China through Asia Pacific Offset, Inc.

Library of Congress Cataloging-in-Publication Data

Mayer, Lance.
  American painters on technique : the colonial period to 1860 / Lance Mayer and Gay Myers.
    p. cm.
  Includes bibliographical references.
  ISBN 978-1-60606-077-3 (hardcover)
  1. Painting--Technique--History. 2. Painting, American. I. Myers, Gay. II. Title.
  ND1471.M39 2011
  751.40973'09033--dc22

                          2011002118

Front cover: William Sidney Mount (American, 1807–1868), *The Painter's Triumph*, 1838. Oil on wood,
49.5 × 59.8 cm (19½ × 23⁹⁄₁₆ in.). Philadelphia, Pennsylvania Academy of the Fine Arts, Bequest of Henry C. Carey
(The Carey Collection), 1879.8.18. Reproduced courtesy of the Pennsylvania Academy of the Fine Arts.

Frontispiece: John Neagle (American, 1796–1865), *The Studious Artist* (Thomas Birch), 1836. Oil on canvas, 76.5
× 63.7 cm (30⅛ × 25¹⁄₁₆ in.). Philadelphia, Pennsylvania Academy of the Fine Arts, Gift of John Frederick Lewis,
1922.1.3. Reproduced courtesy of the Pennsylvania Academy of the Fine Arts.

Back cover: John Singleton Copley, *Self-Portrait*, 1780–84, Washington, D.C., National Portrait Gallery (see fig. 3).

CONTENTS

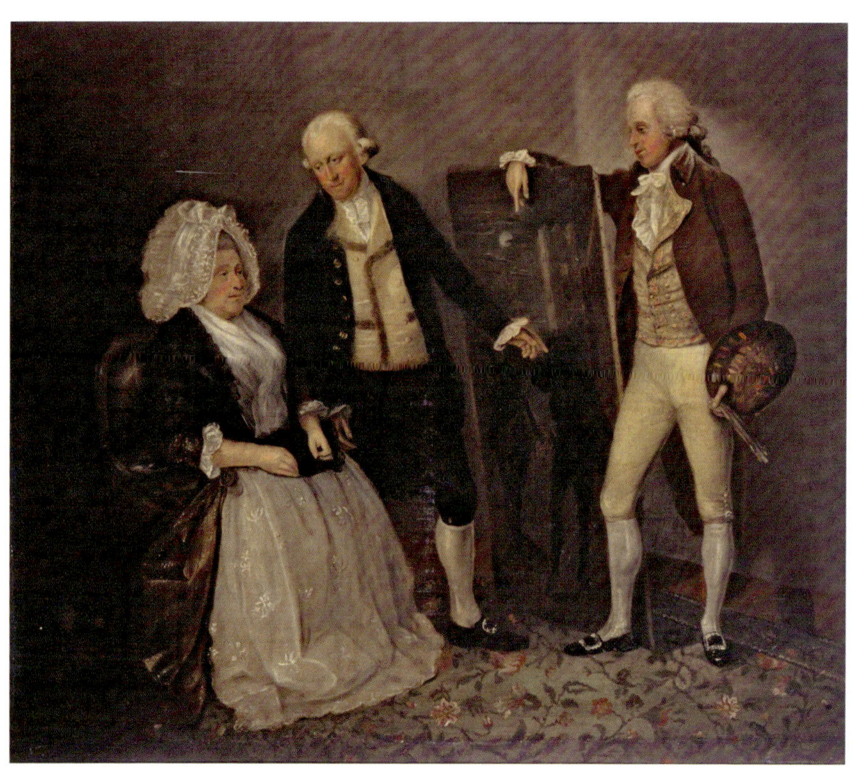

William Dunlap (American, 1766–1839), *The Dunlap Family*, 1788. Oil on canvas, 107.3 × 124.5 cm (42¼ × 49 in.). New York, New-York Historical Society, 1858.87.

PREFACE AND ACKNOWLEDGMENTS

AS CONSERVATORS OF PAINTINGS, our initial goal when we began to collect firsthand descriptions of American painters' methods nearly twenty-five years ago was to better understand the paintings we were treating—why some were more discolored than others, or had patterns of cracks, or were difficult to clean. We found that the written records about artists' techniques often existed only in manuscript form, and after spending many hours in libraries and archives studying recipe books, letters, journals, and other accounts of artists at work, we realized that we were uncovering a largely unknown part of the story of American art. We also discovered that this kind of information was very unevenly distributed—frustratingly sparse for some artists and some periods and almost incredibly rich for others. But eventually we came to believe that we could connect enough pieces of information with one another to construct a coherent story around several themes.

One theme is the importance of Benjamin West, who was a ringleader in the search for the "secrets" of the old masters that was so prevalent in London beginning in the 1760s. Americans who visited West took copious notes about techniques that might have been common knowledge at the time but for that very reason were never written down by British painters. John Singleton Copley, John Trumbull, Washington Allston, and members of the Peale family all carried out experiments in Europe that could be seen as continuations of the experimentation of West and other London painters. Gilbert Stuart was a notable exception to this rule—he had contempt for artists who sought secret recipes and "tricks" and in fact took unusual care to ensure the long-term preservation of his paintings.

By the 1820s and 1830s, increasing numbers of experiments were being carried out by American painters on American soil. Those by Thomas Sully, Rembrandt Peale, John Neagle, and William Sidney Mount are particularly well documented in long manuscript notebooks and often have a different, more scientific feeling than experiments of an earlier time. John Neagle, in particular, brought a surprisingly modern and analytical approach to investigations into why paintings cracked or discolored and how they might be protected from changes of humidity. One can also sense an evolving confidence on the part of Americans that they could improve upon what they had learned from Europe; they tested milk, gums, animal fats, and other unique painting materials and made mechanical improvements to paint tubes, stretchers, and panels for painting. Instead of importing earth pigments from Europe, William Sidney Mount (and other Americans) dug colored earths from American soil and attributed special qualities to the pigments that they found, in a sense, right under their feet. American written sources also provide important documentation of British, German, and French materials of this time. However, while Americans clearly followed the lead of European artists, they sometimes experimented with new pigments and other materials before they were widely used in Europe.

In addition to information about specific materials and techniques, some of our most important information is less concrete and more subjective, such as how artists believed their paintings might change over time, or whether paintings should be colorful or have a brownish "tone." We found much more information than has thus far been discovered in European sources about painters applying overall toning layers to their paintings—especially in the second quarter of the nineteenth century—in the belief that earlier masters did the same.

Other themes include the gradual rise, by the 1830s, of the professional colorman in American cities; Thomas Cole and William Sidney Mount made many observations on (and sometimes had problems with) "store-bought" materials. There is also ample documentation of the use of optical devices such as the camera obscura (a topic of heated debate in recent years) by Americans during the eighteenth and nineteenth centuries. Perhaps most importantly, we have come to believe that painters of the eighteenth and nineteenth centuries have not been given nearly enough credit (as later ones have) for being extremely variable in their techniques.

It is somewhat surprising that there has never before been a book that presents an overview of American painters' methods. (In contrast, there is a fairly large body of books and other scholarly publications about European painters' techniques dating back as far as the 1840s.[1]) This may be, in part, because the recognition of the importance of American art has been a relatively recent development. The uneven distribution of records also makes it a challenge to know how to organize and present information about American painters' techniques. At times we have focused on a particular painter and at other times on a general theme, depending on whether there was sufficient information to build a coherent story around that topic.

Although the generalizations that we have made must be tentative, we hope that this book will stimulate further research and that it will be of interest to curators, art historians, and painters as well as to conservators. At a time when many art historians are discovering new approaches to the history of art, the story of how paintings were made (in the most literal sense) could perhaps be seen as a parallel history to the better-known histories of how styles changed or how paintings were commissioned, exhibited, and sold. Among conservators, at least, this kind of approach is coming to be called "technical art history."[2]

The year 1860 seems a logical ending point for this book. By that date the reach of the colormen was such that manuscript notebooks of recipes and experiments all but disappeared, because artists could buy every type of material ready-made in a bottle (even if they may not have understood exactly what was in the bottle). After 1860, no painter of any ambition could afford not to go to Europe, and Americans brought back from European ateliers a bewildering variety of new and different materials and techniques, although some independent-minded Americans continued to innovate. By the early twentieth century, there was renewed interest in the techniques of earlier masters and an explosion of experimentation with "homemade" grounds and paints that harks back, strangely, to the experiments of the late eighteenth and early nineteenth centuries. We will discuss all of these topics in a subsequent book.

Many, many people have been generous with their time and have shared information with us over the years that we have been collecting material on American painters' techniques.

Above all, we owe an enormous debt of gratitude to the conservators, curators, art historians, and others who read and commented on earlier drafts of the book and thereby helped shape and clarify this vast amount of information. We would like to especially thank Carrie Rebora Barratt at the Metropolitan Museum of Art and Carol Troyen, formerly of the Museum of Fine Arts, Boston, for having taken the time to give us very detailed and thorough comments and criticism on matters of both style and substance. Others whom we are very grateful to for reading and commenting on all or parts of the manuscript include the art dealer and Sargent scholar Warren Adelson, Claire Barry at the Kimbell Museum of Art and Amon Carter Museum of American Art, the private conservator Mark Bockrath, Dare Hartwell at the Corcoran Gallery of Art, Elizabeth Johns of the University of Pennsylvania, Franklin Kelly at the National Gallery of Art, Barbara Martin at the Museum of Fine Arts, Boston, Ross Merrill at the National Gallery of Art, Ellen Miles at the National Portrait Gallery, Norman Muller at the Princeton University Art Museum, Mervin Richard at the National Gallery of Art, Susan Strickler at the Currier Museum of Art, and Joyce Zucker at the New York State Bureau of Historic Sites. We would like to thank Gregory Britton and Ann Lucke of Getty Publications and manuscript editor Cynthia Newman Edwards for believing in the project and helping bring it to fruition, and for aiding us in making the book more readable.

If the Archives of American Art (AAA) did not exist, this book could not have been written. We are extremely grateful to all those involved in founding, supporting, and staffing that extraordinary institution. Visits to the AAA branch at the

Boston Public Library, where the staff diligently fetched roll after roll of microfilm for us, first convinced us that there was enough information on technique to make into a book. Much of the material collected by the AAA is becoming available online, which will make it easier for future generations of scholars to explore American painters' techniques. We would particularly like to thank Joy Weiner for her help and interest during visits to the AAA's New York office.

We would like to give heartfelt thanks to the many people who shared information with us about painters' techniques. These include Ed Ahlstrom of the Montgomery College of Art for information on Thomas Sully; Nancy Anderson at the National Gallery of Art for discussions on Thomas Moran; Mark Aronson at the Yale Center for British Art for sharing material on the Provis manuscripts that relate to the Venetian Secret; Claire Barry at the Kimbell Museum of Art and Amon Carter Museum of American Art for discussion of Thomas Cole's grounds; Elisabeth Batchelor at the Nelson-Atkins Museum of Art for discussions on Benjamin West's *Ophelia and Laertes* at the Cincinnati Art Museum while we were treating that painting; P. J. Brownlee of the Terra Foundation for American Art for discussions on Samuel F. B. Morse while treating *The Gallery of the Louvre* and on color in nineteenth-century American art; Theresa Carbone of the Brooklyn Museum for including so much information about techniques in her catalogue of the museum's American collection; Leslie Carlyle for sharing and comparing information and encouragement over the years; Henry DePhillips of Trinity College for having carried out scientific analyses of samples of pigments from a number of paintings for us over the years; Elise Effmann of the Fine Arts Museums of San Francisco for sharing her thoughts on Cole's use of the camera obscura; Theresa Fairbanks-Harris for sharing material on John Singleton Copley, Sully, and early colormen's catalogues and for many other productive discussions when we were working at the Yale Center for British Art; Michael Gallagher, Dorothy Mahon, Charlotte Hale, Carrie Rebora Barratt, and Kevin Avery at the Metropolitan Museum of Art for fruitful discussions during our treatment of Emanuel Leutze's *Washington Crossing the Delaware*; Marc Gerstein of the University of Toledo for discussions on the toning of sculpture; Dare Hartwell at the Corcoran Gallery of Art for discussions on paneled stretchers and on Albert Bierstadt, and for giving us the opportunity to study paintings at the Corcoran while writing catalogue entries there; Barbara Heller and Alfred Ackerman at the Detroit Institute of Arts for sharing information on Rembrandt Peale when we treated *The Court of Death* at that museum; Alexander Katlan for his pioneering work on American colormen and for his encouragement; Irene Konefal, Rhona MacBeth, and Erica Hirschler at the Museum of Fine Arts, Boston, for discussions on the young Gilbert Stuart; Stephen Kornhauser and Ulrich Birkmaier at the Wadsworth Atheneum Museum of Art for discussions on Benjamin West and on artists' suppliers' catalogues while we were treating West's *Raising of Lazarus* in Hartford; Dan Kushel of the Art Conservation Program at Buffalo State College for discussions on Cole's underdrawings; Elizabeth Lunning for stimulating discussions on a great range of topics over the years; Ross Merrill of the National Gallery of Art for inviting us to study a transcription he shared with us of Rembrandt Peale's "Notes of the Painting Room"; Robert Proctor, who first said: "You should write a book about this stuff!"; Jules Prown of Yale University for discussions on toning and on Copley; Anne Ruggles of the National Gallery of Canada for sharing with us material she collected while she was treating West's *The Death of General Wolfe*; Carol E. Soltis for discussions on Rembrandt Peale; Ken Sutherland for sharing information on shellac; Robert Torchia for information on images of John Neagle; and Joyce Zucker for discussions on early pigments, Frederic Church, and grounds.

We are very grateful for discussions with many other people that shaped our understanding of artists and artists' materials over the years and eventually encouraged us to present this information in book form. We would like to thank Rita Albertson at the Worcester Art Museum; Jeffrey Andersen and Amy Kurz Lansing of the Florence Griswold Museum; Thomas Barwick; Stephen Bonadies of the Virginia Museum of Fine Art; Jonathan Boos; Thomas Branchick and Sandra Webber of the Williamstown Art Conservation Center; Sarah Cash of the Corcoran Gallery of Art; Bruce Chambers; Helen Cooper and Robin Jaffee Frank of the Yale University Art Gallery; Chris Crosman of Crystal Bridges Museum of American Art; John Driscoll; Robert Emlen of Brown University; Scott Ferris; Sarah Fisher, Ann Hoenigswald, Catherine Metzger, and Michael Swicklik of the National Gallery of Art; Sam Forsythe; Fred Giampietro; Mary Anne Goley; David Good; Paul Himmelstein; Susan Hobbs; the late Bill Hutton of the Toledo Museum of Art; Elizabeth Kennedy of the Terra Foundation for American Art; Arthur Liverant; Lisa Long, formerly of the Redwood Library and Athenaeum; Barbara MacAdam of the Hood Museum of Art; Carol Mancusi-Ungaro at the Whitney Museum of American Art; Dara Mitchell at Sotheby's New York; Kenneth Moser and Carolyn Tomkiewicz of the Brooklyn Museum; Larry Nichols, Amy Gilman, and Suzanne Hargrove of the Toledo Museum of Art; Glenn Peck; Eric Pourchot of the Foundation of the American Institute for Conservation; Martin Radecki; William Reese; Bonnie Rimer; Marguerite Riordan; Andrew Spahr, Kurt Sundstrom, and Karen Papineau of the Currier Museum of Art; John Stinson; Joyce Hill Stoner of the University of Delaware and Winterthur Museum; Don Walters; Timothy Whalen of the Getty Conservation Institute; Nelson H. White; Jim Wright; and Frank Zuccari at the Art Institute of Chicago. We would also like to thank our family members and friends who have given us understanding and encouragement even at times when it all seemed like much too much. The project grew so large and took such a long time that we would like to apologize if we have forgotten to include someone who contributed to its realization. Of course, in spite of the help of so many people, we accept responsibility for any errors or omissions in the book.

We would like to thank the grant-giving agencies that gave us the means to take time away from our normal work to write this book. Our research was made possible in part by a Winterthur Advanced Fellowship, a Guest Scholarship at the Getty Research Institute, and a Foundation of the American Institute for Conservation-Kress Foundation Publication Grant. We are particularly grateful to Mark Leonard, formerly at the J. Paul Getty Museum, first for encouraging us to publish, and then for inviting us to be guest scholars at the Getty Research Institute, where we were finally able to begin writing. The staff, librarians, and special collections librarians at the Getty Research Institute were extremely welcoming and eager to help; we would also like to thank Karen Gunterman and Britta McEwen, our Getty research assistants, who tracked down countless references for us.

We are grateful to the patient staff members of many libraries, especially the ones at the Henry F. du Pont Winterthur Museum, where we spent a productive two weeks, and at the New-York Historical Society, Historical Society of Pennsylvania, American Philosophical Society (Rob Cox, formerly head of special collections at the American Philosophical Society, deserves special thanks for seeking out and locating hard-to-find manuscripts by that indefatigable scribbler Rembrandt Peale), and Yale Center for British Art. We would also like to thank the staffs at the Connecticut College Library, New York Public Library, Frick Art Reference Library, American Antiquarian Society, Connecticut Historical Society, British Library, Boston Public Library, the library of the Wadsworth Atheneum Museum of Art, and the Beinecke Rare Book and Manuscript Library and Sterling Memorial Library at Yale University.

Several people deserve special mention for encouraging us to persist in what turned out to be an enormous project. Early on, Ross Merrill of the National Gallery of Art helped us to believe that American painters' techniques were worth studying, and in a sense kicked all of this off. Theresa Fairbanks-Harris of the Yale Center for British Art and Malcolm Warner, formerly of that institution, encouraged us to speak on (and eventually publish on) George Stubbs, which showed us how information from American sources can amplify our understanding of British techniques and vice versa. We would also like to give special thanks to David Bomford and Zahira Veliz for their encouragement and for discussions on many topics over many years.

We would like to single out for special thanks Edward Shein for supporting us and giving us the opportunity to work on many extraordinary American paintings. We would also like to thank Ed and Deborah Shein for generously allowing us to use their guest house on the coast of Maine, where large parts of this book were planned and written.

Lastly we would like to express our gratitude and admiration for some people who inspired us who are long dead. William Dunlap was not only the first historian of American art but a painter himself (see page vi) who believed that painting methods were so important that he included many observations and anecdotes about technique in his 1834 *History of the Rise and Progress of the Arts of Design in the United States*. We would also like to acknowledge our debt to the inquisitive nineteenth-century American experimenters, especially Thomas Sully, John Neagle, and Rembrandt Peale. Because they documented their techniques so thoroughly, they have made it much easier for all of us to understand the processes of painting from an artist's point of view. Sully and Peale were frustrated in their attempts to publish books on technique; we hope they would be happy to see how much of the information they collected has finally made its way into print.

—Lance Mayer and Gay Myers

NOTES

1   The first scholarly books on European painters' techniques are generally considered to be Charles Eastlake's *Materials for a History of Oil Painting* (1847), which identified and interpreted many important primary sources, and Mary Merrifield's 1849 *Original Treatises on the Arts of Painting*, consisting of transcriptions of early documents with extensive commentaries by the author (Merrifield had translated Cennino Cennini's *Libro dell'Arte* into English in 1844).

  In terms of American painters' techniques, the conservator Alexander Katlan has published two books (Katlan 1987 and Katlan 1992) in which he has compiled a great deal of very useful information about American artists' suppliers, with special emphasis on supports. Katlan 1992 includes short monographs on the materials of Cole, Cropsey, and Bierstadt. Especially in recent years, a number of conservators have written about aspects of individual American painters' techniques, occasionally in exhibition catalogues, but more often in journals read mainly by conservators. Leslie Carlyle's comprehensive study of nineteenth-century British treatises (Carlyle 2001) not only provides very useful points of comparison with American materials and techniques but also includes discussion of several American nineteenth-century treatises.

2   See Bomford 1998 for a concise discussion of the developing field of technical art history.

LIST OF ABBREVIATIONS

AAA	Archives of American Art, Smithsonian Institution, Washington, D.C.
AAA/Hart	Archives of American Art, Charles H. Hart Autograph Collection
APS	American Philosophical Society, Philadelphia
CHS	Connecticut Historical Society, Hartford
HSP	Historical Society of Pennsylvania, Philadelphia
LIMAA	Long Island Museum of American Art, History and Carriages, Stony Brook, N.Y. (formerly The Museums at Stony Brook, N.Y.)
N-YHS	New-York Historical Society Library, New York
NYPL	New York Public Library, New York
NYSL	New York State Library, Albany

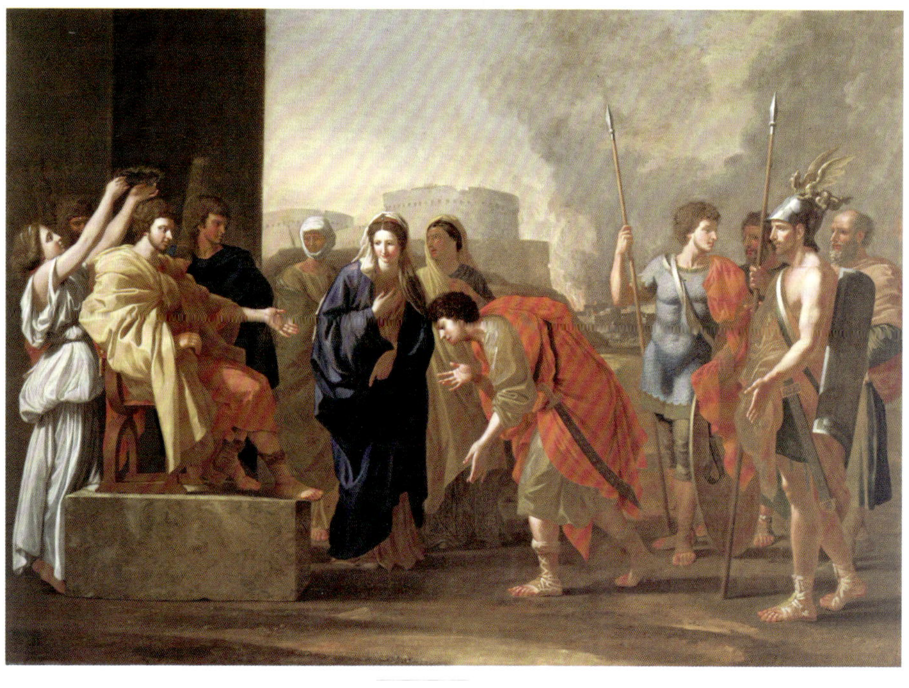

John Smibert (Scottish-American, 1688–1751), *The Continence of Scipio* (after Poussin), ca. 1719–22.
Oil on canvas, 116.2 × 159.1 cm (45¾ × 62⅝ in.). Brunswick, Maine, Bowdoin
College Museum of Art, Bequest of the Honorable James Bowdoin III, 1813.10.

CHAPTER 1
PROVINCIAL PAINTERS AND EUROPEAN CONNECTIONS

FROM THE EARLIEST DAYS of British settlement, North American painters showed the interesting combination of connectedness and provincialism that characterized colonial life in general. In the larger port cities, ships regularly brought people, news, and material goods from the mother country, while life in the hinterlands could be simple and isolated in the extreme.

Although records are sparse and there is still much that we will probably never know about the availability of painting materials during the early colonial period, portraits were being painted in New England by the 1660s, and a modern study of one-half of the known seventeenth-century New England portraits revealed the presence of all of the pigments commonly available to artists in Europe.[1] A detailed 1684 inventory of the estate of the Boston decorative painter Daniel George similarly included most of the pigments that a portrait painter in London might have used, the exception being the most expensive pigment—ultramarine.[2]

By the early eighteenth century, when newspapers began to be published regularly, the importation of artists' materials into cities like Boston can be better documented. Painters' colors were advertised for sale in Boston newspapers as early as 1711, when Zabdiel Boylston offered "Painter's colors, most sorts of," and in 1713, when Nehemiah Partridge advertised "All Sorts of Paints and Oyl to be Sold, by Wholesale and Retayle." Neither of those two advertisers made a distinction between materials for painting houses or furniture and those intended for the fine arts, although Partridge was an accomplished portrait painter himself. By the 1730s, "face painting" (an eighteenth-century term for portrait painting) was specifically mentioned in newspaper advertisements. In 1738 the Boston merchant John Merrett advertised that he sold at least sixteen different pigments, and in 1762 John Gore listed thirty-eight pigments by name, including ultramarine.[3]

In Philadelphia, "colours neatly prepared either for house or face painting" were advertised by James Peters in 1764,[4] although when Charles Willson Peale visited Philadelphia at about this time he bought art supplies at Christopher Marshall's store, which he called "the only colour shop in the City."[5] Fragmentary surviving records from the Marshall shop show that there was at least some inter-colonial trade in painting materials—in 1766 Marshall sent white lead, linseed oil, and whiting and in 1767 "Three Barrells and one Cag [cask?] of Painter's Colours" to Newport. These had most likely been imported from England, but Marshall's papers also show him exporting spirits of turpentine and beeswax (presumably American products) back to London.[6]

John Smibert has a special place among artists' suppliers in the American colonies, in part because of the breadth of his experience. Smibert had painted portraits in London and Edinburgh and had traveled in Italy before arriving in Boston in 1728. In addition to selling artists' materials imported from London, Smibert kept in his studio an art collection that gave many American painters their first impressions of earlier European art. These included copies that Smibert had made in Italy of works by Raphael, Titian, Van Dyck, Tintoretto, and Poussin (see fig. 1), as well as prints and plaster casts of classical sculpture. At least part of the collection was maintained by Smibert's nephew John Moffat after his uncle's death in 1751, and it helped instruct several generations of aspiring American artists until the collection was finally dispersed around 1795.[7] After 1779, Smibert's studio itself was rented by a succession of artists, including John Trumbull, Mather Brown, and Washington Allston.[8]

Surviving letters between Smibert and his nephew and their London agent give details of the materials available in Boston in the 1740s and 1750s. These include, surprisingly early (1743), three dozen three-quarter-length stretched canvases and two full-length canvases (rolled up), and by the 1750s, "Primed Cloaths" (canvases with the ground already applied). When he ordered pigments from London, Smibert specified exactly which grades he wanted of expensive pigments such as red lake and Prussian blue. In one case he ordered equal amounts of red lake "of the Common middling sort" and "good Lake" and on another occasion ordered Prussian blue in four different grades—significantly, he ordered much more of the cheaper grades than of the expensive ones.[9] Even at this early period Smibert also ordered materials for amateurs who practiced the genteel hobby of decorating fans with watercolors, a reminder that many of the brushes and other painting materials that made their way to America were not necessarily intended for the professional oil painters who are the main focus of this book.[10] Smibert also sold palette knives, black-lead pencils, chalk, brushes of various sorts, and gold leaf.[11]

John Singleton Copley's American career is a striking example of how—if a provincial painter desired it badly enough—he could connect himself to the larger world, even at a time when there were few professional painters in America. Before he went to London in 1774, Copley was in contact via letters with the painters John Greenwood and William Johnston, whom he had known when they worked in New England, but who had moved on to London and Barbados, respectively. Copley wrote to Johnston to request information about making boiled oil (linseed oil treated by cooking it with lead compounds to make it dry faster).[12] It was apparently a constant struggle for painters to find a grade of linseed oil good enough to be used in the fine arts. Linseed oil had been manufactured in Boston as early as 1726,[13] but oil continued to be imported into Boston from London much later than this,[14] and the quest by painters for high-quality oil would continue into the nineteenth century. William Johnston's surviving letter to Copley makes it clear that the reason Copley and Johnston wanted to make their own boiled linseed oil was to obtain a better grade than the "common" variety (presumably, the kind used by house painters and decorative painters) and that the chief defect of the common oil was its dark color.[15]

Copley's poignant letter to Jean-Étienne Liotard in 1762, with its awkward spelling and grammar, epitomizes his desire to reach beyond his provincial roots. Copley acknowledged his isolation, writing, "You may perhaps be surprised that so remote a corner of the Globe as New England should have any d[e]mand for the necessary eutensils for practiceing the fine Arts." But Copley made it clear that when it came to materials for making art (in this case, pastels), he wanted only the best: "In a word let em be a sett of the very best that can be got."[16] It must have been because he wanted the best that Copley also ordered oil-painting materials to be sent from London to Boston, including canvases, brushes, poppy oil, and pigments.[17]

Copley put himself in contact more directly than any other colonial artist with the London art world by sending paintings there for exhibition, beginning in 1765, and seeking comments on his work from Benjamin West and Joshua Reynolds. Copley had seen the copies of earlier European paintings, plaster casts, and prints on display in Smibert's studio in Boston, and when he was in Philadelphia in 1771 he viewed the six copies of European paintings that West had painted in Italy in the 1760s.[18] Copley was struck by the warm coloring of West's copies and by the "universal finishing and harmoniseing of all parts."[19] These were points he would have paid particular attention to, for the paintings he sent to London—while praised—had been criticized for "coldness" and "over minuteness."[20]

Copley also overcame the limitations of his provincial background by reading widely. At the age of eighteen he carefully copied the plates and text from two books on human anatomy by Italian and Dutch authors.[21] Copley's familiarity with works on art theory by Francesco Algarotti, Charles du Fresnoy, Roger de Piles, Horace Walpole, and others must have been an attempt to put himself on an equal footing with artists in London who were reading these same books.[22]

A book played an important role in connecting the young Charles Willson Peale to the larger world of the fine arts. Peale served an apprenticeship to a saddle maker and arrived late at his ambition to be a painter. In exchange for a saddle, the painter John Hesselius allowed Peale to watch him paint several portraits. Eventually Peale made his way to Philadelphia, where he not only bought paints but purchased a book at Rivington's bookshop—*Handmaid to the Arts*, by Robert Dossie—and closeted himself away for four days trying to improve his painting by following its directions.[23] Peale called *Handmaid to the Arts* "a very useful work."[24]

In fact Dossie's book gives a great deal of detailed and practical information, not only about oil painting but about topics ranging from gilding to making ceramics to staining wood, which may explain why there were far more copies of *Handmaid to the Arts* in eighteenth-century America than any other similar book.[25] Peale apparently kept and used his copy of Dossie for many years—there is evidence of him still taking notes from it in the 1790s.[26]

Peale traveled to Boston in 1765, where he visited Smibert's color shop.[27] After Peale became "a little acquainted" with John Moffat, Smibert's nephew said he would give Peale a "feast" and led him upstairs to a room lined with green cloth, where he viewed Smibert's collection of paintings, which, in Peale's words, "were in a stile vastly superior to any he had seen before."[28] In Smibert's shop Peale received directions to the home of Copley, who received him graciously and lent him a painting to copy. Making copies of works by other painters was a common practice at this time for artists at all levels, from rank beginners to experienced painters.

The young Benjamin West also copied paintings early in his career, among them, surprisingly, a work by the seventeenth-century painter Bartolomé Esteban Murillo that had been captured from a Spanish vessel.[29] West had taught himself to paint in rural Pennsylvania, but the young man soon attracted the attention of patrons in Philadelphia and New York, who commissioned portraits; a merchant gave him a box of proper paints and brushes and several pieces of prepared canvas.[30] In Philadelphia West met the British immigrant painter William Williams, who lent him books on art theory by du Fresnoy and Jonathan Richardson.[31] Williams also showed West how to use a camera obscura, an optical device that could help an artist record a landscape view by throwing an image via a lens into a darkened chamber, and the budding artist then made his own. (This is the first of many references to camera obscuras and other optical devices being used in America—most likely the event occurred in the late 1740s or early 1750s).[32] Most importantly, West's patrons provided him with funds that allowed him, at the age of twenty-one, to sail for Italy in 1760 with the promise that he would make copies of paintings by European masters and send them back to America.[33]

From the very beginning of his career, John Trumbull always seemed to be able to get the best materials. Trumbull had the advantage of being of a higher social class than any other early American painter;[34] a Harvard graduate who spoke and wrote French fluently, he was the son of the governor of Connecticut, and his relatives were successful merchants. Before he was sixteen, his family's mercantile connections had enabled him to send to London for a copy of Dossie's *Handmaid to the Arts*.[35] At college, Trumbull read still more widely on art and art theory.[36]

Trumbull then began to train himself in earnest as a painter. A letter shows that while he was on active duty with the Continental army outside Boston he was able to obtain high-quality art materials, in this case canvases that a merchant relative had bought for him in New York.[37] Since there was a war on, he was initially reduced to copying prints. But he found another way to train himself. After British troops left Boston, he not only rented Smibert's old studio to learn from its collection of art, but he had the means to buy six paintings from Smibert's descendants, including copies (possibly originals—the paintings have been lost) by Cornelis van Poelenburgh and Jan Breughel the Elder.[38]

Trumbull was so eager to study with West that he sailed to London before the war had ended, and this miscalculation cost him more than seven months in prison on a charge of treason. He employed part of his time in jail copying West's copy of a painting by Correggio.[39] Trumbull eventually made his way back to America, but after the war's end he began the first of several long stays in England, becoming an important member of West's studio.

When he returned to the United States, Trumbull maintained his European connections, especially when it came to high-quality art materials. In 1790 Trumbull, then in New York, received a large variety of brushes from a Flemish merchant named Derveaux who had recently relocated to London; these included brushes described as "extra fine white Roman hair," "fine sable," "fine fitch purified," "tartary sable," "good camel hair," "hog hair pencils in quill," and "hog hair tools." The merchant quoted prices by the gross, clearly hoping that Trumbull would show them to his friends, and perhaps serve as a vendor.[40]

It should be emphasized that many early American artists were not as well connected as Copley, Peale, West, and Trumbull, and many tried and failed to have careers in the fine arts. The self-taught Winthrop Chandler of Woodstock, Connecticut, who in the 1770s painted vivid, detailed portraits that are now widely admired, was reduced to poverty and was called a "house painter" at the time of his death in 1790. Chandler's obituary reads in part: "His genius was not matured on the bosom of encouragement. [Financial] embarrassment, like strong weeds in a garden of delicate flowers, checked his enthusiasm and disheartened the man."[41] Abraham Delanoy Jr., one of the first Americans to study in London with Benjamin West, found that even those credentials did not bring success as a portrait painter in America. Delanoy offered to do all kinds of painting, from portraits to signs, carriages, ships, and houses, as well as selling putty and "paints mix'd at a short notice";[42] toward the end of his life (he died in 1795) he was said to have been poor and "his only employment sign-painting."[43]

The number of painters in America had grown demonstrably by the early nineteenth century—in 1806 a single English ship brought 450 gross of artists' brushes and 144 portrait-size canvases to Boston.[44] Yet many stories have come down about the unusual "make-do" materials that artists used at this time, especially at the beginning of their careers. The young James Frothingham, a coach maker's apprentice, wanted to be a portrait painter but had never seen a palette, so he made one himself by drilling holes in a piece of wood and putting thimbles in the holes to hold his paint.[45] As a young beginner in Pennsylvania, Jacob Eichholtz was said to have used a bootjack as a palette and "anything in the shape of a brush" until he obtained some of Thomas Sully's cast-off brushes when Sully departed for London in 1809.[46] And when Thomas Cole was beginning to paint in Ohio in the 1820s he was described as making his own brushes and obtaining colors from a chair maker.[47]

Many early-nineteenth-century American artists, especially those working outside of major cities, could have obtained painting materials from suppliers who were not selling them specifically for use in the fine arts. For example, a rural Connecticut woodworker named Nathaniel Martin added to his income by selling small amounts of paint and pigments—probably mostly to neighbors who were painting a barn or a wagon. Entries in his account book from around 1800 show, amid income from such activities as mending a harness, mending a rake, and repairing a clock, the sale of "boild oil" and "prepaird oil," as well as "grinding paint." It is possible that some of the pigments and oils that Martin sold to his neighbor Doctor John Brewster were used by the doctor's son, the portrait painter John Brewster Jr. (Martin also made a "stretching frame" for John Brewster Jr., and Ralph Earl had a local woodworker make him a stretching frame when he was painting in rural Connecticut.)[48] Charles Willson Peale supposedly obtained his very first painting materials from a coach maker.[49] The Connecticut portrait painters Richard and William Jennys gave instructions on the reverse of a portrait to varnish it each year with an egg-white varnish. Egg-white varnishes were used as temporary varnishes in Europe, but it seems likely that Americans working far from major cities told their patrons to use this material because it would be available in every household.[50]

A vivid impression of the difficulties of a beginning painter trying to obtain supplies in the early nineteenth century was given by Francis Edmonds, who grew up in Hudson, New York, and recalled buying some of his materials at a store that supplied house painters and making some of them himself:

> You must remember that at this period, about 1819, there were no such shops as we now have retailing artists materials, where colors ready mixed, canvases duly prepared and every article in an artist line are to be found ready made by the modern "colorman"—I had 25 cents capital to start with, and I bought at a house painters store 3 cents worth each of the five primitive colors in the dry state—and paid the same price for a little oil & turpentine—In my fathers yard were some white marble flagging stones. I took up one of these…and commenced grinding the surface of the marble with Sand and water to make it a smooth & even surface—this done I commenced grinding my paints and as I grou[nd] them poured them into clam shells which answered for pots—I then undertook to prepare some canvass to paint upon, but I could not get the surface smooth, I had therefore to paint upon it in its rough state.[51]

On the other hand, John Trumbull, who had been particular about his materials early in his career, continued to take steps to get the best art materials. In 1807 he reached to the other side of the globe when he bought, through his nephew, "1 box painters colors &c" for ten dollars, and one hundred paintbrushes for five dollars, as well as gold and silver leaf, from merchants Lunshing and Yookshing in Canton, China.[52] The quality of oil available in New York in the 1820s apparently did not suit Trumbull—in 1824 a jug of oil was sent from Boston to New York for his use[53]—and in 1825 he wrote to Thomas Sully in Philadelphia, asking him to "procure from Wm Heyl a Gallon of his Nut Oil, of which you were so good as to send me a specimen 3 years ago."[54] With Trumbull, we are clearly a very long way from simply buying what the local house painter or woodworker had available.

In the early nineteenth century, artists sometimes established informal networks to obtain supplies. Thomas Sully was notably active in this kind of thing; he exchanged information with and supplied materials to a number of other artists in addition to Trumbull. In 1819, when William Dunlap was in Norfolk, Virginia, he wrote to Sully asking him to send stretched fabrics, bladders of paint, and mastic from Philadelphia.[55] Another letter from 1819 shows the hand of Sully reaching deeper into the provinces—to Nashville, Tennessee, where Ralph E. W. Earl received a letter from Philadelphia with the following postscript: "P.S. Mr. Sully has informed me that a french merchant here has imported several fine excellent colors. If you wish any, I will send you some under his direction."[56]

This proves that at least some painters working in the provincial parts of America in 1819 could, if sufficiently motivated and well connected, obtain the highest quality materials from other parts of the world. In 1828 Sully even obtained a keg of red pigment from China through the agency of the British artist George Chinnery, who was then working in Canton, and Sully shared the pigment with John Neagle and Rembrandt Peale.[57] But these exchanges also show how the supply of materials from abroad remained to some degree casual and sporadic, not very different from the situation in the eighteenth century, when a ship's cargo containing artists' materials was advertised only after it arrived.

When Samuel F. B. Morse needed to buy oil paint in Philadelphia in 1828, Sully told him to go to Samuel Scarlet, saying: "Scarlett does not keep colours ready ground, but is glad to receive orders for such, and charges moderately: being an artist he knows what is the proper method of doing justice in the preparation of colour."[58] Scarlet advertised in city directories as an artist and picture restorer, so preparing paint must have been only a part-time occupation.[59] But soon, beginning in the 1830s in New York, and not long after in other cities as well, full-time colormen would keep paints "ready ground" as well as selling a great variety of other supplies for artists' use at a moment's notice.

NOTES

1   England and van Zelst 1982; Fairbanks and Trent 1982, 3:455–79. For New York, see Zucker 1980; for South American pigments, see Seldes et al. 2002.

2   The Daniel George inventory is published in Fairbanks 1982, 449; see also Dow 1927 and Vanderhoof 1977.

3   Dow 1927, 237–43; Cummings 1971.

4   Prime 1929, 301.

5   C. W. Peale 1983–2000, 3:174.

6   Marshall Waste Book, various bills of lading from 1766 as well as bills dated April 26, 1763, and December 10, 1767; the beeswax and turpentine were sent in 1763. John Trumbull mentioned using "American turpentine" in England in 1813 (see chapter 3).

7   See Saunders 1995 on Smibert's collection and its eventual dispersal. Shortly after Smibert's death, the collection included thirty-five portraits, forty-one "History pieces & pictures in that taste," thirteen landscapes, and two conversation pieces (ibid., 263).

8   Ibid., 125.

9   Saunders 1995 includes Smibert's surviving correspondence. In 1749 Smibert ordered twenty pounds of the cheapest Prussian blue at four or five shillings, ten pounds of the next expensive at eight or nine shillings, six pounds at twelve or fifteen shillings, and four pounds of the most expensive at eighteen or twenty shillings (ibid., 255–61).

10 Ibid., 257, 259–60.

11 Ibid., 258–61. Smibert ordered both palette knives and "stone knives" that cost twice as much—the latter presumably a larger type of knife used to mix paint on a stone.

12 John Greenwood to Copley, March 23, 1770 (Copley 1914, 81–83); William Johnston to Copley, May 4, 1770 (Copley 1914, 88–93).

13 Cummings 1971, 113.

14 Advertisements of 1738, 1762, and 1766 (Dow 1927, 238–41). In 1794 Tench Coxe reported that the production of linseed oil in America was increasing rapidly but production did not meet demand (cited in N. Evans 2006, 158).

15 Johnston to Copley, May 4, 1770: "instead of its being return'd to you Very black (which is ever the case from the Common method of boilg.) it will be return'd to you as pure as you put it in, and will hold its colour, and that in fact is what you are in pursuit of" (Copley 1914, 90).

16 Copley to Jean-Étienne Liotard, September 30, 1764 (ibid., 26). The letter that survives is a draft, and it is not certain that it was actually sent.

17 Ibid., 115–16, 140–41.

18 West's copies were of paintings by Titian, Domenichino, Guido Reni, a follower of Annibale Caracci, and Anton Raphael Mengs (Erffa and Staley 1986, 441–48).

19 Copley to Henry Pelham, September 29, 1771 (Copley 1914, 163–64).

20 Joshua Reynolds's comments, cited in Prown 1966, 1:48.

21 Prown 2001b.

22 Schimmelman 1984b, 180; Prown 2001b, 25n4. See also Schimmelman 2007.

23 C. W. Peale 1983–2000, 5:16; also C. W. Peale to Rembrandt Peale, October 28, 1812 (ibid., 3:174). The editors of the Peale papers felt Peale purchased the book in December of 1762 (C. W. Peale 1983–2000, 1:33), but the copy of the book at APS identified as Peale's is the second (1764) edition.

24 C. W. Peale 1983–2000, 5:16.

25 Schimmelman 1984a, 193–94, 197–99; Saunders and Miles 1987, 228–29. John Hesselius owned a copy of the first (1758) edition.

26 C. W. Peale Memorandum Book. Notes from Dossie are on p. 1.

27 C. W. Peale 1983–2000, 3:172–73, 5:21.

28 Ibid., 3:172–73.

29 Dunlap 1834, 1:44.

30 Ibid., 1:39–40.

31 Ibid., 1:40.

32 Flexner 1969, 183. See chapters 2 and 10 for more on the camera obscura and camera lucida.

33 Dunlap 1834, 1:39–47.

34 Ibid., 1:340; see also Prown 2001d, 159.

35 Dunlap 1834, 1:342.

36   Prown 2001d, 160–61.

37   Trumbull to David Trumbull, October 5, 1775 (Trumbull Papers CHS, microfilm roll 80006, reel I, frame 31).

38   For Trumbull's bill for the six paintings he bought from Smibert's heirs, see Saunders 1995, 125, 221ff.

39   Cooper et al. 1982, 194–95. The painting was *Madonna and Child with Saint Jerome* (1780–81, Yale University Art Gallery, New Haven, Connecticut).

40   B. Derveaux to Trumbull, May 29, 1790 (Trumbull Papers NYPL; AAA, microfilm roll N26, frames 36–39).

41   Little 1947, 88.

42   Sawitsky 1957, 200–202; Kelby 1970, 8; Gottesman 1970, 1.

43   Dunlap 1834, 1:161.

44   The items were imported on the ship *Galen* for the Boston chair maker and paint shop owner Samuel Tuck (Whitley 1932, 131; N. Evans 1996, 351). Amateur painting, especially watercolor painting by young women, had grown enormously by the beginning of the nineteenth century, which may explain the huge number of brushes, but oil painting on canvas was not commonly done by amateurs at this time.

45   Dunlap 1834, 2:212–13.

46   Wescott 1886, 1270.

47   Noble 1964, 28.

48   Kornhauser 1991, 85–86, 91, 100n24. An entry in 1803 for a half pint of oil "for John," presumably John, Jr., the artist; other entries for Dr. Brewster include ones from 1792 (frame for painting) and 1798 (paint) (Martin Account Book, CHS, microfilm roll 86862, frame 168).

49   R. Peale 1855a, 82.

50   Wolbers 1988, 246. On egg-white varnishes, see Wouldhuysen-Keller 1994.

51   Edmonds 1981, 6.

52   Trumbull Papers CHS, microfilm roll 80006, reel II, frames 145–47.

53   Andrew Allen to Peter Remson, November 11, 1824 (ibid., frame 229).

54   Trumbull to Sully, probably between April and May 1825 (ibid., reel I, frame 301). William Heyl owned a drug and paint store in Philadelphia (C.W. Peale 1983–2000, 3:700n). In 1819 Charles Willson Peale (C.W. Peale to Rembrandt Peale, December 16, 1819) noted that "Mr. Heyl thinks that he now has the best Copal varnish he had ever made" (ibid., 3:782).

55   Lipton 1981, 44.

56   Joseph Deleplaine to Earl, February 6, 1819 (Earl Papers). See chapter 12, note 41, on Sully sending pigments to Thomas Cole in 1828.

57   Sully Journal, AAA, microfilm roll N18, frame 319 (November 2, November 21, and December 7, 1828).

58   Sully to Morse, March 4, 1828 (HSP, Simon Gratz Collection; AAA, microfilm roll 22, frame 476).

59   Katlan 1992, 431–32.

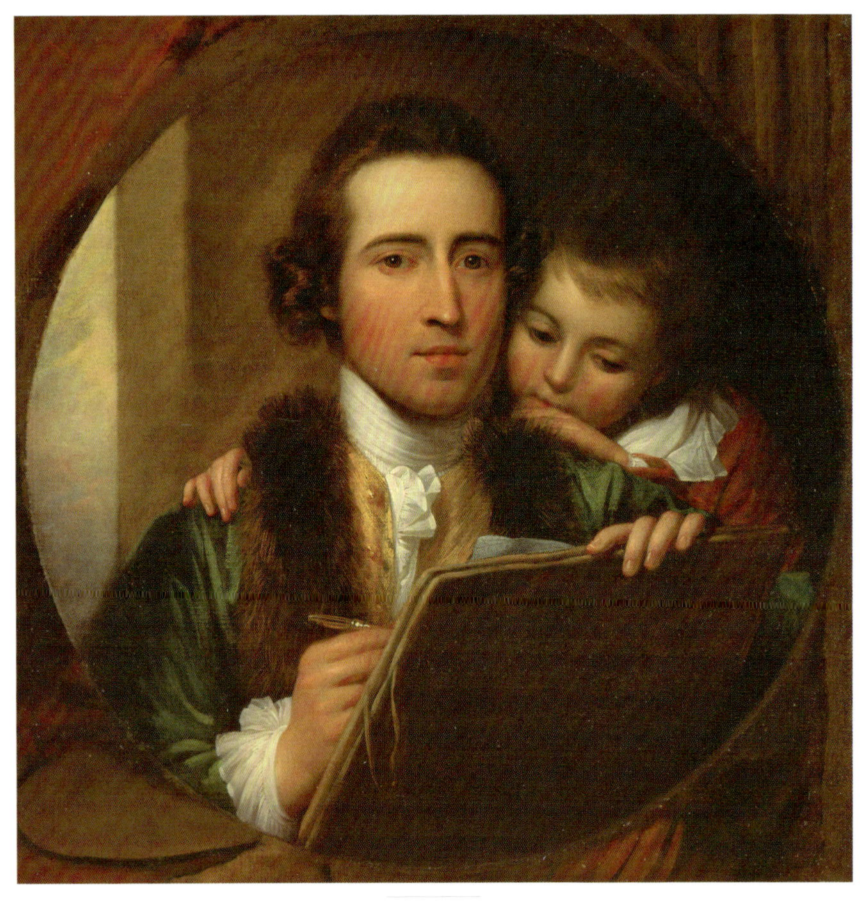

FIGURE 2

Benjamin West (American, 1738–1820), *The Artist and His Son Raphael*, 1773.
Oil on canvas, 63.5 × 63.2 cm (25 × 24⅞ in.). New Haven, Conn., Yale Center for British Art,
Paul Mellon Collection, B1977.14.111.

CHAPTER 2
BENJAMIN WEST AND HIS INFLUENCE

SHORTLY AFTER CHARLES WILLSON PEALE arrived in London in 1767 to study with Benjamin West, he noticed that West painted "in a Differrent Manner from Common Oil Paint:g which gives great luster & Strength to the Coulering—a method or art no Painter here Else knows any thing of."[1] West's interest in new and different techniques would influence artists on both sides of the Atlantic and would help set the tone of painters' discussions about these topics for generations to come.

Upon his arrival in Italy in 1760 at the age of twenty-one, West had received advice from the German neoclassical painter Anton Raphael Mengs, then at the height of his influence. Mengs told West that he should study the old masters, but rather than imitate any single one of them he should travel in Italy to see the best works of the Carracci, Correggio, Titian, Tintoretto, and Veronese.[2] West invented his own style by combining what he learned by studying and copying paintings by these masters; West also copied paintings by Mengs. (Later, when John Singleton Copley saw some of these copies that had been sent to Philadelphia, he mistook West's copy of a painting by Mengs for a copy after Correggio.[3])

Many painters at this time believed that certain "secrets" of the old masters had been lost, and if the secrets were rediscovered, it would be easier for modern painters to achieve the same effects. The search for the secrets of the old masters became so pervasive that it began to attract ridicule within the British colony in Italy. One British artist in Rome in the 1760s asked why British artists "follow chimaeras, dancing about like bewildered travelers after a jack-and-the-lantern."[4] Another artist, James Barry, also writing in the 1760s, poked fun at "such people of ours who are floating about after Magilphs and mysteries."[5]

Barry's use of the word "magilph" is one of the earliest occurrences of a term that was variously spelled megilp, megellup, or macguilp, and which refers to a concoction added to oil paint to give it better handling qualities.[6] Many believed that Titian and other early artists had the advantage of such a medium, but that the recipe had been lost in the intervening centuries. The search for the perfect megilp would turn out to be an important part of the history of painting techniques in both Britain and America, not only in the second half of the eighteenth century but in the nineteenth century as well.

Late in his life, West (through his official biographer John Galt) tried to downplay the importance of a lost "secret" medium, saying that the greatness of Titian "was chiefly owing to…an exquisite delicacy of sight which enabled him to perceive the most approximate tints,—and not to any particular dexterity of penciling, nor to any superiority in the materials of his colours."[7]

However, Galt's biography also alluded to "many unsuccessful experiments" that West had made trying to understand the methods of Titian.[8] West never, as far as we know, wrote anything about his painting processes. But many of the experiments by West and his students can be documented, and their influence on British and American art (and the preservation of paintings from this period) was far-reaching.

WEST IN LONDON

West arrived in London in 1763, during a decade of great change for artists in Britain. In the 1760s there were more painters and more places to exhibit than ever before, which may have increased the level of competition among them. Richard Wilson, a British painter who had studied in Italy, was described as having "his secrets of colour, and his mystery of the true principles in painting, which he refused to explain."[9] At about the same time as Peale's remark on West's unique technique, the leading British painter of the day—Joshua Reynolds, who had studied in Italy ten years prior to West, where he copied and speculated on the techniques of the old masters—began writing down accounts of his experiments with a variety of unusual painting materials. Reynolds was secretive about these recipes during his lifetime; the recipes, written in a mixture of English and Italian, often involved glazing with thin, transparent layers of color over a "dead-colored" underpainting (done in monochrome or in a limited range of colors), which he believed was the method of Titian. Reynolds's methods of glazing, which were said to give a "deep-toned brightness"[10] to his paintings, were greatly admired at the time, although eventually Reynolds would be held up as an example of the perils of experimentation, when it was discovered that many of his paintings lasted poorly[11]

When West described at a later time the process he used in the first commission that he obtained after coming to England, he told Joseph Farington he mixed blue with his white to give it a cooler tone and used only this white, along with red and black colors, to paint the flesh. When these layers were dry, he finished the flesh with warm glazing colors. While West did not acknowledge the debt, the avoidance of yellow in the preliminary layers of flesh colors, and glazing with warm, transparent colors afterwards, is very similar to the procedure that Reynolds used in many of his paintings.[12]

An anecdote of about this time says a great deal about the changes in style and technique embraced by British painters who had been to Italy. At some time between 1766 and 1768, West and Richard Wilson were in charge of hanging an exhibition of the Society of Artists in London. Wilson found many of the paintings deficient in their technique, calling them "a shower of chalk and brick-bats ." Wilson "improved" nearly half of the paintings by applying a black-brown glaze made from ink and licorice, which he said was "as good as asphaltum."[13] "Chalk and brick-bats [pieces of brick]" implies that the paintings were opaquely blended in the manner of older painters such as Thomas Hudson and William Hogarth, and the dark, asphaltumlike glaze presumably added some of the "deep-toned brightness" that Wilson felt was lacking. The use of asphaltum (or bitumen), a rich, transparent blackish-brown color, is very characteristic of painters who had worked in Italy at this time, including Reynolds, Wilson, Mengs, and West.[14]

There is a connection between the passionate admiration that these painters had for old paintings, the copying of old paintings, and love of the "tone" that old paintings acquired when they become darker over the years. A book on landscape painting reflecting the observations of British painters in Italy in the 1760s emphasized the importance of giving green trees a brownish tinge.[15] (Green foliage in early Italian paintings often turns brown over time.) The enameler William Birch, who copied Reynolds's oil paintings in enamel, wrote that he needed to invent a new enamel color to imitate the deep brown tints he found in paintings by Reynolds, and he also invented a new method of preparing enamel underlayers with a thin coating of yellow, "which gives a warmth of colouring not other wise to be obtained for the picture … and effects the beauty of age seen in many of the old Paintings in Oil by the former Masters."[16] The interconnected topics of color, age, taste, and "tone" would come up repeatedly in decades to come, but much of the groundwork for this taste appears to have been laid in the 1760s.[17]

Firsthand accounts by visiting American artists give snapshot views of the methods used by West at different times in his career. During the mid-1770s, John Singleton Copley sent letters back to Boston describing the variability of West's technique at that time. Copley wrote down West's method for giving "richness to your Colours" (echoing Peale's observation eight years earlier that West's technique gave "great luster & Strength to the Coulering"). This method consisted of adding poppy oil that had been cooked with mastic resin. According to Copley, West "sometimes" added copal varnish mixed with poppy oil to his paints, which West told him was another method that gave "great richness to the Colours."[18] Copley also named West as an artist who had tried to imitate the method of Titian by painting underlayers in watercolors, then glazing with oil paint.[19]

Copley reported in 1775 that West used two different retouching varnishes containing a substantial proportion of spermaceti (a waxy product obtained from sperm whales).[20] A retouching varnish would have been understood at the time as a layer applied to a partly completed painting after the paint was dry, so that new paint could be more easily applied. Wax was a popular topic of experimentation all over Europe by this time (see chapter 3), and Reynolds and Alexander Cozens were, like West, using waxy varnishes or intermediate layers in London in the 1770s.[21] But it is significant that West's recipe was unique—in fact, Copley said (twice) that adding spermaceti was West's exclusive formula, implying strongly that West had invented it himself.[22] In 1778 a recipe called "Benjamin West's Spirit Varnish" appeared in the British painter Ozias Humphry's memorandum book; it consisted of sandarac dissolved in alcohol with a little fir balsam added.[23] However, this is the same recipe that Copley had sent to Humphry three years earlier, shortly after he had arrived from the American colonies, and which also appears in Humphry's memorandum book as "Copley's varnish."[24] Most likely West had gotten the recipe from Copley (see chapter 3).

Another aspect of West's experimentation has to do not with paints or varnishes but with optical devices. West seems to have used a camera obscura even before he left America, probably in the late 1740s or early 1750s.[25] In 1777 Horace Walpole described a new version of the camera obscura—William Storer's "Delineator"—and said, "Sir Joshua Reynolds and West are gone mad with it."[26] The direction that Reynolds's and West's madness took is indicated by Walpole's following remark: "it will be all their own faults if they do not excell Rubens in light and shade, and all the Flemish masters in truth."[27] In Walpole's view, the most modern mechanical inventions were best employed to achieve (or exceed) the effects of the old masters. William Dunlap told a story that relates to this or another optical device in West's studio, saying that Gilbert Stuart accidentally dropped a camera lucida and smashed it to pieces while West and his students were examining it.[28] Stuart was probably already familiar with the camera obscura. Dunlap reported that the Scottish immigrant painter Cosmo Alexander had used a camera obscura for taking landscape views in Newport, Rhode Island, in the 1770s, where presumably his student, the young Stuart, would have seen the instrument in use.[29] (These devices were considered especially useful for rendering in two dimensions the complex lines of recession in a landscape.) Further evidence of West's belief in the utility of these technical aids is found in correspondence in 1802 between members of the Scottish-American Robertson family of painters, which included the observation: "[West] would recommend the camera obscura to any artist, whether portrait, history or landscape."[30] (See also chapter 10 on optical devices in the nineteenth century.)

In 1784 John Trumbull recorded a conversation in which West outlined in some detail his theory that fine coloring is best produced by glazing with complementary colors—for instance, glazing a blue drapery that is "too powerful and glittering" with a transparent orange color "will at once reduce the Colour to the depth requir'd & at the same time give the most pleasing Modesty & Union of Tone." For glazing, West recommended mixing paints with "a composition of drying Oil with a small proportion of Mastic Varnish & oil of turpentine." This is a version of megilp, the favorite medium of this period. West made the sensible suggestion that a painting be thoroughly dry before glazing but added somewhat impractically that "if it has stood two or three Years the better." West named the pigments Prussian blue, red lake, and yellow lake as "the substances which in oil painting approach most nearly to the Atmospheric Colours of Nature."[31] These are the most transparent primary colors in use at the time, and would be important for a painter whose technique depended on transparent glazes. (Unfortunately, all of these pigments can fade on exposure to strong light.)

According to Trumbull, West said that asphaltum "is also most wonderfully usefull when great Depth is requir'd, united with clearness."[32] Humphry also emphasized the importance to West of deep-toned glazing colors: "Mr. West used Lake & asphaltum for all the great depth of his pictures."[33] Others described West's fondness for asphaltum.[34] In the early 1780s West gave advice to Copley about glazing the latter's *Death of the Earl of Chatham* with the color called "mummy."[35] Mummy is a pigment made from ground-up Egyptian mummies; the asphaltum used in embalming produced a transparent brown color that was prized by European painters beginning in the sixteenth century.[36] (West apparently had a special liking for this version of asphaltum, for an 1808 book described mummy as "the finest brown used by Mr. West in glazing."[37])

WEST, THE PROVISES, AND THE VENETIAN SECRET

West was reported to have been generous with his advice by many of his students and colleagues. Dunlap, who studied with him and interviewed many of West's former pupils when writing his history of American art, said that West "had no secrets or mysteries."[38] But in 1797 West became deeply involved in an episode—the so-called Venetian Secret—that put his reputation at risk.

The Venetian Secret affair had begun inauspiciously enough. Joseph Farington wrote: "I first heard of the discovery at the Academy Club from Tresham and Daniell, & paid little attention to it, having so frequently heard of discoveries of processes which came to nothing."[39] A man named Provis and his daughter, who was a painter, claimed that a manuscript written by Mr. Provis's grandfather contained the secrets of Titian and other painters that had been given to him in Italy more than seventy years ago by a Signor Barri.[40]

The Provises approached West in his capacity as president of the Royal Academy, seeking money for their secret, eventually asking for £600.[41] West took lessons in the method but then dragged his feet for more than a year, leading Provis to complain to Farington that West "meant to monopolize the discovery to have an advantage at the next Exhibition" and even that West intended "to cheat him."[42] Farington also heard from others that West was claiming that he had discovered most of the process himself.[43] Some of the confusion and controversy are understandable given West's earlier interest in Venetian technique and the fact that—as Provis himself admitted—"The Secret when known appears to be so simple &

obvious, that every one will wonder it did not occur to him."[44] But Farington and others seemed inclined to think ill of West; Farington described a conversation with Peter Francis Bourgeois: "We concurred in condemning the indirect proceedings of West. [Bourgeois] remarked on the habit of West in adopting the thoughts of others & presenting them as his own."[45]

West was to some degree vindicated when Provis supposedly withdrew the worst of his accusations,[46] but Farington clearly remained suspicious. A committee of artists demanded that they, too, be given a chance to learn the secret, and eventually an accommodation was reached. A number of painters, including the American-born John Trumbull and Mather Brown as well as West, his son Raphael West, Farington, Thomas Lawrence, and others, paid ten guineas each to the Provises for the secret, with a £2,000 penalty stipulated if any of the subscribers leaked it to others.[47] Trumbull was included because he was staying in West's house at the time and others suspected that he "from his sagacity" was likely to have discovered the secret; Farington proposed making Trumbull an exception to a rule against foreigners learning the process, and the other British artists agreed.[48]

Secrecy was taken very seriously. Provis suggested that if James Poole, the colorman, stretched any fabrics for subscribers to the method, he should stain the canvas gray on the back to conceal the color of the Provises' ground, which was an important part of the secret.[49] Farington drew up a document to stipulate that even artists who painted large paintings were required to apply their grounds "at home under their own eye" to prevent the secret from spreading via the colormen who normally applied grounds to large canvases.[50] There was great anxiety among the subscribers that William Beechey, who refused to pay for the secret, had obtained it by "scoundrel conduct."[51]

The rise and fall of the Venetian Secret is documented in Farington's diary, and West was involved at every stage. In January 1797 West—at that time the only artist who had actually tried the process—recommended it highly, saying that it answered questions that had "puzzled him and all other imitators of the Venetian colouring. Sir Joshua had tried wax &c & He [West] had attempted by many means, but could not accomplish his attempt."[52] West also approved the process because it allowed artists to paint quickly (always a high recommendation throughout the history of painting techniques): "Artists may paint with double expedition....Half a dozen pictures may be prepared in a row and coloured at once."[53] When West showed fellow artists two paintings done with the method, *Venus Comforting Cupid* and *Portrait of Raphael and Benjamin West,* he made a prediction: "A new Epocha in the Art...would be formed by the discovery."[54]

Farington kept notes on the process. An important part of the method consisted of a dark reddish-brown, absorbent ground made with glue size and earth pigments. On the dark ground, a monochrome underpainting was done, with the lights modeled in pure white, and any shadows darker than the ground in the "Titian shade," an invention of the Provises consisting of red lake, a transparent blue pigment, and ivory black.[55] This was called the "russet" stage, and there are many references in Farington's diary in 1797 to artists "russeting." After the russet was dry, the coloring was applied by extensive glazing with transparent colors. Many specific pigment mixtures were recommended for the various parts of a painting, and the medium was simply linseed oil rather than any more exotic medium.[56] Farington's notes gave the sensible advice that in the interest of good preservation, the artist should mix a moderate quantity of oil into the paint beforehand rather than dipping the brush into oil while painting.[57] The Provises offered hints about other schools than the Venetian—a large part of the manuscript was taken up with more conventional kinds of opaque flesh mixtures for painting different complexions in the manner of Correggio, and there were also hints on paint mixtures for landscape painting.[58]

On the occasion of the first demonstration by Miss Provis in front of Farington and other painters in January 1797, not all artists were convinced.[59] Farington must have known it was a bad sign when on March 3 he heard of "[Paul] Sandby having made a humorous Song" about the Provises' secret.[60] A few days later Thomas Lawrence offered more pointed criticism when he lamented that "He had surrendered himself to Provis & his daughter *as if He had never held a pencil*, and afterwards was surprised at having done so to two fools who knew so much less than himself."[61] The list of disappointed artists soon became longer. John Hoppner "found it too humpy & meagre a manner of painting,"[62] implying that he was accustomed to working with materials that allowed him to spread his paint more easily—perhaps the absorbent ground kept his paint from gliding as smoothly as he liked. Other artists were variously "disappointed and mortified" when their russets came out too white, had "some doubts of the process answering," or felt "apprehension" that they had to guard against a "coaly appearance."[63]

As spring approached, artists' dissatisfaction led them to try to make improvements on the Provis process. West suggested underpainting with flesh color rather than pure white,[64] and he described painting *Cicero at the Tomb of Archimedes* "in a mixed manner, partly Venetian, partly with body colours."[65] This must mean that parts were blended opaquely rather than "russeted" and glazed. Newspaper reviews of the Royal Academy exhibition that spring were critical of the Venetian pictures, calling them too cold,[66] which is not surprising given that the pure white modeling over a dark ground would tend toward blue, while the Titian shade made with red, blue, and black would be purplish. Unless substantial yellow was added at the glazing stage, paintings could very well end up cold in tone.[67]

After the bad reviews of the Academy exhibition, some of the subscribers tried additional variations on the Provis method.[68] There was also much second-guessing. Farington did something that, astonishingly, no one else seems to have done at this time. He studied the paintings attributed to Titian owned by West and found "the grounds much warmer than Provis's grounds—and the objects are painted in *Colour* not russetted."[69] West was also backpedaling fast, and in June 1797 Farington wrote that West "*now says* Provis's grounds are too *cold & purple*."[70] West tried to rewrite history that July on a day when he was peevish with the gout; as Farington described the scene, West "has painted a small picture on a warm ground—complained of Committee who examined Provis's process—said He knew the *Black Ground would not do*."[71] The final nail in the coffin was a cartoon by Gillray in November 1797, which ridiculed the believers and depicted West slinking away at the corner of the scene.[72] It is difficult to document precisely the end of the Venetian Secret affair. As in the case of many bad ideas for which people have paid money, there were few expressions of regret; they simply stopped talking about it.[73]

AFTER THE VENETIAN SECRET

The Venetian Secret affair by no means convinced West to give up his search for the secrets of earlier painters. Like many others, he continued to believe that the ground layer was an important part of Venetian technique. As early as 1797, the year of the Venetian Secret, Sebastian Grandi had promoted an alternative secret recipe for a ground; at first he tried to sell it for a fee,[74] but in 1806 published the recipe and was awarded a silver medal and twenty guineas by the Society of Arts. Initially, Farington recorded that West "does not like Grandi's grounds,"[75] but by 1806 West's name appeared along with many other British artists who gave testimonials in favor of them. Grandi's absorbent grounds (made from calcined sheep's trotters and wheat flour) were said to be "in the old Venetian stile; an art which has been long lost."[76] At about this time there are indications that West was also working with the London colorman James Poole to make special absorbent grounds according to West's recipe.[77] This is significant because Poole's firm was taken over in the early nineteenth century by Thomas Brown,[78] and many American artists would eventually use Brown's absorbent grounds. The origin of this kind of ground may possibly be the relationship between West and Poole in 1803.

In the year 1800, West had a new idea about the medium of the old masters: he confided to John Trumbull that he believed the Venetians "must have employed *Gum Sandarac*, adding that he had made many experiments, but could find no means of dissolving it in oil, or of combining it so as to work with any facility."[79] This set Trumbull off on an elaborate series of experiments of his own, which will be described in chapter 3.

Even while involved with the Venetian Secret, West had speculated on the techniques of Northern painters, placing great importance on their use of thin washes of color over a white ground. West believed that "Vandevelde glazed a sized White ground with Brown Pink and Ivory Black, or with Vandyke Brown & Blue, which served for middle tints, then outlined and laid in respective colours thin & so went on to finishing."[80] West was among those who traveled to Paris in 1802 during the brief Peace of Amiens to see the treasures that Napoleon had brought there from all over Europe, and this must have deepened his interest in art from all periods and nations.[81] In the next few years he copied works by both Rembrandt and Van Dyck and incorporated the lessons into his own paintings. He believed that Rembrandt, like Van de Velde, painted with multiple thin glazes over a white ground.[82]

When Rembrandt Peale visited London in 1802–3, he recorded conversations in which West continued to recommend color mixtures that sound very much like the Provises'—for instance, asphaltum, red lake, and blue were recommended by West as a "general shade" for glazing.[83] At about this time a British publication described another aspect of West's technique:

> According to Mr. West, when you intend to re-paint, re-touch, or glaze your picture, let it first be tolerably dry, then give the whole, or the part you intend to paint, a coat of varnish a day or two before, after which you may mix some of the same varnish with the colors you put on, which will make them bear out with great force and clearness, insomuch that there will not be the least occasion for varnishing those parts when the whole is finished, only covering the other parts that appear dull or sunk in.[84]

Paint to which varnish has been added—applied on top of varnish—could set up an alarming situation in which the retouching would be likely to be damaged during cleaning. Thomas Sully had concerns about the long-term preservation of a variation of this technique, which was also said to be the method of William Beechey. According to Sully:

> When finishing the picture, no matter how large it may be, [Beechey] brushes it over with a mixture of drying oil and spirits of turpentine, and then adds upon it a mixture of turpentine and gold-size, upon this mixture he retouches the work, and it serves as a varnish.
>
> I am persuaded this practice would hasten the destruction of the picture, and at all events change the tone. Mr. West followed the same process in his picture of "Christ Healing the Sick" and the defect of it is already visible. (T.S. 1822)[85]

It appears that Sully was seeing noticeable problems on West's picture only seven years after it was painted, although he did not specify whether the defect was a change of tone or another problem, such as cracking. Sully apparently had been in direct communication with West about this painting, because Sully wrote that West told him to varnish with a mixture of drying oil and turpentine any parts of *Christ Healing the Sick* that needed "bringing out."[86]

West had problems with cracking on some of his paintings. In 1806 he retouched (and dated a second time) paintings done fourteen years earlier. On one of these paintings, West's retouching and his second inscription clearly go over and into a pattern of wide drying crackle, indicating that concealing the disfiguring crackle was the likely motivation for the retouching.[87] Applying varnishes or other fast-drying layers such as gold size, as described above, could cause cracking if the underlayers of oil paint were not yet dry. A waxy coating between the layers of paint (as Copley described in West's paintings of ca. 1775) could also contribute to cracking by keeping the layers from sticking to one another. When William Beechey, in the nineteenth century, painted over a layer of wax as an experiment, he found his painting "cracked all over."[88]

Cracking may also be aggravated by the pigment asphaltum, a tarry material that never completely dries. West's method for glazing with asphaltum at one time included mixing it with copaiva balsam, another unstable material that may have exacerbated the problem.[89] But problems of preservation are a relative thing at this period, and West's work was considered to have lasted well compared to that of Reynolds, whose paintings deteriorated alarmingly even during Reynolds's lifetime. Around 1840, Benjamin Robert Haydon (obviously not an admirer of West) could write: "While West's detestable surface has stood from the simplicity of his vehicle, half of Sir Joshua's heads are gone."[90]

The overall impression given by West's technique is that it was far from simple—he used an ever-changing variety of materials and techniques throughout his career. He played an important role during the initial period of enthusiasm about the "secrets" of the old masters in Rome and London in the 1760s, and over the course of his long presidency of the Royal Academy he encouraged and gave prestige to this search for secret recipes. It is thus somewhat surprising that toward the end of his life he seemed to repent of this, as seen in the quotation from Galt cited previously, and in the following posthumous comment from his pupil Charles Robert Leslie: "Mr. West…thought we had better colours and oils than were known to Titian and Veronese. I believe he was right, and that the *Venetian* secret, as it is called, was not a chemical secret. We must study nature, as they did, in the *fields* and in the *streets*, to arrive at it. Most of us confine our observations too much to our painting rooms."[91]

This sensible advice was becoming more fashionable in some quarters during the period after West's death, and it was becoming correspondingly less fashionable to claim that a single formula was the "secret" of Titian or any other old master painter. But this did not stop painters from trying out new materials, and by the second quarter of the nineteenth century a younger generation of painters would experiment with techniques even more varied than those used by West.

NOTES

1   C.W. Peale to John Beale Bordley [March 1767] (C.W. Peale 1983–2000, 1:47–48).

2   Galt 1820, 122. For a modern study of Galt's book, see Rather 2004.

3   Copley to Henry Pelham, September 29, 1771 (Copley 1914, 163–64); Erffa and Staley 1986,

445–46. The work in question was West's copy of Mengs's *Holy Family* (1762, Ferens Art Gallery, Kingston-upon-Hull, Humberside, U.K.).

4   Oram 1810, 82 (quoting a 1762 letter from Matthew William Peters).

5   Gage 1964, 38 (quoting a 1769 letter from James Barry to Joshua Reynolds).

6   The earliest use of the word "megilp" so far found is in Joshua Reynolds's ledgers from 1767 (Townsend et al. 1998, 205).

7   Galt 1820, 130.

8   Ibid., 131.

9   Cunningham 1879, 1:161. William Beechey on Wilson: "How he made his vehicle he would never say"(Haydon 1853, 3:397).

10   Beechey used these words to describe Reynolds's goal (Haydon 1853, 3:401). Reynolds himself wrote that the method of the Venetians proceeded from "breaking down these fine colors that would appear too raw, to a deep-toned brightness"(cited in Gombrich 1962, 52–53).

11   Cormack 1968–70; Haydon 1853, 3:389–402; Talley 1986.

12   Farington 1978–84, diary entry of January 26, 1808, describing how West painted *Venus and Cupid* (1765, The Parthenon, Nashville, Tennessee) (cited in Erffa and Staley 1986, 232). On the methods of Reynolds, see Talley 1986.

13   Dunlap 1834, 1:66.

14   On Reynolds's use of asphaltum, see Cormack 1968–70, and Talley 1986, 64. On Wilson, see Carlyle 2001, 404 (citing Wilson's recipe for asphaltum from *Practical Treatise* 1795). On Mengs, see Schmid 1948, 89–90 (citing British publications of 1795 and 1810 illustrating Mengs's palette with an inscription saying that "a little asphaltum must be used in all the warm tints").

15   Oram 1810, 30, 89–90 (discussing the importance of asphaltum and yellow glazes for British painters in Rome in the 1760s).

16   Birch "Life" (AAA, microfilm roll P20, frames 640–41).

17   For discussions (from a variety of points of view) concerning admiration of the effects of age on paintings at different periods, see Gombrich 1962, Kurz 1962, Plesters 1962, Mahon 1962, and Talley 2005.

18   Copley to Henry Pelham, June 25–July 2, 1775 (Copley 1914, 333–43).

19   Ibid., 341.

20   Ibid., 336–37.

21   On Cozens, see Rice 1979, 99. For more on wax painting, see Rice 1979, Mayer and Myers 2004, and Mayer and Myers 2006.

22   Copley to Henry Pelham, June 25–July 2, 1775 (Copley 1914, 336–38). West's use of spermaceti in 1775 is the earliest use by an artist we know of, but spermaceti became a topic of interest again in Britain in the 1790s (Mayer and Myers 2004, 135).

23   Humphry Memorandum-Book, April 2, 1778. Our thanks to Anne Ruggles for giving us a copy of her 1990 notes on West.

24   Copley to Ozias Humphry, July 2, 1775 (AAA/Hart, microfilm roll D5, frames 42–44); Humphry Memorandum-Book, March 22, 1779.

25   See chapter 1, note 32.

26   Simon 1987, 133. A camera obscura that belonged to West is owned by the Science Museum, London (illustrated in Kemp 1990, 198).

27   Simon 1987, 133.

28   Dunlap 1834, 1:87. Dunlap must have misremembered, because the camera lucida was only invented in 1806, by which time Stuart had been gone from London for nineteen years. The difference between the two is that the camera obscura throws an image via a lens onto a surface within a dark chamber (*camera obscura*); the camera lucida, which appeared in many variations after 1806, allowed an artist to copy an image in daylight (Kemp 1990, 188–202; Ayres 1985, 69–71). Dunlap may have been thinking of the "Delineator" or another improvement on the camera obscura.

29   Dunlap 1834, 1:166.

30   Andrew Robertson to Alexander Robertson, September 18, 1802 (Robertson 1897, 84).

31   Trumbull Papers Yale (cited by Sizer 1967, 134–35).

32   Ibid.

33   Humphry Memorandum-Book, 113. The entry is undated, but Humphry's memoranda date from 1777 to 1795.

34   R. Peale Miscellaneous, undated sheet beginning, "Asphaltum: Mr. West was fond…" See also notes 83 and 87 below.

35   Farington in 1806 (cited in Erffa and Staley 1986, 218). *Death of the Earl of Chatham* (1779–81, Tate Gallery, London).

36   Gettens and Stout 1966, 132; Woodcock 1996; Languri and Boon 2005.

37   *Compendium of Colours* 1808, 221.

38   Alberts 1978, 68.

39   Farington 1978–84, diary entry of January 17, 1797. See also Trumble and Aronson 2008.

40   Farington 1978–84, diary entries of January 6, January 11, and February 13, 1797. Gage 1964 states that the manuscript was claimed to be an authentic sixteenth-century Italian manuscript, but Farington at least never said this. Farington wrote that Provis's grandfather had died about seventy years before, which means he must have died fairly young, in about 1727, making the probable date of the alleged manuscript about 1700–1727.

41   Farington 1978–84, diary entries of January 5 and 6, 1797.

42   Ibid., January 10 and 17, 1797.

43   Ibid., January 12 and January 17, 1797.

44   Ibid., January 6, 1797.

45   Ibid., January 16, 1797.

46   Ibid., January 25, 1797.

47   Gage 1964; Alberts 1978, 225–32; Erffa and Staley 1986, 174–75, 226–27, 230–31, 234–35, 460–61, 545–46; D. Evans 1982, 191 (citing Whitley 1928, 2:210). George Beaumont also paid for the secret, but as an amateur he paid twenty guineas instead of ten (Farington 1978–84, diary entry of March 9, 1797).

48   Farington 1978–84, diary entry of February 22, 1797.

49   Ibid., January 24, 1797. Poole was active in London ca. 1780–1800 (Katlan 1992, 461, fig. 223).

50   Farington 1978–84, diary entry of February 13, 1797. See also Farington "Provis." Our thanks to Mark Aronson for providing us with a photocopy of this document.

51   Farington 1978–84, diary entries of February 23, March 9, and March 15 and 16, 1797.

52   Ibid., January 17, 1797.

53   Ibid., January 23, 1797.

54   Ibid., January 18, 1797. Both paintings, from 1796–97, are at the Nelson-Atkins Museum of Art, Kansas City, Missouri.

55   The blue colors Farington lists for making the Titian shade are: "Indigo or Hungarian (Prussian) Blue (or Antwerp) (Indigo softest)" (Farington "Provis"). This is somewhat confusing, because Hungarian blue is an uncommon term but most likely refers to one of the copper pigments, since Hungary had been a source of azurite in earlier times (Harley 1982, 47). Indigo and various copper pigments could have been used in Titian's time. Farington put "Prussian" in parentheses next to Hungarian blue; if he believed that the two were the same, this would be an historical anachronism, for Prussian blue had not been invented in Titian's time. Prussian blue, invented in 1704, would, however, have been available in the lifetime of Provis's grandfather, the alleged source of the manuscript. Antwerp blue is also a somewhat confusing term. After the middle of the nineteenth century, a variation of Prussian blue was called Antwerp blue. But in the late eighteenth and early nineteenth century various copper pigments, including artificially made copper blues—versions of which *could* have been used in the time of Titian—were called Antwerp blue (Carlyle 2001, 474). See also Trumble and Aronson 2008, 27–29; Gage 1964, 38; and Whitley 1928, 2:211–12. On Antwerp blue, see also chapter 4, note 70.

56   In November 1797, Miss Provis showed Farington and others that "White of Egg well beat up would serve as a drying vehicle when russetting with *white*. The[n] oil out with Linseed oil & dabbing of the superfluous oil, Glaze with Colours as in the process manner." The egg medium seems to have been a late development in the process, when many artists had already become disenchanted (Farington 1978–84, diary entry of November 27, 1797).

57   Farington "Provis" and Farington 1978–84, diary entry of January 25, 1797, where West said "the poorest [purest?] oil best, that oil which is most watery (new oil)."

58   Farington "Provis."

59   Farington 1978–84, diary entry of January 30, 1797. Opie was "dissatisfied"; Stothard was "alarmed, said it was only a glazing System."

60   Ibid., March 3, 1797. The lyrics to the song are printed in Trumble and Aronson 2008, 50–51.

61   Faringron 1978–84, diary entry of March 6, 1797. Later, on June 25, when other artists were making modifications to the Provis process, he wrote, "Lawrence told me today He had been painting in body color—on Provis' dark ground & thought it an advantage."

62   Ibid., March 20, 1797.

63   Ibid., March 18 and April 6, 1797.

64   Ibid., April 5, May 21, June 6, 1797.

65   Ibid., April 6, 1797. For a discussion of *Cicero at the Tomb of Archimedes* (1797, private collection), see Trumble and Aronson 2008.

66   Farington 1978–84, diary entry of May 1, 1797.

67   Much later Farington described Smirke doing exactly this: "Smirke has passed Yellow Lake over *Angersteins process pictures* as a ground for correcting coldness. I think it will be a good way to pass Yellow Lake over Russett *at first* and then tint, in order to get rid of coldness. Sometimes to mix it with Asphaltum to avoid greenish color" (Farington 1978–84, diary entry of November 1, 1797).

68   For instance, some tried a variation of the Provises' method on "oil umber ground" with "no size or Spanish brown to avoid cracking," implying that cracking had been a problem (Farington 1978–84, diary entry of May 22, 1797). George Beaumont seems to have put aside dark grounds and was painting on bare canvas or on white grounds (ibid., May 26 and 28, 1797).

69   Ibid., June 6, 1797. For modern studies of the grounds and other materials actually used by Titian, see Birkmaier, Wallert, and Rothe 1995, 119–20; and Dunkerton, Foister, and Penny 1999, 282.

70   Farington 1978–84, diary entry of June 6, 1797.

71   Ibid., July 17, 1797. The last entry in Farington's diary that associates West with the Provises' technique was on August 26, when West was apparently simultaneously trying to make improvements to and complaining about the process: "West has painted a Bacchanti on a Buff-Col'd. ground, adhering *to the process* except in Flesh which in the body colour becomes a contrast which He think luminous—He says 'twas the way of Titian—the other *process that* of Bassan. Said He made this objection to Provis formerly."

72   Farington mentioned a discussion with another artist about the Gillray print (ibid., November 23, 1797).

73   References to the Venetian Secret in Farington's diary fell off dramatically after the spring of 1797, but sporadic mentions of attempts to improve upon it appeared in the fall and early winter. On December 10, 1797, Farington transcribed, without comment, a number of favorable newspaper reviews of his paintings using the Provis process shown at the Academy the previous May. In the run-up to the next Academy exhibition in May 1798 there was complete silence in Farington's diary about matters of technique. The first definite mention of Farington trying out a system of painting other than the Provis system, involving a "simple palette," occurred on June 13 and 16, 1798.

74   Farington 1978–84, diary entries of March 30, May 21, and June 6, 1797. On May 21 Farington claimed that "Grandi carried abt. a picture painted by Tresham by the Provis *Process* & shewed it as being painted with Grandis process & got subscribers for his secret."

75   Ibid., diary entry of June 6, 1797.

76   *Transactions of the Society for the Encouragement of Arts, Manufacturers, and Commerce* 24 (1806): 85–89. Grandi also had methods for purifying oil and making pigments that he said were unique. For more on Grandi, see Carlyle 2001, 39n7.

77   "Today Daniell shewed me the Canvasses prepared in West's manner at Poole's Shop,—which absorb and require only Linseed oil" (Farington 1978–84, diary entry of January 3, 1803). "Daniell called in morning to ask abt. drawing in outlines on absorbing ground for Linseed oil, agreeable to his & West's process" (ibid., January 10, 1803).

78   Katlan 1992, 456.

79   Trumbull Inventories (recalling a conversation from 1800, recorded following an entry dated April 1814), unpaginated. See also chapter 3.

80   Farington 1978–84, diary entry of February 3, 1797, probably referring to Willem Van de Velde the Elder or the Younger, both of whom worked in England.

81   Dunlap 1834, 1:80–81.

82   Erffa and Staley 1986, 200, 443.

83   "Mr. West, mentions that asphaltum, blue and lake produce a fine deep tone" and, as a footnote:

"General shade Glazing asphaltum, lake & Blue"(R. Peale Miscellaneous, undated sheet signed by Rembrandt Peale, "James Peale" written on reverse). West recommended glazing with mummy, which could be mixed with blue, red, "or any other glazing colors"(*Compendium of Colours* 1808, 221). According to Rembrandt Peale, West "glazed [*King Lear*] with Asphaltum, Lake & Blue, & retouched it previous to Fulton's bringing it to America" (R. Peale Miscellaneous, undated sheet beginning, "Asphaltum: Mr. West was fond…").

84   *Compendium of Colours* 1808, 218.

85   Sully "Hints," AAA, microfilm roll N18, frame 79 (1822); see also Sully, "Memoirs," 11. The story was repeated almost verbatim in Dunlap 1834, 2:126. "Gold size," also called "Japanners' gold size," was a quickly drying oil of variable composition (Carlyle 2001, 37–38). *Christ Healing the Sick* (1815, Pennsylvania Hospital, Philadelphia).

86   Sully, "Hints," AAA, microfilm roll N18, frame 230 (June 25, 1854).

87   Paintings by West that are signed and dated twice include *Ophelia and Laertes before the King and Queen* (1792/1806, Cincinnati Art Museum) and *King Lear* (1788/1806, Museum of Fine Arts, Boston), both of which are signed: "Retouched 1806" (Erffa and Staley 1986, 271–73). Rembrandt Peale wrote of *King Lear* that: "Our dry atmosphere by contracting these thick glazings & retouches, which were on a soft varnish, has nearly destroyed it,—the cracks being more than the eighth of an inch wide" (R. Peale Miscellaneous, undated sheet beginning, "Asphaltum: Mr. West was fond…"). The authors treated *Ophelia and Laertes* and believe that in that case at least, the fact that West's retouching and his second signature go over and into the cracks proves that the crackle existed prior to the retouching, rather than having been caused by the glazing.

West justified the practice of extensive retouching, saying that when he signed a painting a second time he considered it "a new picture"(West to the members of the Council of the Royal Academy, April 16, 1803 [HSP; AAA, microfilm roll P23, frame 225]); see also Alberts 1978, 280–85.

In 1819 Farington, at the request of Lawrence, Mrs. West, and Benjamin West, Jr., talked to West "about the injury he does to his pictures long since painted, by touching upon them with fresh colour which would not assimilate with the old colour." West replied that "in eleven or twelve years the colours would harmonize"(Farington 1978–84, diary entry of September 3, 1819 [cited in Alberts 1978, 383]).

88   Haydon 1853, 3:396.

89   *Compendium of Colours* 1808, 11–12.

90   Haydon 1853, 3:400.

91   Dunlap 1834, 2:247.

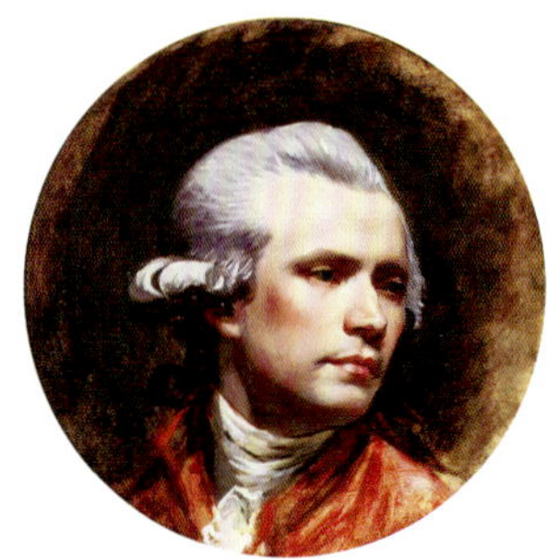

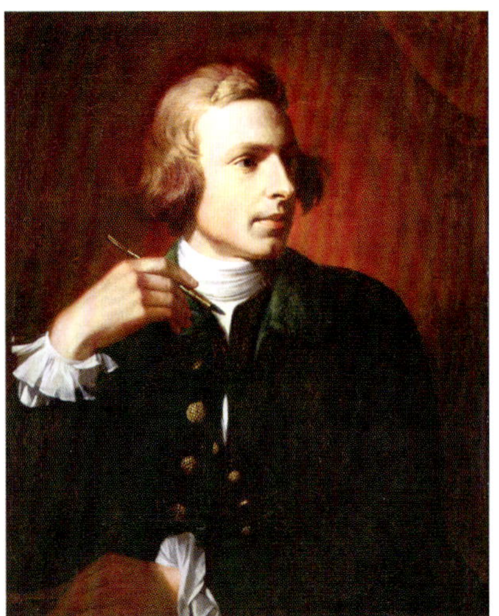

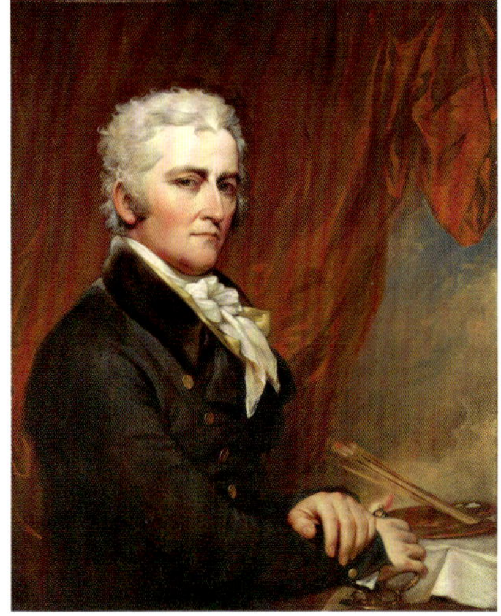

FIGURE 3

John Singleton Copley (American, 1738–1815), *Self-Portrait*, 1780–84.
Oil on canvas, diam. 56.5 cm (22¼ in.). Washington, D.C., Smithsonian Institution,
National Portrait Gallery, Gift of the Morris and Gwendolyn Cafritz Foundations
with Matching Funds from the Smithsonian Women's Committee, 77.22. Photo: National Portrait
Gallery, Smithsonian Institution/Art Resource, N.Y.

FIGURE 4

Benjamin West (American, 1738–1820), *Portrait of Charles Willson Peale*, 1767–69.
Oil on canvas, 71.7 × 58.4 cm (28¼ × 23 in.). New York, New-York Historical Society, 1867.293.

FIGURE 5

John Trumbull (American, 1756–1843), *Self-Portrait*, ca. 1802.
Oil on canvas, 75.5 × 62.4 cm (29¾ × 24 9/16 in.). New Haven, Conn., Yale University Art Gallery,
Gift of Marshall H. Clyde Jr., 1981.129.1.

CHAPTER 3
AMERICANS IN THE OLD WORLD:
COPLEY, THE PEALES, AND TRUMBULL

JOHN SINGLETON COPLEY

JOHN SINGLETON COPLEY WAS BORN the same year as Benjamin West and was already an accomplished painter when he moved to London at the age of thirty-six in 1774. He did not seek instruction from West but embarked on a course of self-improvement based on a close study of the old masters, although letters that he sent back to Boston show that he also learned a great deal about West's painting techniques. After a month and a half in London, Copley set off for France and Italy, where he was finally able to see the original paintings he had known in America only from copies. Copley's letters to his half-brother Henry Pelham, who was also a painter, spoke at length of the appearance of Italian paintings. Now that he had seen the originals, he criticized John Smibert's copy of a painting by Raphael, saying that the original had "none of the olive tint" and was "not so bricky" and that the drawing of the hands in Smibert's copy was "very incorrect." He also remembered the copy by West of a painting by Titian as being "less broken and variegated in the tints of Flesh than the original. I think it has more of the look of Putty or leather."[1]

Copley's study of the old masters led him to speculate immediately about what materials and techniques he might use himself to imitate these effects. For Copley at least, the search for "Magilphs and mysteries" was still as much alive in Italy of the mid-1770s as it had been in the Italy that West had known in the early 1760s. Copley proposed imitating the effects of Titian by applying an underpainting, or "dead-coloring," on an absorbent ground (which would absorb the oil), coating this underpainting with mastic varnish, then finishing with glazes. The object seems to have been to keep the brightness of the underpainting from being darkened by too much oil.[2]

In Italy, Copley learned by making copies, and he also painted original compositions based on biblical and classical subjects. British painters in Italy remarked on his slowness as a copyist. Joseph Wright of Derby wrote to Ozias Humphry: "It is with infinite labours that he produces what he does, but that is *entre nous*."[3] Others noted Copley's unique, methodical way of making many "tints" (colors mixed on the palette beforehand), probably a sign of his provincial self-training.

As Dunlap described it: "Mr. West told me he [Copley] was the most tedious of all painters. When painting a portrait, he used to match with his palette-knife a tint for every part of the face, whether in light, shadow, or reflection. This occupied himself and the sitter a long time before he touched the canvas."[4]

Unfortunately, nothing is known about the experiments in the manner of Titian that Copley proposed in the 1770s, and there are only tantalizing shreds of written evidence about any aspect of Copley's technique after this time.[5] Back in England, he apparently took technical advice from West on occasion—when Copley painted his *Death of the Earl of Chatham* in 1779–81, "it was under the eye of West that Copley harmonized it," using the brown pigment mummy.[6] West's advice about harmonizing implies that he felt the coldness and/or "over minuteness" which Copley had been criticized for when he sent paintings to London from America in the 1760s remained a problem.

The two artists eventually became rivals, but there are hints that Copley continued to share West's fascination with the secrets of the old masters. Copley's early biographer wrote that "He sometimes made experiments in colours; the methods of the Greeks, the elder Italians, and the schools of Florence and Venice, he was long in quest of; and he wrote out receipts for composing those lustrous hues in which Titian and Correggio excelled."[7] Except for those contained in his 1775 letters, Copley's "receipts" (recipes) are lost, but in 1802 Copley's son wrote to his sister to impart a "great secret" that she should tell to no one. The secret was that their father had discovered the method of the Venetians, "which the artists of three generations have in vain been endeavoring to explore." Copley's son went on to say that the greatness of the Venetians "is principally ascribed to the medium, or vehicle, of which they made use, which was peculiar to themselves, which they carefully concealed from others, and which was lost with the decline of their school. Henceforth, then, you may fairly expect that my father's pictures will transcend the productions even of Titian himself."[8] Unfortunately, we do not know the composition of Copley's alleged Venetian medium of 1802, and we hear no more about it in Copley's correspondence.[9]

VARNISHING IN THE EIGHTEENTH CENTURY

Copley's letters from the 1770s give many insights into the question of varnishing, which is an extremely important and sometimes perplexing topic for painters (and for conservators as well). A clear coating of varnish protects a painting from dirt and accidents, and this protective function was recognized in the eighteenth century.[10] But British and American eighteenth-century artists also knew that the saturation of a layer of varnish improved the appearance of a painting: it could make "the effect stronger and the colours the clearer."[11] Artists also knew that varnish was a two-edged sword—a clear varnish coating would eventually grow dark over time, obscuring instead of enhancing a painting's appearance. Charles

Willson Peale wrote that removing and replacing old, darkened varnishes from his own paintings "wonderfully improved their appearance."[12]

While he was still in Italy, Copley sent a varnish recipe to Humphry. From other references in his letters, it seems clear that Copley considered this "his" varnish, and he believed that it was not known to British painters.[13] Presumably this was the varnish that he normally used on his American paintings. As a newcomer and a provincial, Copley may have not realized that his varnish was unknown because it was somewhat old-fashioned. It was made of sandarac,[14] a resin that had been used since medieval times, dissolved in "spirits of wine," or alcohol, with a little fir balsam added.[15]

A very different kind of varnish that, according to Copley, was in "general use" by painters in London, but which Copley had not known about previously, consisted simply of mastic dissolved in spirits of turpentine.[16] The authoritative contemporary French book on varnishing by Jean-Félix Watin said that mastic in turpentine was the only varnish appropriate for oil paintings.[17] Copley's testimony is important because it documents the fact that British painters were coming to believe this as well, in spite of the fact that many other exotic and elaborate varnish recipes continued to be listed in British painting manuals during this period and long afterward.

Sandarac, the main ingredient in Copley's American varnish, had been imported into Boston as early as 1738.[18] We have not seen mastic listed for sale in America prior to Copley's time, although in his letters of 1775 he seemed to assume that Pelham could obtain mastic in Boston if he wanted to. It is worth speculating about why the varnishing practice of the most famous American colonial painter was so different from that of his English contemporaries. Mastic varnish might have been less well known in America simply because it had only recently become the varnish of choice in Britain. But cost may have also been an issue. A price list from a French varnish seller from nearly the same time as Copley's letter shows that the cost of mastic in Paris was five livres per pound, while sandarac cost only one to two livres, depending upon its grade. The cheaper sandarac might have been considered good enough for the bulk of British exports to the colonies.[19]

Copley's 1775 sandarac varnish recipe appeared in Humphry's notebook in 1779 as "Copley's varnish," but in a slightly different form (with additional directions that would ensure the safety of the varnish maker by keeping the bottle from bursting while being heated).[20] However, almost exactly the same recipe appeared in Humphry's notebook a year earlier, in 1778, this time called "Benjamin West's" varnish.[21] The incident may possibly show how West "made his own" any technical tricks that came his way, as Farington had claimed. It is also significant that in this period, when anything that resembled a "secret" was highly treasured, a slightly out-of-date varnish from the colonies could come back to London and be passed around as something special. If British artists knew that sandarac had actually been used since the earliest days of Italian painting, it might have been seen as an additional recommendation. This may also have been a factor in West's coming to believe, by the year 1800, that sandarac—not as a final varnish, as Copley used it, but as a medium—was the secret of the early Venetian painters.

Humphry's recipes make it clear that he knew that Canada gum, or Canada balsam, from North America, was the near equivalent of European fir balsam (also called Strasbourg turpentine). Strasbourg turpentine, like sandarac, had been used as an ingredient in varnishes since the earliest days of medieval Italian painting. It is possible that the influence of the North American painters Copley and West made British painters aware of a North American product—Canada balsam—at this time.[22]

In a period when so many "discoveries" turned out to be mistakes or outright nonsense, the growing realization that mastic dissolved in turpentine was the best varnish, which Copley documents so well, was an important step forward. Since all traditional varnishes turned dark and needed to be periodically removed, it was a great advantage that mastic varnish could be removed much more easily from an old painting than any other varnish known at the time. In fact, the apparent lack of awareness prior to 1775 of simple mastic varnish, even by so particular an artist as Copley, may go some way toward explaining the poor condition of many American paintings of the pre-Revolutionary period, which often have rock-hard residues of old-fashioned oil varnishes stuck in the hollows of the paint texture, accompanied by damage to the paint where the varnish has been scrubbed off the high points. Robert Dossie described the problem of removing oil varnishes: "[Oil varnishes] are greatly out of use now; as such varnishes are slow in drying, and the linseed oil will turn yellow, besides the disadvantage arising from the impracticability of ever taking them off the painting again."[23]

It should be said that Copley's sandarac varnish, which does not contain any oil, would be easier to remove than those made with oil, and in fact many of Copley's American portraits are very well preserved. But the discovery, by Copley and others, that mastic varnish was the best varnish would make it the predominant varnish in Britain and America for many years. Rembrandt Peale documented this when he wrote in the margin of his copy of a 1795 British treatise (which discussed a great variety of varnishes): "use none but mastick."[24]

Retouching Varnishes

Copley's letters also shed light on the topic of retouching varnish, which was applied to a layer of dried paint to allow subsequent layers of paint to be easily applied. This was especially important in helping portrait painters make smooth transitions in flesh tones. Copley's letters tell us that when he was still in America he rubbed dried underlayers with "a little Oyl" to prepare them for additional painting.[25] This was called "oiling out," and a British book of 1760 described it as a common practice.[26]

The new retouching varnishes that Copley learned about from British painters were quite different. One was a variety of what would be called, in the early nineteenth century, "gumtion," a mixture of mastic, sugar of lead, and oil,[27] similar to megilp, but thought by some to have better aging properties.[28] Benjamin West's unique recipe for retouching varnish, which contained spermaceti as well as mastic varnish and poppy oil, has been described above. Ingredients in these varnishes could possibly remain soluble enough to put a painting at risk when it came time to clean it, although even more alarming is Copley's report that "some persons" simply applied a thick layer of mastic varnish to a portrait between sittings.[29]

A thread that runs through Copley's discussion of varnishes is a concern for permanence. He said that West's retouching varnish "will never change," and his discussions about imitating the effects of Titian hinged upon the assumption that adding varnish to paint would make it yellow less. However, both oil and varnish-containing mixtures will discolor over time, especially if used to excess. It is likely that the yellowish cast to the flesh tones in some of Copley's American portraits is due to excessive "oiling out" between sittings. This could have been a particular problem for Copley if he required many sittings for a portrait, as some of his sitters alleged.[30] Faces are the parts of a portrait most likely to suffer from this kind of problem, because they require more sittings in order to capture a likeness and because smooth transitions are especially important in a face (fig. 6). Gilbert Stuart objected specifically to the practice of applying oil to a portrait between sittings, because it might cause discoloration (see chapter 4).

If a layer of oil or retouching varnish was kept very thin, it would of course discolor less, and Copley emphasized this in a letter to Henry Pelham: "You must observe than when you have put the retouching Varnish on your Picture that you wipe it off as clean as you can with a little Cotton Wool, or Peice of Woolin Cloath."[31] Similar advice was given in British treatises of the day,[32] but Copley's insistence upon it to his fellow painter may indicate that this was new information to him, and it hints that he might have suspected that he had used too much oil when "oiling out" his American portraits.

Copley's English pictures have generally lasted quite well, and one sees less of the yellowing of flesh tones than one sees in his American portraits. A theme that will be returned to again and again in this history of painting techniques—which has lessons for modern painters as well—is that problems with the aging of paintings often result from the ways in which materials are employed as much as from the nature of the materials themselves. *Any* oil or natural resin, if applied copiously, can produce yellowing. Copley's desire to paint portraits that lasted well, and his eventual success in doing so during his career in Britain, are documented in an anecdote that has come down from one of his British sitters. The sitter reported that Copley told him he had disdain for contemporary

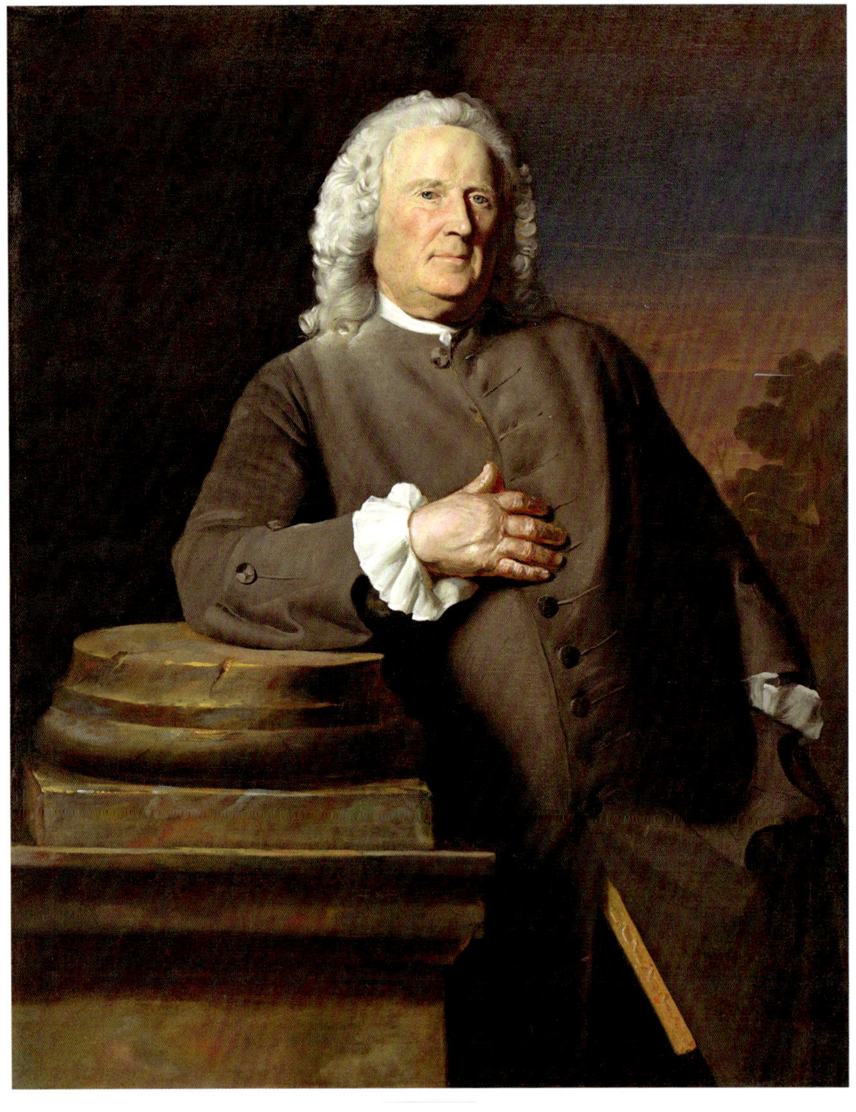

John Singleton Copley (American, 1738–1815), *Portrait of Epes Sargent*, ca. 1760.
Oil on canvas, 126.6 × 101.7 cm (49¹³⁄₁₆ × 40¹⁄₁₆ in.). Washington, D.C., National Gallery of Art,
Gift of the Avalon Foundation, 1959.4.1.

theories that a painting would "ripen in forty years," the sitter adding that his own portrait by Copley had proved the point by lasting without change for more than half a century.[33]

Thick and Thin Varnishes

One striking thing about Copley's varnish recipes—to the modern reader at least—is that the "new" varnishes recommended by British painters would produce very thick solutions. The normal solution of mastic in turpentine that Copley recorded was about 50 percent, and an alternative ("Some Persons make their Varnish much Stronger") was over 70 percent, which would make a very thick and glossy varnish indeed. Copley's own alcohol-based varnish was thinner, about 26 percent, perhaps because it would have been difficult to brush out a thicker solution in such a fast-evaporating solvent as alcohol.[34] It is likely that there were differences of opinion about the appropriate thickness of a varnish layer even at the time. In 1794 a London critic appeared to criticize the American-born Mather Brown for a thick varnish, describing one of his paintings as "filthily beplaistered with a varnish, which will inevitably crack in all directions."[35]

It is possible that, as in some other aspects of technique at this time—such as the classification and naming of varnishes (see note 15 of this chapter)—the British and Americans were still relatively unsophisticated about varnishing compared to the French. Jean-Félix Watin wrote that a varnish layer should be just thick enough to bring the colors together and protect them, but not so thick as to make a glare that would get in the way of seeing the design. This is a subjective judgment, of course, and in another place Watin described an ideal varnish layer (not necessarily on a painting, for Watin dealt with varnishes for other kinds of decorative functions as well) as the thickness of a piece of paper, which is of course variable.[36] Evidence that some eighteenth-century artists and critics viewed glossy varnishes as a bad thing can be seen, in a roundabout way, in the French and English literature about wax painting. It was claimed to be an advantage that wax painting did not require varnish, and therefore "you are capable of seeing the picture in any light, or in whatsoever situation you place it; in short there can be no false glare or light upon the picture for the spectators."[37] The thickness, gloss—and even the appropriateness of any varnish at all—would continue to be topics of discussion on both sides of the Atlantic in the nineteenth century as well.

CHARLES WILLSON PEALE, REMBRANDT PEALE, AND WAX PAINTING

When Charles Willson Peale came to London to study with West in 1767, he almost immediately bought several books.[38] One of these, *Encaustic, or Count Caylus's Method of Painting in the Manner of the Ancients*, by J.H. Müntz, connected him with the latest fad among European painters and set him on a course that would have consequences for American painting for years to come. According to Peale, he had gone out intending to buy that particular book and had its name written down beforehand.[39] West, or another artist, may have recommended it, or Peale's curiosity may have been piqued by having read the excerpts from Müntz that were included in *Handmaid to the Arts*.[40] Müntz's book was the introduction, for most British painters, to the investigations into wax painting that had begun in France in the 1750s. Wax painting had great resonance in the neoclassical period because it supposedly revived the methods of the ancient Greeks as described by Pliny; Pliny's account was so vague that it also provided fertile ground for scientific experimentation, another favorite activity of the age. Joshua Reynolds and George Stubbs were among the British painters who used wax in many of their paintings during this period; eventually, wax painting spread to locations as far-flung as Scandinavia and Russia.[41]

Peale's account of his experiences with Müntz's book tells us, first of all, that the book was so popular in London in 1767 that a pirated edition existed. But Peale also tried out the process and recorded exactly what he thought of it, which is the only unbiased firsthand account of an eighteenth-century artist trying any of the wax processes. Peale wrote: "I have Muntz's encaustic painting and at first was much pleas'd with it; but found on tryal that the fixing the wax darken'd the coulers too much, therefore we cannot have so great an Effect as with Oil besides being much deceiv'd in the changing by fixing them."[42]

The difficulties Peale found in using Müntz's wax process—which involved applying pigments ground in water to a specially prepared support, then heating it in front of a fireplace to "fix" or saturate the colors with wax—helps explain why the method never really caught on. The water-based paint became matte when it dried, and it was difficult for an artist to anticipate the degree of darkening that would take place when the painting was then saturated with wax. These sorts of problems may explain the seemingly endless number of "improved" wax methods that came out of Italy and Germany in the 1770s, 1780s, and 1790s, some of which eventually made their way to England.[43]

In spite of his disappointment with Müntz, Charles Willson Peale never completely lost interest in wax painting, even after he returned to America. He appears to have painted the majority of his paintings in oil; however, a memorandum book kept by Peale beginning in 1794 contains several items relating to encaustic. These include a reference to a 1798 article on encaustic from a London magazine and recipes that are apparently Peale's attempts to make improvements on Müntz's method. The experiments did not always go smoothly, given the following comment: "New Encaustic / Have tried experiment & find it to answer better than the method of Muntz with this defect which is the same in his method." This is rendered ambiguous by the fact that it has been decisively crossed out. Especially notable is another wax recipe that is given in French measure (*gros*) and is attributed in Peale's memorandum book to his son, Rembrandt Peale.[44]

Rembrandt Peale carried his father's interest in wax painting into the nineteenth century. During a visit to France in 1809–10, Rembrandt Peale announced in letters to America (which were immediately published) that he had discovered a new process of encaustic painting. Peale said his invention "succeeded beyond my expectations.…Beauty shall come to me for immortality, for its texture flows from my pencil as I trace its forms; to create flesh is no longer difficult." He effused: "I have not only gained durability in my canvass and colours, but a facility of execution and a spendour of effect that absolutely equal my romantic speculations or waking dreams.…I now paint entirely in encaustic—oil painting appears to me too dirty, too sticky, and too stinking." At this time, Rembrandt Peale used his encaustic method to paint portraits of many of the illustrious Frenchmen of the day, including the painter Jacques-Louis David.[45]

Although Rembrandt Peale claimed he had invented this encaustic process himself around 1810 after nine years of experimentation, the true story may be more complex. Around the same time, the French painter Jacques-Nicholas Paillot de Montabert was promoting in Paris a technique that involved applying paint made from wax mixed with various resins, then fusing them with heat.[46] We do not know exactly what Rembrandt Peale's process was, but it is clear that it, too, involved melting his paints with heat after applying them.[47] (By this time, wax recipes that involved the application of heat appear to have been losing ground in Britain, and British painters who continued to use wax more often employed the simpler procedure of adding a small amount of wax or wax/resin to ordinary oil paint on the palette.[48])

It is significant that Rembrandt Peale never mentioned the ancient Greeks; it was ease of execution and longevity that were claimed as the main advantages of his method. Nor did Paillot de Montabert claim that he was re-creating the methods of antiquity when he finally published his theories on wax painting in a multivolume compendium on technique in 1829. The different emphases, on the part of both Rembrandt Peale and Paillot de Montabert, are perhaps a sign that the neoclassical period had ended, or at least that experimentation could now take on a life of its own independent of ancient precedents.[49]

This extraordinary episode ended in something of a mystery. After the fanfare of Rembrandt Peale's announcement of his encaustic discovery in 1810, and indications that Charles Willson Peale was trying out his son's process in 1811 and was pleased with it,[50] nothing more about encaustic appeared in the Peale family correspondence.[51] John S. Cogdell saw some of Rembrandt Peale's wax paintings in 1816 but was not overly impressed with their style, which he called "very soft" and said that the only benefit was that the technique could be done quickly and repaired easily if necessary.[52] In fact many of Rembrandt Peale's paintings from this time have been found to be unusually sensitive to solvents and/or have been damaged during previous cleanings.

The only other clue to the fate of Rembrandt Peale's grand plans of 1810 came much later, in John Neagle's account of a discussion between himself and Peale in 1832, when Peale tried to sell him a "secret" method of coloring for a sum of money. Neagle rebuffed Peale's offer tartly, saying, "I reminded him of the failure of his wax painting."[53] It is worth considering why Peale's encaustic was considered a failure. Some eighteenth- and early-nineteenth-century wax paintings have suffered from flaking, a flaw all the more poignant since proponents of encaustic had claimed from the earliest days that wax was more permanent than oil.[54] Rembrandt Peale's final verdict on wax painting may be inferred from his manuscript "Notes of the Painting Room," compiled with the intention to publish it and completed about 1850–52. In this document, in which he summed up—as he described it—"the experience of more than half a century," encaustic painting was not even mentioned. However, the addition of wax to oil paint, sometimes in small amounts, remained a topic of discussion for many American painters well into the nineteenth century.

JOHN TRUMBULL, THE EXPERIMENTER

While West, Copley, and Reynolds left only few or cryptic accounts of their attempts to discover the materials of the early Venetians, John Trumbull recorded in some detail a number of his experiments. He recalled that Benjamin West had set him off on his trail of experimentation:

> In the year 1800, conversing with Mr. West, on the subject of the vehicle used by the Venetians in their paintings, which time has proved to be so superior to all others; he stated it as his conjecture, "that they must have employed *Gum Sandarac*, adding that he had made "many experiments, but could find no means of dissolving it in oil, or of combining it so as to work with any facility.—This conversation put me upon the enquiry; and going soon after to Bath, where I had leisure, I made several trials, and found that Sandarac dissolved readily in Alcohol, & in the essential oils of Lavender and Rosemary; and when so dissolved might be combined with colours ground in oil, but not without some difficulty, nor perfectly without a second grinding;—a number of experiments were made specimens of which are preserved in my Colour box.[55]

Trumbull wrote that he used this method of adding sandarac (with a little sugar of lead to promote drying, and sometimes Canada balsam as well) in paintings that he did in Britain and in America until 1809. He noted that "the pictures which were done at that time seem to have preserved their colour & Tone much better than those which I before painted with drying Oil and Mastic Varnish [probably mixed together to form megilp]." Being in Britain seemed to stimulate his creative juices, and upon returning to England in 1809 he embarked on some new experiments, still having as his goal uncovering the secret of the earlier Venetian painters:

for altho in some respects this System [adding sandarac] seemed to approach to
those qualities, which contemporary authors describe as having been possessed by
the Venetian vehicle, yet there remained some striking differences:—it was difficult
to work the colours—and it was expensive:—whereas the paintings particularly of
the *Bassans* were wrought with evident facility:—and they were poor Men:—so poor
that their pictures are often seen, painted on different scraps of linen sewed together:
it is not therefore probable that they employed a vehicle which was expensive; or a
process which required time, and was difficult.

Trumbull described experiments with gum Arabic ("complex and difficult"),
Venice turpentine ("sticky, and does not dry hard"), Chio turpentine ("it works
pleasantly, but does not seem to possess the requisite hardness"), and Canada
balsam (turbid, and it did not dry well). He finally settled upon "common resin,"
by which he meant rosin, or colophony, the residue left after distilling turpentine. "I
painted the Picture of Peter the great at Narva, with this vehicle, as well as several
portraits; and think it equally beautiful & durable, and much more easy than the
Sandarack system."

Trumbull summarized the results of many of his experiments when he had
the bad luck to be caught in England at the outbreak of the War of 1812. He was
not allowed to leave the country, but anti-American feeling was such that he could
not find work as an artist, so he had plenty of free time. He changed his focus of
investigation to "the common American turpentine," which is closely related to
rosin, being the semisolid material that comes from pine trees before it is separated
into the solid rosin and liquid spirits of turpentine. This seemed to fulfill all of his
requirements, and he felt finally able to say: "This mixture appears to be to possess
all the qualities of the Venetian Vehicle.…The Vehicle is cheap, & formed without
Science or Labour. And the System has perhaps been lost from its very simplicity &
cheapness. But whether this System be the Venetian or not, it is at least one of the
best I have known; future trials will ascertain completely its relative merit."[56]

Over the "tedious winter" of 1813–14, while waiting for the war to end,
Trumbull painted out an elaborate series of trial mixtures containing various additives, labeling each with a letter. We do not know exactly what his final conclusions
were, but Trumbull saw immediately that some of the experimental mixtures were
not going to work, writing in his book, for instance, that raw linseed oil and sugar
of lead, or this mixture plus white vitriol, were "useless."

Trumbull also collected recipes on a variety of other topics from many
different sources, including articles by Timothy Sheldrake that speculated on the
secret of the Venetians.[57] In 1813 he tried a method of making drying oil that he
had read about and mixed the resulting oil with several pigments that he knew to
be fugitive to see whether it would preserve their color. He also computed the profit
that could be made by manufacturing drying oil according to this recipe and selling

it. He recorded that in 1813 he varnished a portrait of Wellington with Canada balsam, a material that Charles Willson Peale had also used as a varnish—but which Peale blamed for the darkening of his pictures.[58]

Trumbull read in a journal how a painter could obtain a better color of burnt umber by heating raw umber in a crucible, and he proudly wrote: "I have tried this experiment successfully." He then tried to make ivory black from chips of genuine ivory ("The Ivory black of the Shops is generally only burnt bones"). But his crucible cracked, and he was only partly successful, "so that I have two qualities, one excellent, the other not better than blue Black." He read about and carefully calculated the profit that could be made from a system of refining fish oil or whale oil to make paint, but then concluded: "This appears to be a miserable troublesome System."[59]

Documents from late in his life hint that Trumbull never decided what the secret of the Venetians actually was. In a conversation with Thomas Sully in 1828, in his seventy-second year, Trumbull apparently reverted to his earlier opinion that rosin was the secret.[60] But the next year, Trumbull painted a picture in which he recorded that his medium was "nut oil and sandarach"[61]—sandarac being the very medium that Benjamin West had suggested to him twenty-nine years (and innumerable experiments) earlier.

In Trumbull we see the last of the continuous line of experimentation inspired directly by Benjamin West's pursuit of the secrets of Titian and other early painters. We also sense in Trumbull some of the contradictions inherent in artists' search for the secrets of earlier times. Many of Trumbull's paintings suffer from the type of crackle called traction or drying crackle, or sometimes "youth crackle," because it can appear early in a painting's life. Trumbull may well have seen these problems during his lifetime, and he may have known that paintings by Titian did not suffer similarly.

In fact, there are some hints that toward the end of his life Trumbull, like West, may have shown some regret about his experimentation. Thomas Sully recorded two episodes in which Trumbull's earlier paintings were held up as examples of how simple techniques lasted better than complicated methods. In one case Sully wrote: "Trumbull showed me a copy he had made of Correggio's *Marriage of St. Catherine* 40 years ago—and owing to the fact that it is painted with simple materials, it is yet in excellent order."[62]

NOTES

1   Copley to Henry Pelham, March 14, 1775 (Copley 1914, 304–7).

2   Ibid., 306–7. He amplified on these proposed experiments in another letter to Pelham, June 25–July 2, 1775 (ibid., 334–35).

3   Wright to Humphry, July 24, 1775 (Prown 1966, 2:253–54). Copley had been working on his copy of Correggio's *Holy Family* for five weeks and told Wright that it would take him twice as much time to finish it, but "he will get it like the original."

4   Dunlap 1834, 1:126. Other anecdotes from Dunlap about Copley's slowness include a sitter

complaining that painting her head required fifteen or sixteen sittings, "six hours at a time!!" (ibid.). A sitter told Rembrandt Peale she sat for Copley twenty times for her hands only (R. Peale 1855b, 290).

Copley must have become quicker after spending some time in England; John Quincy Adams described only seven sittings when he was painted by Copley in 1796 (Neff 1995, 172). As a counterpoint to Copley, it was said that West—one of those who pointed out Copley's slowness—"paints quicker than any other artist" (Samuel F. B. Morse to his parents, May 3, 1815 [cited in Morse 1914, 1:178]).

5   In 1797 Ozias Humphry described a particularly dark black pigment that Copley made himself from pigs' trotters calcined in a crucible (Humphry Memorandum-Book, October 7, 1797).

Other hints about Copley's painting methods date from after his death. In 1826, Thomas Sully wrote: "Copley I remember to have heard, recommended the free use of it [spirits of turpentine]" (Sully "Hints," AAA, microfilm roll N18, frame 106 [1826]). In 1827 Sully believed that Copley added mastic varnish to his paint by "first dropping the liquid in the white" (ibid., frame 117 [May 26, 1827]).

On Copley's techniques, see also Shank 1984, Vagts, Gerber, and Newman 1996, and Webber 2001.

6   Farington Diary, entry of July 2, 1806 (cited in Erffa and Staley 1986, 218). *Death of the Earl of Chatham* (1779–81, Tate Gallery, London).

7   Cunningham 1879, 2:242.

8   Amory 1882, 229–31; see also Whitley 1928, 2:212.

9   Around this time Timothy Sheldrake published several articles suggesting that copal or amber varnish was the secret of the Venetians (Carlyle 2001, 123).

10   Dossie said varnish was applied "to secure the colours from the injuries of the air or moisture, and to defend the surface from scratches or any damages the painting might receive from slight violences" (Dossie 1764, 1:224).

11   The comment is by Joseph Wright of Derby, who knew Copley in Italy (Jones 1991, 18). Charles Willson Peale also noted that varnishing "would improve the appearance of some [paintings] to have the force of colour brought out" (C. W. Peale to Rubens Peale, December 9, 1818 [C. W. Peale 1983–2000, 3:662]).

12   C. W. Peale to Rembrandt Peale, June 26, July 3, 1808 (C. W. Peale 1983–2000, vol. 2, part 2, p. 1093).

13   Copley to Ozias Humphry, July 2, 1775 (AAA/Hart, microfilm roll D5, frames 42–44). Prown says that this letter may actually date from August 1775 (Prown 1966, 254n28). See also Copley to Henry Pelham, June 25–July 2, 1775 (Copley 1914, 337).

Vagts, Gerber, and Newman 1996 believe it is unclear what the varnish recipe given to Humphry was used for. We believe internal evidence argues that this was the one Copley called "my spirit varnish" and that it had been his standard varnish for a final coating. Three passages refer specifically to using a spirit varnish or "his" spirit varnish as a final coating: "My spirit Varnish is unknown to them and I think if these Varnishes would bear the Spirit at last it would be very well" (Copley 1914, 337); "but I could like to finish then with Spirit Varnish, that is when my Picture was intirely done Varnish with it" (ibid., 338); and "Your Picture, when dry, Varnish with Mastick Varnish, or Spirit Varnish if it will bear it" (ibid., 335).

14   See Dunkerton, Kirby, and White 1990. Carlyle reports that sandarac "appears to have been restricted mainly to the eighteenth century" (Carlyle 2001, 131).

15   Copley called his varnish a "spirit" varnish. There has been confusion about the use of this term since the eighteenth century. French eighteenth-century sources divided varnishes into three types: spirit varnishes (dissolved in alcohol, also called "spirits of wine"), turpentine-based varnishes (dissolved in turpentine), and oil varnishes (dissolved in oil); see Watin 1778, 217. Eighteenth-century British sources got these terms hopelessly confused. This most likely happened because the word "turpentine" was used in various ways in English. The word alone meant a semisolid resin, while the liquid that we nowadays call "turpentine" was sometimes called "spirits of turpentine" and sometimes "oil of turpentine." Hence, English varnish recipes containing the liquid turpentine sometimes were classified as spirit varnishes and sometimes as oil varnishes. Modern books continue to confuse by calling varnishes made with turpentine "spirit varnishes," although in the eighteenth century a spirit varnish was properly one like Copley's, made with alcohol.

16   Copley's lack of familiarity with simple mastic varnish is indicated by the fact that he sent the recipe for it to Pelham (along with recipes for retouching varnishes) followed by: "these are the Varnishes used among Painters. my spirit Varnish is unknown to them....I have never yet

try'd any of these, but as they are in such general use I think there is no Danger in useing them" (Copley 1914, 337).

17   Watin 1774, 239–40. Watin's picture varnish included semisolid turpentine as well as mastic and spirits of turpentine; he specifically stated that oil varnishes and varnishes made with alcohol were unsuitable for paintings. On the authority of the French in eighteenth-century varnish making, see *Practical Treatise* 1795, 178.

18   Advertisement of John Merrett, Boston (Dow 1927, 238); sandarac was also mentioned in the 1768 advertisement of John Gore, Boston (ibid., 242).

19   Watin 1778, 331, 4 (supplément). Of course, materials like sandarac were not used only by painters; the preferences of furniture makers and other craftsmen (and the price they were willing to pay) would have influenced availability.

     In 1808 a British book listed sandarac at one-third the price of mastic (*Compendium of Colours* 1808, 50), and this could have led at that time to sandarac being used as "a cheap substitute for mastic" or as an adulterant (Carlyle 2001, 131).

20   Humphry Memorandum-Book, March 22, 1779. Humphry was a compulsive collector of recipes, not only from his contemporaries but also from earlier written sources (Mayer and Myers 2004, 138n4).

21   Humphry, Memorandum-Book, April 2, 1778.

22   Charles Willson Peale had a low opinion of Canada balsam as a varnish ingredient: "I very much suspect that the Canada Balsam was the cause of the dark appearance which the oldest pictures had"(C. W. Peale to Rembrandt Peale, June 26, July 3, 1808 [C. W. Peale 1983–2000, vol. 2, pt. 2, p. 1093]).

23   Dossie 1764, 1:231, 244.

24   R. Peale / *Practical Treatise*, 63 (written in ink, with a long "s," which makes it one of his earlier comments). Next to "sandarach gum," Peale wrote: "not," which in his shorthand means "not used"(p. 55). Next to copal, Peale wrote: "use none" in ink; however, the words "use none" were crossed out with pencil (p. 35). In fact, we know that by the middle of the nineteenth century, Peale did experiment with copal as an ingredient in media and varnishes (see chapter 11).

25   "Mr. Hamilton used none for retouch[ing] his Pictures but a little Oyl as I used to do," Copley to Pelham, June 25–July 2, 1775 (Copley 1914, 342).

26   Müntz 1760, 60; see also *Practical Treatise* 1795, 206.

27   For the 1775 recipe, see Copley 1914, 336. Copley's is the earliest recipe we have seen for this kind of material, although sugar of lead had been used earlier in the eighteenth century as a drier (Dossie 1758, 2:152). The painter Julius Caesar Ibbetson announced in 1803 that he had invented "gumption" (Carlyle 2001, 106–9).

28   Field 1835, 208.

29   Copley 1914, 336, 342.

30   See note 4 above.

31   Copley to Pelham, June 25–July 2, 1775 (Copley 1914, 337n).

32   *Practical Treatise* 1795, 170.

33   Neff 1995, 123n.

34   Dossie recognized that alcohol-based varnishes needed to be thinner solutions and wrote: "Indeed less than two or three coats of this kind of varnish is not sufficient" if a painting became "sunk in" (Dossie 1764, 1:229).

35   D. Evans 1982, 189. In contrast, a British treatise of 1795 claimed "the mastich varnish of the shops is in general too poor and thin," hinting that the author preferred a thicker varnish (*Practical Treatise* 1795, 195–96).

36   Watin 1774, 239–40, 274.

37   Müntz 1760, 8–9. See also Caylus and Majault 1755, 65, 129.

38   On C. W. Peale in London and the books he bought, see Prown 2001c and Ward 2004, 34.

39   C. W. Peale to John Beale Bordley, March 29, 1772 (C. W. Peale 1983–2000, 1:118).

40   C. W. Peale's copy of Dossie's *Handmaid to the Arts* (now at APS) was the second (1764) edition. The first (1758) edition did not mention wax painting at all, but the second quoted at length from Müntz and called wax painting "of practical importance"(Dossie 1764, 1:xi.) See also chapter 1, note 23.

41   On wax painting in Britain, see Rice 1979, Mayer and Myers 2004, and Mayer and Myers 2006. When Edward Gibbon was preparing for his trip to Rome in 1764, Caylus's book was among those he read (Ford 1974, 451).

42   C. W. Peale to John Beale Bordley, March 29, 1772 (C. W. Peale 1983–2000, 1:118).

43   Mayer and Myers 2004, 132–33; Mayer and Myers 2006, 56–57.

44   C.W. Peale, Memorandum Book, 32, 41–46. The improvements included applying pigments in sugar water (presumably later infused with wax) and mixing pigments and wax with a hot solution of turpentine. The recipe attributable to Rembrandt Peale is: "Memo: from R. Peale's book 1 oz Yellow oker add 10 gros wax. (Gros. French measure)." There follows a list of quantities of wax to be mixed with each pigment, also with measurements in *gros*. Rembrandt Peale also took notes on wax painting, describing Greenland's method of encaustic painting that was published in the 1807 *Transactions of the Society for the Encouragement of Arts, Manufacturers, and Commerce* (R. Peale Miscellaneous, four undated sheets titled "Jane Greenland's method of encaustic painting.").

45   R. Peale 1810. See also a transcription of his letters from Paris in C.W. Peale 1983–2000, 3:33–40; Hevner 1992, 262–65; and Oedel 1992. On September 10, 1810, Peale presented a report of his method to the Institut de France (Oedel 1992, 8).

46   Rice 1979, 170–74. Paillot de Montabert described his encaustic process in 1829 (Paillot de Montabert 1829, 8:526–662). In 1875 his pupil amplified on the process and illustrated some of the utensils used to melt the wax (Carpentier 1875).

47   C.W. Peale to Rembrandt Peale, August 27, 28, 1811 (C.W. Peale 1983–2000, 3:101, 103n). In his letter he described a special stove with which "the painting of today may be melted in on tomorrow."

48   Mayer and Myers 2006.

49   Rembrandt Peale wrote: "To me it was a circumstance of little consequence to ascertain with count Caylus and other antiquarians whether the great painters of the time of Apelles, who have left us none of their works to admire, painted with wax" (R. Peale 1811, 14). For Paillot de Montabert's scientific approach, see Rice 1979, 179–82.

50   C.W. Peale to Rembrandt Peale, August 27, 28, 1811 (C.W. Peale 1983–2000, 3:101–3); C.W. Peale to Thomas Jefferson, September 9–10, 1811: "I have painted a few portraits with encaustic Colours from my son Rembrandt's instruction" (C.W. Peale 1983–2000, 3:114).

51   Much later, Rembrandt Peale wrote that he learned an important secret about drying oil in 1812, implying that by this date he was already using more conventional oil paints rather than encaustic (Rembrandt Peale to Mary [Jane Patterson Peale], December 18, 1850 [R. Peale Miscellaneous, APS, Peale Family Papers, B P31]). In 1818–20, Charles Willson Peale became interested in adding wax to oil paint when he saw the British immigrant painter Charles Catton do so and admired the effect. However, this was a relatively small amount of wax ("one oz. of white wax into a pound of white"), in a manner that was common in Britain in the early nineteenth century (C.W. Peale 1983–2000, 3:633, quoting C.W. Peale's diary from November 5, 1818–January 29, 1819; also C.W. Peale 1983–2000, 3:795, quoting C.W. Peale to Rembrandt Peale, February 10, 14, 15, 1820).

52   Cogdell Diaries/Letterbooks, vol. 2, entry titled "Museum" (probably 1816).

53   Neagle "Hints," "about 14th Septr 1832."

54   See Mayer and Myers 2004, 136.

55   This and the following quotations are (unless otherwise specified) from the Trumbull Inventories at N-YHS, which are unpaginated. The idiosyncratic use of quotation marks follows Trumbull's manuscript. On the incompatibility of sandarac with spirits of turpentine and with oil, which was responsible for some of Trumbull's difficulty, see Mills and White 1987, 90.

56   Conservators have found that the addition of resinous materials like rosin has made some of Trumbull's paintings difficult to clean without risking damage to the paint.

57   Sheldrake believed that the secret of the Venetians involved copal or amber varnish as a medium (Carlyle 2001, 123). Trumbull also obtained varnish recipes from "Mr. Rederschein, a Physician in the service of Mr. Beckford of Fonthill," as well as recipes from "Hewlett's (of Bath)" and "Sir Harry Englefield."

58   Sizer 1967, 136. About Peale, see note 22 above.

59   The foregoing all from Trumbull Inventories [unpaginated].

60   "Col. Trumbull is persuaded that Titian and the Bassans used oil in their colours that had rosin dissolved in it" (Sully "Hints," AAA, microfilm roll N18, frame 121 [April 9, 1828]).

61   Cited in Sizer 1967, 137.

62   Sully "Hints," AAA, microfilm roll N18, frames 106 (March 27, 1826) and 125 (August 11, 1829). Sully also recalled (in 1851): "Sir Martin Archer Shee warned me against using strange vehicles in painting. He said that simple materials were safest, and best. Trumbull expressed the same opinion" (Sully "Memoirs," 11).

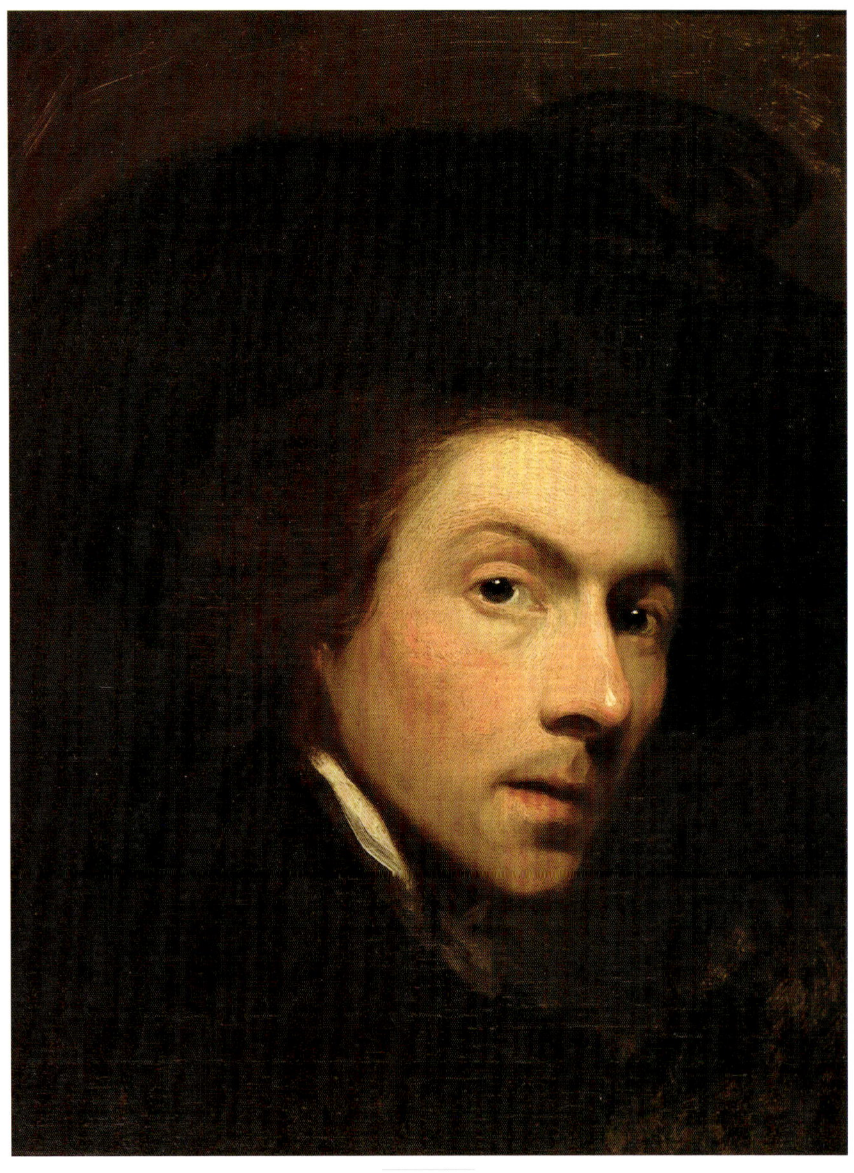

Gilbert Stuart (American, 1755–1828), *Self-Portrait at Age 24*, 1778.
Oil on canvas, 42.5 × 32.4 cm (16¾ × 12¾ in.). Newport, Rhode Island, Redwood Library
and Athenaeum, Bequest of Louisa Lee Waterhouse, RLC.PA.113.

CHAPTER 4

GILBERT STUART: THE FIRST AMERICAN OLD MASTER

GILBERT STUART WAS BORN in Rhode Island in 1755 and grew up in the busy coastal city of Newport. Beginning at the age of about thirteen, he studied under the Scottish immigrant painter Cosmo Alexander, then traveled to Scotland with him, but his training was cut short by Alexander's sudden death. Stuart returned to Newport in 1773, and the seventeen-year-old, now on his own, began to paint portraits. Stuart's earliest known portraits, done under the influence of Alexander, have a stiff, almost primitive appearance, but Stuart had an urge to improve himself, and he and a friend hired a muscular blacksmith so they could learn to draw the human body properly.[1]

Several early portraits by Stuart show problems that often afflict beginning painters. Some have wrinkled surfaces, while others have spotty, dark areas of discoloration, each a sign that too much oil or other medium was mixed with the paint.[2] Adding another medium will make paint flow and spread more easily, which can be attractive to a beginner. A tyro might also think that if adding a little megilp or other medium was a good thing, adding a lot might be even better, while veteran painters would have seen the wrinkling and discoloration that inevitably develop over a period of months or years.

In 1775 Stuart left America again, this time for London. He entered Benjamin West's studio, and West immediately "employed him in copying."[3] Soon afterward, Stuart painted a self-portrait that shows how much a beginning artist can learn from the imitation of earlier paintings (fig. 7). Stuart's self-portrait, inspired by a portrait by the seventeenth-century British painter William Dobson, has been called "the greatest leap in his artistic career."[4] Benjamin Waterhouse reported that when Stuart saw the painting more than twenty years later, "I heard him talking to it thus: 'Gibby, you needn't be ashamed of that—there is the perfection of the art or I know nothing of the matter.'…I remarked that most people took it for a very old picture. He replied, 'Yes, I suppose so; I *olified* it on purpose that they should think so,' punning on the Latin word *oleum*—oil."[5]

Stuart implied that it was not only the costume, pose, and style of the painting but also the technique—and perhaps even the look of darkened oil and varnish which an old painting acquired over time—that had inspired him.[6] This "old-looking" self-portrait reflects one aspect of London taste at the height of the influence of Joshua Reynolds and West, but it is in sharp contrast to Stuart's known preference, expressed later in life, that the white parts of his paintings not become darkened by discolored oil or varnish.

During his time in West's studio, Stuart painted other experimental portraits based on those of Van Dyck and Thomas Gainsborough, but as he gained experience, he discovered his own manner. Some of the anecdotes that have come down about the relationship between Stuart and West have as their theme the contrast between a natural painter and one who needs special recipes or technical "tricks." The most famous is West's remark: "It is no use to steal Stuart's colors: if you want to paint as he does you must steal his eyes,"[7] which implies jealousy of Stuart's talent on the part of the other students, and perhaps on the part of West himself. West must have known that Stuart was developing greater facility with a brush than he would ever have, while Stuart must have known that a less facile painter had a greater motivation to discover secret processes. Later in his life, Stuart told tales at the expense of painters (like West and Reynolds) who believed in odd recipes and "secrets." His daughter reported the following (which again reinforces the important role that copying played in the lives of painters at this time):

> [Stuart] had been commissioned to copy a very fine head of Sir Joshua Reynolds, and while at work on it, in a warm room, he thought he saw one of the eyes move and take a downward course. A second glance showed this to be true, and it instantly occurred to him that Sir Joshua must have used wax with his colors (as is well known was the case), to give greater transparency. In an agony of mind, for the picture was one of great value, he hurried with it into the cold air, and gradually worked the eye back into place.[8]

Stuart eventually perfected a method of capturing a likeness with freshness and spontaneity that surpassed West and rivaled the best British portrait painters. He set up on his own, and his prices were said to have been exceeded only by Reynolds and Gainsborough.[9] Stuart earned the praise of artists and critics in London and in Ireland before returning to the United States in 1793 to be acclaimed as America's greatest living painter.

In his attitude toward technique, Stuart makes a sharp contrast with many other painters of this time. In 1816 Stuart recalled his period of study under West—when all of London (and most of Europe) was abuzz with the urge to discover new kinds of megilps and secrets—in a stream-of-consciousness rant to Matthew Harris Jouett, who apparently wrote it down as fast as he could: "Cry in England Sir Joshua why Stuart you are not a migelpist & whether or no does Reubens shade with body or transparent colours. The storys recollectd to prove the folly of attending too closely to the mere mechanical processes of the art. Does Reubens paint on a blue or yellow ground. Ansr he paints on just what ground he pleases."[10]

Others verified Stuart's contempt for the processes of technique. John Neagle recalled that in discussing painting, Stuart "made use of fewer technicals than any other artist with whom I ever conversed."[11] In one section of Jouett's account, he described how Stuart used different kinds of brushes and brushstrokes for different complexions, then added parenthetically: "The result of my observations on his pictures—He disdains such system business."[12] Stuart's daughter summarized her father's views on tricks and secrets:

> He treated with contempt whatever looked like a trick in art. Artists frequently brought him some wonderful discovery in colors or oil, or some composition that Titian or Veronese was supposed to have used; to all which he would listen pleasantly, and then say "Take my advice and have nothing to do with anything of the kind, for certainly you cannot pretend to know what may be the ultimate effect on your work." But some persons, unwilling to accept his views, would insist on leaving their wonderful concoctions with him, all of which were immediately thrown from the window.[13]

William Dunlap told a story about the young Stuart that supposedly took place at an antique drawing class at Somerset House in London, when each of the students named the old master whom he sought to imitate. Stuart alone said that he would strive to see nature with his own eyes rather than through the eyes of the old masters, and (according to Dunlap), Gainsborough overheard this and praised him for it.[14]

THE LEGEND OF STUART'S TECHNIQUE

Ironically (given that Stuart believed "the mere mechanical processes of the art" to be overrated), his fellow artists were in such awe of his technique that they discussed Stuart's processes endlessly. Details of his methods were recorded and passed from one painter to another, by word of mouth and in writing, during his lifetime and long after his death.[15]

Adding to the legend was the fact that Stuart was eccentric, funny, and opinionated, and therefore eminently quotable. When asked if he was tired after a session with Stuart, one sitter replied, "Yes, with laughing."[16] But sometimes Stuart's eccentricity and impetuosity exasperated his sitters, as when Stuart painted the wife of Commodore Isaac Hull. She found sitting for her portrait very tedious, and at what was supposed to be the last sitting, a friend told her something very interesting "which occasioned a turn of her head which no sooner caught Stewarts eye, than he daubs out all his likeness, and turning the canvass upside down, began sketching in a new head." The horrified Mrs. Hull burst into tears and went home, and the portrait was never completed.[17]

Additional gloss was given to the legend of Stuart's technique by the fact that he made painting appear easy. There are stories dating back to Stuart's time in London about his ability to make a likeness surprisingly quickly.[18] As opposed to John Singleton Copley, who was described as an extremely slow worker (see chapter 3), Stuart was said to have required only four or five sittings—and frequently only three—to do the bulk of the work on a portrait head.[19] Horace Binney recalled Stuart painting the head of his portrait in two sessions of one hour each (doing the hands, clothing, and accessories afterward without the model present): "At the end of [the first] hour I rose to go, and looking at the portrait, I saw that the head was as perfectly done as it is at this moment, with the exception of the eyes, which were blank. I gave one more sitting of an hour, and in the course of it Stuart said, 'Now, look at me one moment.' I did so. Stuart put in the eyes by a couple of touches of the pencil, and the head was perfect."[20]

Despite his facility as a painter, Stuart can be documented to have used some kind of mechanical device—possibly a set of proportional dividers or calipers—to enlarge a composition when making a copy of a portrait.[21] He also used tracings made on a translucent piece of sized linen called a "tracing cloth" as an aid when making replicas of paintings.[22] Both of these examples reinforce the impression given by Dunlap and other writers that the use of various sorts of mechanical and optical aids was taken for granted in the early nineteenth century, even by the most skilled American painters (see chapter 10).

STUART AND SUPPORTS

With so many stories about Stuart repeated over and over, it is sometimes difficult to disentangle fact from fiction. A case of this is Stuart's well-known use of wooden panels having an inscribed texture that imitates the diagonal pattern of a twill canvas. Stuart's daughter Jane claimed that a cabinetmaker named Ruggles in Boston invented a way to inscribe mahogany panels with diagonal lines at Stuart's request.[23] The story was later elaborated to say that this use of wooden panels was necessary because disruptions of trade caused by the Napoleonic Wars made it impossible for Stuart to obtain the English twill canvases that he preferred.[24]

This topic has been studied in recent years by conservators and art historians, who have found it somewhat more complicated than might first appear. The technique is not limited to Stuart (a number of other artists used similar supports), nor is it limited to times of wars and embargoes.[25] In addition, some examples of textured panels were scored with a toothed plane (as Jane Stuart described), but in other cases the ground was applied with a tool so that a ridged or "twill" effect was produced independently of the texture of the wood.[26]

Manuscript sources provide further information. A firsthand account from John Neagle tells us that, at least in 1825, Stuart's preferred canvas was in fact a twill fabric prepared by Thomas Brown of London.[27] Neagle also discussed Stuart's use of wooden panels and gave Stuart's reason for scoring their surfaces, although scarcity of canvas because of war was not mentioned. Neagle said only that Stuart painted on canvases from London "or upon slightly coated panels, which to avoid smoothness, were frequently *toothplaned* to imitate the English twilled canvas, which he was fond of. He disliked a slippery surface."[28] It makes sense that Stuart, who loved to apply dragging strokes of paint that caught in the texture of his support, would find a smooth or "slippery" surface uncongenial.

On another occasion, when John Neagle compiled, in one of his notebooks, all the information that he could think of about wooden panels, his thoughts again ran to Stuart. Neagle owned a portrait painted by Stuart on a wood panel, and he struggled to remember the type of wood it was painted on, first guessing holly, but later correcting this to "Basswood or *Baywood* not *Holly*," adding that "whatever it be, it came from the neighborhood of Boston, Mass." Such was the power of Stuart's recommendation that Neagle attributed wonderful properties to this wood "that neither warps, nor splits, nor throws out sap….it requires no double backing of cross stays of wood, or glued canvas on the back to support it."[29] Modern investigators have found that Stuart in fact painted on a variety of different kinds of wood, including mahogany, yellow poplar, and yellow pine.[30]

The use of wood panels is somewhat unusual at this time, although a revival of their use had begun in France in the mid-1700s, especially for wax painting, and in fact a French publication from 1755 included instructions for making diagonal striations in a panel with a steel tool.[31] This technique may have been discovered independently in America, or Stuart could have seen or heard about the process during his time in England.

Some artists believed that a wood panel would last longer than canvas.[32] In 1800 Stuart was said to have believed that this was particularly true in the American climate: "Mr. Stewart observes, that the heat of our climate will destroy canvas exposed in a public building, in about twenty years, & he recommends Mahogany Pannells, in lieu of canvass—he says, that the Pannells can be so constructed as not to warp or crack—I should suppose his judgement founded on experience ought to be relied upon."[33]

A conservator might disagree with Stuart's opinion, at least with regard to large paintings—the subject of Stuart's remarks was a pair of life-size portraits of George Washington. Although mahogany warps and cracks less than many other woods, the construction of a large wooden panel involves joining many boards and consequently multiplies the risk of splitting and warping along the joins. In any event, the esteem in which Stuart was held guaranteed that his use of scored wood panels would be noticed by other American painters, and some American artists who used them may have been following his lead. Regardless of wars and embargoes, it was probably also convenient for some American painters, especially those in the provinces, to use a support that could be provided by any local woodworker.

A final anecdote about Stuart and his wooden panels deals with the principal disadvantage of wood: it sometimes splits. When this once happened to a painting by Stuart, a cabinetmaker told the artist he could rejoin it perfectly. After Stuart saw the result, he said he was forced to simultaneously swear at the cabinetmaker and "laugh at the absurdity of the thing," for the cabinetmaker had planed the edges before gluing them together, and the process "ran the nostrils into one, brought the corners of the mouth nearly together, and did away wholly with the bridge of the nose."[34]

STUART AND GROUNDS

Stuart's grounds also attracted the attention of other American painters. Four different firsthand sources from 1800 and later agree that Stuart preferred a gray color for his grounds, calling it variously "light grey or lead colour," "a cool and pearly hue," or "fog-colored." Gray grounds were often used by British and American painters in the eighteenth century; Stuart's reason for using a gray ground was given as "being of no colour it receives any colour well."[35] However, the color of his grounds is in fact quite variable. Some of Stuart's earliest paintings done in Newport have gray grounds, but others tend toward a light tan color.[36] Paintings from the 1780s and 1790s sometimes have gray grounds, but many—most notably the unfinished Athenaeum portraits of 1796, in which a great deal of the ground remains visible—were painted on white or very slightly off-white grounds. Some paintings done after 1800 also have white or off-white grounds.[37] A painting from 1796, on a preprimed fabric labeled by the London colorman James Poole, has a ground with a distinctly blue-green cast.[38]

Firsthand sources give contradictory information about the absorbency of Stuart's grounds. This may seem an arcane point, but it was an important one for late-eighteenth and early-nineteenth-century painters. The early Venetians were thought to have used absorbent grounds, and painters argued constantly about the advantages and/or dangers of absorbent grounds (typically made using glue as a binder) versus nonabsorbent grounds (having an oil medium). The painter Nathaniel Jocelyn visited Stuart in 1823 and later wrote a short account of his observations, including the remark "It was always *oil grounds*, not absorbent."[39] But other accounts contradict this. Matthew Harris Jouett watched Stuart begin a portrait "on the naked white wood,"[40] and this practice of painting on a wood panel without any ground at all has been verified in another painting by Stuart.[41] John Neagle provided one of the most thorough accounts of Stuart's practice, based on his having spent considerable time with him in 1825, while painting Stuart's portrait. Neagle wrote that Stuart "confined himself usually, to the *absorbent grounds* of canvas prepared by Brown of London, or upon slightly coated panels."[42] Neagle was in a position to know about the absorbency of Stuart's grounds, because Stuart gave him one of his own twill canvases prepared by Brown on which to paint his portrait.[43] Neagle went on to discuss the effects of Stuart's use of absorbent grounds (or "slightly coated" panels or canvases—he equated the two). He believed that Stuart's wood panels were "just absorbent enough to draw in the oils from the outer surface & keep the effect of the painting bright."[44] Neagle also wrote: "Some of the portraits of G. Stuart, painted many years ago on absorbent panels or thinly coated canvas, have a surprizing freshness of color.…Where the ground is absorbent, the oils gradually are drawn in, leaving less matter to turn brown on the surface."[45]

Neagle (in this comment and on other occasions) is such a thoughtful and objective observer that it makes us favor his opinion about Stuart's grounds over Jocelyn's. However, we must also admit that artists can be variable in their practice, noting that our most careful observer—Neagle—used the word "usually" to qualify Stuart's preference for absorbent grounds.

STUART'S USE OF ADDED MEDIUM

Thomas Sully, who received instruction from Stuart for three weeks in 1807, later wrote that "the vehicle which he used, to moisten the colours while painting or to assist the application of glazing, was the common macguilp used by most painters, composed of mastic varnish, mixed with drying oil, in equal portions."[46] An account of Stuart's methods in 1809, written down much later by Obadiah Dickinson, confirmed that Stuart used a "maggylp of oil & mastack."[47]

Neagle watched Stuart make megilp in 1825: "I saw Gilbert Stuart make a cup of *megellup* which he said was excellent & was useful in painting—İt was such as he used. He poured into the cup as much as would about half fill it, of *drying oil* & then added about as much *mastic varnish*, which he stirred with his palette knife & it became somewhat thickened—He observed then that by standing it bye for a while it wd form into a jelly & would stand up on the knife, which would then be fit for use."[48]

But Neagle also explained that Stuart sometimes added different materials in different parts of a painting. Stuart told him that certain fugitive pigments, such as orange mineral and orpiment, were durable only "if secured by mixing it with varnish & varnishing over it immediately" (Neagle claimed to have found this to be true in his own experience).[49] Even more importantly, Neagle indicated that in white passages, Stuart mixed his colors with turpentine (which would evaporate) rather than megilp, so that the white areas would not discolor from excess medium, and this is confirmed in the 1816 account by Jouett. Neagle attributed to this practice the fact that the white cravats in Stuart's portraits are "many of them *very white*; staringly white."[50]

Stuart's concern with preserving the freshness of his colors is shown by another peculiarity of his technique. It had long been a common practice among portrait painters to anoint a portrait with oil or megilp before beginning a new sitting (see chapter 3). But two different sources say that Stuart specifically objected to this, because if the oil or megilp was not completely covered with paint it would become discolored and make the portrait blotchy.[51]

Jane Stuart worried that some of her father's later paintings suffered from cracking because some "unscrupulous dealer in artists' materials" made a megilp from copal instead of mastic varnish, implying that her father may not have always made his megilp himself as Neagle described. However, her remarks were made in 1879, long after her father's death, and may reflect painters' concerns after the middle of the nineteenth century, when commercially prepared megilps were more readily available.[52] Another remark by Jane Stuart is equally puzzling: she reported that her father "never glazed his pictures, nor ever attempted in this way to strengthen his shadows, for he thought it a trick."[53] This is contradicted by every other account of painters who watched Stuart work, who agree that as his final step he used transparent colors mixed with megilp to strengthen his shadows. Of course, Stuart did not glaze as extensively as an artist like Allston, whose paintings were sometimes called "all glazes." Jane Stuart may have exaggerated the fear of her father (and other artists) that the megilp used in glazes could make a painting discolor, as Stuart recognized in his admonition about not "anointing" a painting with oil or megilp between sittings.[54] Stuart also knew that glazing could be ephemeral, because thin layers of paint mixed with megilp might be sensitive to the solvents used by picture cleaners, and this fear may have led him to use glazing sparingly. Jouett reported that in 1816 Stuart advised: "Never to glaze on the face no where in fact unless you have such a body of colour underneath the glaze as stand against all accidents, from picture cleaners."[55]

STUART'S PIGMENTS AND PAINT APPLICATION

In spite of West's statement that "it is of no use to steal Stuart's colors," American painters were extremely curious to know which pigments Stuart used to achieve his dazzling effects. As a result, we probably know more about his pigments than about those of any other early American painter.

The most remarkable thing about Stuart's colors is that they are not very remarkable. Portrait painting can be done (and has been done for centuries) with relatively few pigments. In fact, all contemporary observers agreed that Stuart used a limited number of pigments and mixtures on his palette. It was traditional for a painter to place dabs of pure colors around the edge of the palette (usually beginning with white next to the thumbhole and proceeding left to the darker pigments) and also to place some premixed "tints" in the area below this row. Stuart apparently placed seven or eight pure pigments and nine or ten premixed tints on his palette, which is fewer than many other artists whose palette arrangements have been recorded.[56] For instance, Thomas Bardwell, in his 1756 book, recommended twelve pure colors and twelve mixed tints for portraits.[57] In the early nineteenth century, some writers recommended up to sixty-six mixed tints![58] Jocelyn's description of Stuart's actual wooden palette took a gentle poke at artists who thought that a large number of mixed tints would help them; he said Stuart's "pallet-board" was "smaller than the large pallets affected by some lesser artists."[59]

A limited number of pigments and mixtures makes sense given Stuart's style of painting, and in fact it was his method of applying his paints that was unique, rather than the nature of his pigments. In the use of his palette and the application of his paints, Stuart was nearly the opposite of Copley, who was said to have spent hours premixing the exact tint with his palette knife for every flesh tone and shadow (see chapter 3). Stuart, by comparison, "condemned the practice of mixing a colour on a knife, and comparing it with whatever was to be imitated.—'Good flesh colouring,' he said, 'partook of all colours, not mixed, so as to be combined in one tint, but shining through each other, like the blood through the natural skin.'…[Stuart] could not endure Copley's laboured flesh, which he compared to tanned leather."[60]

Stuart used, in Jouett's words, "chopping" strokes of distinct colors to give the effect of translucent flesh, thereby avoiding the leathery look that he disliked in Copley's work.[61] Jouett also reported Stuart's advice to "keep your colours as separate as you can. No blending, tis destruction to clear & bea[u]tiful effect."[62] Others noticed this as well; John S. Cogdell, after describing how Stuart combined different colors, added: "Tho this is not done on his pallette but only as they are wanted with the pencil[.] Mr. Stewart lays one tint over another."[63] In a detailed account of Stuart's method, Obadiah Dickinson described how a portrait became more distinct as it progressed: "Mr. Stewart endeavours in the first sitting to give the appearance of the person at 20 yards distant and in each succeeding sitting to advance its effect nearer until it be completed at 2 yards distance."[64] But Dickinson noted that even in final touches, Stuart advised: "What you do in the shadows over the glazing must be finished if possible with a single touch or you will spoil the beauty of your work."[65]

Stuart also had opinions about Titian and Rubens that may have influenced his own method of applying paint. In sharp contrast to painters who loved the mellowness and deep tone of Titian's paintings, Stuart believed that "Titian's works were not by any means so well blended when they left the esel.…Rubens…must have discovered more tinting, or *separate tints*, or distinctness, than others did, and that, as time mellowed and incorporated the tints, he (Rubens) resolved not only to keep his colours still more distinct against the ravages of time, but to follow his own impetuous disposition with spirited touches."[66]

One oddity in the layout of Stuart's palette, as reported in three different accounts,[67] is that the color blue was placed farthest to the right, next to the thumbhole. This position of honor (nearest to the hand that holds the paintbrush) was traditionally given to the white pigment and is shown that way in most other palettes of all periods.[68] It is tempting to think that Stuart had a special reason for placing his blue in this prominent position—he loved to commingle bluish strokes with his flesh to imitate the effect of blue veins under the skin. But this unusual arrangement is contradicted by five other accounts that have him placing the blue more conventionally on the other (left) side of the palette,[69] so it is possible that Stuart sometimes arranged his palette this way, and sometimes not.

Stuart's principal blue pigment (and in some accounts the only one) was Antwerp blue. Unfortunately, this is an imprecise term, and we cannot say exactly what "Antwerp blue" meant in the eighteenth and early nineteenth centuries. By the middle of the nineteenth century, the term had come to mean a weaker variety of Prussian blue, but modern authorities point out that in earlier times colormen may have also sold completely different copper-based pigments—or even mixtures of pigments—under the name Antwerp blue.[70] During Stuart's lifetime, the finest and most permanent blue color was known to be ultramarine, but it was extremely expensive (the much cheaper artificial ultramarine becoming available only after the artist's death in 1828).[71] The expense of ultramarine helps explain some of the slightly confusing explanations of various observers about Stuart's use of blue pigments. Jouett said Stuart "uses no ultramarine but keeps it by him."[72] Jocelyn gave the most complete explanation: "though he [Stuart] preferred Antwerp Blue to all other ordinary Blues, he would doubtless have used Ultramarine…but for the expense, and especially the trouble & uncertainty of procuring it."[73] The final word on this matter should be given to Stuart himself, who would probably have been impatient with the discussion: "I can produce what I wish from these colours, nor can any man say whether or no I put into my faces ultramarine. Colouring is at best a matter of fancy & taste."[74]

Stuart did not change his palette very much during the time when there are good records of his colors (from 1807 to 1825). This is quite different from some American painters of the next generation, who experimented endlessly with pigments. Stuart said that at one point (in 1823) he had simplified his process by using pure black instead of a tint mixed up from black and red, because "mingling it in his brush [with the neighboring tint] it came to the same thing."[75] It is also possible that Stuart used different or more exotic pigments on occasion for special purposes, as he hinted when he told Neagle how to use the unusual pigments orange mineral and orpiment.[76]

A pattern of change over time can be seen in Stuart's use of brown pigments. The earlier recorded palettes tend to contain the opaque earth pigment burnt umber for dark tones, while the later palettes are more likely to contain the more transparent (but more fugitive) Van Dyke brown.[77] Three different accounts from 1822 and 1823 document a period when Stuart was using Van Dyke brown and burnt umber mixed together in a ratio of 2:1 for the brown color on his palette. Stuart explained: "The former is a bad drier & not in all circumstances permanent, the latter is a fine drier, gives permanence to the former &, for Hair, improves the colour."[78] A few years later, in 1825, Neagle said nothing about Stuart's use of this kind of mixture but recorded that Stuart advised him not to use umbers in flesh, because raw umber was "too earthy or muddy" and burnt umber "too foxy."[79] Jane Stuart recalled, long after her father's death, his use of both Van Dyke brown and burnt umber, saying that Van Dyke brown was "a favorite color" of his, while burnt umber was used "sparingly."[80] Stuart was ahead of many others in believing as early as 1823 that Van Dyke brown might not be permanent. Nineteenth-century British sources generally recommended it as permanent, although the American Laughton Osborn questioned its stability in 1845.[81]

Stuart's mixing of umber with Van Dyke brown is an unusual variation on a theme that will recur with other artists as well: Stuart clearly knew that the more transparent organic brown colors might not last, but there must have been something in their transparency or in the beauty of their color that made him want to use them in spite of this. Painters have often had to wrestle with this kind of trade-off, of a beautiful immediate effect against permanence, and it is an example of Stuart's practical nature that in this case he hedged his bets by adding a portion of the more permanent pigment to the less permanent one. On another occasion, in a story passed along many times (as such stories often were), from Stuart to Washington Allston to Thomas Sully to William Dunlap, Stuart was said to have "condemned" the bright red pigment vermilion, which was known to turn blackish under certain circumstances, but "could not relieve himself by a substitute," so he—like many other American painters—continued to use it.[82]

STUART AND VARNISHING

Stuart told Jouett that an artist should varnish with vertical strokes, followed by horizontal ones, as "this prevents inequalities."[83] He also gave the commonly held opinion that a painting should not be varnished too soon, or it will crack.[84] However, he contradicted himself when he said that certain fugitive pigments should be varnished immediately. It is not clear if he meant those areas should be varnished locally or that the whole painting in this case should be varnished soon after it was painted.[85] The question of how soon an artist can varnish would be an important topic of discussion and experimentation for the next generation of American painters.

One opinion about varnishing attributed to Stuart is possibly unique among American painters. We have already described how Stuart painted the white cravats in his portraits using turpentine rather than adding megilp, which might eventually discolor. In his discussion of this topic, John Neagle added: "I have understood that he was loath to varnish over that part of his portraits when he varnished the rest."[86] In context, this must have been out of fear that the varnish would discolor and make the cravats darker and more yellow than Stuart had intended. Neagle left open the question of whether Stuart ever actually did this, or only lamented the fact that his cravats would appear dingy after a few decades as the varnish on top of them gradually turned darker and more yellow.

The care that Stuart took to avoid discoloration in his paintings—not only in his varnishing practice but in the grounds, pigments, and media that he used—make him a conspicuous exception to the tendency for artists at this period to experiment (sometimes recklessly) with painting materials. It was not Stuart's materials, but his way of using them, that was extraordinary. In most cases, his paintings, done with simple materials, have remained as fresh as any painter of that time could have wished.

NOTES

1   Dunlap 1834, 1:166–67; Barratt and Miles 2004, 14.

2   The authors have treated three paintings from Stuart's Newport period that show noticeable spottiness: *John Bannister*, *Christian Bannister*, and *William Redwood* (ca. 1773, Redwood Library and Athenaeum, Newport, Rhode Island). The painting with the most noticeable wrinkling is *Francis Malbone and His Brother Saunders* (ca. 1774, Museum of Fine Arts, Boston).

3   Dunlap 1834, 1:174.

4   D. Evans 1999, 15. *Self-Portrait* (1778, Redwood Library and Athenaeum, Newport, Rhode Island).

5   Dunlap 1834, 1:208.

6   The authors cleaned the *Self-Portrait* in 2002 and found that it is indeed painted with oil-containing layers that tone down the flesh colors and give it an antique look.

7   Mason 1879, 38; see also Dunlap 1834, 1:178–79.

8   Jane Stuart in Mason 1879, 40–41. This story sounds suspiciously like an episode in a parody written by James Northcote, in which an artist invented a special ground. In Northcote's fictional account, a portrait by "a very celebrated artist…was hung over a chimney of a very close warm room, and from the great heat, the ground became soft to such a degree, that the eye floated down the face as low as the mouth; and really I must own that it quite spoiled the likeness" (Northcote 1815, clvi–clvii). It is possible that Stuart enjoyed this story and retold it, and the story eventually metamorphosed into Stuart copying a painting by Reynolds.

9   Dunlap 1834, 1:188; D. Evans 1999, 148n16.

10   Jouett 1816, 83.

11   Dunlap 1834, 1:215.

12   Jouett 1816, 86.

13   Jane Stuart in Mason 1879, 40.

14   Dunlap 1834, 1:181.

15   For example, Matthew Harris Jouett's 1816 account of Stuart's technique was printed on a single sheet of paper by the painter James Bogle, who gave a copy to John Durand, who published it in *The Crayon* in 1861 (Mason 1879, 67). The account in *The Crayon* (Stuart 1861) is abridged, rearranged, and the wording often changed from Jouett's sketchy notes.

16   Dunlap 1834, 2:115.

17   Mason "Recollections," 2:23–24.

18   Dunlap 1834, 1:178–79.

19   Jane Stuart in Mason 1879, 37; see also Dickinson "Remarks," 1–5, which gives highly detailed descriptions of Stuart's palette settings and process during each sitting.

20   Miles et al. 1995, 219–20. *Horace Binney* (1800, National Gallery of Art, Washington, D.C.).

21   Henry Sargent described the device that Stuart used in about 1806 to enlarge a composition as a "small instrument" that he "held in his hand" (Dunlap 1834, 2:61). Stuart owned a boxed set of

mechanical drawing instruments given to him by Ozias Humphry that still survives (illustrated and discussed in D. Evans 1999, 85, 148n17).

22   Ibid.

23   Stuart 1877, 381; Mason 1879, 58.

24   Whitley 1932, 151.

25   Goldberg 1993, 33, 36–37. Stuart's use of a grained wooden panel in 1800 (Miles et al. 1995, 221) occurred long before the Embargo Act of 1807. In September 1815 (more than six months after the Treaty of Ghent) Ethan Allen Greenwood "Grained 20 panels for painting" (Barnhill 1993, 124). On Ezra Ames's use of a scored panel ca. 1815, see Kelly et al. 1996, 7. For two paintings with scored lines by Samuel Waldo ca. 1820–25, see Carbone et al. 2006, 2:1049; for Waldo's use of scoring on an 1828 portrait, see Torchia, Chotner, and Miles 1998, 224. As late as ca. 1835, Francis Alexander (who sought and apparently received advice from Stuart when Alexander lived in Boston) used a similar technique of diagonal cross-hatching on a panel without any ground (Kelly et al. 1996, 3). A ca. 1841 painting attributed to Joseph Alexander Ames is also on a scored panel (Kelly et al. 1996, 10).

26   Goldberg 1993, 36; Kirsh and Levenson 2000, 25–27.

27   Neagle Commonplace Book, 1. Neagle made entries in this book from 1839 until at least 1854, but the entries about Stuart on p. 1 presumably date from about 1839.

28   Ibid.

29   Ibid., 74. Basswood is usually considered to mean wood from trees of the linden family (*Tilia*), but the term is used loosely to describe wood from the tulip tree (also called tulip poplar or yellow poplar) (*Webster's Dictionary*).

30   Goldberg 1993, 37. A number of panels described in Miles et al. 1995 were found to be yellow poplar, as is *George Bethune* (ca. 1820, Corcoran Gallery of Art, Washington, D.C.), which was analyzed by Michael Palmer at the National Gallery of Art in 1987 (report in Corcoran files).

31   See Mayer and Myers 2004, 135–36; the tool is illustrated in Mayer and Myers 2006 and Caylus and Majault 1755, 121–22, pl. 1.

32   Caylus and Majault 1755, 17–18.

33   Oliver Wolcott, Jr., to John Trumbull, May 17, 1800 (cited in Barratt and Miles 2004, 130, 189). Stuart's observation related to the proposed purchase by the state of Connecticut of two copies of his life-size Munro-Lenox portrait of George Washington. The one painting that was eventually done (1800–1801, Old State House, Hartford, Connecticut) was painted on canvas, as were most large paintings by Stuart. One large painting that was done on panel is *Washington at Dorchester Heights* (1806, Museum of Fine Arts, Boston, deposited by the City of Boston).

34   Mason 1879, 59.

35   Jouett 1816, 83. For Stuart's use of gray grounds, see D. Evans 1999, 86; Morgan 1939b, 133; and Neagle Commonplace Book, 1. On Copley's use of gray grounds in his American portraits, see Vagts, Gerber, and Newman 1996 and Webber 2001. On gray grounds in eighteenth-century British paintings, see Talley and Groen 1975, 54–59. On gray grounds in Britain being replaced by white grounds around 1820, see Townsend 1995, 176.

36   For instance, of four early paintings in the Redwood Library and Athenaeum, *John Bannister* and *Christian Bannister* have gray grounds, *William Redwood* is a light color between gray and tan, and *Benjamin Waterhouse* (1775) is light tan.

37   See Miles et al. 1995, where the colors of the grounds on the many paintings by Stuart at the National Gallery of Art are described.

38   *Edward Shippen* (1796, Corcoran Gallery of Art, Washington, D.C.); James Poole was active ca. 1780–1800 (Katlan 1992, fig. 223). Another Stuart portrait on a fabric bearing the stamp of James Poole is *George Washington* (the Vaughan-Sinclair portrait) (1795, National Gallery of Art, Washington, D.C.); the color of the ground on this painting cannot be determined (Miles et al. 1995, 206).

39   Morgan 1939b, 133.

40   Jouett 1816, 88. The portrait was that of Mrs. Shaw, probably Mrs. Robert G. Shaw (see Morgan 1939a, 254–55).

41   Mark Bockrath noted this on the portrait of *George Reignold* (Pennsylvania Academy of the Fine Arts, Philadelphia), cited in Goldberg 1993, 40.

42   Neagle Commonplace Book, 1.

43   Ibid.

44   Ibid., 74.

45   Ibid., 4.

46   Sully "Memoirs," 3.

47   Dickinson "Remarks," 2, 4. Dickinson noted that Stuart used megilp for the second, third, and
       fourth sittings, preferring only turpentine and drying oil as a vehicle for his first sitting. Thomas
       Sully, when recording in 1851 the method he (Sully) had used "for many years," also noted that
       he used megilp only after the first sitting ("dead-coloring") (Sully "Memoirs," 107–11.). Cogdell
       wrote that Stuart's medium was "a mixture of boiled oil and Mastic varnish which looks like
       Magilp & is a jelly" (Cogdell Diaries/Letterbooks, vol. 3, entry of September 13, 1816).

48   Neagle Commonplace Book, 12.

49   Ibid., 20. "[Stuart's] dark colours he grinds up with sugar of lead" (Cogdell Diaries/Letterbooks,
       vol. 3, entry of September 13, 1816); Dickinson said that in 1809 Stuart sometimes added sugar
       of lead to slow-drying colors but in the summer simply exposed the back of his canvases to the
       sun (Dickinson "Remarks," 2).

50   Neagle Commonplace Book, 4. Jouett quoted Stuart as saying: "Always use spirits of turpentine in
       your white draperys[.] It assists to evaporate the oil & leaves the white a standing white, & free
       from the yellowness occasiond by the oil"(Jouett 1816, 87). This was simplified to "Always use
       spirits of turpentine with white. It carries off the oil in evaporation" when reprinted later (Stuart
       1861, 50).

51   "Some painters have a custom of rubbing over their pictures some oil before they proceed in
       the second painting. This is a practise that Mr. Stuart condemns for should it be expedient to
       leave some part of the flesh in the first sitting unchanged through the succeeding progress of
       the painting those parts will be discolored by the oil in the course of a few months"(Dickinson
       "Remarks," 2–3); and "Bad practice of migelping a picture before you work on it unless workd
       entirely over. apt to be blotchey"(Jouett 1816, 86). John Neagle disparaged this practice himself
       in a remark probably made in the mid-1820s, about the time he painted Stuart's portrait and took
       advice from him: "The practice of oiling the lights of a picture after coloring is dry, in order to
       work the fresh colors into it, is dangerous in the extreme; I have observed that great changes take
       place by means of the oil turning brown, and frequently where the whole face has been oil'd and
       the colors spread but partially—wherever the flesh has not been retouched with color there has
       [sic] been dark splotches" (Neagle Student Notebook, unpaginated).

52   Jane Stuart in Mason 1879, 40. Jane Stuart's remarks about her father's techniques should
       be treated with caution not only because they were made so long after his death but also
       because—according to Dunlap, at least—she received little encouragement or instruction directly
       from her father (Dunlap 1834, 2:445).

53   Jane Stuart in Mason 1879, 39.

54   Osborn 1845, 137–39, warned about glazes turning brown and said that glazing was not
       practiced in this country "to anything like the extent that it was once prevalent." Jane Stuart's
       remarks may reflect this change in opinion over the course of the nineteenth century.

55   Jouett 1816, 90. In the same year, Cogdell wrote: "[Stuart] glazes the dark tints with asphaltum"
       (Cogdell Diaries/Letterbooks, vol. 3, entry of September 13, 1816), while in 1809 and 1823
       Dickinson described him glazing with a variety of colors (Dickinson "Remarks," 5).

56   Jouett 1816, 85; Morgan 1939b, 132; Dickinson "Remarks," 1, 5.

57   Bardwell 1756. Bardwell's system was reprinted in *Practical Treatise* 1795; Thomas Sully tried out
       Bardwell's palette in 1837 and did not find it useful (see Neagle Commonplace Book, 73). See also
       Talley and Groen 1975.

58   Bouvier 1827; Schmid 1948, 64–67, pl. 3. Rembrandt Peale criticized Bouvier for his excessive
       number of tints (R. Peale "Notes," 101–2). However, Laughton Osborn's 1845 translation and
       interpretation of Bouvier's book would become the most influential book on technique in America
       in the second half of the nineteenth century (Osborn 1845).

       It should be noted that books may have recommended larger numbers of mixtures than
       professional painters actually used, because beginners might use a book without benefit of a
       teacher, and more mixtures might give a beginner confidence.

59   Morgan 1939b, 133. Dunlap agreed that Stuart's palette was small and said it had been used
       previously by the British painters Nathaniel Dance and Thomas Hudson (Dunlap 1834, 1:192).

A palette of Stuart's—apparently this same one—is owned by the National Portrait Gallery, Washington, D.C. (illustrated in Barratt and Miles 2004, 8).

60   Neagle, quoted in Dunlap 1834, 1:217.

61   Jouett 1816, 83.

62   Ibid. Neagle said Stuart told him he used a "blender" or "sweetener"—a large, soft brush, to "tease" his distinctly applied strokes together, but no other artist mentioned this, and Neagle did not actually see him do so. Stuart told Neagle that Rubens's method was to "lay each tint in its place, separately & distinctly, along side of each other, before any blending was used, & then they were united by means of a large soft sweetner or brush, & without teasing or corrupting the freshness of the tints; Mr. Stuart also said that this was his own practice, & declared that even Rubens' colors after being laid together in his masterly manner might be totally destroyed by unskillfully teasing them while fresh" (Neagle Commonplace Book, 36). It is somewhat surprising to see Stuart connected with this technique, but not surprising is his insistence that the sweetener be used with great restraint or the effect will be too smooth.

63   Cogdell Diaries/Letterbooks, vol. 3, entry titled "Conversations over Mr. Stewart's Pallette," September 10, [1816].

64   Dickinson "Remarks," 2.

65   Ibid., 5.

66   Neagle, cited in Dunlap 1834, 1:217.

67   Jouett 1816, 83, 85; Dunlap 1834, 1:192n, 193n (describing a palette of 1822); Jane Stuart in Mason 1879, 39. The latter two lists do not say specifically that blue was rightmost, but the order of the pigments does not make sense otherwise, especially in light of Jouett's 1816 diagram.

68   See, for example, Schmid 1948.

69   Dunlap 1834, 1:192n (citing a palette of 1813); Jocelyn's 1823 description in Morgan 1939b, 132; Dickinson "Remarks," 1, 5 (two different palettes of 1809 and 1823); Sully "Memoirs," 3. In marked contrast to Stuart giving the color blue a prominent place on some of his palettes, some eighteenth-century portrait painters excluded blue from their palettes altogether, using only black and white to obtain cool tones (Schmid 1948, 54–56). In three of John Trumbull's palette settings that have been preserved, none have blue (Sizer 1967, 136–37).

70   See Harley 1982, 74–75; Carlyle 2001, 474–75. When Osborn translated Bouvier's 1827 book for an American audience in 1845, he reported that Antwerp blue was a "modification of Prussian blue" and should never be used because it will either fade or darken (Osborn 1845, 3–4). On Antwerp blue, see also chapter 2, note 55.

71   In London in 1785, most pigments cost three to six pence for a bladder ground in oil, while the cheapest grade of ultramarine (the pigment only) was three guineas an ounce (Williams 1937, 23). In Paris in 1778, Watin sold most pigments for between 2 and 12 livres per pound, although Prussian blue was 40, the best grade of red lake 96, and ultramarine 1,536 livres per pound (Watin 1778, supplément, 1–2).

72   Jouett 1816, 90. Also confusingly, in 1809 Dickinson described Stuart setting his palette with Prussian blue but said, "Antwerp blue or Ultramarine are preferable in flesh" (Dickinson "Remarks," 1).

73   Morgan 1939b, 133.

74   Jouett 1816, 83.

75   Morgan 1939b, 133.

76   "Orange mineral" may mean the naturally occurring orange mineral realgar, which is related to and often associated with orpiment, or possibly a variety of red lead (Fitzhugh 1997; Carlyle 2001, 501).

77   Sully "Memoirs," 3; Sully "Memoirs" (1859 addendum), 3; Dickinson "Remarks," 1–5; Jouett 1816; Dunlap 1834, 1:192n, 193n; Jocelyn in Morgan 1939b, 132–33; Neagle Commonplace Book, 26; Jane Stuart in Mason 1879, 39.

78   Dunlap 1834, 1: 192n, 193n; Jocelyn in Morgan 1939b, 132; Dickinson "Remarks," 5.

79   Neagle Commonplace Book, 32, 35. In another, probably earlier notebook, he recorded Stuart's comments on earth colors slightly differently: "Never use Naples Yellow, Siena or Raw Umber in flesh—G. Stuart, 1825 to Neagle. He says Bt. Umber [inserted: & Siena] is too foxy—Raw umber is too clayey & muddy, & Naples Yellow is too brassy" (Neagle "Receipts," 8). On another occasion, Neagle quoted Sully about the British artist Martin Archer Shee: "*Umbers* he discards," then added his own remark: "(so does G. Stuart—J Neagle)" (Neagle Commonplace Book, 26).

80   Jane Stuart in Mason 1879, 39.

81   Carlyle 2001, 482–84; Field 1835, 160 (saying that Van Dyke brown is "durable both in water and oil"); Osborn 1845, 31–34, 56–57.

82   Dunlap 1834, 2:140. This comment appeared first in Sully "Hints," AAA, microfilm roll N18, frame 128 (June 30, 1831). Sully added that Allston was of the same opinion about vermilion, although Allston had experimented with red earth pigments as substitutes.

83   Jouett 1816, 86.

84   Ibid. On one occasion Stuart received a letter from a former client in Ireland asking him to have a bottle of varnish sent so that another artist could varnish his portrait. Stuart may therefore have left the portrait unvarnished, presumably because he wanted a period of time to elapse before varnishing (Dean Butson to Stuart, undated [Morgan 1939a, 75]).

85   Neagle Commonplace Book, 20.

86   Ibid., 4.

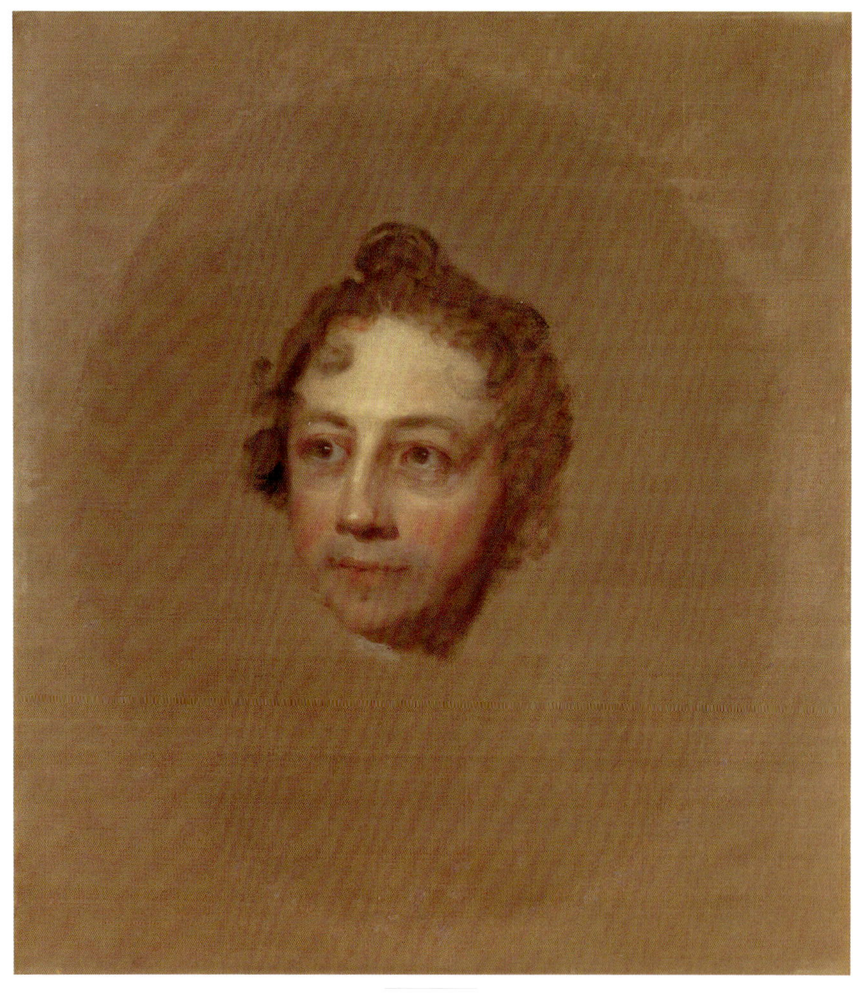

Gilbert Stuart (American, 1755–1828), *Portrait of Washington Allston*, ca. 1818.
Oil on canvas, 61 × 54.6 cm (24 × 21½ in.). New York, The Metropolitan Museum of Art,
Alfred N. Punnett Endowment Fund, 28.118. © The Metropolitan Museum of Art/Art Resource, N.Y.

CHAPTER 5
WASHINGTON ALLSTON: "THE PAINTER-POET"

CONNECTIONS BETWEEN AMERICAN AND BRITISH ARTISTS remained strong during the first part of the nineteenth century. Samuel F.B. Morse was perhaps being only slightly chauvinistic when he wrote from London in 1813, fifty years after Benjamin West had arrived in that city:

> The American character stands high in this country as to the production of artists.... Mr. West now stands at the head, and has stood ever since the arts began to flourish in this country, which is only about fifty years. Mr. Copley next, then Colonel Trumbull. Stuart in America has no rival here. As these are now old men and going off the stage, Mr. Allston succeeds in the prime of life, and will, in the opinion of the greatest connoisseurs in this country, carry the art to greater perfection than it ever has been carried in ancient or modern times.[1]

Washington Allston's reputation in London grew to the extent that he was apparently considered a serious candidate for the presidency of the Royal Academy after West's death in 1820, despite the fact that Allston had moved back to the United States by that time.[2] Allston's innovations in technique also attracted attention and were greatly admired, both during his lifetime and afterward. It has long been recognized that understanding Allston's technique is integral to understanding his art, and in fact his technique has been discussed by modern scholars as much as that of any other American artist.[3]

ALLSTON, THE OLD MASTERS, AND GLAZING

Allston made his first experiments in painting while a student at Harvard in the last years of the eighteenth century. Already at this time a theme appeared that would persist throughout Allston's career—his love of the "rich, deep tone" of old paintings: "There was an old landscape at the house of a friend....It was of a rich, deep tone, though not by the hands of a master...but of one who lived in a *good age*, when he could not help catching something of the good that was abroad."[4]

Allston also learned, as so many other Americans had, by copying one of the copies made by John Smibert in Italy and brought to America in 1728. He later said of Smibert's copy of the portrait of Cardinal Bentivoglio by Van Dyck: "At that time, it seemed to me perfection."[5]

Allston arrived in London in 1801 and studied under Henry Fuseli, although he also sought the advice of West and made himself familiar with the old paintings in West's collection. Allston would have found the admiration of the old masters, and the striving after their effects, very much alive in London at this time. Joshua Reynolds had been dead for nine years, but the techniques of Reynolds lived on in several of his pupils. The excitement of the Venetian Secret episode of 1797, which relied heavily on the application of colored glazes to a monochrome underpainting, was still only a few years old. During these years, West was still speculating on the techniques of the Venetians (see chapter 2), and Allston said that West helped him to understand the merits of Venetian painting.[6]

Armed with methods learned in London, in 1803 Allston went with John Vanderlyn to the Low Countries and eventually arrived in Paris, where he said he "worked like a mechanic"[7] copying old pictures and producing his own compositions. Allston recalled that when he was copying at the Louvre, French artists did not understand the technique of glazing. As they watched him prepare an underpainting "different in actual color, to be modified afterward by glazing," they "tittered together in groups" and told Vanderlyn "there was a countryman of his in the gallery whom they pitied very much." As Allston told the story, once he began applying glazing to his underpainting, a cardinal who was a connoisseur of art praised his work, and some of the French artists made amends for their previous remarks. Allston disclaimed any credit for the process of glazing, saying that the technique that the French were unaware of was simply "the English school of color, where I had learned this process."[8]

Allston traveled to Rome in 1805, and there he also played an important role in passing on English glazing techniques. There is confirmation of this from German sources, which refer to a painter "named Alston, from the North American Republic," who taught them to paint like the old masters.[9] An 1806 German periodical said that Allston had "discovered the secret" of earlier painters: "The secret is said to be the use of asphaltum."[10] As in Paris, Allston demonstrated his technique of glazing over dried paint with mixtures containing megilp, asphaltum, and other colors, again saying that he did not invent the system but brought it from England.[11] It was the German community in Rome that first began to call Allston "the American Titian."[12]

The idea that glazing had been forgotten in large parts of Europe is somewhat surprising, but the neoclassical style as taught by Jacques-Louis David and others emphasized smooth blending of paint rather than glazing. In a novel by Allston's friend Henry Greenough, which incorporated many of Allston's views, the main character criticized contemporary Italians for not glazing and for thinking a painting was finished "when the impasto is dry."[13] It may have been the extreme form of glazing advocated by Allston that made others take notice—an observer in

1825 described one of his paintings as "all glazes"[14]—rather than that these artists were completely ignorant of the practice of applying thin layers of color to deepen and enliven parts of a design.

Allston's influence must have been partly due to his education and intellect. He mixed easily with leading intellectual lights of the day, including Samuel Taylor Coleridge.[15] Allston wrote florid romantic poetry of his own, including a bizarre invention called *The Paint King*, in which a painter marries a beautiful young woman only to murder her and grind up the various parts of her body into paint.[16] In bringing to fruition the Romantic period of British and American painting, Allston connected romantic subject matter, style, and technique.[17] When describing one of his paintings, he claimed that applying and reapplying layers "at least twenty times" was "the secret of the diaphanous effect"; this kind of technique not only produced a dreamy vagueness that appealed to the romantic imagination, but it must have resonated in viewers' minds with Titian, who was reported to have said that "glazes—thirty or forty" were the secret of his technique.[18]

Early in his career, Allston painted a copy after Veronese and an adaptation of Titian's *Adoration of the Magi*. He gave the "Titian" to Coleridge, who told Ralph Waldo Emerson that a collector wanted to buy it, but when he touched it, he exclaimed, "By Heaven, this picture is not ten years old!"[19] Coleridge inscribed in a book of Allston's: "Born to renew the 16th century."[20]

Allston returned to America in 1808, setting up in John Smibert's old studio in Boston.[21] In 1811 Allston went back to London, bringing with him the young American Samuel F. B. Morse, who would become his principal pupil. Morse, in a letter home to his parents, described some awkward moments when Allston commented on his early efforts: "Very bad, sir; that is not flesh, it is mud, sir; it is painted with brick-dust and clay."[22] At this time Allston met the young Charles Robert Leslie, who was born in London of American parents and spent his youth in Philadelphia—where he met Thomas Sully—but had come back to Britain to study painting. Leslie remained in England for the rest of his life (except for a brief return to America as an instructor at West Point in 1833–34). Leslie wrote: "It was Allston who first awakened what little sensibility I may possess to the beauties of color. He first directed my attention to the Venetian school, particularly to the works of Paul Veronese, and taught me to see, through the accumulated dirt of ages, the exquisite charm that lay beneath."[23]

Leslie and other painters working in London would keep the tradition of glazing in the manner of the early Venetians alive in the decades to come. Because he kept in close contact with many Americans, Leslie played an important role in injecting these ideas into discussions about "tone" that were taking place in Philadelphia in the 1820s (as we shall see in chapter 6).

While in London in 1811–18, Allston showed himself willing to change his technique in response to criticism. *The Dead Man Revived* was praised by West,

who said, "Why, sir, this reminds me of the fifteenth century; you have been studying in the highest school of art."[24] But a reviewer for the *Morning Chronicle* wrote:
"The colouring, too, is without any strongest contrasts or general gradations,
and is half-toned and half-tinted away, between reddish-brown flesh and wan-red
drapery, till all effect, union, and relief, is lost."[25]

Allston reacted immediately, and soon wrote to Morse: "I have repainted
the greater part of the draperies—indeed, those of all the principal figures, except-
ing the Dead Man—with powerful and positive colors, and added double strength
to the shadows of every figure, so that for force and distinctness you would hardly
know it for the same picture. The 'Morning Chronicle' would have no reason now
to complain of its 'wan red.'"[26]

ALLSTON IN AMERICA

Allston came back to Boston for good in 1818, taking with him his albatross, the
huge picture *Belshazzar's Feast*,[27] which would remain unfinished at the time of his
death in 1843.

There is a well-known, detailed, but undated account of Allston's painting
methods written by his friend Henry Greenough,[28] who said that Allston had used
these techniques for fifteen years. Greenough knew Allston over a long period
of time, so it is difficult to know exactly when these techniques were used.[29] The
account seems to reflect the criticism that Allston suffered at the hands of the *Morning Chronicle,* that his coloring lacked "force and distinctness," a complaint that is
reinforced by other accounts. Thomas Sully, for instance, reported after a visit to
his studio in 1831 that "Allston recommend emphatically solid tinting in painting
flesh…'Paint pure decided tints; if too raw you may correct them by scumbling.'"[30]

Allston told Greenough that to paint flesh color, he began with a "dead-
coloring" in white, black, and red, painted "solidly, with good body of color, and in
a broad manner." The next stage was his most distinctive contribution. He set his
palette with the three primary colors (red, blue, and yellow) and then mixed each
with white to make a series of three increasingly lighter "tints" of each color. He
then mixed a neutral olive color out of pure yellow, red, and blue, and used this
to define the shadows of his composition on top of the dead-coloring. Then, he
would take up on the tip of a brush some of each of his bright-colored tints, "not
grinding them together with my knife, but by a few turns of my brush, mingling
them in a light and delicate manner," and begin to define the flesh tones next to the
shadows with mixtures of the pure colors, then with mixtures of the increasingly
lighter tints. "My head is now covered, and each of the three colors enters into the
composition of the whole. In every part there is a blue, red, and yellow, as there is
in flesh, even in the highest part."

Allston recalled a conversation he had in his student days when William
Hazlitt was copying a painting by Titian: "[Hazlitt] remarked upon the singularly

varied character of the tints. 'It looks,' said he, 'as if Titian had twiddled his colors.' I don't know whether this expression strikes you as it did me. To me it is very expressive, and first gave me the idea of catching up each of the three colors and merely twiddling them together instead of grinding them with the knife."[31]

Another painter described Allston's "mottled" manner somewhat differently as "painting with blue, red, and yellow mingled, taking the color which he wished to be predominant as the last upon the brush, and carefully stippling over the work."[32] Allston would vary and add more pure tints if he felt at this point that his color was incorrect, always trying to keep the colors from becoming muddy. He believed that the bright admixture of varied colors at this stage would show through the final glazes and provide the *luce di dentro*, or light from within, that was said to be the effect of Titian.

Allston then glazed in two stages, first applying a very thin, neutral "general glazing" made from megilp with a very little asphaltum plus red and blue—"just enough to discolor my megilp a little." When this was dry, he made a deeper shade of megilp tinted to a neutral color with asphaltum, red, and blue, which he called "Titian's dirt," and with this he modeled the shadows of the face. Allston's "standard" method of painting flesh colors ended here, although he made it clear that he kept open the option of painting into the glazing at this stage. Allston believed that painting into glazing was a "secret" that William Beechey and Thomas Gainsborough also knew.[33]

Allston's process for painting flesh is related to but distinct from other British theories about the glazing techniques of the Venetians. Reynolds's technique varied, but in at least some cases he applied a cold-colored underpainting (not using any yellow at all), applying whatever yellow was needed later in the form of transparent glazes. The Venetian Secret advocated pure white underpainting over a dark ground in preparation for extensive glazing—the local color would presumably be added by applying brightly colored glazes, as opposed to Allston's neutral glazes, although the "Venetian shade" for shadows was similar in color to Allston's "Titian's dirt." West's system, as described by Trumbull in 1784, of applying bright-colored glazes that were the complementary color of a bright-colored underpainting (to dim its color) was also quite different. Benjamin Robert Haydon wrote an entry for *Encyclopaedia Britannica* in 1838 describing a Venetian glazing technique that sounds somewhat similar to Allston's, saying that it was "the present practice of the British school." Haydon said the Venetians "placed their colours purely and crudely, and then by spreading thin transparent tones, took down the rawness, without losing the force of the tint," although unlike Allston he emphasized the importance of a white ground, which should always remain visible and was the source of Titian's *luce di dentro*.[34]

These competing ideas about glazing would result in very different outcomes if glazes were accidentally removed from a painting—as can happen when glazes darken and are mistaken for discolored varnish by a picture cleaner. Paintings by Haydon and West (at least West's system in 1784) would be brighter in color. Reynolds's paintings might be colder and lack yellow, while in a Venetian Secret painting, removing the glazes might remove the coloring altogether. If paintings by Allston were overcleaned, they would be brighter and more mottled and lack the final modeling in the flesh tones. Allston renounced authorship of one of his paintings that he said was ruined by cleaning.[35] Allston's particular method of using asphaltum may in fact have contributed to his paintings' sensitivity to solvents; in a letter to Morse in 1812, Allston told him to add turpentine to asphaltum, rather than oil.[36] If he had added oil to asphaltum, as many other painters did,[37] his glazes might have better withstood cleaning.

Allston's method was unusual in that he did not insist on maintaining the transparency of shadow tones, and he emphasized this several times to Greenough. Allston described sketching in the background of his *Angel Delivering Saint Peter from Prison* with umber, and, instead of following West's advice that a dark background should always be painted thinly, he applied bright, opaque colors to the background and counted the experiment a success, saying "he never had occasion to retouch it, except to give it one general wash of thin asphaltum glazing."[38] It may have been this or a similar example that Allston was thinking of when he spoke to John Neagle: "Allston told me that a good plan of *coloring bright*, was to *glaze* with great richness the general effect of your work upon a light ground, & afterwards to paint *solidly* over all. The rich tone produced by the glazings underneath, would *force your eye* to see bright tones of color.—He said he had practiced this mode upon some work of his, & it was, he thought, his finest coloring."[39]

Allston's dark, neutral glazes would make his pictures look, to some degree, like old paintings, even when new (although the glazes are certainly darker now than they were originally). This "oldness" must have been part of their appeal. Allston once told the young Thomas Cole: "I have been frequently told by friends of yours, sir, that they were *afraid* you were running after the old masters. *Now if that frightens them, I would make every hair on their heads stand on end!*"[40]

Allston's expression "Titian's dirt" was unique to him and is the most explicit case of an American artist acknowledging that one of his goals was imitating the dirt of the ages. This is something about which painters would disagree. In 1825 Thomas Sully commented on this question of "dirt" in relation to Allston's pupil Samuel F. B. Morse, whom Sully said was "too fond of process in his colouring—loading—glazing &c. &c. until the work looks soiled."[41] In 1818 John S. Cogdell wrote that Morse's *Dying Hercules* was "too brown."[42] And upon learning of Allston's death in 1843, Thomas Cole criticized this aspect of Allston's paintings: "I feel confident that his great admiration for the Old Masters led him somewhat astray, for in some of his pictures he imitated the effects of time & they have often put me in mind of what Fuseli has said 'Those pictures which anticipate the beauties of time are pregnant with the seeds of decay.'"[43]

Allston used especially complex methods on certain paintings. For example, he told Greenough that in *The Spanish Girl* he painted the mountain landscape first in strong tints of blue. "Then to mitigate the fierceness of the blue I went over it, when dry, with black and white, and afterward with Indian red and white, not painting out each coat by the succeeding one, nor yet scumbling, but going over it in parts as seemed necessary....I went over that mountain, I suppose, *at least twenty times*, and that is the secret of the diaphanous effect."[44]

Allston also reported an unusual method for painting a sky:

I dead-color it with orange, grading my tints from deep orange at the top down to light yellow on the horizon, just as if I were going to paint an orange sky instead of a blue one. When this is dry, I then paint a sky over it of pure blue and white, grading my tints from dark to light as before, the orange underneath modifies the blue just enough to prevent it looking cold. I finally give it a slight glazing of umber, asphaltum, or any neutral color, which not only gives harmony and atmosphere, but takes away the appearance of paint.[45]

Allston described other unconventional methods, including painting the leaves of a tree with pure yellow ochre, later glazing them down with asphaltum or a mixture of asphaltum and blue.[46] If Allston wanted to glaze several times in one day, he used quick-drying Japanners' gold size instead of megilp as a glazing medium.[47]

He sometimes used even more uncommon materials. Allston told Greenough that he used, as an experiment, milk as a binder for the underpainting of *Elijah in the Desert*, which he varnished with copal, "touched into with transparent oil colors" while the varnish was still wet, and then glazed. One of the motives for this may have been speed—because the milk binder dried much more quickly than oil, Allston reported that this painting "was finished in an inconceivably short time."[48] *Elijah in the Desert* had been painted in England in 1817–18, but Allston's use of milk became known shortly afterward to American painters—Thomas Sully knew about it in 1822.[49] Allston's student Morse apparently also experimented with milk as a binder in 1823.[50] In the mid-1830s, Morse tried painting with beer as a medium and passed this idea on to Sully. Sully, who was game to try anything, tried both beer and milk after a visit to Morse, but he found that if the colors ground in beer were applied too thickly, they cracked. However, he said he had used milk successfully.[51] There is little evidence that unusual media like milk and beer were ever used widely in America, but their use by Morse and Sully indicate the power of Allston's influence. Allston's use of milk gained still wider circulation when it was mentioned in William Dunlap's 1834 book, and it was also one of the nuggets of information about Allston included in Sully's posthumously published *Hints to Young Painters* in 1873.[52]

CHANGES IN ALLSTON'S TECHNIQUE

There are indications that Allston changed his mind about technique more than Greenough's account might indicate. In 1816 John S. Cogdell visited the Academy of the Fine Arts in Philadelphia and described *The Dead Man Revived*: "The whole has been softened down and glazed I believe in every part with asphaltum."[53] But when Cogdell visited Allston in Boston in 1825, he wrote that Allston "says he paints now boldly not as before," although glazing continued to be a part of his technique.[54] Thomas Sully and Bass Otis noticed more radical changes in Allston's method when they visited him in 1836 and 1837, respectively. Sully said Allston told him his method "was more simple than formerly; had in great measure banished process."[55] In Sully's jargon, "process" meant preparing for glazing, and then glazing as a separate step. Otis explained further when he told John Neagle that Allston

> had abandoned his old practice of *toning with asphaltum* & that his present custom is to make out all the modeling & character with a *neutral tint* composed of *white, brown oker, Indian red, & black* for the shades—the lights are *light red & white* for general color, & into this are dragged the three primary colors—*Red, blue & yellow,* with their variations. The effect of flesh color, is thus wrought up to as perfect an imitation of nature as possible at one painting, for which purpose no drying vehicle is used in order that the work may be repeatedly gone over & improved.[56]

This is a surprising development for a man who had for so long relied on glazing with asphaltum, although Sully's expression "in great measure banished process" hints that Allston may not have *completely* given up glazing. But it appears that in Allston's new technique the principal modeling was done in one long session of wet-into-wet painting. Another change described by Sully in 1836 was that Allston "never uses Prussian blue."[57] This reinforces the idea that Allston had largely given up glazing, for in Greenough's account Allston had criticized Prussian blue when used to paint skies, but said, "Prussian blue is a most useful color for glazing" when mixed with asphaltum.[58]

Allston's changes in his technique—and his uncertainty about the correctness of his methods implied in these changes—may have contributed to his well-known inability to finish paintings. It was not only the large painting *Belshazzar's Feast* that remained unfinished at the time of his death—Allston left many other paintings only partly completed.[59] As Gilbert Stuart pointed out, "the work of this month or year was felt to be imperfect the next. And must be done over and over again, or greatly altered, and therefore could never come to an end."[60] Ironically, it was Stuart who precipitated Allston's greatest crisis in painting *Belshazzar's Feast,* when he criticized the perspective, which made Allston attempt major changes from which he was never able to extricate himself.[61]

Upon Allston's death in 1843, there was an outpouring of critical acclaim tempered by dismay that he had not completed the painting on which so many had pinned their hopes. But the influence of Allston's technique was destined to live on. There was a retrospective exhibition of his work in 1839 (the first of a living American artist), and a flurry of exhibitions and general interest immediately after his death. The influence of Allston's methods would be felt even more strongly in following decades by younger artists as different as William Page, George Fuller, William Morris Hunt, and George Inness.

NOTES

1   Morse to "a friend," May 13, 1813 (Morse 1914, 1:102–3).

2   Alberts 1978, 381; Gerdts 1979, 111.

3   Johns 1977; Stoner 1990a; Stoner 1990b; Bjelajac 1997.

4   Dunlap 1834, 2:155.

5   Ibid., 2:156.

6   Sweetser 1879, 57.

7   Richardson 1944, 41.

8   Henry Greenough (cited in Flagg 1892, 189).

9   Richardson 1944, 40; Gerdts 1969.

10   *Elysium* 1806.

11   Gerdts 1969, 184; Greenough in Flagg 1892, 188.

12   Gerdts 1969, 183.

13   Cited in Allston 1993, 39.

14   This comment, "all glazes—but the flesh beautifully clear and transparent," referred to Allston's painting *Edwin Seated in a Wood* (which may be *Italian Shepherd Boy*, 1819, Detroit Institute of Arts) (Cogdell Diaries/Letterbooks, vol. 4, entry of September 23, 1825).

15   On Allston and Coleridge's friendship see Johns 1977, Gerdts and Stebbins 1979, and Allston 1993, 538–41.

16   *The Paint King* is printed in Dunlap 1834, 2:171–75. See also Richardson 1948, 94 and 94n. Richardson points out that Allston's poem was apparently well known enough that Ralph Waldo Emerson referred to it in one of his lectures.

17   While much of his approach to art was emotional and intuitive, Allston was pleased when he received a visit to his studio from the color theorist George Field, who told him that Allston's painting *The Sisters* (ca. 1816–17, Fogg Art Museum, Harvard University, Cambridge, Massachusetts) "was painted exactly in accordance with his theory of color" (Flagg 1892, 192). Allston owned Field's 1817 book *Chromatics* and took notes from Field's later (1835) book *Chromatography* (Johns 1975, 36; Allston 1993, 548).

18   Greenough in Flagg 1892, 194.

19   Gerdts 1979, 100–101.

20   Johns 1977, 18.

21   Gerdts 1979, 56.

22   Prime 1875, 42.

23   Sweetser 1879, 57.

24   Cited in Johns 1979, 90. *The Dead Man Revived by Touching the Bones of the Prophet Elisha* (1811–14, Pennsylvania Academy of the Fine Arts, Philadelphia).

25   Ibid., 94.

26   Ibid.

27   *Belshazzar's Feast* (1817–43, Detroit Institute of Arts).

28   Greenough in Flagg 1892, 181–201.

29 Greenough knew Allston well from his student days (1823–25) until Allston's death, except for Greenough's years abroad in 1830–33 (Allston 1993, 553). Stoner (1990b, 5) believes Greenough wrote his account down in 1844.

30 Sully "Hints," AAA, microfilm roll N18, frame 128 (June 30, 1831).

31 Greenough in Flagg 1892, 182–86.

32 Mr. Spear, quoted in Sweetser 1879, 144.

33 Greenough in Flagg 1892, 182–87.

34 Haydon and Hazlitt 1838, 176. Allston knew both Haydon and William Hazlitt well and saw them often prior to his final return to America in 1818 (Allston 1993, 557–58).

35 The painting he disavowed was *Diana and Her Nymphs in the Chase* (1805, Fogg Art Museum, Harvard University, Cambridge, Massachusetts) (Johns 1979, 89n79); a painting that Stoner (1990b, 9) says still has intact glazes is *Taming of the Shrew* (1809, Philadelphia Museum of Art).

36 Allston to Morse, February 18, 1812 (Allston 1993, 60).

37 Carlyle 2001, 403–7.

38 Greenough in Flagg 1892, 189–91. One of Allston's main points was the need to use bright, hot colors—in some cases pure yellow and red—to keep a background from looking cold and chalky. Hot colors compensate for the so-called turbid medium effect, which makes a lighter color applied thinly over a darker one look bluish. *Angel Delivering Saint Peter from Prison* (1814–16, Museum of Fine Arts, Boston).

39 Neagle Commonplace Book, 25. The entry is undated but probably dates to Neagle's visit to Allston in July 1825. See Allston 1993, 568.

40 Greenough in Flagg 1892, 197.

41 Sully Journal, AAA, microfilm roll N18, frame 290 (July 21, 1825).

42 Cogdell Diaries/Letterbooks, vol. 2, entry titled "The Academy of Arts" [1816]. *Dying Hercules* (1812–13, Yale University Art Gallery, New Haven, Connecticut).

43 Cole Journals [July–August 1843].

44 Greenough in Flagg 1892, 194. *The Spanish Girl in Reverie* (1831, The Metropolitan Museum of Art, New York).

45 Ibid., 194–95. Underpainting a sky with a warm color was also done by Cole, the young Frederic Church, and on some occasions by William Sidney Mount. See chapters 12 and 13.

46 Ibid., 195.

47 Ibid., 196.

48 Ibid. Allston on another occasion said that *Elijah in the Desert* (1817–18, Museum of Fine Arts, Boston) required only three weeks to paint (ibid., 129).

49 Neagle Commonplace Book, 1.

50 Prime 1875, 247; Morse 1914, 1:436. The experimental painting is *Lucretia Pickering Walker Morse and Her Children* (1823, High Museum of Art, Atlanta).

51 Neagle Commonplace Book, 73; Sully "Hints," AAA, microfilm roll N18, frame 140 (June 22, 1836).

52 Dunlap 1834, 2:184; Sully 1873, 29–30. It is not exactly clear where Allston and Morse got their ideas about milk and beer as media, but a French book of 1801 extolled the virtues of milk as a binder for exterior and interior house painting, and English and German editions of this book appeared shortly thereafter (Cadet-de-Vaux 1802). Bouvier (1844, 647) wrote that Cadet-de-Vaux's use of milk as a binder was only a revival of ancient practice. The use of beer and milk as media (allegedly by Northern Gothic or Renaissance painters) was mentioned in 1859 when *The Crayon* printed an article on tempera painting (Gullick and Timbs 1859). In Carlyle's survey of British nineteenth-century technical literature no references to milk or beer were found (Carlyle 2001).

53 Cogdell Diaries/Letterbooks, vol. 2, entry titled "The Academy of Arts" [1816].

54 Cogdell Diaries/Letterbooks, vol. 4, entry of September 28, 1825; the passage continues: "glazing in all his Pictures—but boldly I think & glazes afterwards as he wishes it."

55 Sully "Hints," AAA, microfilm roll N18, frame 142 (August 11, 1836). Sully also described this visit to Allston in "Memoirs," 49, (mis?) dating it to 1835.

56 Neagle Commonplace Book, 25–26. In his "Hints for a Painter" Neagle recorded Otis's testimony in slightly different words (Neagle "Hints," July 21, 1837).

57 Sully "Hints," AAA, microfilm roll N18, frame 142 (August 11, 1836).

58   Greenough in Flagg 1892, 201.

59   Thomas Cole wrote: "The sketches & half finished pictures which I have seen in his studio were charming & it is to be regretted that the[y] were never finished—"(Cole Journals, [after July 30] 1843).

60   Gilbert Stuart to William Ellery Channing (cited in Gerdts 1979, 161). Stuart died in 1828, so his remarks are all the more striking because they do not reflect the documented changes in technique near the end of Allston's life, nor the increasing evidence during the 1830s and later that Allston would never finish *Belshazzar's Feast* or the other paintings that remained unfinished in his studio.

61   See Gerdts 1973a and 1973b. Issues of condition became important with *Belshazzar's Feast* after Allston's death. Allston left it with several figures of a much larger scale partly painted in and the central figure of Belshazzar painted out. A restorer, Darius Chase, removed the paint that Allston applied to cover up Belshazzar, and the painting remains in this state.

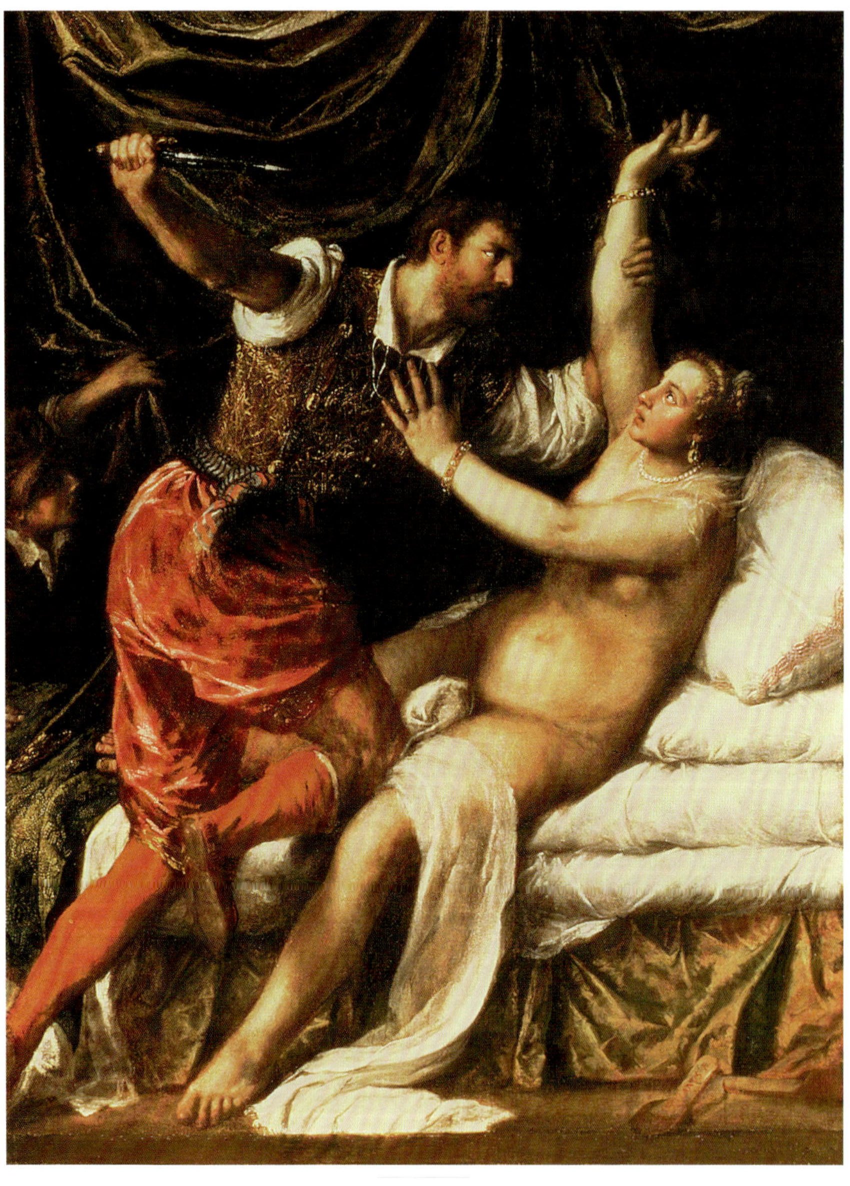

Titian (Tiziano Vecellio) (Italian, ca. 1488–1576), *Tarquin and Lucretia*, ca. 1571.
Oil on canvas, 188.9 × 145.1 cm (74⅜ × 57⅛ in.). University of Cambridge,
Fitzwilliam Museum, Gift of Charles Fairfax Murray, 914. Photo: The Bridgeman Art Library.

CHAPTER 6

SULLY, THE OLD MASTERS, AND "TONE"

LATE IN HIS LIFE, REMBRANDT PEALE recalled the excitement caused in 1799 when Americans had an extraordinary opportunity to see high-quality European old master paintings on American soil. This was the collection of Henri-Joseph Stier of Antwerp, who had brought his paintings to Maryland for safekeeping during the Napoleonic Wars. The paintings may have included Rubens's celebrated *Chapeau de Paille* among others by Rubens, Van Dyck, and Titian.[1] Stier kept the majority of his paintings hidden in packing crates, but at one point Peale convinced Stier that they needed to be unpacked and "aired." Charles Bird King was put in charge of the airing, and for two weeks visitors flocked to see the pictures. Peale said "it was a new and pleasant sight to witness such an animated and pleasant assemblage of artists and amateurs."[2] Gilbert Stuart traveled to Maryland to see the paintings "and admired them much."[3] Decades later, and after several trips to Europe, Peale still remembered what he had learned about the effects of time and varnish from the Stier collection:

> There was a Roman Daughter by *Rubens*—rich & glowing in colour. Mr. Steir to show the effect of cleaning, removed the old Varnish, about the size of a half dollar, from the cheek of the female. This spot appeared as if the flesh had been painted with Vermillion & white, whilst the contiguous parts, owing to the Varnish (if not the glazing), which had become yellow would have led a copyist to mix much Yellow with his Vermillion tints. It is therefore supposed that Rubens' Pictures when new, must have been raw, though brilliant. Time has given them the warm mellow hue, so much admired now.[4]

THOMAS SULLY AND TONING

As the nineteenth century advanced, there were increasing opportunities for Americans to see European paintings—of varying quality—on American soil as well as in Europe.[5] An artist who tells us more than any other about the complex relationship between the old masters and American painters' techniques at this time is Thomas Sully.

Sully was formed as an artist by two trips to England, the first as a young man in 1809–10, when he studied with Benjamin West, became acquainted with

Thomas Lawrence, and began to emulate Lawrence's style. In England, Sully began to keep journals describing interesting things that he saw, including many observations on artists' techniques. Sully returned to England in 1837–38 as an accomplished portraitist, painted the young Queen Victoria, and took additional notes about the techniques of British artists as well as speculating about the techniques used on the old master paintings that he saw.[6]

The sheer volume of Sully's various manuscript notebooks is numbing. Some information is repetitive, but occasionally it clarifies a point to hear the same story told (slightly differently) a second or a third time. Even during Sully's lifetime, he shared his notebooks with other artists. Charles Robert Leslie remembered that at the beginning of his career Sully "lent me his memorandum books, filled with valuable remarks, the result of his practice."[7] This was in 1811, so the volumes would have been slim at that time—Sully continued to add material until 1871, the year before his death.

In 1851 Sully collected and organized a large amount of his material and rewrote it into more high-flown prose, most likely intending publication.[8] A direct observation that had appeared in an earlier notebook as "The specimens of Reynolds' pencil disappointed me; and Opie's seemed raw, crude and dirty" was rewritten to: "The specimen by Reynolds did not come up to my [crossed out: warm] ardent imagination of his excellence, and the [crossed out: one] picture by Opie, seemed crude and unfinished."[9] Similarly, a passage about Reynolds's *Repose on the Flight to Egypt,* "The fingers of the Virgin have turned into the resemblance of lumps of chalk," was rewritten to: "The fingers of the Virgin have changed into a lilac tint."[10]

Sully's manuscripts shed light on a topic that is important for anyone who is curious about exactly what nineteenth-century paintings looked like when they were new, and how their appearance may have changed over time. The practice of "toning" (applying a thin glaze or glazes to lower the tone of a painting) appears to have been inspired by the appearance of old master paintings and by the belief that the old masters themselves toned their paintings. Of course, artists knew that as paintings aged, paint and varnish could turn darker and more yellow; Rembrandt Peale was shocked at the degree of discoloration of Stier's Rubens, but his comments make it clear he was not certain that Stier had not taken off some of Rubens's original glazes as well. An additional complication is that restorers in the first part of the nineteenth century often applied toned layers to an old painting to hide damages and/or make a painting look more "mellow."[11] Sully was far more eloquent than any other nineteenth-century artist in trying to puzzle out how the old masters intended their paintings to look and what this meant in terms of his own practice.

It is worth telling the story of Sully's involvement with toning in some detail because sources of information on this topic are so limited, and the ramifications are so large. On his first trip to England, Sully saw a practice that was apparently new to him. In 1851 he transcribed and amended his original notes:

> Toning the whole picture, is a practice frequently resorted to by [crossed out: the] artists here. Beechey always oils the surface slightly before he spreads the toning....After spreading a tone of Burnt terra de Sienna, when that was dry, and hard, [inserted: he had] oiled out the surface again, and passed over [inserted: it] a mixture of blue, lake, and brown, mixed to an ink colour. In this process, the brush should be moved from corner to corner, as is the practise in laying on varnish.[12]

Comparing this passage with other manuscript accounts makes it clear that when Sully said "artists here" he meant artists in London in 1809–10.[13] It is also an important amplification that—in this telling—the brush should be moved from corner to corner, "as is the practise in laying on varnish," making it clear that Sully is talking about a tone that is uniformly applied overall. This is reinforced by Sully's expression "toning the whole picture" as opposed to "toning the picture," which is the phrase that appeared in a short book published after his death by Sully's grandson.[14] "Burnt terra de Sienna" is a reddish earth color. Beechey's second, ink-colored toning mixture, containing blue pigment and red lake pigment in addition to brown, is similar to the "Titian shade" recommended by the Provises during the Venetian Secret episode of 1797.[15] The mixture of brown, blue, and red is also the same combination of colors that Benjamin West used for glazing during the first decade of the nineteenth century.

Immediately following his account of Beechey's toning practice, Sully described an opposing view by John Trumbull, who was working in London at the time of Sully's visit in 1809–10: "Trumbull condemns the practice of toneing. He thinks a better plan to produce harmony of hue, is to mix with the white which is to be used in the work, colour to produce the desired hue, and employ that white only, in painting the picture."[16]

Sully recognized from the beginning that toning was not universally done but was a method chosen by some painters and not others. This is reinforced by the passage from his 1851 "Memoirs" mentioned above, where Sully's editing of "the artists here" into "artists here" shaded his meaning toward the implication that some artists did it while others did not.

Trumbull's method of adding another color to "tone down" the white on his palette is confirmed by three palette settings of Trumbull's that have been preserved, all of which have a little yellow earth or red earth pigment added to the lightest white.[17] Sully believed that he saw this practice of adding a little color to the whites confirmed by earlier masters as well. When in London in 1809–10 he commented that Van Dyck "used Naples yellow and white for the highest light."[18] Sully also recorded two different palettes of Henry Raeburn's that had been described at a meeting of the Pennsylvania Academy, neither of which contained pure white.[19] In succeeding years, Sully appears to have followed this practice himself in palettes dating to 1829 and 1838.[20] He explained his reasons for doing so in 1835: "By painting on a ground of deep yellow (of raw terra di Sienna and white) and by changing the white which I mix with my colours, into a yellow by the addition of Naples—or raw Sienna, I have produced a more glowing tone."[21] Sully seems to have returned to using pure white on his palette later in his life (at some time before 1851),[22] confirming our general sense that the peak of interest in various aspects of tone and toning was from about 1810 to the 1840s.

The practice of adding a little yellow pigment to the whitest white is very different from the ideas of Gilbert Stuart, who not only used pure white on his palette but took pains to ensure that the cravats in his portraits remained white. In fact, Stuart's coloring was occasionally criticized during and after his lifetime— his flesh tones were called "too strong,"[23] and Neagle called Stuart's cravats "staringly white."[24]

As Sully's observation about Van Dyck demonstrates, the love of a yellow tone must have been connected with emulating the appearance of old paintings. At the time of the Venetian Secret episode in 1797, Joseph Farington wrote: "There is now an acquired prejudice in favor of brown & yellow hues."[25] When Rembrandt Peale used white mixed with yellow ochre for his lightest flesh tones in 1820, he made it clear that he was looking to the past by calling this mixture "historic flesh."[26] (See more on Rembrandt Peale's pigment mixtures in chapter 10.)

If there was a prejudice in favor of brown and yellow, there was an equivalent prejudice in some quarters in both Britain and America against the use of bright colors, which were seen as unsophisticated. As the British writer John Burnet wrote in his 1837 *Essay on the Education of the Eye*: "We observe that children and rude nations are most attracted by strong colors."[27] These sorts of ideas were used to comic effect by popular writers—for example, when Charles Dickens described, in *Nicholas Nickleby* (1838–39), the "bright salmon flesh-tint" and "sky-blue veins"[28] in Miss La Creevy's portrait miniatures, he was clearly inviting readers to laugh at her lack of sophistication. Mark Twain poked fun at the bright colors on provincial upper-middle-class American portraits: "In big gilt frame, slander of the family in oil…these persons all fresh, raw, and red—apparently skinned."[29] Americans might have been particularly prey to worrying that they would be seen as unsophisticated if they painted with colors that were too bright. Rembrandt Peale made this explicit when he recommended to artists that they apply a black toning layer "on the supposition that your Portrait has been solidly & well painted in with tints perhaps a little too bright & raw."[30]

Thomas Cole and William Sidney Mount also had opinions about the proper tone of a painting (discussed in chapters 12 and 13). Cole even suggested at one point that the fad for "toning down" bright whites in the first half of the nineteenth century extended to sculptors in marble as well. In 1838 he wrote that ancient Greek sculpture "might have been *tinted*, as the best modern sculptures are, to take away the cold effect of the marble."[31]

Artists had differing opinions about the original appearance of old paintings and the degree to which they might have darkened or yellowed over time. Rembrandt Peale's somewhat confused reaction to the cleaning of a spot on Stier's Rubens bears comparison to Stuart's opinion that Rubens "made his tintings distinct, that they might bear up the longer against time which destroyed their luster & rendered them, by incorporation, monotonous."[32]

When the Clive family portrait by Reynolds was exhibited in America in 1833–34, its coloring must have appeared unusually warm, and at least some observers knew that it was not originally that way—a pamphlet printed in America at that time stated: "Sir Thomas Lawrence was of the opinion that this picture was originally painted cool and quiet in color."[33] Thomas Sully later saw the picture in England after its owner had it cleaned and noted the difference, saying, "it appears fresh and forcible."[34]

In 1826 Sully saw a major late work by Titian (fig. 9) in the collection of Joseph Bonaparte (Count Survilliers), the brother of Napoleon, who was living in exile in Bordentown, New Jersey, and reported: "It is remarkable how much glazing has been used in the picture of the Lucretia which I examined closely—even the white drapery has been glazed or toned down—the effect is a subdued splendor, far preferable to the oily smoothness of the opposite system."[35]

During the mid-1820s toning and glazing were very much on Sully's mind. There exists a flurry of references in Sully's manuscripts to artists who had spent time in London using intermediate toning layers—applying a thin, overall layer, then continuing to paint on top of that layer. Sully reported that his friend Charles Bird King did this, using a mixture of mastic varnish and the red pigment vermilion.[36] In 1825 Sully paraphrased one of several letters from his nephew Robert Sully, in which Robert gave a detailed account of methods that he and Charles Robert Leslie were using in London at that time: "[A portrait] was in its progress toned with black made thin with magyllip, the shadows glazed with asphaltum and with lake and the lights retouched while moistned with the toning—the black was used to take off the rawness of hue—He informs me as follows: 'Leslie tones his pictures in their various stages—the colour is made very thin with magyllip and afterwards nearly taken off with a dry brush, in this state the picture is retouched.'"[37]

Another comment from Leslie hints at the motivation for this: "Leslie's advice is never to think of the modern masters but study the old masters altogether."[38] This is a radical statement, but it is not too different from Washington Allston's boast that he was proud to be "running after the Old Masters."

Sully also read widely on art and artists, and one passage he wrote down in 1826 from Northcote's supplement to his *Memoirs of Reynolds* was: "Hodges, the landscape painter, said of Reynolds 'Infant Hercules' when he first noticed it in the exhibition room—from the extraordinary rich tone of colouring, warm and glowing in the extreme, he said 'that it looked as if it had been boiled in brandy.'"[39]

In May 1830 Sully studied the Abrams collection of old master paintings in New York. His notes make it clear that he discriminated between localized glazing and overall toning, and that he was trying to discover the methods used by earlier painters with an eye toward re-creating the effects himself. He wrote: "I find that the practice of toning the whole picture with a warm colour—like raw Sienna—and some instances with a dark colour like asphaltum, was common to their practice." He thought a copy after Correggio and a portrait by Velázquez were "much toned." In a landscape by Hobbema, "asphaltum had been used over all the surface—sky and all," and a painting by Murillo was described as "the whole much toned." Of a landscape by Claude, Sully wrote "and finally the whole picture, sky also, was toned with raw sienna, or a colour like it."[40] In another notebook, he summarized his overall opinion: "On a careful consideration of several pictures, in Abrams collection at New York, I find most of the works of the Old Masters were toned after the picture was completed."[41]

Robert Sully had returned to America by 1830, but he was still in contact with Leslie in London and was more enthusiastic than ever about toning and glazing paintings with asphaltum and megilp. Late that year Neagle recorded that Robert Sully emphasized the lineage of this technique as attributable to Reynolds:

> R. Sully declares that [John] Jackson and Northcote & Leslie & [Gilbert Stuart] Newton all approve of this plan, and that it was the method practiced by *Reynolds*, and that the toning will not grow dark nor change more than any other mode of painting.…It is a mistaken idea, says Robt Sully, that Sir Joshua's pictures all faded—some of them now in England are in a high state of preservation and the coloring is magnificently rich and juicy.…Jackson is at the head of living colourists, and that he (Jackson) worships the tone and colouring of Reynolds with a kind of idolatry.[42]

Robert Sully felt so confident about the correctness of the methods learned from this Anglo-American coterie of Reynolds worshippers that he and Leslie criticized his uncle's paintings, saying they "wanted tone."[43] Thomas Sully may have felt he needed Allston's guidance at this point, and the next year—1831—he traveled to Boston to see him. Among other advice, Sully seemed to get confirmation from Allston that his nephew and the other English painters were right: "He [Allston] recommends the use of a very slight glazing of asphaltum to a portrait—face and all."[44]

Twenty years later, Sully remembered this conversation and elaborated further in his "Memoirs" manuscript:

He recommends to use a very slight glazing or toneing over every portrait I paint. Asphaltum, generally speaking, he thought most fit for the purpose.

Any opinion on the subject of painting from Alston, is entitled to grave consideration.[45]

It is significant that upon reflection Sully added the word "toning," which more clearly refers to an overall layer as opposed to a glaze (which might be applied to only part of the composition). John Neagle came up with a definition of what "toning" meant in the second quarter of the nineteenth century:

> To "*tone*" in the usual acceptation, is to glaze some color or colors, transparent or semitransparent, over the whole work while it is dry.—Some artists repeat this process between the different coatings of solid color; others who do not tone between the sittings, glaze at last for a rich hue over the work. There are others again who begin each painting or sitting by glazing & then into this preparation [inserted: while moist] work the different changes of colour required, with solid tints, half transparent colors & glazes.[46]

In 1832, the year after Sully's visit to Allston, Neagle recorded a remarkable conversation that showed Sully's conflicted thoughts about toning, even when Allston's advice must have been fresh in his mind. The conversation also incorporated Robert Sully's opinions about intermediate toning layers:

> In the conversation also of this day with Mr Sully he did not *condemn toning, except a regular process of it, in portraits.* He did not think however that otherwise good painting required toning in every instance and gave that of the head of Col Gibbs by Stuart, above mentioned [which Sully had praised very highly], as an instance, which was not toned. But in the same conversation acknowledged that Allston recommended to him as his own practice never to let a portrait go out with out a thin glaze of asphaltum all over the work.—In a letter a few days ago from Robt M. Sully now in Richmond, he avers that no one can colour well who does not pass some glaze colour all over the work when finished, and into this vehicle drag some warm colours into the shades & half tints leaving the lights untouched after toning. Mr. Sully thinks that *toning by process,* that is, preparing the work for tone, and depending on tone for true effect, was not only too tedious but required too much time and then was not so apt to be durable.[47]

Neagle went on to mention other painters who had arrived at a successful result by painting directly, without resorting to toning. Gilbert Stuart was again brought up as an artist who had not toned.

> Reynolds, Rubens, Vandyke have painted heads up at once *without toning* which
> were said to be exquisite for colour & effect—Mr Sully says that Vandykes head of
> Gervatious was *not toned* and it is considered the crack portrait in London. It was
> said Reynolds painted the head of Mr. Johnson in *one long sitting.* Vandyke painted
> (according to Vertue & Walpole) *a full length portrait* in one day! Gilbert Stuart *never
> toned* but often painted shadows with glazed colours.[48]

In spite of Thomas Sully's misgivings about "toning by process," he
employed this method on some paintings in following years. For instance, in
1836 he wrote two different accounts of his experience in toning a portrait. In a
notebook that he often shared with other artists, he wrote: "Toned the portrait of
Kane with asphaltum—note that when it is intended to pursue that process, the
flesh should be of a cooler hue."[49] But in his more private journal—in a remark
made the same day but intended for his eyes only—he was more frank: "Toned the
portrait of Paul—and made it too brown."[50]

By late 1837, Sully was back in England, where he took further notes on
old masters' techniques. As might be expected, he was especially interested in the
question of toning, and he believed that he saw artist-applied toning on paintings
by Velázquez and Titian.[51] A remark by Sully's daughter when she and Sully were
visiting the collection of Lord Ashburton is a reminder that the admiration of the
effects of time on paintings was not universal: "Father fell to work instantly to
admire the quantity of pictures by the old masters that adorned the walls—bad
taste in me, for I cannot admire those black dirty looking things."[52]

When in London, Sully made an insightful comment about Titian's *Noli Me
Tangere* that may have pertained not only to that painting but perhaps also implied
dissatisfaction with his own efforts at "toning by process": "It is pure in every
respect and of exquisite truth—The tone is not a subdued hue as we find produced
by a glazing of asphaltum over the whole work, but a rich golden atmosphere that
is produced by the proper tempering of his tints."[53]

Sully also observed J. M. W. Turner on varnishing day at the British Institution in 1838: "He [Turner] was busily engaged in retouching his sea piece, I
observed an opened box of water colors by him; but I did not see him use them.
But whatever he did use in retouching I saw the whole picture toned with a brown
liquid before he left it."[54]

Turner is known to have glazed his pictures extensively, but we know of no
other reference to his having applied an overall toning layer. Sully's anecdote goes
against the testimony of Leslie (cited below), who wrote that Turner never toned
his pictures. Sully's account also goes against his own description of Turner as the
champion of the painters who were nicknamed the "Bianchi" as opposed to the
"Neri"—in Sully's words, "the first named, colour very bright, and pure of tint;

avoiding the process of toning. The other class on the contrary, cherish deep toned hues of colour…Turner is an ultra Bianchi."[55]

On three other occasions Sully wrote slightly different versions of his story about Turner on varnishing day. In one account he called the toning layer "a yellow varnish" instead of a brown liquid, in another "a yellowish varnish," and in yet another version he added that the toning was done on the day *after* the retouching. Taking the accounts together, Sully's use of the words "toned" and "varnish" and the fact that the toning apparently took place as a separate operation on the following day, make it likely that what Sully saw—or at least *thought* he saw—was an overall toning layer rather than extensive local glazing.[56]

Shortly after his return to Philadelphia in 1838, Sully wrote a memorandum to himself: "Mem.: To paint lighter than you intend the finished part to appear—When you mean to tone or glaze." This may be because when he saw his own pictures on display in London, he was sometimes critical of their lack of force, remarking, "My pictures look dingy and vapid," or "My own works, I see, are on too low a scale of color."[57]

At this time, Sully also read about and wrote down that he agreed with the theory of Reynolds that *atramentum*—the secret of the ancient Greek painter Apelles—was in fact a glaze of bitumen.[58] The precise nature of Apelles's atramentum, a kind of unifying layer and/or varnish that had been described in vague terms by the Roman author Pliny, had been a favorite topic of speculation since the Renaissance.[59] Reynolds's opinion might have reinforced in Sully's mind the correctness of employing this kind of toning layer. In any case, Sully's notebooks occasionally contain notes like the following from 1842: "Toned with asphaltum the portrait of Mrs. Allston.…it will therefore not require varnish." And in 1849: "Toned picture of a child praying with asphaltum."[60] These sporadic descriptions imply that not every picture was toned. In fact, the paintings described in Sully's notebooks are most likely the exceptional ones, or ones using experimental materials that he wanted to watch carefully to see how they lasted.

When Sully collected his thoughts on technique with an eye to publication in 1851, his respectful treatment of Allston's advice about overall toning showed that he still believed this to be a valid way to paint. Sully gave his final reference to overall toning in 1855, when he wrote that he toned a copy he had painted after Guido Reni with "raw Terra de Sienna." This last case is somewhat different from the previous examples—raw sienna is a dull yellowish earth color that Sully thought he had seen used as a toning layer on paintings by earlier European masters, and his use of it on a copy of an old painting may have been (consciously or unconsciously) an attempt to reproduce the appearance of the old, yellowed varnish layers frequently found on old pictures.[61]

REMBRANDT PEALE AND TONING

Just as Sully wrote a manuscript for a book in 1851, Rembrandt Peale—between 1850 and 1852—compiled his notes on technique into a long manuscript that he intended to publish, entitled "Notes of the Painting Room." An important part of his idea of "tone" involved mixing warm pigments with the white on his palette (see chapter 10). But Peale also had theories about the atramentum of Apelles. Ever the salesman, Peale claimed that he had discovered an improvement over Apelles's atramentum:

> My improvement…will give to the modern painter the advantage so much praised as the means employed by Apelles alone, in toning his Pictures into the soft & shadowy reality of Nature. Ivory Black ground very fine, & diluted with the Magnesia Vehicle [a medium of Peale's invention, made of oil plus magnesium carbonate], becomes an *Atramentum* to soften & subdue the intensity of every colour and tint. It may be used alone, or in combination with any Colour, & should be put on with a new brush. It may sometimes be spread with a sponge or rag, or rubbed with the finger, & then retouched with the brush.[62]

On an undated manuscript sheet, Peale gave a detailed account of how a similar sort of layer might be used as an intermediate toning layer during the painting of a portrait:

> Toning with Black: On the supposition that your Portrait has been solidly & well painted in with tints perhaps a little too bright & raw, I think it is often well, especially in a Male Portrait to glaze it over especially the lower part of the face [inserted: very thinly] with Ivory black, finely ground & used with the Copal Vehicle (magnesia & Copal). This prepares the surface well for Painting.…If too much is put on the lights, it may be removed with a rag or buckskin.[63]

Peale's black-pigmented intermediate toning layer was very similar to the technique that Robert Sully, Leslie, and Jackson were using in London in the 1820s.

It is also significant that Peale noticed and thought worth writing down (in 1850–52) one of the very few British references to overall toning (or a "general glaze," as the British tended to call it), from an 1850 book on portrait painting by John Burnet: "It may be safely recommended gradually to strengthen the colours as the various sittings proceed, both by a general glaze over the whole, and, while wet, painting into it both with opaque and transparent tints, which will give it a higher refinement and solidity than any other process; still reserving the power of adding a general glaze at the finishing sitting, if his practice is to be founded upon such principles."[64]

CHANGES OF OPINION ABOUT TONING

Even if one knows a great deal about a painter's technique at a particular moment in time, artists may change their opinions. This is true of Charles Robert Leslie and toning. In the 1820s Leslie was one of the most enthusiastic advocates of toning paintings in their various stages with asphaltum and megilp. At that time he told Robert Sully to use megilp freely, it "being a pleasant vehicle and will stand [last] well."[65]

But by the middle of the nineteenth century painting techniques were being discussed with a new urgency in Britain, and many people's opinions were in flux. The controversy that revolved around the cleaning of paintings at the National Gallery in London between 1846 and 1853 focused debate on the original appearance of old paintings.[66] Another catalyst for change was the publication in Britain of several scholarly books about painting techniques, including Mary Merrifield's translation of Cennino Cennini's *Libro dell'Arte* (1844),[67] Charles Eastlake's *Materials for a History of Oil Painting* (1847), and Merrifield's collection of a number of early documents with her own extensive commentaries called *Original Treatises on the Arts of Painting* (1849).

Most of the discussions at this time concerned the techniques of earlier European masters. However, Leslie made some comments in 1855 that relate directly to the question of toning on nineteenth-century paintings:

> The attacks that have been so unsparingly directed against the cleaning of pictures in the National Gallery have been generally founded on the assumption that the tone of a fine picture is always imparted to it by a general glazing, and that, in the removal of this, its most valuable quality is destroyed. But it is so far from being true that the best colourists finished their pictures with a general glaze, that I believe the cases in which they have done so have been exceptional. Reynolds sometimes, but not always, did this; and it appears, by his own account, to have been the invariable practice of Mr. Haydon: but I know it was not the practice of Turner, of Etty, of Constable, or of Willkie, and I feel confident it was not of Paul Veronese, Rubens, Claude, the Poussins, or Cannalletti.[68]

By the 1850s, Leslie had also changed his mind about asphaltum and megilp, saying they were unstable, and pointing out that in his understanding of painting materials he had benefited from the scholarly research of Eastlake.[69] After Leslie's death, his son went so far as to say that his father "had a particular objection to the practice of preparing his work in one colour, to be afterwards altered to another by glazing"[70]—in other words, exactly what he had been doing in the 1820s. Leslie was (in 1855) also critical of George Beaumont, who was close to Allston and was a champion of the "Neri," and who was said to have admired the effect of a dark varnish.[71] Leslie was also critical of the application of toned varnishes to old master paintings earlier in the century, which he spoke of as if it were a practice of the past: "About the beginning of the present century it was not unfrequent for the possessors of old pictures to have them *toned*, as it was called."[72] One senses that those who saw themselves as progressives during the mid-century National Gallery cleaning controversy were trying to distance themselves from the practices of the earlier part of the century—in the case of Leslie, he was distancing himself from his own previous practice.

In Leslie we see not only a change in his opinion over time, but also how opposing opinions could be held by different artists at the same moment. Leslie was the source for the famous debates about "tone" between John Constable, who advocated fresh, natural colors, and George Beaumont, who said that a painting should have the brown color of an old violin. According to Leslie, "in these matters, each was disposed to set the other right," but the two men remained friends.[73] Leslie also reported a disagreement between Constable and the sculptor Francis Chantrey about Constable's landscapes being too bright and cold in color and needing (according to Chantrey) a glaze of asphaltum.[74] The discussions that revolved around Constable all took place in England, but, as we have seen, Leslie was an important conduit between British and American artists.[75]

It is important to note that the most popular mid-nineteenth-century American book on technique, compiled in 1845 by Laughton Osborn but based primarily on a book by Pierre-Louis Bouvier, did not mention overall toning, although Osborn (following Bouvier) described locally applied glaze layers called "preparations," which were similar to intermediate toning layers but applied only to parts of the design.[76] It is also significant that a recent, very thorough study of British nineteenth-century painting treatises found only passing references to overall toning and no specific instructions about how to do it. The most explicit reference was contained in a book on art theory from 1838, but there were no descriptions as detailed as those given by the Americans Sully, Peale, and Neagle.[77] This may imply that the process was not done by British artists as frequently as Sully thought (or at least not by the kinds of painters who wrote instruction books) or—perhaps—that it was considered a disreputable method.

Laughton Osborn's book gave some hints about why some artists may have thought toning was disreputable. Just as Sully was afraid that toning "was not so apt to be durable," Osborn warned his readers that glazes might be accidentally removed at a later time by picture cleaners or might turn brown because of the high proportion of medium that they contained.[78] Rembrandt Peale was also keenly aware of the danger that glazes might suffer at the hands of picture cleaners, saying that a painter's final glazes might be for the benefit of the first owner of the painting only.[79] These concerns about glazes would apply to a toning layer, or "general glaze," as well.

The British restorer Henry Merritt shed additional light on these questions in a short book on the cleaning of paintings in 1854, in which he decried the taste for brown pictures and said that the old masters did not use overall glazes. Although Merritt's comments focused on earlier masters, some remarks could be seen as criticism of recent practice: "The more skilful the artist the less need is there for scumbling, toning, or any final operation to unite the component parts into a 'whole.'"[80] The casting of toning in such a negative light marks a distinct change from Sully's opinion that toning was a legitimate choice that some artists might make and others might not.

NOTES

1. Rembrandt Peale insisted that he saw *Le Chapeau de Paille* when the Stier collection was shown in Maryland, although William Dunlap quoted Robert Gilmor to the effect that this painting never came to America (R. Peale 1855c, 175; Dunlap 1834, 2:458). *Le Chapeau de Paille*, also called *Portrait of Susanna Lunden (?)*, (ca. 1625, National Gallery, London).

2. R. Peale 1855c, 175.

3. Dunlap 1834, 2:458–59.

4. R. Peale "Notes," 70.

5. See Craven 1990. On exhibitions in New York during the period 1825–60, see Barratt 2000a.

6. On Sully's manuscripts, see Prown 1964 and Barratt 2000b, 75. Barratt 2000b includes parts of the Journal relating to Sully's second London visit with cross-references to "Hints for Pictures."

7. Dunlap 1834, 2:242.

8. Sully "Memoirs." Sully's grandson Francis T. S. Darley wrote in the preface to a short volume, *Hints to Young Painters*, which he published in 1873 (Sully 1873, 3), that the book was "prepared for the press by the late Thomas Sully in the year 1851," presumably referring to the much longer "Memoirs of the Professional Life of Thomas Sully" manuscript. There are editorial changes and spelling corrections in "Memoirs" in a different hand, as if someone had intended to publish it closer to its present size instead of Darley's much smaller book. The "Memoirs" manuscript was once the property of Darley, so Darley may well have done the editing and then abandoned the project as too unwieldy.

9. Sully "Hints," AAA, microfilm roll N18, frame 77 (July 21, 1809); Sully "Memoirs," 7. (The cruder original version was printed almost exactly in Dunlap 1834, 2:119.) A late (1871) Sully manuscript (Sully "Incidents") at the Frick Art Reference Library is somewhat puzzling because in many ways, including the cited passage about Reynolds and Opie, it is much closer to "Hints" than to "Memoirs."

10. Sully "Hints," AAA, microfilm roll N18, frame 150 (December 12, 1837); Sully "Memoirs," 63.

11. *Exhibition of Cleaned Pictures* 1947, vii; Anderson 1990, 6; L. Mayer 1998, 28–29.

12. Sully "Memoirs," 15.

13. Sully "Hints," AAA, microfilm roll N18, frames 80–81 (1809–10).

14. Sully 1873, 37.

15. See chapter 2.

16. Sully "Memoirs," 15.

17. Trumbull's palettes are from 1813, 1820, and 1829 (Sizer 1967, 136–37). In a modern collection of European palette settings, the only other palette that similarly excluded pure white was that of George Romney, who added a little yellow ochre to his whites (Schmid 1948, 96). For more detail on Romney's palette, see Williams 1937.

18. Sully "Hints," AAA, microfilm roll N18, frame 80 (comment from 1809–10, recalled in 1822).

19. Ibid., frame 102 (August 13, 1825).

20. Ibid., frame 126 (December 23, 1829); Barratt 2000b, 59; Fabian 1983, 95. On Sully's procedure during various stages of painting a portrait, see Fabian 1983, 19–20.

21. Sully "Hints," AAA, microfilm roll N18, frame 139 (October 25, 1835).

22. Sully "Memoirs," 107–11. The palette reproduced in Sully 1873 is unusual in that it has tints (none of them pure white) around its rim, but a pile of pure white in the interior of the palette.

23   Jane Stuart in Mason 1879, 37; see also D. Evans 1999, 152n8.

24   Neagle Commonplace Book, 4.

25   Farington 1978–84, diary entry of May 3, 1797. Around this time, Lawrence asked Farington "if I thought He might glaze the whole to a lower tone, I said *the lower the tone short of obscurity the better*, there is a solemn grandeur in low tones" (ibid., March 19, 1797).

26   R. Peale to Sully, July 4, 1820 (C. W. Peale 1983–2000, 3:384). Later, Peale wrote: "Excessive White is offensive to the Organs of sight, especially in contrast with extreme black. Yellow gives to white the most pleasing luminousness even when slightly tinged with Orange" (R. Peale "Notes," 38).

27   Burnet 1837, 63–64.

28   Charles Dickens, *Nicholas Nickleby* (1838–39), chapters 5, 10.

29   Mark Twain, *Life on the Mississippi*, chapter 38. (The book was published in 1883, but Twain was clearly recalling a much earlier time.)

30   R. Peale Miscellaneous, undated sheet, beginning "Toning with Black…"

31   Thomas Cole to Mr. Adams, September 10, 1838 (cited in Noble 1964, 200).

32   Neagle Commonplace Book, 36. See chapter 4 for a slightly different version of Stuart's conversation with Neagle.

33   *Descriptive Catalogue of Paintings, by the Great Masters, of the Italian, Venetian, Spanish, Flemish, Dutch, French, and English Schools; by permission, in the Rotunda of the Capitol; and Submitted to the Government, and Patrons of the Arts in General, as Suited for the Foundation of a National Gallery* (Washington, D.C., 1834), 19. *George Clive and His Family with an Indian Servant* (1765–66, Gemäldegalerie, Berlin).

34   Sully "Hints," AAA, microfilm roll N18, frame 151 (February 5 [?], 1838).

35   Ibid., frame 107 (April 30, 1826). *Tarquin and Lucretia*, (ca. 1571, Fitzwilliam Museum, Cambridge). On the Bonaparte (Survilliers) collection, see Stroud 2002.

36   Sully "Hints," AAA, microfilm roll N18, frames 99–100 (January 2, 1825); Neagle Commonplace Book, 36.

37   Robert Sully to Thomas Sully, September 12, 1825 (Sully "Hints," AAA, microfilm roll N18, frame 104).

38   Robert Sully to Thomas Sully, April 29, 1825 (Sully "Hints," AAA, microfilm roll N18, frame 101).

39   Sully "Hints, AAA, microfilm roll N18, frame 111 (September 1826).

40   Ibid., frame 127 (May 17, 1830).

41   Sully Journal, AAA, microfilm roll N18, frame 346 (May 17, 1830).

42   Neagle "Hints," December 1830.

43   Ibid.: "R. Sully declared that Leslie said of the two recent pictures painted by T. Sully which went to England that they *wanted tone*, and that his own opinion was that *tone & colouring* were neither of them his Uncle's *forte*."

44   Sully "Hints," AAA, microfilm roll N18, frame 128 (June 30, 1831).

45   Sully "Memoirs," 31.

46   Neagle Commonplace Book, 26 27.

47   Neagle "Hints," September 23, 1832.

48   Ibid.

49   Sully "Hints," AAA, microfilm roll N18, frame 143 (November 21, 1836).

50   Sully Journal, AAA, microfilm roll N18, frame 411 (November 21, 1836).

51   Sully "Hints," AAA, microfilm roll N18, frame 145 (November 8, 1837); frame 152 (February 5, 1838); frame 170 (July 6, 1838); Sully "Memoirs," 67.

52   Blanch Sully, March 4, 1838 (Sully Letterbook, 2:43–44).

53   Sully "Hints," AAA, microfilm roll N18, frames 147–48 (December 1, 1837). The painting Sully saw was probably *Noli Me Tangere* (1514, National Gallery, London).

54   Ibid.: frame 151 (February 5, 1838). The painting was *Fishing Boats, with Hucksters Bargaining for Fish* (1838, Art Institute of Chicago).

55   Townsend 1996, 66; Sully "Memoirs," 57; Sully "Hints," AAA, microfilm roll N18, frame 147 (November [14?], 1837).

56   Thomas Sully to Jane Sully, February 5, [1838] (Sully Letterbook, 1:134–35); Sully "Memoirs," 65; Sully Journal, AAA, microfilm roll N18, frame 436 (February 5, 1838).

57 Sully "Hints," AAA, microfilm roll N18, frame 151 (February 5, 1838); frames 171–72 (December 1837).

58 Ibid., frame 176 (1839).

59 The question of atramentum, tone, and toning were debated in a series of articles in *Burlington Magazine*. See Brandi 1949, Gombrich 1962 and 1963, Kurz 1962 and 1963, MacLaren and Werner 1950, Mahon 1962, and Plesters 1962; see also Bomford and Leonard 2004, pt. 6; and Talley 2005.

60 Sully "Hints," AAA, microfilm roll N18, frame 190 (July 22, 1842); frame 209 (January 25, 1849). In an undated entry, John Neagle recorded: "Sully sometimes toned his portraits all over the flesh & bkground with Bt terra de Siena and sometimes with other colors added which should approach the hue he wants and then paints solidly upon it when dry" (Neagle "Receipts," 49).

61 Sully "Memoirs," 31; Sully "Hints," AAA, microfilm roll N18, frame 230 (August 28, 1855).

62 R. Peale "Notes," 70–71.

63 R. Peale Miscellaneous, undated sheet, beginning with "Toning with Black…" The British author T.H. Fielding wrote in a similar vein: "[Flat brushes] are used as well in the beginning as towards the completion of a large picture, when, instead of firm undiluted colours, they are used with varnish or other vehicles, in order to glaze and tone down the brightness of those colours that have been laid in for this purpose, or which may be accidentally too gay or vivid" (Fielding 1846, 199).

64 Burnet 1850, 40 (cited in R. Peale "Notes," 169).

65 Robert Sully to Neagle, September 12, 1825 (Neagle "Receipts," 38). To his credit, Neagle disagreed with Leslie's opinion about megilps even in the 1820s, saying that "they certainly, with most vehicles, will turn dark; particularly when not mixed with colors. J.N. 1826" (Neagle "Receipts," 39).

66 *Exhibition of Cleaned Pictures* 1947, xii–xx; Anderson 1990.

67 Merrifield's was the first translation of Cennino d'Andrea Cennini's *Il libro dell'arte* into English, but the book had been published in Italian in 1821, so artists who read Italian could have known it then. On the possible influence of eighteenth- and early-nineteenth-century manuscript copies of Cennini on William Blake and other British artists, see Stemmler 1984.

68 Leslie 1855, 218.

69 Ibid., 213–14, 218ff.

70 Leslie and Taylor 1860, xv.

71 Robert Smirke wrote a satire on Beaumont's views in 1816: "This year he will admire a Yellow Picture, next year a brown one; however, it is but just to acknowledge, that for 24 summer moons, he has been constant in his dislike to green leaves and blue skies"(cited in Egerton 1998, 374–75).

72 Leslie 1855, 218–19.

73 Leslie 1845, 113–14.

74 Ibid., 177.

75 It is also interesting that Dunlap went to some length to claim Leslie as an American artist (Dunlap 1834, 2:239–40).

76 Osborn 1845, 140–42. Osborn, while urging caution when cleaning paintings, wrote: "And as for the embrowning of the varnish, there are even cases where it is rather an advantage," although he did go on to give methods for removing a varnish (ibid., 288).

77 Carlyle 2001, 221–22, 248–50.

78 Osborn 1845, 137–39.

79 R. Peale "Notes," 44.

80 Merritt 1854, 26.

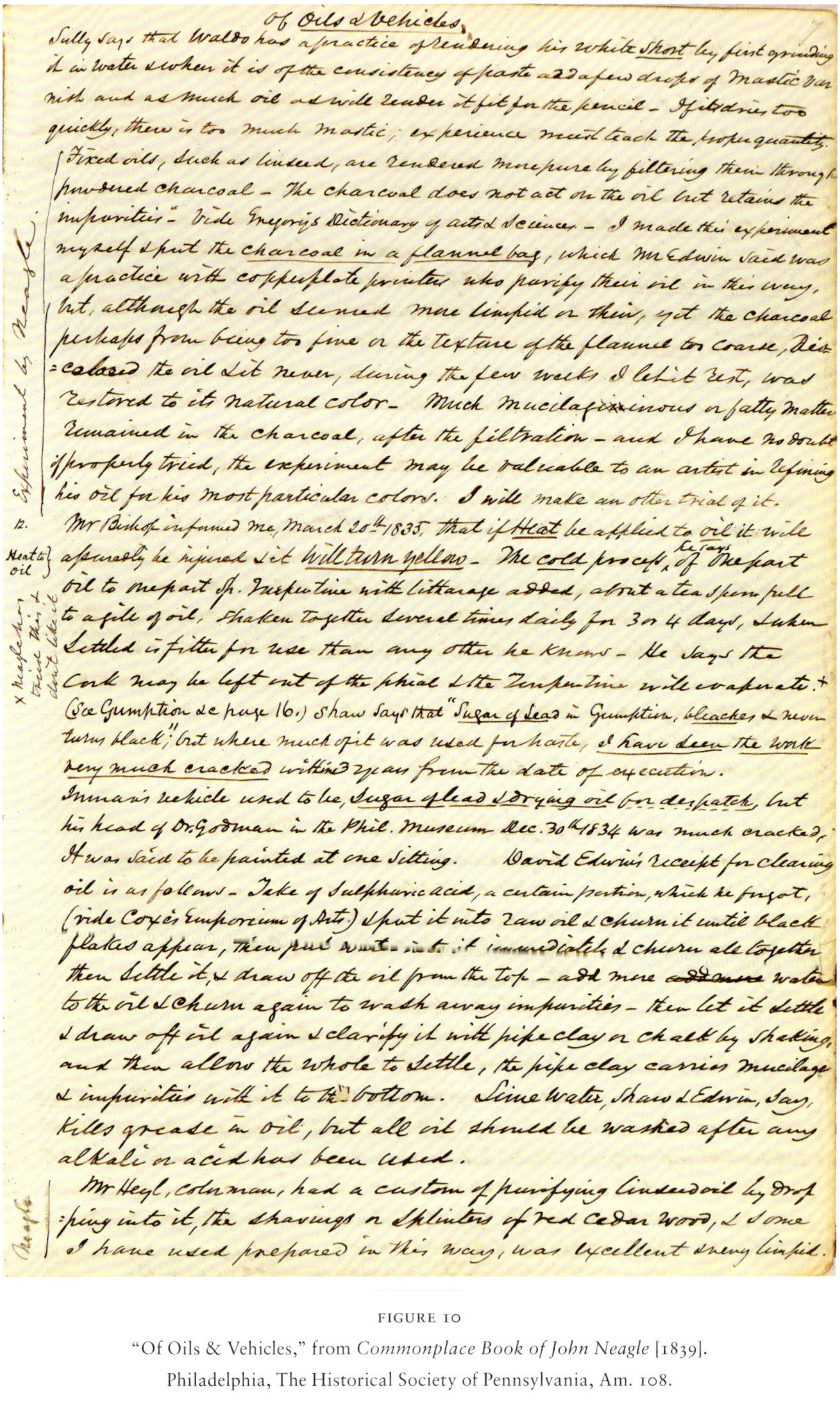

Of <u>Oils & Vehicles</u>.

Sully says that Waldo has a practice of rendering his white Short by first grinding it in water & when it is of the consistency of paste add a few drops of Mastic Varnish and as much oil as will render it fit for the pencil — If it dries too quickly, there is too much Mastic; experience must teach the proper quantity.

Fixed oils, such as linseed, are rendered more pure by filtering them through powdered charcoal — The charcoal does not act on the oil but retains the impurities" — vide Gregory's Dictionary of Arts & Sciences — I made this experiment myself & put the charcoal in a flannel bag, which Mr Edwin said was a practice with copperplate printers who purify their oil in this way, but, although the oil seemed more limpid on their, yet the charcoal perhaps from being too fine or the texture of the flannel too coarse, dis=colored the oil & it never, during the few weeks I let it rest, was restored to its natural color — Much mucilaginous or fatty matter remained in the charcoal, after the filtration — and I have no doubt if properly tried, the experiment may be valuable to an artist in refining his oil for his most particular colors. I will make an other trial of it.

Mr Bishop informed me, March 20th 1835, that if Heat be applied to oil it will assuredly be injured & it <u>will turn yellow</u> — The <u>cold process</u>, he says, of One part oil to one part Sp. Turpentine with litharage added, about a tea Spoon full to a pile of oil, Shaken together several times daily for 3 or 4 days, & when Settled is fitter for use than any other he knows — He says the Cork may be left out of the phial & the Turpentine will evaporate + (See Gumption &c page 16.) Shaw says that "Sugar of Lead in Gumption, bleaches & never turns black"; but where much of it was used for haste, I have seen the work very much cracked within 3 years from the date of execution.

Inman's vehicle used to be, Sugar of lead & drying oil for despatch, but his head of Dr. Godman in the Phil. Museum Dec. 30th 1834 was much cracked, It was said to be painted at one sitting. David Edwin's receipt for clearing oil is as follows — Take of Sulphuric Acid, a certain portion, which he forgot, (vide Cox's Emporium of Arts) & put it into raw oil & churn it until black flakes appear, then put water into it immediately & churn all together then settle it, & draw off the oil from the top — add more water to the oil & churn again to wash away impurities — then let it settle & draw off oil again & clarify it with pipe clay or chalk by shaking, and then allow the whole to settle, the pipe clay carries mucilage & impurities with it to the bottom. Lime Water, Shaw & Edwin, Say, Kills grease in oil, but all oil should be washed after any alkali or acid has been used.

Mr Heyl, coloniman, had a custom of purifying linseed oil by drop=ping into it, the shavings or splinters of red cedar wood, & some I have used prepared in this way, was excellent & very limpid.

FIGURE 10

"Of Oils & Vehicles," from *Commonplace Book of John Neagle* [1839].
Philadelphia, The Historical Society of Pennsylvania, Am. 108.

CHAPTER 7
THE "EXPERIMENTALISTS"

BY THE 1820S, INCREASING NUMBERS of experiments with painting materials were being carried out by American painters on American soil. This trend is documented especially well in lengthy manuscripts written by Thomas Sully, John Neagle, and Rembrandt Peale. (The notebooks and experiments of William Sidney Mount, a somewhat younger artist, are different in character and will be discussed separately in chapter 13.)

In a note under the heading "Experiments," Peale explained his motivations: "Since there is no Prescription, furnished with the Accuracy of a Physician, every Painter must in some degree be an Experimentalist, in testing the various processes of other Painters, & comparing his own efforts with each other."[1]

This "golden age" of American experimentation, which reached its high point in the second quarter of the nineteenth century, was the result of a unique combination of circumstances. On the one hand, there were more painters working in America than ever before and more ideas about techniques that artists could discuss and compare. On the other hand, there were still relatively few merchants who sold ready-made artists' supplies. Artists needed to take the initiative to obtain the best oils and varnishes, and they mixed up many of their materials themselves from raw ingredients.

There is a somewhat different feeling in the accounts of experiments in this period as opposed to previous decades. Artists were less likely to make unsubstantiated guesses about the methods used by Titian or Rubens and tended to be more methodical or even scientific in their search for new and improved materials. As William Dunlap described Sully, "He was incessantly making experiments, but not losing his time in search of nostrums and secrets."[2] This more objective kind of experimentation fits in with the growth of scientific inquiry in America during the nineteenth century. In fact, two pioneer American scientists encouraged our "experimentalist" painters—Dr. Benjamin Rush was the initiator of Sully's first journal, which contained notes about technique, and James Woodhouse, professor of chemistry at the University of Pennsylvania, encouraged Peale in the early part of his career.[3]

Another difference in feeling in the accounts of American artists' experiments at this period is less easy to define. Americans continued to hold European art in high esteem, but at least some American painters had enough confidence in their own opinions about painting techniques that they began to believe they might be able to improve upon what they had learned from Europe. It is tempting to connect this with other currents of thought at this time, such as Daniel Webster's famous 1825 exhortation: "Let our age be the age of improvement,"[4] or Ralph Waldo Emerson's Phi Beta Kappa lecture of 1837, which has been called an intellectual declaration of independence from Europe. No American artist said this as explicitly as Emerson did, but pride in America and Americanness runs deep in another important document of this period—Dunlap's *History of the Rise and Progress of the Arts of Design in the United States*, which was published in 1834. Dunlap predicted that the arts in America would eventually equal or surpass not only modern European art but would be "upon an equality at least with those of the best days of Greece and Italy."[5] Dunlap was a painter himself, with a strong interest in practical technique. His book put into print—for the first time—specifically American ideas about technique as reported by several artists, including Sully and Neagle, thereby making this information available to a wide audience.

Sully, Neagle, and Peale knew each other well. There may have been an element of competition in their note taking and experimenting, but they shared ideas and new materials freely. When Sully obtained a keg of the pigment Indian red from China in 1828, he wrote in his journal shortly afterwards: "Gave Neagle and Mr. Peale some Indian Red."[6] Sully and Peale exchanged recipes all through the first half of the nineteenth century, both early and late in their careers. Neagle was related to Sully by marriage (he married Sully's niece, who was also his stepdaughter), and his notebooks show that he had access to Sully's notebooks and cited them frequently. Neagle also mentioned Peale's opinions in his notebooks a number of times, although their relationship was less consistently friendly; Peale nominated Neagle for membership in the Pennsylvania Academy in 1824,[7] but in the 1830s Neagle quarreled with Peale about Peale's attempt to make a profit from technical "secrets" (see chapter 10).

Both Sully and Peale intended to publish books summarizing their lifelong study of artists' materials. A few observations on technique from Sully's journals were printed in Dunlap's book in 1834,[8] but in 1851 Sully compiled and organized his notes into a long manuscript called "Memoirs of the Professional Life of Thomas Sully." Peale completed his "Notes of the Painting Room" at about the same time and launched a campaign to publish it in June 1852. But neither book was ever published in its intended form (although a very slim volume of extracts from Sully's manuscripts was eventually published by Sully's grandson in 1873, the year after the artist's death). Potential publishers must have noticed that both manuscripts were long and fairly undigested, perhaps the result of the artists competing to be the first to finish. But in the bigger picture, Sully and Peale were both too late. The world of American art had become very different from the period earlier in the century when Sully and Peale were at the peak of their fame. By the 1850s, ready-made art materials were becoming more easily available. Peale acknowledged this when, in "Notes of the Painting Room," he quoted George Field on the situation in Britain: "Pigments, & fine ones too, so abound that it requires nearly as much *experience* for a judicious selection of them, as was formerly required for their acquisition or production.…the necessity for, & the practice of, the Artist's preparing his own materials have ceased."[9]

Sully and Peale were too late in another sense: a number of books on painting technique written by European authors in the 1820s, 1830s, and 1840s had become available to American painters. Perhaps most importantly, in 1845 the American Laughton Osborn published *Handbook of Young Artists and Amateurs in Oilpainting*, a partial translation of a book by the Swiss artist Pierre-Louis Bouvier, with considerable additions by Osborn himself. Osborn's book contains a great deal of very useful and practical information; artists must have noticed this, for the book was reprinted without alteration in many editions until at least 1883. In the years before his death, Peale must have realized that "Notes of the Painting Room" would never be published, and he wrote instead a number of reminiscences and other short contributions for the journal *The Crayon*. To his credit, he included brief reviews of the books—by Bouvier, Osborn, J.-F.-L. Mérimée, George Field, and Charles Eastlake—that had beaten him to the punch and made his proposed magnum opus obsolete before it could appear in print.

It is tempting to connect the experimentation of Sully, Neagle, and Peale with a kind of inventiveness that many Americans have come to see as particularly American. However, it should be said that during the first half of the nineteenth century many experiments were being carried out by British and French painters as well—Americans were clearly aware of these developments and, to a degree, were following the lead of the British and French in technique just as they were in terms of style. Sully was on friendly terms with the British painter William Beechey, who tried out many experiments with unusual materials that are documented in Sully's notebooks as well as in British sources.[10] The British author and colorman George Field also carried out experiments in preparation for his 1835 book *Chromatography*.[11] Experimentation was going on in France as well during the early nineteenth century. Paillot de Montabert's massive ten-volume 1829 treatise on painting technique had little influence in America because it was never translated into English. But J.-F.-L. Mérimée's theories became easily available to English speakers when his much shorter book was published in translation in 1839, and all of our American experimenters took note of his ideas, just as they had taken note of the theories of Field.

What we can say is that artists' experiments with painting materials during the period 1820–50 are particularly well documented in America. These manuscripts are sometimes the only surviving records of artists trying out the multitudinous materials that European and American authorities were recommending at this time. And it is clear that—in some cases—the curiosity of the American experimenters led them to use new pigments and other materials before they were widely used in Europe.

Some of the experimenters' accounts have a peculiarly American accent, especially in the pride that Americans took in practical, rolling-up-the-sleeves kinds of know-how. It is difficult to imagine a British or French painter saying—as Rembrandt Peale did—that knowledge of materials and techniques was as important to a painter "as good materials & tools & modes of using them are to the mechanic in the production of watches or Steam Engines."[12] By the 1830s, Americans' pride in their inventiveness and ability to improve things was showing itself in many fields other than the fine arts. Americans were proud of the democratic system of government that had attracted the attention of the French visitor Alexis de Tocqueville and proud of American technological innovations in fields as diverse as steamboats and telegraphy. In fact, Samuel F.B. Morse's pupil Daniel Huntington argued that his master's inventions in telegraphy were connected to his activities as a painter: "He had studied hard under Allston and West, and was an accomplished composer; but his fondness for experiment in natural philosophy manifested itself also in the domain of art. He was always trying different textures, vehicles, and methods.…When I knew him, he had his wires strung around his studio, and his chemical apparatus side by side with his easel."[13]

Morse took a special interest in the most "scientific" branch of picture making, photography, and was a pioneer in bringing this new art to America.[14] Huntington elaborated further on the connection between science and art: "Every studio is more or less a laboratory. The painter is a chemist, delving into the secrets of pigments, varnishes, mixtures of tints, and mysterious preparations of grounds and overlaying of colors; occult arts, by which the inward light is made to gleam from the canvas and the warm flesh to glow and palpitate."[15]

Peale also made explicit his understanding of the connection between invention and the fine arts when he pointed out that Morse and Robert Fulton had both been painters;[16] Peale was also proud of the role that Americans had played in perfecting the collapsible paint tube (see chapter 11).[17]

Another American who drew connections between innovative technology and the fine arts at this time was the scientist and inventor James Jay Mapes, who lectured at the National Academy of Design in the 1820s and 1830s on the chemistry of colors and who was an amateur painter himself.[18] Neagle sought his advice about painting materials on several occasions. Mapes was one of those who worked along with Morse to perfect the photographic process when it was first brought to America in 1839. He was also the founder and editor, in 1840, of a short-lived periodical called *The American Repertory of Arts, Sciences, and Manufactures*, which featured articles on such topics as the manufacture of white

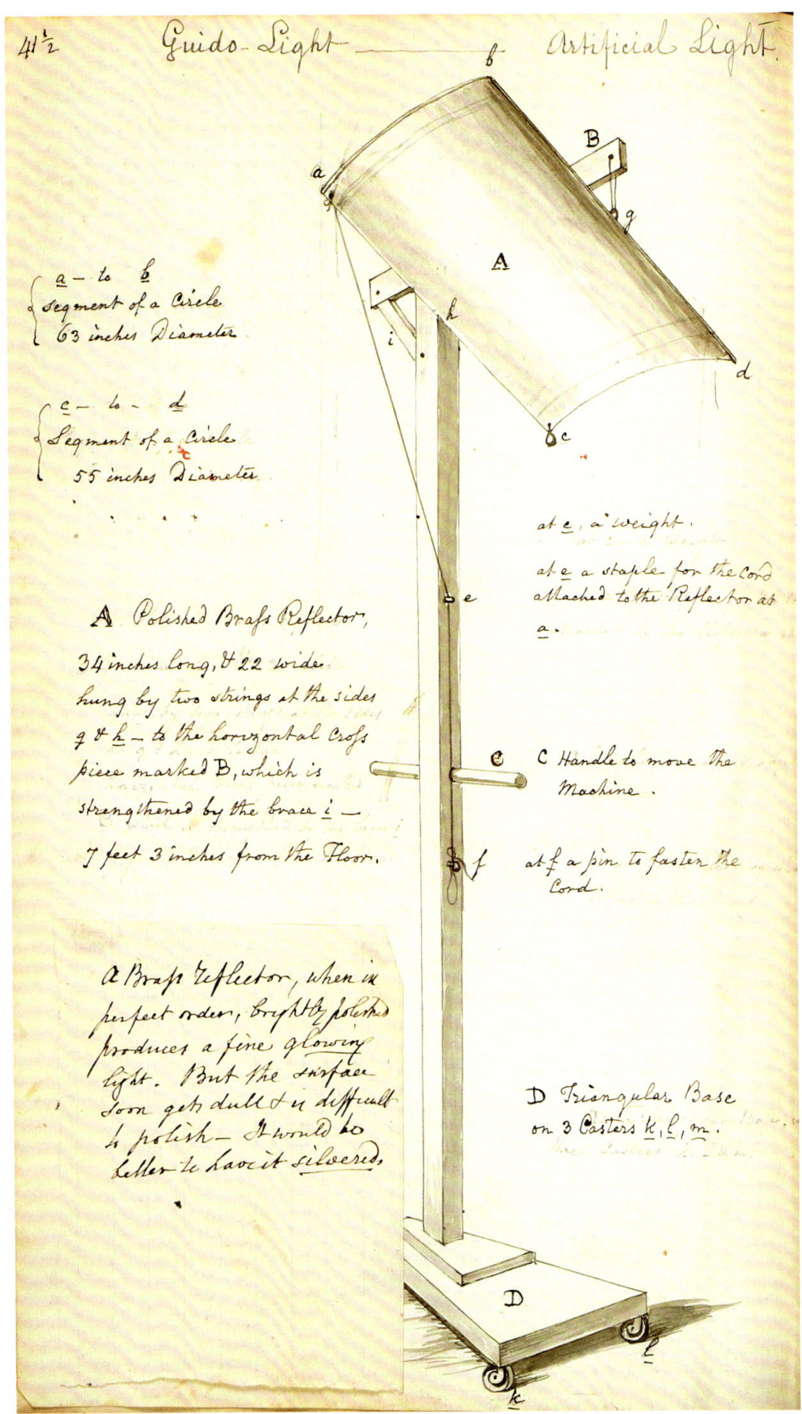

FIGURE 11

"Guido-Light," from *Notes of the Painting Room* by Rembrandt Peale, ca. 1852.
New York, National Academy of Design.

lead, theories of color, reviews of art exhibitions and books on art, as well as many other subjects that had nothing to do with the fine arts. Mapes's introduction to the first volume of *The American Repertory* was a trumpet call for innovation and cross-fertilization between the arts and sciences:

> The time, we hope, has forever gone by, when those who were actively engaged as artisans, mechanics, manufacturers, or artists, were contented to obey mere directions, or to follow beaten tracks, in the performance of their avocations, without any curiosity as to the laws by which their several operations were guided, or the principles upon which they were founded. The march of science is now giving fresh improvements to art, and the progress in art affords continual stimulus to science.[19]

Mapes claimed that advances of the last thirty years proved that "in all the useful arts, and the sciences connected therewith, we [Americans] may proudly consider ourselves as not inferior to any people whatsoever."[20]

Another aspect of the connection between art and technology is embodied by Rufus Porter, now best known as a painter of landscape murals and small portraits in a simple, almost primitive style. Porter took out countless patents[21] and was a writer, editor, and publisher of books and periodicals. In 1841 he began the journal *New York Mechanic*, later renamed *American Mechanic*, and in 1845 founded *Scientific American*. In 1845–46 he wrote a series of articles in *Scientific American* about painting techniques, encompassing everything from house painting to painting portraits. The articles are poignant in the equivalency that Porter gave to the various branches of the art, describing on the one hand how to paint a door without leaving brush marks, while on the other hand instructing a budding portrait painter to begin painting his subject at the top of the head. Porter's confidence that he could reduce each branch of painting to a set of brief, simple rules strikes a naïve but democratic—and perhaps peculiarly American—note. These kinds of attitudes must have helped contribute to the flowering of American "folk" portraiture in the period from the 1820s to the 1840s.[22]

As the nineteenth century advanced, a germ of an idea began to grow that would help guarantee that the "golden age" of American experimentation would be in decline by mid-century. This was the belief that experimentation with artists' materials could be useless or even dangerous. Joshua Reynolds's experimental methods had attracted negative comments even before the artist's death in 1792,[23] but it was only beginning in the 1840s that the recipes contained in his ledgers were published and the lessons to be learned from his experiments discussed in print in any detail. Eastlake, in 1847, explained in scientific terms why Reynolds's paintings had lasted so poorly,[24] while William Beechey and Benjamin Robert Haydon contributed lurid commentary on Reynolds's ledger entries, such as: "'This manner is the MOST extraordinary.' It is insanity. He had at his elbow a mocking fiend!"[25]

Some Americans had already begun to take similar positions; in 1834, Dunlap reported the following observation by Robert Weir about his teacher, a British immigrant painter named Cook: "He consumed his precious hours in making fruitless experiments in search of some other and better vehicle than oil to paint with….I learned one salutary lesson from him which has been repeatedly confirmed by others—that time is too valuable to be consumed in making experiments."[26] Late in life Rembrandt Peale himself acknowledged that time spent experimenting was time taken away from improving oneself as an artist.[27]

Another argument against experimentation began to be made with greater frequency as the nineteenth century neared its midpoint: an artist who sought "secrets" too enthusiastically might be suspected of lacking true talent. Laughton Osborn's 1845 book included Haydon's remark: "It is curious to see how imbecile and weak men dwell upon the importance of their vehicles, how every fault is palliated by the want of some spirit or some oil."[28] In a similar vein, Peale cited the German author Libertat Hundertpfund's opinion that the old masters did not know about megilp or gumtion, "to which the mechanical mixers of the present day resort, in order to effect what *genius* denies them."[29] George Field, the British author whose work was well known to Sully, Peale, and other American experimenters, echoed yet another version of this theme when he quoted a bit of doggerel by Martin Archer Shee that put experimenters in a truly bad light:

> How many fondly waste the studious hour
> To seek in process what they want in power;
> Till, all in gums engross'd, macgilps, and oils,
> The painter sinks amid the chemist's toils.[30]

British and American artists had come a long way from the starry-eyed experimentation of the eighteenth and early nineteenth centuries, when many painters believed that a single, secret ingredient or process would make it easy for modern artists to paint like the old masters.

NOTES

1   R. Peale Miscellaneous, undated sheet, beginning with "Experiments."

2   Dunlap 1834, 2:138–39.

3   Sully "Hints," AAA, microfilm roll N18, frame 76 (April 23, 1809). On Peale and Woodhouse, see Oedel 1992, 8.

4   Webster 1853, 64.

5   Dunlap 1834, 2:258.

6   Sully Journal, AAA, microfilm roll N18, frame 319 (November 2, November 21, and December 7, 1828).

7   Torchia 1989, 28.

8   Dunlap 1834, 2:119–20, 124–26n, 137–41.

9   R. Peale "Notes," 5–6 (quoting Field 1841, x, xi).

10   For example, Farington 1978–84, diary entries of March 4 and March 7, 1798; and Haydon 1853.

11   Harley 1982, 27–28, 216n24; Harley 1975; Harley 1979.

12   R. Peale "Notes," 6.

13   Sheldon 1881, 105.

14   Prime 1875, 400–408; Morse 1914, 2:141–46.

15   Prime 1875, 713.

16   R. Peale 1856, 101–2.

17   Ibid., 102.

18   Fink and Taylor 1975, 109, 111.

19   *American Repertory of Arts, Sciences, and Manufactures* 1 (1840): 1.

20   Ibid., 1:2.

21   Lipman 1980, 27–48.

22   In fact the itinerant "folk" portrait painter Joseph Whiting Stock owned bound issues of *Scientific American* at the time of his death in 1855 (Tomlinson 1976, 56).

23   Talley 1986.

24   Eastlake 1847, 1:538–46.

25   Haydon 1853, 3:393.

26   Dunlap 1834, 2:385–86n.

27   R. Peale "Notes," 6–7. Peale used the argument to underline the importance of his own work as an experimenter—because he had invested so many hours, other artists need not do so.

28   Osborn 1845, 82.

29   R. Peale "Notes," 119–20.

30   Field 1841, 341.

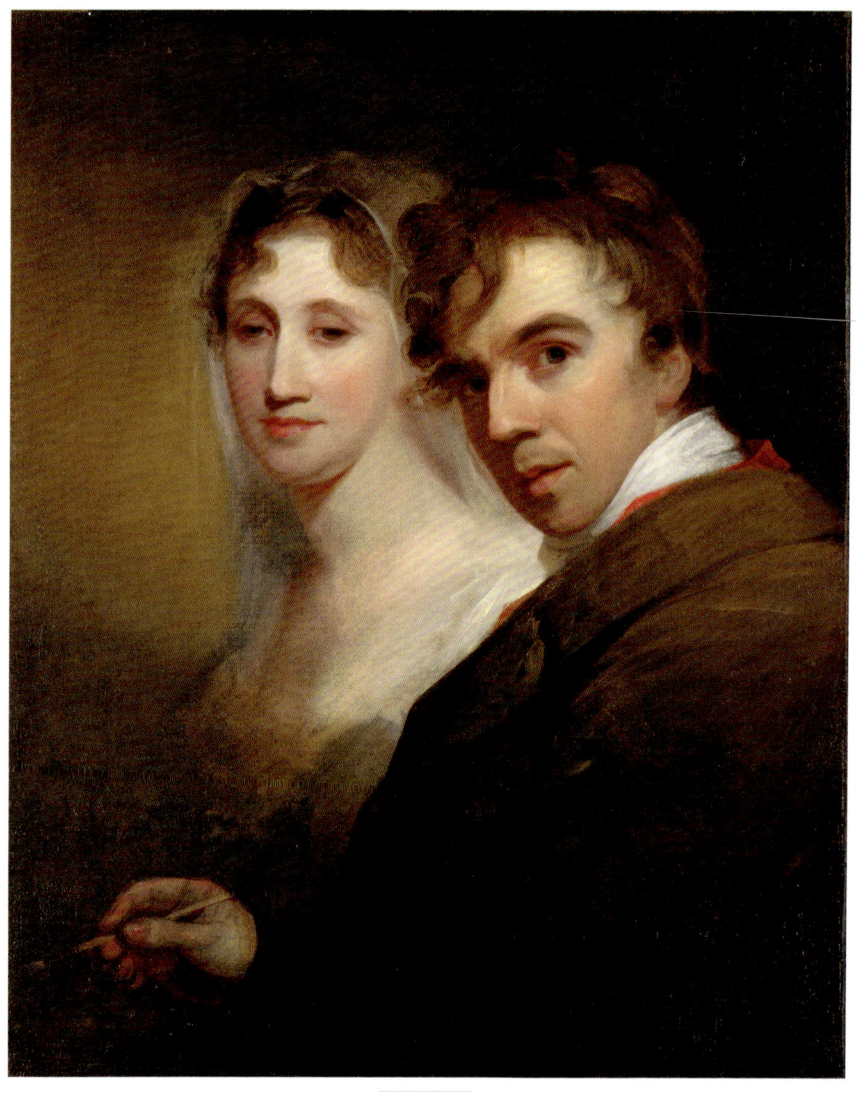

FIGURE 12

Thomas Sully (American, 1783–1872), *Self-Portrait of the Artist Painting His Wife (Sarah Annis Sully)*,
ca. 1810. Oil on canvas, 67.9 × 55.6 cm (26¾ × 21⅞ in.). New Haven, Conn.,
Yale University Art Gallery, Mabel Brady Garvan Collection, 1937.15.

CHAPTER 8

THOMAS SULLY: COMPILER AND EXPERIMENTER

THOMAS SULLY TRIED OUT and recorded in his notebooks a greater variety of different techniques and materials than any other painter we have studied. It is a legitimate question to ask whether his methods were actually more varied than those of other artists or whether his copious note taking made his practice simply better documented (most likely there are elements of both). By studying, in some depth, several of the topics that interested Sully, we can get an inkling of the many directions that his experiments took.

SULLY AND "HOMEMADE" GROUNDS

Around the time that Sully first went to England, there were many competing theories about what constituted the ideal first layer to paint upon: the ground. James Northcote, the pupil of and biographer of Joshua Reynolds, must have been thinking of the special grounds promoted by the Provises and Sebastian Grandi (see chapter 2) when he wrote a parody in 1813 about an artist who invented a ground "by which means every painter should be enabled to paint exactly like Titian." In Northcote's fictional account, the ground was initially a great success, but "in a short space of time some of the pictures which had been painted on my grounds became exceedingly cracked, and others fell piecemeal from the canvas; so that I have been informed, that the house-maids used to bestow curses on the painter for dirtying the rooms with his *dropping* pictures."[1]

Prepared (or preprimed) canvases, with the ground layer already applied, had been imported into America from England since the eighteenth century, although as long as prepared canvases had existed, artists had complained about them. Dossie's *Handmaid to the Arts* disparaged the quality of prepared fabrics available in London in the 1750s and 1760s.[2] In 1808 Charles Willson Peale told Robert Fulton that the prepared canvases available in Philadelphia were liable to crack, so he prepared his own.[3] Later, John Neagle wrote: "I have often suspected that the ordinary English prepared canvas, altho' well adapted to the climate there, is too flimsy for the sudden changes of an American climate."[4] Thus there were incentives for Americans to try to figure out for themselves how to make a ground that would last.

During his first visit to England in 1809–10, Sully noted that "the English painters generally use absorbent grounds,"[5] and this set Sully off on a course of ad hoc experimentation, with many twists and turns, over the next several decades. Shortly after returning to America, he made his own absorbent ground "which I prepared myself with weak size[,] whiting and a small portion of treacle."[6] Other Americans were experimenting with absorbent grounds during this decade. In 1817 John Trumbull tried to get the American canvas maker Isaac McCauley to imitate an English absorbent ground, telling him to carry out experiments to avoid using too much glue: "No Oil is used in the preparation of the ground, which I presume is simply weak glue or size. By making some experiments before you prepare the large Cloth, you will find that if your size is too strong, the ground will crack which would be a miserable defect."[7]

Neagle painted some portraits on English absorbent grounds in the mid-1820s,[8] but around this time he and Sully were both experimenting with "home-made" grounds containing mixtures of water-soluble materials (such as starch paste or glue) plus oily or resinous ingredients. For instance, in 1826 Sully tried a variation of "Mr. Delonpery's" ground, made with paste plus white lead in oil with litharge, but his normal ground at this time consisted of paste plus Venice turpentine, which when dry he coated with one or two layers of oil paint (a recipe he said he originally obtained from Rembrandt Peale).[9] On one occasion in the 1820s Neagle prepared a canvas "mostly with watercolors and size, with turpentine paint mixed into the composition. It produces a good surface and is *absorbent*."[10] A painting at the National Gallery of Art has a lengthy inscription on its reverse documenting the difficulties Neagle encountered while preparing a similar kind of ground containing starch, whiting, oil, and turpentine.[11] In 1828 Neagle experimented with fish glue plus whiting, saying, "It appears to answer very well, except where the composition had been laid on too thick, where I am fearful it will crack and scale off."[12] At another time Sully described how Neagle prepared a textured surface by covering a canvas with paint and then, while the paint was still wet, would "sift over some fine sand procured at the marble cutters."[13]

One of the more unusual ideas among artists who applied their own grounds at this time was to add soap, apparently to give flexibility and thereby avoid cracking. Charles Willson Peale described "Andersons New Method of preparing Canvas," which consisted of dissolving soap in water, and mixing this with "common paint."[14] In the late 1820s Sully, Neagle, and Charles Bird King all experimented with adding soap to their grounds. Sully noted King's claim that canvases prepared this way two years previously still remained pliant and in good condition, and Neagle commented: "I have known soap and oker to be used and it was thought to be excellent."[15] (As late as 1857, when Sully heard that soap was added to oil paint to keep firemen's capes flexible, he made a note to try this himself again.[16])

Sully and Neagle experimented with a variety of different grounds in the 1830s and 1840s. Neagle found, as Sully had earlier, that the combination of wheat starch and Venice turpentine (sometimes with a little oil) had the qualities that he was seeking and none of the disadvantages. Neagle noted, for instance, that a ground prepared with glue as the sole binder was too brittle, and he disapproved of a recipe for an absorbent ground that he had tried earlier (containing glue plus oil) because it was "liable to chip off."[17]

On his second trip to England in 1838, Sully found he liked the absorbent grounds (also called "half prepared") made by the London colorman Thomas Brown: "I intend to bring some home to Phil_a_ with me, and if I continue to like it will adopt it entirely."[18] Two years later (perhaps when he had run out of Brown's canvas), he had an unfortunate experience that proved the validity of Trumbull's warning about getting the proportion of glue exactly right: "I prepared some absorbent ground canvas by first giving the Russia sheeting a coat of size and then a coat of whiting from Earl's workshop, such as is used to prepare frames for gilding. This preparation cracked all over after I had painted a beginning of a picture on it."[19]

Shortly after this, in 1841, Sully wrote down Brown's address and a list of his prices for various kinds of prepared canvases, as if he thought that ordering canvases from London might be a better idea than making his own;[20] the same year he in fact "sent an order for absorbent canvas to Brown of London…amount about $100."[21] A painting from 1845 was done on a canvas labeled by Brown and stamped "Absorbent,"[22] and other Brown stamps appear on paintings by Sully from 1843 and 1853.[23]

But at the same time Sully was also beginning to take a very different, innovative approach to making his own grounds. Beginning in the early 1840s, he mixed pigments with skim milk to make a ground, in the spirit of the experiments that had been carried out with milk as a binder earlier in the century by Allston and Morse (see chapter 5). By the late 1840s Sully claimed that this kind of ground "does not crack or show any defect," and he appears to have used skim milk grounds with some regularity for at least a decade and a half.[24] In 1867 he had still "not found any fault" with a painting done in this manner twenty-six years earlier.[25]

In a survey of nineteenth-century British treatises, no recipes quite like Sully's skim milk ground were reported, which may indicate Sully's skim milk ground really was—as he claimed—his own discovery.[26]

SULLY AND A MULTIPLICITY OF MEDIA

Many of Sully's observations and experiments have to do with adding various kinds of media to oil paint to give it better handling qualities or make it last longer. Sully did not carry out experiments as methodically as a scientist, but he took notes on many of the materials he used, often adding comments if he noticed problems (like cracking or darkening) at a later time. He occasionally used an ingredient that he wanted to test "to excess in order to prove what may be the result."[27] This can be a simple but effective experimental technique that would make any flaws in the procedure more apparent and might make them appear sooner.

Even before he first went to England, Sully wrote down a recipe for a wax megilp that probably came from Rembrandt Peale.[28] In London, Sully saw British painters mix wax with mastic varnish, then add it to their paint,[29] and in 1812 he recorded a portrait that he "painted in wax,"[30] perhaps in emulation of Peale's encaustic technique of this time (see chapter 3). The Peales most likely stimulated a renewed interest in wax in the early 1820s as well (this was shortly after Charles Willson Peale had become interested in adding wax to oil paint, and Sully's first notebook entry at this time dealing with waxy painting media was adjacent to two other pieces of information from the Peales). As Sully noted in 1822, when he made a copy after Leslie's copy of Hogarth's *The Gate of Calais*, he painted the figures "with colour tempered with wax…To a dessert spoonful of mastic, add a piece of bleached wax melted by fire; when this mixture is cold, it will form a thin jelly which may be either used as a magyllip by tempering it with oil, or by adding to the colours ground in oil."[31]

The next year Sully continued to experiment with a different kind of wax medium used as a retouching varnish, and he tried to improve it when he found that it dried too quickly: "Used a mixture of wax and spirits of turpentine to spread over the surface of a picture to prepare it for retouching—but I discovered that it dried too fast. I afterwards tried a jelly composed of wax and linseed oil, which has answered the purpose very well—I am only anxious that it may not turn yellow—also used some in the colour used in the background of the same picture. (Mr. Vaughan—the one intended for myself)."[32]

In this case Sully experimented on a painting "intended for myself," and he could therefore observe any problems that might develop. Sully did not in fact write down any further information on the results of these experiments with wax, although much later (about 1858) he questioned the wisdom of adding wax to oil paint.[33] Later still, Sully's grandson had the last word on one of his grandfather's wax experiments from the 1820s: "In fifty years (1872) the colors flake off, defying all efforts at restoration or cleaning."[34]

An artist who watched Sully paint in 1818 reported that his normal practice was to add conventional megilp—made from mastic and drying oil—to his paint rather than anything more exotic.[35] But by the 1820s, recipes for other media appeared in his notebooks, some of them quite unusual. For instance, in 1822 Samuel Waldo suggested a method for making white paint "short" (stiff) by grinding pigment in water to a pastelike consistency, then adding a few drops of mastic varnish and as much oil as would allow it to be brushed.[36] In 1826 Sully wrote down the following information from Charles Leslie's sister Anne: "Miss A. Leslie tells me that her brother makes free use of magyllip even in beginning his pictures—in toning, finishing, etc."[37] Sully was clearly interested in how *much* megilp an artist should use—something that is difficult to quantify because a painter would add the megilp as needed while painting, without measuring. But it was an important question in Sully's time, as it is now, because painters have long known that medium added copiously can discolor or crack, while a smaller quantity might not.

As early as his first trip to England in 1809–10, Sully wrote down recipes for two different versions of gumtion (made with mastic, sugar of lead, and oil),[38] although there is no sign that he tried them. In 1825 Sully recorded a recipe for preparing gumtion (which he called "painters' cream") obtained from Samuel Scarlet, a painter, restorer, and vendor of paint who had been trained in England before emigrating to Philadelphia.[39] But in 1830 Sully had a bad experience when he tried to add sugar of lead directly to his paint, which might have made him wonder about the stability of gumtion: "I put sugar of lead as a dryer to the black drapery of Guy Bryan and when I washed the picture previous to finishing it—the sugar of lead came up in a white powder."[40]

In the 1830s Sully continued to be alert to the question of how much megilp could be safely added to paint and recorded that Robert Weir told him "[David] Willkie uses very freely magyllip—says it gives a 'Rembrandt richness.'"[41] Sully said of William Page: "He uses plenty of megyllip and abundance of paint—the effect is juicy and rich."[42] It was also during the 1830s that Sully tried weird experiments with beer and milk as paint media after a visit to Samuel F. B. Morse (see chapter 5).[43]

The 1840s saw Sully change his opinions about gumtion. In 1842 he cited an elaborate recipe for gumtion published in the *Art-Union*, which proposed different proportions of ingredients for different purposes. Sully dutifully tried the various mixtures but had strong opinions about how the mixtures worked in terms of the time they took to dry, and he noted with dismay that the recipe he thought would last the best was unfortunately the most difficult to use. Sully's account ended on a skeptical note, in which he asked himself: "Would not the use of turpentine and drying oil in the chief conduct of a picture do as well?"[44] A little later that year—in an entry that sounds like it was based on personal experience—Sully wrote that gumtion dried firmer than ordinary megilp, but it turned a deeper yellow.[45]

Further negative opinions about gumtion appeared in 1843 and 1844, when Sully noted that gumtion "clouds over" or gave "a dull brown cast," and he wrote that he had changed back from gumtion to using ordinary megilp.[46] He then tried a medium containing copal, but soon wrote that he had "again returned to the common megilp with confidence and satisfaction," only to almost immediately experiment with Canada balsam, copal megilp (again), and rosin (which "works ungratefully").[47] Still later, in 1849, Sully recorded that he had received a recipe from a German painter for "Painter's Butter"—"This is English Gumption, but I think purer."[48] This was Sully's last word on gumtion, and there is no indication that he ever tried the recipe from Germany.

Sully was much less preoccupied than artists of a previous generation with discovering the "secret" medium of the old masters—his main goal was simply to find materials that had good handling and aging properties. However, an episode during Sully's second visit to England proved that the search for the secrets of the early Venetian painters was not yet over. In 1838 Sully was excited to learn the following: "Brett told me that a portion of starch ground up in my paint would produce a permanent loading of an agreeable and Venetian-like quality—indeed it was supposed to be practiced by those excellent colorists."[49]

John Watkins Brett was a British collector who had previously sent a widely admired group of paintings on tour to America. Sully must have put great confidence in Brett's opinion,[50] for he wrote from London to his daughter in Philadelphia: "Jane I want you to try the following mixture which it is said is a discovery of the Venitian mode of preparing their colours—Grind up with your colour in oil—a portion of *starch*—I cannot say what proportions but try several, both with white lead and I. [ivory] black—lay the colour very thick and put it away until I return and we will then have had time to prove its value."[51]

In sending this starch recipe back to America, Sully was a little ahead of the curve—adding starch to paint would become a topic of discussion in Britain a year or two later, and Sully's is apparently the earliest written description of the process.[52] As with many of the recipes that Sully recorded, we do not know whether he followed up on it.

Later in his life, Sully seems to have become more cautious about adding megilp or other additives to oil paint. In his 1851 "Memoirs" he wrote: "The search after macguilps or vehicles to improve the quality of the colours, has misled many excellent artists. They have persuaded themselves that the ancient painters who excelled in colouring, and especially the Venetian painters, used a menstruum which greatly improved the texture of their work. Sir Joshua Reynolds was constantly engaged in the vain endeavor to discover this delusion."[53]

"Vain" and "delusion" are strong words from an artist who had made so many experiments with added media himself. Sully's language fits in with the changed tone of discussions about artists' materials around the middle of the nineteenth century; many artists altered their opinions at this time (see chapter 7). However, when Sully described his "present practise of painting" in 1851, he made it clear that he still kept megilp on his palette "in case I need to make any of my tints more liquid," and he even said, "I use macguilp freely."[54] But by the time he gave another account of his method twenty years later, in 1871, he had eliminated megilp, saying that he added to his paint "no other liquid than a mixture of drying-oil and spirits of turpentine in equal quantities."[55] Instead of using this medium "freely," Sully now said that the medium "should be used sparingly."[56] He may have been influenced by the generally bad press that megilp received around the middle of the century (see chapter 11), but it is also possible that the results of his own experiments with paint additives had led him to the same conclusion.

PIGMENTS

Sully wrote a great deal about the various pigments and pigment mixtures used by himself and others. In fact it was a pigment that was the subject of Sully's longest-running experiment, when he made notes in 1859 on a test begun thirty-two years earlier: "I placed some Antwerp blue in the sun light in January 1827, where it has been since; on inspection I found it changed to an ashen color."[57] In 1859 Sully was compiling information for an addendum to his "Memoirs" manuscript, which included a list of pigments used by Gilbert Stuart. Antwerp blue was the principal blue used by Stuart, and Sully's experiment was one reason that he could say with confidence about Stuart's palette: "I do not quite approve it, as many of the colours are fugitive."[58]

Although Antwerp blue was favored by Stuart, Sully never mentioned painting with it himself. He seems to have used cobalt blue as his only blue until 1838,[59] but in 1839 he began substituting ultramarine and eventually used it exclusively for the rest of his life.[60] Sully's ultramarine was presumably the artificial variety that was invented in 1828, making this formerly exorbitantly expensive pigment available to all. It is now known that artificial ultramarine has the same chemical composition and stability as the natural product, but some nineteenth-century authorities were slow to recognize this—even the highly respected George Field had reservations about artificial ultramarine in the 1835 and 1841 editions of his book *Chromatography*.[61] But the 1839 English translation of Mérimée correctly noted that artificial ultramarine was identical to the natural mineral in its appearance and stability,[62] and it is possible that the information contained in this book influenced artists' acceptance of artificial ultramarine. By 1845 the American Laughton Osborn seconded Mérimée's opinion, adding that artificial ultramarine made cobalt blue unnecessary.[63] Sully apparently agreed.

As a portrait painter, Sully was extremely interested in the family of brown, dull red, and dull yellow pigments that were used to paint the shadows of the human face. The origin and nomenclature of these pigments are extremely confusing to modern readers and were probably confusing to eighteenth- and nineteenth-century artists as well. Many of them are naturally occurring earths, but earth pigments were sometimes altered by heating, and some colors that look like earth pigments were actually manufactured outright. For example, as early as 1764 Robert Dossie told English readers that the pigment called "Spanish brown" did not come from Spain but was actually dug in England.[64] Similarly, "Indian red" originally meant a naturally occurring earth from India, but even in Dossie's time this pigment was rarely encountered, and the term Indian red was used for a manufactured iron oxide.[65] When Sully ordered Indian red from China in 1828, it is impossible to know what he actually received, but he may have believed that by sending to Asia, he was more likely to get the genuine article.

One of the vexing questions for portrait painters using earth pigments was how to mix them with white to give shadow tones the correct degree of warmth. In the 1820s and 1830s, Sully was greatly concerned with the question of the "tone" of his pictures (see chapter 6). Seeking warmth in flesh tones, in 1827 he followed up on a suggestion by Benjamin West and tried the aforementioned (misnamed) "Spanish brown" in flesh mixtures, finding it "the best colour for such purpose that I have tried.…If the raw umber teints are occasionally found to be too green and cold, the Spanish brown warms them into a fine general tone."[66] But after this entry, Sully never mentioned Spanish brown again as an ingredient in his paint mixtures.[67]

In 1834 John Neagle documented a change in Sully's palette, again involving the troublesome pigment raw umber, which tends toward green in mixtures. Sully had made a copy of a painting by John Hoppner and told Neagle that burnt umber had helped him to attain Hoppner's colors. Neagle wrote: "Mr Sully has for many years, used *raw* instead of the *Burnt Umber* here marked. He thinks he will discard the raw umber in future."[68] Burnt umber would give flesh mixtures a much redder tone than raw umber, and Sully seems to have abandoned raw umber for some time—it does not appear in a detailed list of colors he used in 1851, for instance.[69] But by 1852 he was experimenting with mixtures for shadows that included raw umber as well as burnt umber, although he noted that the mixtures containing raw umber were "very green."[70] Raw umber reappeared on a palette that he recommended toward the end of his life (1871), with a note that if the shadows required a warmer color "in some places," burnt sienna could be added to the raw umber.[71]

Sully kept asphaltum on his palette all through his life, to be used in final glazes. Both Field and Osborn cautioned artists against using asphaltum too liberally,[72] but Sully may have felt that by using it only as a glaze in the final stages of painting, he would not be putting his paintings at risk. His desire for permanence clearly had its limits. When late in his life he wrote that he had reluctantly given up Van Dyke brown, it was not for reasons of permanence, but because it was a poor drier, although artists as far back as Gilbert Stuart's time had questioned the stability of Van Dyke brown.[73]

SULLY AND THE FINE POINTS OF VARNISHING

Sully's experiments with varnishes show what a perplexing variety of varnishing practices were possible in the nineteenth century, and he himself believed that deciding which varnish to use was "the plague of artists."[74] We often sense Sully's frustration with a process that has always been (and remains) difficult to do. He also had a difficult time balancing the desire of an artist that a painting look its best immediately after completion against its long-term preservation.

In 1825 Sully staked out a sensible, conservative position on the length of time that an artist should wait before it was safe to varnish a painting: "I have made up my mind on the evil practice of varnishing a picture which has been freshly painted—they infallibly crack—3, 6 or even 12 months is the best space of time to leave them untouched with varnish."[75] In 1844 he was shocked to learn that his friend Charles Bird King "varnishes his portraits with mastic the instant they are dry enough to bear it. I cannot approve of the practice."[76]

But Sully could not resist trying to get away with varnishing soon after a painting was finished. To this end, he tried an experiment suggested by Samuel Scarlet in 1846: "It is allowed to be improper to varnish a recently painted picture and yet without its aid many of the colors look dead. In one day, after finishing the sketch mentioned, I covered it with egg varnish, (The employment of which does not disturb the fresh paint) and in one or two hours afterwards I varnished over that with mastic varnish."[77] Sully also tried a much weirder variation of this experiment, using fish glue instead of egg varnish, but he found that the sticky fish glue made it "almost impossible to cover the oil painting with the size previous to varnishing."[78]

Sully sold his experimental egg-and-mastic-varnished painting five months after its completion, and therefore probably lost track of it, but he did not note any problems at the time of the sale.[79] In any case he was emboldened, seven months later, to varnish two paintings with mastic only a week after their completion "according to King's custom who has no fear of injury from the varnish."[80] As is frequently the case with Sully, he did not make any further notes on this experiment, although he often did comment if something went wrong, so it may be that on this occasion he got away with varnishing soon after completion without any bad results.

However, at around this time Sully also noted that no less an authority than Cennino Cennini advised artists to wait at least a year before varnishing.[81] Sully also seemed to have been on the lookout for an entirely different kind of varnish that would allow him to varnish sooner with safety. In late 1848 he applied samples of paint to a test panel and two days later "varnished it with a mixture of gum arabic and lump sugar, in equal parts, dissolved in water." But a little more than three months later, Sully wrote: "found it cracked."[82]

Another new material, dammar, came to Sully's notice in 1849—in fact, his mention of dammar during a visit to his nephew Robert Sully in April of that year is the earliest firmly datable example of an American artist using this material (see further discussion of dammar in chapter 11).[83] Sully seemed to have initially believed that dammar had a special quality that allowed it to be used on a fresh painting, and he said so when he compiled his ideas in the "Memoirs" manuscript in 1851.[84] However, around this time he had a bad experience when he applied dammar too soon and the varnish "disturbed the painting."[85]

This kind of problem may have led him to renew his experiments with a water-soluble initial layer that would not dissolve freshly applied paint. By this time he believed that egg varnish was "pernicious."[86] But, inspired by a passage he had read in Rembrandt Peale's manuscript "Notes of the Painting Room" in 1852, he tried another water-soluble material—gum tragacanth—applying it to a new painting and immediately following with a layer of dammar. He mentioned using gum tragacanth sporadically throughout the 1850s and into the 1860s, sometimes on its own, sometimes mixing oil into it, but most often following it with a layer of dammar or mastic.[87] Sully may have felt he needed to experiment because in the 1850s he was often "perplexed" with varnishes not drying well or making an uneven surface (something with which modern artists and conservators can sympathize).[88] His trials with gum tragacanth led Sully to ruminate on the experimental process: "I know of no future injury to the painting [from gum tragacanth] as I have little systematic knowledge; but at all events, I prefer experience and this is an experiment."[89] Sully's persistence in using gum tragacanth over a period of years implies that he did not notice any bad effects during these experiments, although on one occasion he called gum tragacanth "a poor varnish, but better than none,"[90] presumably because it did not wet up his colors very well.

During this time Sully tried out other kinds of varnishes, including drying oil diluted with turpentine (see chapter 11), an old idea that he had learned from Benjamin West. Sully was interested in new commercial products as well, and he experimented with Rowney's Siccatif as a varnish in 1861, the year after it had first appeared in the British company's catalogue. This material was most likely based on copal resin plus driers, and the first time he tried it, Sully found that it dried with "a fine surface," but when he diluted it with alcohol and made more elaborate experiments on a test panel, he found "it stirred up the paint," and he never mentioned Rowney's Siccatif again.[91]

Some of the varnishing experiments that Sully tried in the 1850s and 1860s were odd. He sometimes added calcined magnesia to dammar varnish, believing this would make it dry faster, and at one point in 1861, when he was frustrated with getting his varnish to dry, he added "a great quantity of magnesia"; on another occasion he added a few drops of "severe drier" to dammar.[92] Perhaps strangest of all, on at least two occasions in 1864 and 1865 he varnished a picture three or four days after painting it by rubbing it with lard or bacon fat, which he said "produced a tolerable varnish."[93] He never seems to have given up hope of finding a water-soluble material that could be used as a varnish. For instance, in 1866 he noted that someone had suggested varnishing with isinglass (a pure form of the fish glue that Sully had tried unsuccessfully to brush onto a painting twenty years earlier), but another man warned that if the glue was too strong, it would crack the painting, and Sully seems to have let the matter rest there.[94]

To the end of his days, Sully had wavering opinions about the proper time to wait before varnishing. As late as 1859 he varnished "a picture barely dry" with dammar varnish.[95] But two years later, while in the midst of some varnishing experiments that had gone wrong when the varnish "stirred up" his paint, he wrote: "I have concluded that permanent varnish must not be used soon after painting. When the painting appears to be dry, no less than six weeks should elapse before applying varnish."[96]

Sully's last opinion on the topic, in 1871, the year before his death, was that a painting should be allowed to dry "about four or five weeks."[97] This was much less time than most other authorities recommended (or than Sully himself believed in 1825). Sully's experiments may have given him confidence in his opinion, but he followed with a sentence leaving open the possibility that others would want to wait longer. Sully also could not resist returning to the old argument that had led him to make so many experiments to find methods that would allow him to varnish sooner: "Should [a painting] remain without varnishing for years, it will not suffer for the want of it; it will only look dull, and some colors will not show their effect."[98]

NOTES

1   Northcote 1815, clvi–clvii.
2   Dossie 1764, 1:217–18.
3   C. W. Peale to Robert Fulton, September 1, 1808 (C. W. Peale 1983–2000, vol. 2, pt. 2, p. 1125).
4   Neagle Commonplace Book, 15.
5   Sully "Hints," AAA, microfilm roll N18, frame 80 (comments from 1809–10, recorded in 1822).
6   Ibid., frame 81 (August 1810); see also Fabian 1983, 52–53. Treacle (molasses) was presumably added as a plasticizer to keep the ground from cracking. Later, Neagle reported that Sully made grounds this way "many years ago" (Neagle Commonplace Book, 4).
7   Trumbull to Isaac McCauley, March 31, 1817 (John Trumbull, Letterbook, 1810–17, New-York Historical Society, Trumbull Papers, Mss. coll. BVTrumbull).
8   Neagle Blotter, September 7, 1826.
9   Sully "Hints," AAA, microfilm roll N18, frames 111–12 (November 11, 1826); frame 139 (October 1, 1835).
10   Neagle "Receipts," 66.
11   Torchia, Chotner, and Miles 1998, 21, 24. *The Rev. John Albert Ryan* (1825/29, National Gallery of Art, Washington, D.C.). Part way through the procedure, Neagle applied water with a sponge to keep following layers from "soaking in" too much, but by accident he removed part of his ground; he suggested in the future dipping the ground face down into a tub of water.
12   Neagle "Receipts," 63 (February 11, 1828); Neagle Commonplace Book, 14.
13   Sully "Hints," AAA, microfilm roll N18, frame 100 (1825). On textured grounds, see Carlyle 2001, 174.
14   C. W. Peale Memorandum Book, 47–48.
15   Sully "Hints," AAA, microfilm roll N18, frame 121 (April 9, 1828, and June 30, 1828); Neagle "Receipts," 62–63. Later, Rembrandt Peale criticized soap as an addition to grounds (R. Peale "Notes," 19).
16   Sully "Hints," AAA, microfilm roll N18, frame 231 (May 30, 1857).
17   Neagle "Receipts," 71–75 (also p. 21).
18   Sully to his family, March 24, 1838 (Sully Letterbook, 2:115); see also Sully "Hints," AAA,

microfilm roll N18, frame 163 (March 31, 1838). Sully called this preparation only "half prepared," but Neagle equated it with absorbent ground: "Sully prefers Brown's half finished absorbent canvas, 1838" (Neagle Commonplace Book, 4).

19   Sully "Hints," AAA, microfilm roll N18, frames 181–82 (January 24, 1840).

20   Ibid., frame 182 (1841).

21   Torchia, Chotner, and Miles 1998, 186.

22   Ibid., 184. *Andrew Jackson* (1845, National Gallery of Art, Washington, D.C.).

23   Ibid., 188n12.

24   Sully "Hints," AAA, microfilm roll N18, frame 188 (September 10 and October 1, 1841); frame 190 (June 25, 18, 1842); frame 209 (August 28, 1848); frame 230 (May 8, 1855, recalling process from 1848); frame 231 (September 24, 1855, and July 19 [1856]); Sully 1873, 18.

25   Sully "Hints," AAA, microfilm roll N18, frame 251 (September 1867); see also Fabian 1983, 114–15.

26   Carlyle 2001, 169, 433–34.

27   Ibid., frame 117 (May 26, 1827). In this case it was adding mastic varnish to his paint.

28   Ibid., frame 77 (April 23, 1809).

29   Ibid., frame 79 (1809).

30   Torchia, Chotner, and Miles 1998, 148n2.

31   Sully "Hints," AAA, microfilm roll N18, frame 95 (April 1822). This was also reported in Dunlap 1834, 2:137.

32   Ibid., frame 99 (August 19, 1823). This may be related to other entries concerning wax emulsion or "wax milk" (ibid., frames 93–94 [ca. 1822, amended May 22, 1841]).

33   After having taken extensive notes from Eastlake's *Materials for a History of Oil Painting*, Sully wrote: "The excellence of wax in a vehicle is to be doubted" (Sully "Hints," AAA, microfilm roll N18, frame 245 [undated, but immediately prior to an entry dated November 1858]).

34   Sully 1873, 36n. Sully's wax/turpentine retouching varnish could have produced poor adhesion of the following layers as well as problems of solubility.

35   Cogdell Diaries/Letterbooks, vol. 2, entry titled "Mr. Sully's Room," 1816. Cogdell gave a detailed account of Sully's method, including his use of an absorbent ground, his use of "very much" asphaltum, and a description of the painting room and its furnishings.

36   Sully "Hints," AAA, microfilm roll N18, frame 96 (1822).

37   Ibid., frame 105 (February 16, 1826). On Anne Leslie as a painter, see Dunlap 1834, 2:398–99.

38   Sully "Hints," AAA, microfilm roll N18, frame 78 (1809) and frame 81 (1809–10). Sully did not refer to gumtion by name, but called it in each case a kind of megilp. On gumtion, see Carlyle 2001, 106–9.

39   Sully "Hints," AAA, microfilm roll N18, frame 103 (1825).

40   Ibid., frame 127 (April 1830).

41   Ibid., frame 172, May 17, 1830.

42   Ibid., frame 141 (June 22, 1836).

43   Ibid., frame 140 (November 5, 1835, and June 22, 1836).

44   Ibid., frames 190–92 (1842). Sully did not call it gumtion but "sugar of lead megilp,"

45   Ibid., frame 192 (December 11, 1842).

46   Ibid., frame 203 (September 25, 1843) and frame 204 (July 20, 1844, speaking of a painting done in 1842). As previously, Sully referred to the gumtion as "sugar of lead megilp."

47   Ibid., frames 203–5 (December 14, 1843, and June 15, July 8, July 23, and October 25, 1844).

48   Ibid., frame 210 (October 8, 1849).

49   Ibid., frames 151–52 (February 28, 1838).

50   Brett would send Sully a copy of Field's *Chromatography* in 1842, and Sully began taking detailed notes from it in 1843 (Sully Journal, AAA, microfilm roll N18, frame 556 [1842]; Sully "Hints," AAA, microfilm roll N18, frames 193–203 [April 2, 1843–prior to July 1843]).

51   Sully to Jane Sully, February 20, 1838 (Sully Letterbook, 2: 26).

52   On adding starch to paint, see Carlyle 2001, 110, 135n17. Starch was recommended in the second (1841) edition of Field's *Chromatography*. Brett's recommendation was just prior to the publication of the 1839 English translation of Mérimée, which also suggested starch as an ingredient. This was noticed by both Neagle (Neagle Commonplace Book, 40) and much later by Sully (Sully "Hints," AAA, microfilm roll N18, frame 252 [ca. 1867–68]).

53   Sully "Memoirs," 3. In the same vein, he recalled in 1851 some advice he had received in England

years before: "Sir Martin Archer Shee warned me against using strange vehicles in painting. He said that simple materials were safest, and best. Trumbull expressed the same opinion"(ibid., 11).

54   Ibid., 111.

55   Sully 1873, 8; on p. 10 he reiterated: "In all painting I use only this mixture."(These comments are in the section of the book dated June 1871.)

56   Ibid., 8.

57   Sully "Hints," AAA, microfilm roll N18, frame 246 (May 1859).

58   Sully "Memoirs" (1859 addendum), 2–3. See chapter 2, note 55, and chapter 4, note 70, on what "Antwerp blue" may have meant at this time.

59   Sully used cobalt blue as his only blue in palettes described in 1820 (Dunlap 1969, 531 [April 25, 1820]); in 1826 (Sully "Hints," AAA, microfilm roll N18, frame 104 [February 4, 1826, saying that blue black may be substituted for cobalt blue]; this was repeated in Dunlap 1834, 2:138); in 1829 (Sully "Hints," AAA, microfilm roll N18, frame 126 [December 23, 1829]); and in 1838 (Barratt 2000b, 59, illustrating the palette used to paint Queen Victoria in 1838).

60   Sully "Hints," AAA, microfilm roll N18, frame 204 (July 20, 1844, but citing a palette used in 1839). See also ibid., frame 211 (1849); and Sully "Memoirs,"107–11. In a description of his palette dated June 1871, the recommended blue is "ultramarine (or permanent blue)"(Sully 1873, 11, 13); Sully (or perhaps his grandson, who edited the book after Sully's death) may have used "permanent blue" as a synonym for artificial ultramarine or to designate a variety of artificial ultramarine having a particular shade of blue (see Carlyle 2001, 473), although Osborn in 1845 was confused by the term and did not know what it meant (Osborn 1845, 27n).

61   Field 1835, 110; Field 1841, 202–3.

62   Mérimée 1839, 166.

63   Osborn 1845, 24, 27. Osborn followed the opinion of Bouvier (1844, 27n–28n), who wrote that artificial ultramarine was as beautiful and durable as the original mineral. Rembrandt Peale wrote that "the best preparations" of artificial ultramarine were said to be as permanent as the natural product (R. Peale "Notes,"211–12).

64   Dossie 1764, 55–56; see also *Practical Treatise* 1795, 56–57; and Harley 1982, 119–20.

65   See Carlyle 2001, 506.

66   Sully "Hints," AAA, microfilm roll N18, frame 120 (September 22, 1827).

67   Spanish brown was an old-fashioned term by this time. It was mentioned in *Practical Treatise* 1795, 56–57, but not by Osborn 1845. Field (1835, 95) referred to it only as an "absurd appellation" for red ochre.

68   Neagle Student Notebook, unpaginated. Neagle also recorded an 1830 letter from Robert Sully describing the palette of John Jackson, a devotee of "tone" and a worshipper of Reynolds (see chapter 6): "*Umber* [presumably raw, because burnt is not specified] is totally discarded as being too green and *untrue* in the tone, and even unmanageable" (Neagle "Hints," unpaginated).

69   Sully "Memoirs," 107–11.

70   Sully "Hints," AAA, microfilm roll N18, frame 221 (February 20, 1852). Sully also cited the authority of Allston in 1835 as a reason he had abandoned using raw umber in flesh (Sully "Memoirs," 49).

71   Sully 1873, 11–14.

72   Field 1835, 161; Field 1841, 282–83; Osborn 1845, 86–87.

73   Sully 1873, 15. On Gilbert Stuart and Van Dyke brown, see chapter 4.

74   Sully "Memoirs," 17.

75   Sully "Hints," AAA, microfilm roll N18, frame 102 (August 3, 1825). An 1833 American book aimed at amateurs told readers (in the few pages dedicated to painting in oil) to wait "several weeks" before varnishing an oil painting (Turner 1833, 68).

76   Sully "Hints," AAA, microfilm roll N18, frame 204 (October 25, 1844).

77   Ibid., frame 207 (August 10, 1846). This panel must be the one that appears in Sully's *Record of Pictures*: "Aug. 7 1846 14" x 10" Sketch for the purpose of experiment in Varnish $10 [finished] Aug. 8"(Biddle and Fielding 1970, 385). Thanks to Karen Schoenewaldt and Katherine Haas at the Rosenbach Library in Philadelphia and to Ed Ahlstrom of Montgomery College, Rockville, Maryland, for this reference.

78   Sully "Hints," AAA, microfilm roll N18, frame 207 (September 6, 1846).

79   Ibid., frame 208 (January 23, 1847).

80   Ibid., frame 209 (September 29, 1847).

81   Ibid., frame 208 ([1846]).

82   Ibid., frame 209 (December 18, 1848).

83   Ibid., frame 210 (April 1849).

84   "[Dammar] can be applied, without risk, to a freshly painted picture" (Sully "Memoirs," 17) and "It may be used on a freshly painted picture"(ibid., 103).

85   Sully "Hints," AAA, microfilm roll N18, frame 219 (October 31, 1851). He had finished the painting on October 15 and varnished it two weeks later.

86   Sully "Memoirs,"17.

87   Sully "Hints," AAA, microfilm roll N18, frame 224 (1852; in the midst of other passages clearly taken from Peale's "Notes"); Sully "Hints," frames 228–29 (July 13, 1853); frame 232 (August 1858); frame 245 (November 7, 1858); frame 246 (February 19 and March 14, 1859); frame 247 (July 2, 1859); frame 249 (March 2, 1862); frame 250 (January 13, 1863). Sully may have been further encouraged to experiment with gum tragacanth when he noted that Benjamin Robert Haydon suggested that this combined with powdered gum mastic would make a good varnish (ibid., frame 232 [August 1858]).

88   Ibid., frame 232 (August 1858) and frames 245–46 (November 1858).

89   Ibid., frame 232 (August 1858).

90   Ibid., frame 249 (December 27, 1862). Earlier, Sully had complained about gum tragacanth as a varnish: "it hardly brings out the sunken parts" (ibid., frame 232 [August 1858]).

91   Ibid., frame 249 (June 17, July 8, and November 28, 1861). On Rowney's and other siccatives, see Carlyle 2001, 49–50.

92   Sully "Hints," AAA, microfilm roll N18, frame 248 (March 24, 1861) and frame 249 (April 10, 1861); on his belief that magnesia would make varnish dry faster, see also frame 210 (April 1849). Sully said that "severe" drier was the same as Japanner's gold size (Sully "Memoirs," 95).

93   Sully "Hints," AAA, microfilm roll N18, frame 250 (April 1865). A painting at the Rosenbach Museum and Library, Philadelphia, is inscribed: "June 22 Painted the above / 26 Rubbed it over with / a piece of Bacon Fat / which produced a tolerable varnish / T. Sully 1864." Our thanks to Ed Ahlstrom for bringing this to our attention.

94   Ibid., frame 250 (March 26, 1866).

95   Ibid., frame 247 (October 2, 1859).

96   Ibid., frame 249 (November 28, 1861). In 1869 Sully again wrote that six weeks was the proper drying time for a painting before varnishing (ibid., frame 253 [1869]).

97   Sully 1873, 16 (description dated June 1871).

98   Ibid.

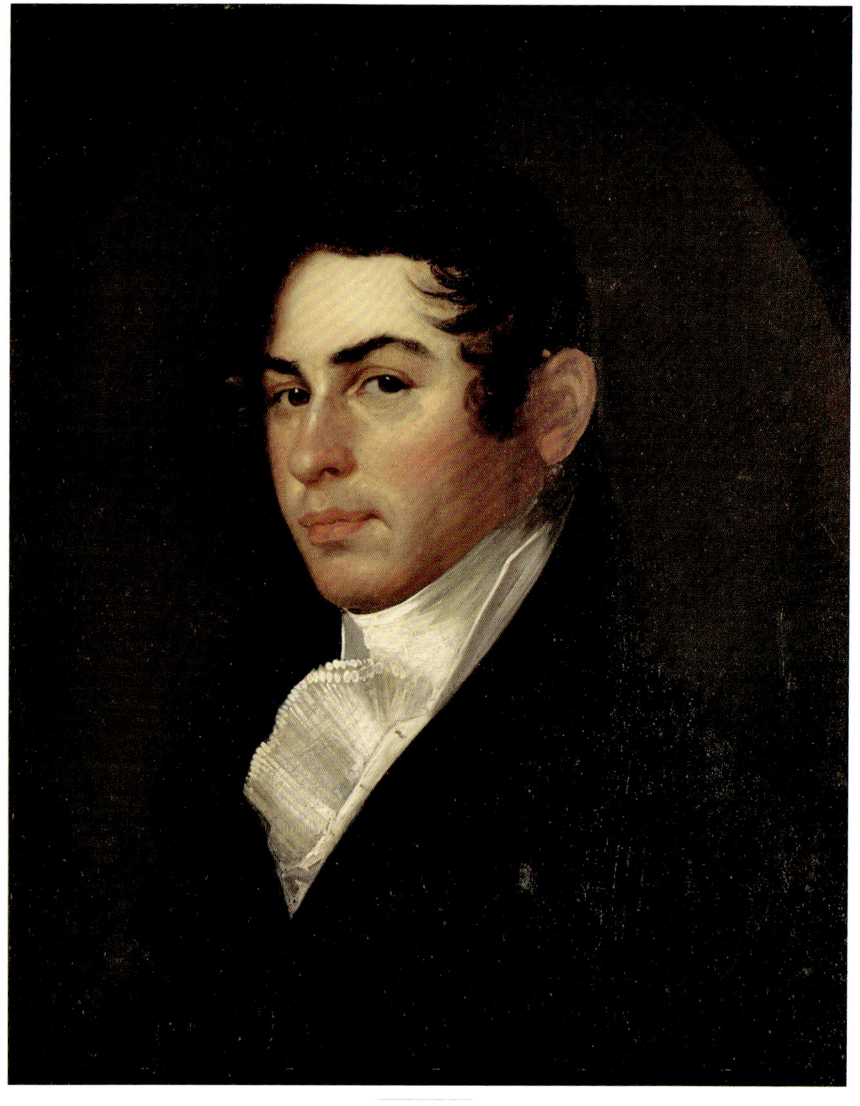

Bass Otis (American, 1784–1861), *Portrait of John Neagle*, ca. 1815.
Oil on wood, 55.9 × 45.7 cm (22 × 18 in.). Philadelphia, Pennsylvania Academy of the Fine Arts,
Gift of Garrett C. Neagle, 1944.24. Reproduced courtesy of the
Pennsylvania Academy of the Fine Arts.

CHAPTER 9
JOHN NEAGLE: METHODICAL EXPERIMENTER

JOHN NEAGLE WAS FIRST APPRENTICED to a coach decorator, then obtained a short period of instruction from the portrait painter Bass Otis, and from this beginning he made himself a competent artist and began to obtain portrait commissions.[1] He never went to Europe, but he improved his knowledge of art by amassing a large collection of prints.[2] Eventually Neagle met Thomas Sully, married his step-daughter, and benefited in many ways from a connection with the most prominent painter in Philadelphia.

In his notebooks dealing with painting materials, Neagle comes across as a more methodical observer than Sully, sometimes designing a series of experiments rather than simply trying out recipes and making notes if things went wrong. Like Sully, he compiled his observations about technique into several long manuscripts, although unlike Sully and Rembrandt Peale there is no sign that Neagle ever intended to have these published. It is characteristic of Neagle's thoroughness that in his longest document—his Commonplace Book, in which, beginning in 1839, he collected and organized information from earlier notebooks for his own use—he made a very complete index of the topics covered in the volume (fig. 14). (None of Sully's documents has an index, and Peale began an index to "Notes of the Painting Room" but never completed it.) Neagle's index is a good indicator of the topics that interested him. For instance, "Cracking, cause of" has six page references; "Grounds" (another preoccupation) is discussed as a general topic in eight different places, followed by detailed subcategories in the index such as "Grounds, beer, *cracks*, Why?" which is discussed on four pages. In all of his writings Neagle's skeptical, inquiring mind shines through.

Neagle copied many entries from Sully's manuscripts, but he often disagreed with his father-in-law. Following is a typical example in which Neagle bolstered his difference of opinion with direct observation:

> Sully says Egg varnish "will not hurt a new picture, but tis dangerous for an old one"—Note by Neagle—I have found it bad for a *new* one. My 1/2 length of Dr. Chapman was varnished with it, & I found it very difficult to get it off again, even with repeated washes of water, both cold & warm, with a soft sponge—Dr. Dewees's

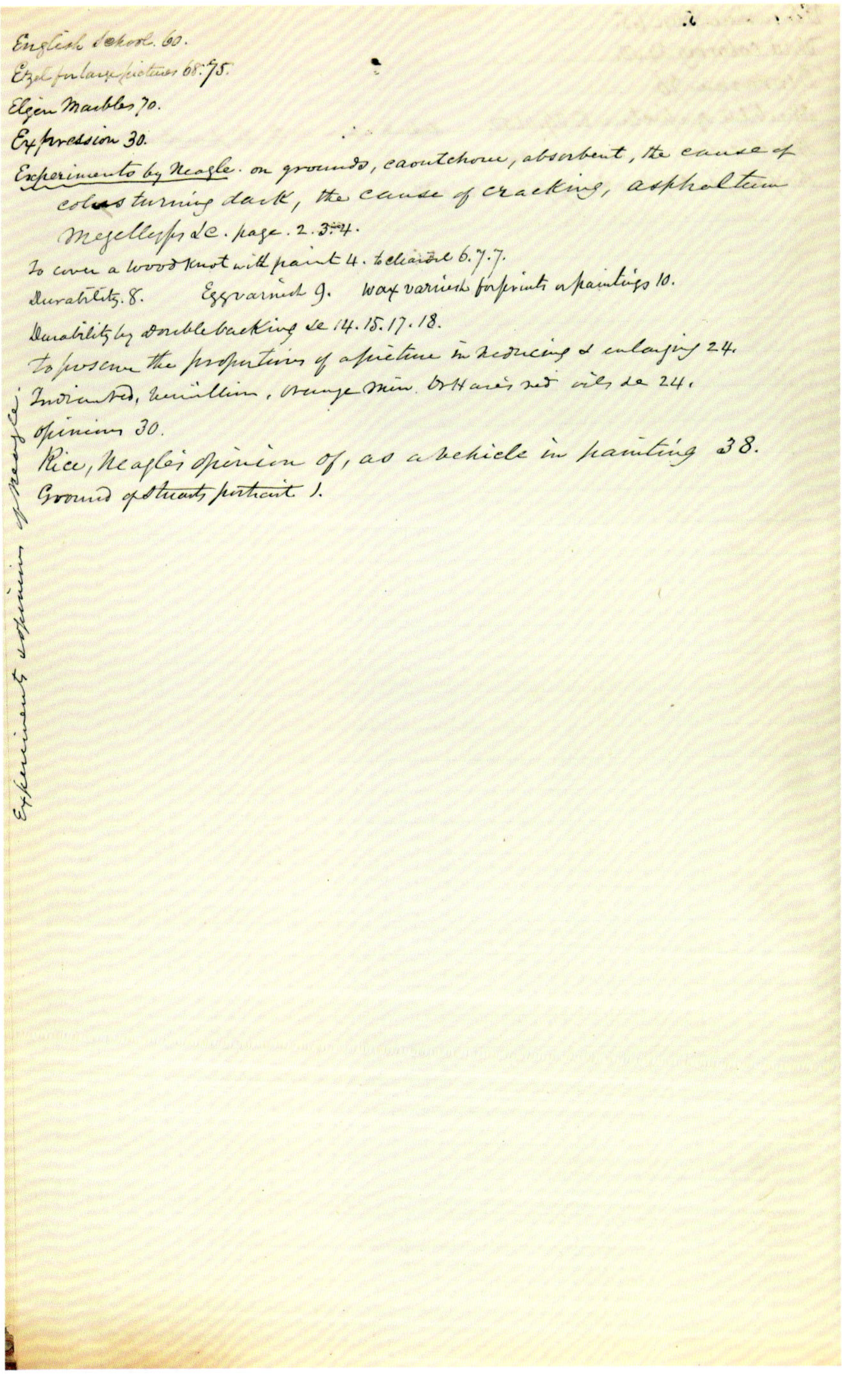

English school. 60.
Etzel for large pictures 68. 75.
Elgin Marbles 70.
Expression 30.
Experiments by Neagle. on grounds, caoutchouc, absorbent, the cause of
colors turning dark, the cause of cracking, asphaltum
Megelleps &c. page. 2. 3. 4.
To cover a wood knot with paint 4. to clean it 6. 7. 7.
Durability. 8.   Egg varnish 9.   Wax varnish for prints & paintings 10.
Durability by Double backing &c 14. 15. 17. 18.
To preserve the proportions of a picture in reducing & enlarging 24.
Indian red, vermillion, orange mineral or Hare's red oils &c 24.
Opinion 30.
Rice, Neagle's opinion of, as a vehicle in painting 38.
Ground of Stuart's portrait 1.

FIGURE 14

Page of Index, from *Commonplace Book of John Neagle* [1839].

Philadelphia, Historical Society of Pennsylvania, Am. 108.

half length too in which I used this vehicle, looks bad.—I saw it the other day [inserted: 1839] at the Penna Academy full of spots which disfigures the whole work. By the way, I must record, that in Summer the flies cover the surface of the picture & eat off the *candy* which was mixed with the Egg, & they make a sweet mess of it in truth.[3]

In Neagle's notebooks we often see a degree of follow-up and attention to detail that are lacking in Sully's investigations. On one occasion Neagle painted out samples of Indian red pigment from four different sources and observed the appearance of the samples seven and a half years later.[4] When he used an experimental fabric and ground for his second version of *Pat Lyon at the Forge*,[5] he checked up on it repeatedly. He recorded: "Jan 1830 I have just examined again my Pat Lyon in the Academy and find the canvas & all my colours without the least change," later adding "Sept. 1833" and "Dec. 1837."[6]

FABRICS AND GROUNDS

Entries in Neagle's notebooks show how American painters needed to make special efforts to obtain fabric for large paintings. For his first full-length portrait of *Pat Lyon at the Forge*,[7] he used a piece of fabric "purchased from the widow of the late Mr. Robinson, an English miniature painter.…It was of a light color and well seasoned."[8] When he painted the second version of this painting, he used "*imitation Russian Sheeting*, in which the threads are not tightly twisted nor wove."[9] And in 1832, when he painted another full-length work he ordered yet another kind of fabric and had comments on the shortcomings of the fabric prepared by the London colorman Thomas Brown for large paintings: "Recd 1 piece of Barnsley Sheeting 45½ yards long & about 7 feet wide. 80 cts per yd $36.40. This is for portraits—Brown's preparation of canvas (of London) is too flimsy for a large picture, but of excellent surface."[10]

Many American paintings were getting larger in the first half of the nineteenth century.[11] Rembrandt Peale's *The Court of Death*[12] was 13 feet high and 24 feet wide and was made from four fairly narrow pieces of fabric (about 40 inches wide), sewn together in horizontal bands.[13] Sewing together pieces of fabric to make a large painting had been common in earlier centuries, when looms for weaving fabric were fairly narrow. But by 1820 this was somewhat old-fashioned—fabrics much wider than 40 inches had been used by British artists (and some Americans) even in the eighteenth century.[14] In fact, while Peale was working on *The Court of Death*, his father wrote to tell him of "an advertizement in the papers of a manufactory of Canvis for painters use" that wove fabric "24 feet wide to any heigth."[15] This "manufactory" may possibly have been the one outside Philadelphia owned by Isaac McCauley. Three years earlier, in 1817, John Trumbull had given specifications to McCauley for 12-by-18-foot canvases for his paintings at the U. S. Capitol. Trumbull also kept open the option of sending to Thomas Brown in London if McCauley were not to be successful,[16] but Trumbull clearly wanted to encourage the American. Trumbull sent McCauley a sample of the fabric he normally used for smaller paintings, then tried to describe the ideal fabric for a much larger one: "The thread of the cloth must be strong and even, much stronger of course, than this specimen which is of the texture employed in moderate sized and small pictures. The surface when finished must be even & free from knots, but not polished or absolutely smooth."[17]

Trumbull appears to have used London canvases for his Capitol paintings, not McCauley's.[18] But McCauley must have eventually made canvas in large sizes successfully, because twenty-five years later, in 1842, Thomas Sully ordered from him a 12½-by-9½-foot canvas, although when the fabric arrived, Sully complained that it was "rather heavy and unnecessarily thick."[19] Perhaps McCauley had taken a little too seriously Trumbull's hint to make a fabric "much stronger" when it was to be used for large paintings.

Neagle's fascination with grounds led him to extrapolate from Sully's wax experiments during the 1820s, and in the early 1830s Neagle tried adding wax to grounds. Unlike Sully, he recorded his observations as his samples aged, writing in 1835, "I have made up my mind under a complete conviction after full experience, that canvas prepared with a composition of *wax* & other ingredients will chip off and is in other respects unfavorable as a preparation for a durable painting. In cold weather the wax grows brittle & in hot weather soft and tacky. It is apt to crack in circles & frequently to peel off entirely by being bruised from the back."[20] Four years later, Neagle added, "I can now say 1839 that the *wax did 'chip off,' as I dreaded, wherever the canvas received a blow on the back,* & I now think it well to record this dangerous practice, so as to bear it in mind."[21]

Rubber Grounds

Neagle's notebooks provide the best documentation of a fad for grounds made with an unlikely material—natural rubber—that blossomed in England during the 1830s and 1840s. The British authors George Field and Theodore Henry Fielding praised this new invention,[22] but in 1837 Neagle tried it out and noted its shortcomings:

> I have recently tried 5 pieces of India Rubber canvas prepared in London by Corven & Waring and find that although it is as pliant as a glove & may resist the injurious effects of contraction & expansion on the back which takes place with the ordinarily prepared stuffs, yet I find that it will not answer. A few days ago, I discovered, in a background, half finished, of the portrait of *I. H. Brolaskey* that it had cracked most frightfully in the course of about *four hours* exposure to the sun; and in the face of an unfinished portrait of *Mrs. Monro* which I am now copying for bishop Delancey from my original portrait of that lady, I perceive many deep cracks.[23]

Ironically, the motivation behind the use of rubber grounds was to prevent cracking by making a ground more flexible.[24] Neagle did not, however, categorically dismiss rubber grounds even after his paintings "cracked most frightfully." He noted that the misbehaving canvases had been coated with a *thick* layer of rubber and guessed that a more thinly coated variety might be successful: "I should however observe here that some *thick English twilled* canvas prepared with India rubber in a less quantity, I think by the same house, of which I gave Mr Sully some, & used some myself, appears to be excellent; and that Joshua Shaw who saw it, pronounced it to be the finest prepared surface he ever saw."[25]

We do not know whether Neagle, Sully, or Shaw carried out further tests with this different variety of rubber ground. But evidence that rubber grounds were an international trend is found in a painting by John Vanderlyn from 1839 on a French canvas that bears the stamp "toile anhygrometrique"; the French patent says that the active ingredient was rubber.[26] A few years later, in 1842, Neagle recorded a recipe from James Jay Mapes for making a liquid solution of rubber.[27] Neagle did not reveal the use to which this liquid rubber might be put, but a hint may be found in a passage in which Sully described an unfortunate experiment that he carried out in 1847: "I spread some India-rubber water-proof for leather on the back of the absorbent canvas on which I was about to paint a half-length of Secretary J. Y. Mason. It penetrated the cloth, and my paint not drying, I had to abandon the picture and begin another."[28]

The firm of Winsor & Newton still carried "India Rubber canvas" in 1846, although it did not appear in their catalogues of the 1850s.[29] But this was not the last word on rubber in the nineteenth century—in 1855 Sanford Gifford reported seeing in G.P.A. Healy's studio outside Paris a portrait of Charles Goodyear, "the India rubber celebrity," painted on a rubber panel that Healy said was "delightful" to use.[30] In this case the rubber may have been a gimmick inspired by the fact that the sitter was the inventor of vulcanized rubber, but the next year *The Crayon* picked up on the story and printed a joking account of the advantages of a rubber support prepared with a rubber ground: "Its great charm here is, that a painting upon it may be changed to suit the whim of the moment. By stretching, it may be made into an upright, or an oval; a mountain may be high or low; the child's figure may be pulled out as he grows."[31]

It was perhaps lucky that rubber grounds (and supports) never really caught on, for natural rubber is not a stable material. If a ground contained a large proportion of rubber, it would likely deteriorate over time, in the same way that a rubber band forgotten in a drawer becomes cracked and brittle after a period of years. However, a painting of about 1847, bearing a Winsor & Newton label and the stenciled inscription, "India Rubber Canvas," is still in good condition—perhaps the amount of rubber in this formulation was relatively small.[32]

PAINT ADDITIVES

Neagle made many observations about megilps and other added media that related directly to his concerns about cracking and yellowing. Neagle noted Thomas Sully's opinions about megilp: "T Sully tells me that megellup *will certainly stand well.* He knows it from long experience, and the only disadvantage from the use of it is that if your color is not well loaded the picture grows weak in effect from the circumstances of this vehicle *thinning* the body of the colors—but he thinks no other danger is to be apprehended."[33] But Neagle followed these remarks with his own opinion: "NB Although megellups may not *crack*, they certainly, with most vehicles, will turn dark; particularly when not mixed with colors. J.N. 1826."[34] Modern observers would tend to agree with Neagle.

A few years later—in 1829—Neagle developed an experiment to test for himself the aging properties of various oils and mediums. He was able to observe ten years later that raw poppy oil mixed with white pigment and kept in a brightly lit room remained "*many degrees brighter*" than the same white pigment mixed with megilp (drying linseed oil and mastic 1:1, with white wax added in this case), concluding that "*megellups* at least with *wax* in them *have a tendency to turn dark!!!* And it is most likely the case with all oils that have been *heated.*"[35]

In 1829 Neagle also did tests to see whether it was the medium or the quality of the white lead pigment that had a greater effect on whether samples of white paint lasted well. After ten years his experiments had convinced him that "both *oils* & *leads* have much to do with durability & beauty of color,"[36] but in his detailed comments on this experiment he described mostly the effects of different oils and other vehicles. He thought that the linseed oil purified by Heyl (the Philadelphia colorman also mentioned by Charles Willson Peale, Sully, and Trumbull) using cedar shavings was the best. Boiled oils tended to turn darker, and darkest of all was paint made with bene [sesame] oil obtained from the estate of Charles Willson Peale.[37]

In 1832 Neagle tested another aspect of the aging of paint samples. He made two strips of canvas, painted them with various mixtures, and exposed one to the light but left the other in the dark. He found that the samples kept in the dark generally grew browner in color, but that white paint made with varnish and *no* oil stayed as white in the dark as in the light. Neagle confirmed what artists have long known—that freshly applied oil paint kept in the dark will discolor (although modern observers have found that a relatively moderate exposure to light will reverse this discoloration). Neagle, however, wondered whether his tests proved that old master painters used something other than oil in their paint. He ended his comments on this experiment by bringing up the question of absorbent grounds: "Or did their grounds absorb the oil *from* the *surface*?"[38]

Like Sully, Neagle was interested in gumtion, the variety of megilp made using sugar of lead. In the mid-1820s Neagle obtained information about gumtion from the British immigrant painter Joshua Shaw, who had gotten the recipe in England directly from its inventor, Julius Caesar Ibbetson. Shaw claimed that the "common" megilp made with mastic and drying oil would turn yellow but told Neagle that for fourteen years he had successfully used gumtion: "This he says is the finest composition for driving colour into when you merely wish to glaze and finish.…it must be laid over the surface of your painting with a large brush as *thinly as possible*, then work your tints into it while fresh. This he says will allow you to work pleasantly for a whole day without drying and cannot injure the perfect durability of the colours."[39]

Neagle must have asked Sully's opinion about gumtion shortly after this, and recorded his response: "Mr Sully is fearful that the megellup described by Mr Shaw will *crack* and recommends the following which is his custom" [raw linseed oil plus litharge, mixed with an equal portion of mastic varnish] "and you will have a good clear megellup to be depended upon when used sparingly." Neagle went on to say that Sully had just given him some, and it looked very clear and was "short" and would stand up so that one might cut it—Neagle also said that a little beeswax would stiffen it.[40]

Neagle could not resist going back to Shaw to report Sully's criticism of gumtion and was told: "Shaw assures me that megellup made from gum Mastic and Sugar of Lead *ground* together of equal weights will neither crack nor turn yellow and will positively *bleach* in the Sun or light."[41]

Some years later (after 1839) Neagle again recorded Shaw's reassurances about the stability of gumtion, although by this time Neagle had noticed problems when he used large amounts of it: "Shaw says that 'Sugar of Lead in Gumption, bleaches & never turns black;' but where much of it was used for haste, I have seen the work very much cracked within 3 years from the date of execution."[42]

Neagle went on to describe another case in which haste led to bad results. He reported that Henry Inman had used both sugar of lead and drying oil to make his paint dry so fast that he could do a portrait in one sitting: "Inman's vehicle used to be, Sugar of lead & Drying oil for dispatch, but his head of Dr. Godman in the Phil. Museum Dec. 30th 1834 was much cracked. It was said to be painted at one sitting."[43]

Neagle reported yet another example of cracking, in this case on one of his own paintings. After glazing it repeatedly with asphaltum, he applied a layer of paint containing Japan drier and placed it in the sun, only to find "*it cracked in deep long gashes down into the body of the work underneath, in the short space of a few hours.*"[44] Neagle believed that if he had allowed his underlayers to dry more completely, he would not have had this problem; like many other painters of this time, including Sully, he apparently did not think that asphaltum itself was at fault. But he added—correctly, according to modern authorities—that the proper sequence of layers for a painting would consist of lean paint first, followed by more "elastic"(medium-rich) layers.[45]

Neagle applied the lessons learned from cases like this when his colleague Thomas Birch was baffled by a painting that had developed long cracks all through the sky during the process of painting it. Neagle noted: "Having had some experience myself in this matter to my sorrow, I asked him *what oils or dryers he had used.*" It turned out that Birch had applied paint containing a drier over an underlayer that was still tacky, and Neagle wrote that "this, in my mind, accounted for it."[46]

PROTECTING THE BACKS OF CANVASES

Neagle provided some of the most sophisticated commentary on a topic that Americans became interested in during the 1820s and 1830s—protecting the backs of their paintings from deterioration. In 1828–29 John Trumbull infused molten wax into some of his paintings that were suffering from cracks and/or were being harmed by damp walls behind them.[47] Other artists took note; Sully, always one to weigh both sides of an argument, said that the paintings "are now in excellent shape," but he also noted that the New York dealer Michael Paff "says the new way of waxing pictures at the back, prevents the recanvassing [lining] them, and he also condemns the waxing [of] the surface for the purpose of filling up the cracks."[48] (In 1836, however, Sully would deem Trumbull's process good enough to try out himself, when he faced the unpleasant task of repairing a portrait that he had painted only seven years earlier that had become "much cracked."[49])

Neagle agreed with Michael Paff that it was not advisable to melt wax into a painting: "Wax will not do upon the immediate back of the cloth on which the picture is painted, because it could never be *lined* successfully, for the wax wd prevent the material from sticking, & I apprehend, even the wax, in time, would become brittle & injure the painting."[50]

Neagle's discussion of this topic sounds surprisingly modern, as does his understanding that paintings suffer not only from dampness but also from "the sudden changes from cold to hot, or from damp to dry weather."[51] He proposed what he called "doublebacking"—stretching a painting over a second, unattached fabric that had been previously infused with wax—"to prevent the sudden action of the atmospheric changes."[52] (Today, this would be called a "loose lining.") Neagle went on: "I am fully persuaded, that a painting, if cut in half—the one part *Doublebacked* as I have suggested, or by means of a *board* loose on the back to protect it behind, & the other half without protection in the ordinary way, and both were exposed in the same place, to some changeably dry & moist, & hot & cold atmosphere, that the result, in due time for trial, would prove my notion to be correct."[53] Modern conservators would agree with Neagle. His discussion of a loose board behind a canvas shows that he was also aware of the principle behind the preservative qualities of a panel stretcher (see chapter 11).

But by 1842, a conversation with James Mapes made Neagle change his mind about "doublebacking." Mapes apparently told Neagle that mold or fungus could grow behind his waxed fabric and convinced him that a "column of air" created by an unattached, unwaxed canvas, stretched so it did not touch the painting, would provide a safer buffer against climactic changes.[54] Like Neagle, Mapes was ahead of his time, especially in anticipating by more than a century the idea that every painting should have a backing board, not only to buffer the canvas against changes in humidity but to contain a volume of static air that will keep the painting from moving when it is transported or otherwise subject to vibration.

Rembrandt Peale also weighed in on the question of protecting the backs of paintings, writing down (in an undated note) a recipe that sounds exactly like the wax procedure used by Trumbull.[55] By the time he completed writing "Notes of the Painting Room" in 1850–52, Peale also believed that saturating the back of a *newly* prepared canvas with a solution of wax in turpentine would "be a great protection from the influence of damp."[56] Materials other than wax were occasionally applied to the backs of canvases. Sully's attempt in 1847 to coat the back of a canvas with liquid rubber before beginning painting had disastrous results. William Sidney Mount had an offbeat theory about protecting canvases; in 1858 he wrote: "To varnish over the back of your canvas with demar varnish would perhaps add to the durability of the painting. I[t] might set the canvas."[57] At least one American canvas maker was thinking in a similar direction. In 1842, the same year that Mapes and Neagle were debating this topic, Sully noticed that the large fabric he had ordered from Isaac McCauley was "painted on the back; t'is unusual but will no doubt protect the cloth from damp."[58]

PROBLEM SOLVING AND EXPERIMENTATION

Neagle had thoughts on a variety of other topics. For instance, he read about a method of purifying oil with charcoal, and he tried it himself (with added innovations), but his experiment was only partly successful: "Much mucilaginous or fatty matter remained in the charcoal, after the filtration," but the oil was discolored by the charcoal. He resolved to "make another trial of it."[59] But Neagle also recorded Rembrandt Peale's sensible opinion that purifying oils—at least in the sense of making them lighter in color—might be pointless, because the lighter oils could eventually revert to a darker color. As Peale told Neagle: "While you use Dark oil, you know what you rely upon in the strength of your tints, while in using light oils that may become brown, by being kept in the shade, the general tone of your work is destroyed."[60]

Neagle's scientific approach to materials is apparent in many of his notes. He sought out some fairly obscure written sources, such as J.H. Müntz's 1760 book on wax painting. In notes that Neagle took from Müntz's book, it is clear that he was mainly interested in Müntz's opinions on the drying of oil layers.

Müntz theorized that "dessicated saline particles" in an oil ground were redissolved when new paint was applied and that they caused "fermentation," which gave a yellowish-gray cast to the surface. The terms are quaint, but it is clear that Neagle was willing to plunge into scientific discussions in order to better understand the subtle effects that occur at the boundaries of paint layers and can have important effects on the appearance of a painting.[61]

Like many Americans at this time, Neagle was fascinated by new technology and new inventions. In 1840 he took detailed notes on how two different panorama paintings were displayed in Philadelphia. One was lit with artificial lamps having tin reflectors, and the other with natural light that was carefully directed and screened. Neagle actually took over the operation of a panorama in Philadelphia as a money-making venture for six months and made drawings in his notebooks of such details as how the rollers were made to turn easily.[62] Neagle also made inventions of his own. His notebooks contain two novel designs for an easel that would support a large picture by attaching light pieces of wood to the ceiling, making the easel steady by suspending weights from it.[63] He also improvised a kind of folding stretcher, variations of which are now frequently used by contemporary artists for large paintings. He described this device in connection with his 1843 portrait of Henry Clay: "The finished full length not being sufficiently dry or hardened, I was afraid to roll it lest the paint would stick, and to render it safe in carriage to Frankfort [Kentucky], I had recourse to two pairs of hinges, which by cutting the stretching frame, I was enabled to fold the canvas over without touching, & it came safely in a box."[64]

Neagle's methodical, scientific approach to problem solving embodies something that many Americans like to think of as typically American. At times, he could be almost chillingly scientific. He was apparently present at the autopsies of three of his children and wrote "Memorandum of the Illness and Death of Margaret Dickson Neagle," a detailed account of the postmortem carried out by four doctors after the death of one of his daughters. In this document Neagle described with objectivity and precision his daughter's diseased internal organs and wondered why several doctors were unable to discover her illness while she was still alive. His account ended with a bitter question: "After all, is not the system of medical treatment, a system of *guessing*?"[65] The same might have been said about the systems that artists had long used to choose painting materials, and Neagle's experiments could be seen as an attempt to substitute scientific inquiry for mere guessing.

NOTES

1   Neagle's youth and education are discussed by Dunlap 1834, 2:372–74; and Torchia 1989, 23–28.
2   Torchia 1989, 31, 51.
3   Neagle Commonplace Book, 9. The "candy" he refers to is sugar, which was often added to egg varnishes. By 1851, Sully also believed that egg varnish on a new picture was "pernicious" (Sully "Memoirs," 17).

4   Neagle Commonplace Book, 20.

5   1828–29, Pennsylvania Academy of the Fine Arts, Philadelphia.

6   Neagle "Receipts," 66.

7   1826–27, Museum of Fine Arts, Boston.

8   Neagle Commonplace Book, 17.

9   Ibid., 14. Earlier, he had tried painting on "white drilling" but disliked it because the threads were "too close" and the paint threatened to peel off (Neagle "Receipts," 66).

10   Neagle Blotter, March 14, 1832; Neagle "Receipts,"70.

11   Of course some of the largest paintings were panoramas; see below in this chapter on Neagle and panoramas.

12   1820, Detroit Institute of Arts.

13   Mayer and Myers 1996, 5.

14   Ralph Earl did a painting in New York about 1791 on an unseamed fabric that was 56 inches wide, although when he was working in Connecticut, his fabrics were no more than about 36 inches wide, sewn together when he needed a wider support (Kornhauser 1991, 86). A late instance of a seamed fabric is Thomas Cole's *A Wild Scene* (1832, Baltimore Museum of Art), which is 48 inches high by 75¾ inches wide and has a horizontal seam across its center (Silberfeld 1965, 31).

15   C.W. Peale to R. Peale, February 10, 14, 15, 1820 (Peale 1983–2000, 3:796). The editors of the Peale papers could not identify the factory.

16   Trumbull to Mr. Brown, March 31, 1817 (Trumbull Papers CHS, microfilm roll 80006, reel I, frame 286).

17   Trumbull to Isaac McCauley, March 31, 1817 (John Trumbull, Letterbook, 1810–17, New-York Historical Society, Trumbull Papers, Mss. coll. BV Trumbull).

18   The only proof of this is in correspondence revolving around the deterioration caused by damp walls in the Capitol: "The cloth on which this work is executed, was prepared in the most approved and perfect manner, by the same person who is employed by Mr. West, to prepare those which are the basis of his admirable works" (Trumbull to John Quincy Adams, February 18, 1819 [cited in Trumbull 1841, 279]). West collaborated with James Poole in making absorbent grounds, and Brown took over Poole's firm in the early nineteenth century (see chapter 2).

19   Sully "Hints," AAA, microfilm roll N18, frame 192 (September 12, 1842).

20   Neagle "Receipts," 70 (1832) and 78–79 (January 6, 1835).

21   Neagle Commonplace Book, 15.

22   Carlyle 2001, 170–71 (citing Field 1835 and Fielding 1839).

23   Neagle "Hints," unpaginated. This story was repeated in Neagle Commonplace Book, 2.

24   Increased flexibility was the same reason that Field and Fielding had recommended adding wax to grounds (Field 1841, 386; Fielding 1846, 171–73).

25   Neagle Commonplace Book, 2–3.

26   Zucker 1999, 6. The painting is a fragment of a study for Vanderlyn's *Landing of Columbus*, 1839, New York State Bureau of Historic Sites, Senate House State Historic Site, Kingston, N.Y. Our thanks to Joyce Zucker for this information.

27   Neagle Commonplace Book, 13.

28   Sully "Hints," AAA, microfilm roll N18, frame 208 (June 4, 1847).

29   Katlan 1992, 374–75; Winsor & Newton catalogues of ca. 1840 and ca. 1842 also advertised rubber grounds (Carlyle 2001, 170).

30   Sanford Gifford to his father, October 24, 1855 (AAA, Gifford Papers [online], Letters, series 1, frame 124). For the story of the portrait and an illustration of it, see DeMare 1954, 32, 176–77.

31   Burnt Umber 1856, 283.

32   John Woodhouse Audubon and Victor Gifford Audubon, *Startled Deer—A Prairie Scene* (ca. 1847, Brooklyn Museum), as described in Carbone et al. 2006, 1:243. The Vanderlyn painting on a French rubber-containing canvas described above is also still in very good condition (Joyce Zucker, personal communication, 2007).

33   Neagle "Receipts,"39.

34   Ibid.

35   Neagle Commonplace Book, 8.

36   Ibid.

37   Ibid.

38   Ibid., 11.

39   Neagle "Receipts," 54. Shaw also advocated an unusual method of laying in the heavily textured parts of his design with a lean paint made from pigments ground in turpentine and copal (Sully "Hints," AAA, microfilm roll N18, frame 127 [November 1830] and frame 141 [July 2, 1836]). Eventually, Neagle and Shaw became enemies and exchanged insulting letters in local newspapers (see Torchia 1989, 42–47, 63–67).

40   Neagle "Receipts," 56–57.

41   Ibid., 58.

42   Neagle Commonplace Book, 7. In 1835 Neagle had reported the claims of a Mr. Bishop that heating linseed oil (as was done to make the drying oil used in "common" megilp) would make it turn yellow, recommending instead a cold mixture of oil, spirits of turpentine, and litharge (ibid.). Neagle later added a comment in the margin next to Bishop's recipe: "Neagle has tried this & didn't like it."

43   Ibid.

44   Ibid., 3.

45   Ibid.

46   Ibid., 4; see also p. 3 (on cracking); and Neagle "Receipts," 71.

47   For a fuller discussion of this topic, see Mayer and Myers 2006.

48   Sully Journal, AAA, microfilm roll N18, frame 339 (September 1829). In another telling, Paff was quoted as saying: "picture-cleaners have a pernicious habit of covering the surface of damaged pictures with wax—he condemns the use of it entirely—it is certain that a picture which has wax on the back cannot be re-canvassed" (Sully "Hints," AAA, microfilm N18, frame 125 [August 11, 1829]).

49   Ibid., frame 143 (November 22, 1836). The painting was a portrait of Mrs. Leslie.

50   Neagle Commonplace Book, 14–15.

51   Ibid., 14.

52   Ibid.

53   Ibid., 15.

54   Ibid., 17–18.

55   R. Peale Miscellaneous, undated, four sheets beginning with "Jane Greenland's Method of Encaustic" and containing section with "Crack—in pictures—to repair." (APS, Peale-Sellers Papers, B P31).

56   R. Peale "Notes," 18, 20; also 92 (which discusses using wax to render an absorbent ground nonabsorbent).

57   Mount's diary [1858] (cited in Frankenstein 1975, 315).

58   Sully "Hints," AAA, microfilm roll N18, frame 192 (September 12, 1842).

59   Neagle Commonplace Book, 7.

60   Ibid., 12.

61   Ibid., 18. Neagle attributed his notes to "Count Caylus," but his page numbers show he was actually using Müntz's 1760 English interpretation of the 1755 book by Caylus and Majault.

62   Torchia 1989, 69; Neagle Commonplace Book, 76–79.

63   Ibid., 75.

64   Neagle to Levi Dickson, March 18, 1843 (Neagle Miscellaneous). The *Portrait of Henry Clay* (1843, Union League of Philadelphia) is over nine feet tall and six feet wide. For later British examples that may be hinged stretchers, see Carlyle 2001, 186. Albert Bierstadt's *A Storm in the Rocky Mountains, Mt. Rosalie* (1866, Brooklyn Museum) is still on its original two-part stretcher, which is not hinged but is held together with metal braces and screws (Carbone et al. 2006, 1:287–88). For other folding stretchers, both American and European, see Buckley 2008, 208–9.

     Sully explained a different kind of folding stretcher in 1812: "Whole length stretching frames should be made to fold up near the bottom so as to bring the drawing of the head within reach while you are painting from the subject" (Sully "Hints," AAA, microfilm roll N18, frame 81 [February 9, 1812]; see also frame 182, dated 1841). However, this would be of no use for Neagle's purpose of keeping a wet, painted surface from touching itself.

65   June 26, 1853 (Neagle Miscellaneous); Torchia 1989, 13.

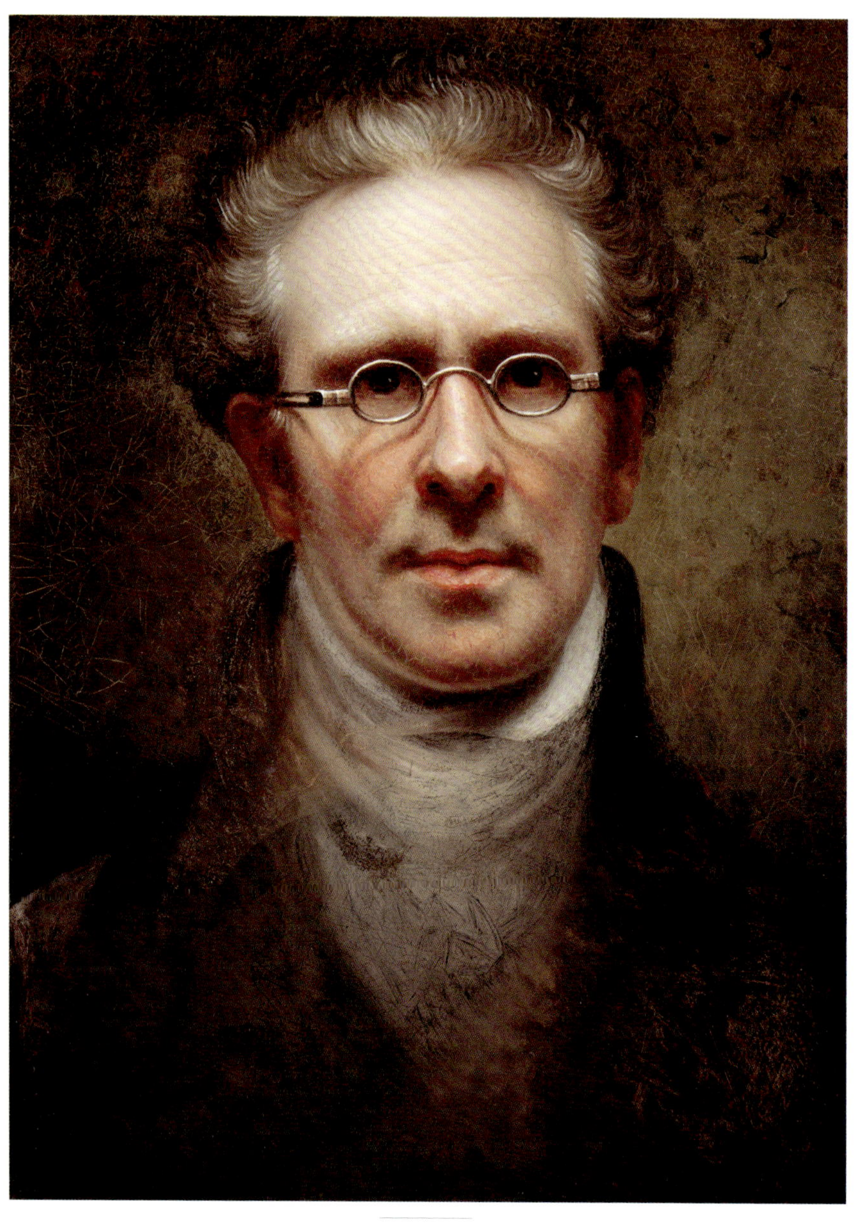

Rembrandt Peale (American, 1778–1860), *Self-Portrait*, 1828.
Oil on canvas, 48.3 × 36.8 cm (19 × 14½ in.). Detroit, Michigan, Detroit Institute of Arts,
Founder's Society Purchase and Dexter M. Ferry Jr. Fund, 1945.469.

CHAPTER 10
REMBRANDT PEALE: EXPERIMENTER AND ENTREPRENEUR

REMBRANDT PEALE HAD A LIFELONG INTEREST in innovative painting techniques. In 1795, when still a teenager, he acquired a copy of a British painting manual, *Practical Treatise on Painting in Oil-Colours,* that had been published the same year and signed it with his name and the date. Peale made numerous annotations to this book over the course of his lifetime, often disagreeing strongly with the authors.[1] Professor James Woodhouse of the University of Pennsylvania encouraged the young artist's scientific studies,[2] and by 1806 his father could boast of "my Son Rembrandt, who is not only a Phylosopher but an experimentor on Colours and Oils," who pursued the "mystery of Chymistry for the discovery of perfect & durable materials."[3]

THE PEALE FAMILY AND OPTICAL DEVICES

The Peale family's interest in scientific and technological innovations ran wide and deep. To take just one example, they had an early interest in optical instruments and other mechanical devices that could help artists draw an image more efficiently. The camera obscura can be documented to have been used by other artists in the American colonies as early as the 1740s or 1750s, as well as in Benjamin West's London studio (see chapters 1 and 2). Charles Willson Peale used a kind of homemade perspective machine as an aid when drawing landscapes in the 1770s, and he devised a more elaborate optical device by the late 1780s.[4] He also worked with an instrument maker to build a "polygraph" (a kind of pantograph that could copy and change the size of documents or images), and in 1804 he sold one of these machines to another American who was interested in scientific and technical innovations—his friend Thomas Jefferson.[5] The Peales became involved with yet another type of reproductive device beginning around 1802, the "physiognotrace." This term referred to various instruments used to take profile likenesses, and one was soon set up at the Peale Museum so that visitors could take home a miniature version of their own image at a moderate price—8,500 silhouettes were cut at the museum in the first year.[6]

By 1816, Rembrandt Peale had introduced his father to an optical device that produced an image that could be traced. This may have been a camera lucida—in any event, a camera lucida called by that name was in Charles Willson Peale's estate in 1827–28 and was then purchased by Titian Ramsey Peale.[7] Cameras, both obscura and lucida, were perhaps more widely used by American painters in the eighteenth and nineteenth centuries than has been previously thought. For instance, in 1814 Thomas Sully took notes from a book (by A. Robertson) that included the comment: "The study of the Camera Lucida + Camera Obscura is highly recommended."[8] Samuel F. B. Morse remembered working with a camera obscura in his student days (about 1811–15).[9] Later—in 1820–22—when he faced the tricky perspective problem of drawing the interior of the U. S. House of Representatives, Morse asked his wife in a letter to send him a camera obscura.[10] William Dunlap mentioned that the young Thomas Cole was so poor in the early 1820s that he needed to sell his camera obscura, as if it were normal for a painter of landscapes to own one.[11]

Optical devices may have played a role in "democratizing" American art in the nineteenth century by helping artists (both amateurs and professionals) render a likeness even if they had limited drawing skills. Bass Otis made this explicit in 1815 when he advertised an invention called the "perspective protractor" as follows: "The outline of any object may be correctly delineated…by any person who can draw a line or has the least idea of holding a pencil."[12] Otis's advertisement included testimonials from the painters Thomas Sully and Thomas Birch; various models of his machine cost between fifteen and fifty dollars. At a more humble level, the "folk" painter and author Rufus Porter built a camera obscura in 1820 that allowed him to paint a rudimentary portrait in fifteen minutes, and in 1825 he published instructions describing how any painter could make his or her own camera obscura "for drawing landscapes, or even portraits."[13]

A FAMILY OF ENTREPRENEURS

For all of the Peale family's qualifications as scientists and experimenters, Rembrandt Peale's experiments sometimes have a different character than those of Sully or Neagle. Peale seems at times to be less a scientific researcher and more an entrepreneur, in the sense that—unlike Sully and Neagle (as far as we know)—he tried to make money from his innovations. As early as 1810 Peale hinted that he would not reveal the secret of his encaustic technique unless he was financially compensated.[14] In 1832 he offered to sell Neagle a secret process "for a certain consideration which he named"; Neagle was shocked, saying that he "was surprized that Mr P. should think of keeping or retailing *secrets* in the art."[15]

The Peale family had a tradition of combining science and technology with showmanship, and they made money from a variety of activities, including the display of curiosities in their museums in Philadelphia and Baltimore and in traveling exhibitions. Charles Willson Peale clearly believed that Rembrandt's interest in chemistry would not only lead to permanent painting materials but made good business sense. On one occasion he urged his son to continue to "make your experiments in Chemestry, for I am sure that it will add considerably to your income and I doubt not that by such an exhibition you will acquire considerable popularity."[16] William Dunlap apparently found this kind of attitude unseemly and took a swipe at Charles Willson Peale by writing that his "*genius* was devoted to making money."[17]

It is difficult for a modern reader to fault the Peale family for expecting to make money from their multitudinous projects. American artists lacked the royal and aristocratic patrons who supported many British artists, and Americans needed to be innovative, flexible, and sometimes hard-nosed in figuring out ways to make a living from the arts. For instance, in 1809 Rubens Peale developed a plan to manufacture the pigment chrome yellow from ore mined in Maryland, but he gave it up when it turned out that the color darkened upon exposure to light. The Peales' business partner, a high-strung French chemist, allegedly became deranged when the project failed, but the Peales avoided what might have been a costly venture. American artists were spared—for a time—one more fugitive pigment (although chrome yellow soon became available from European sources).[18] It should also be pointed out that the members of the Peale family were not alone in trying to profit from inventions in painting techniques—the Provises and Julius Caesar Ibbetson had set precedents earlier in England by selling their innovations, and John Trumbull calculated the profit that might be made by manufacturing oils for painting.[19]

EXPERIMENTATION AND PIGMENTS

Some of Rembrandt Peale's opinions and experiments with art materials were recorded in the family's correspondence, and others were written on undated single sheets of paper, but it was only late in his life (1850–52) that Peale systematically collected many of his ideas in the manuscript "Notes of the Painting Room."[20] It is therefore less easy to map the progression of his changing ideas over the years, as we can often do in the notebooks with datable entries kept by Sully and Neagle.

"Notes of the Painting Room" contains some original thoughts; Peale urged artists to become experimenters themselves by painting out test canvases.[21] However, many passages were frankly taken from other authors, and the general tone of much of the advice is conservative rather than experimental. Perhaps Peale had learned a lesson from having seen his wax method fail after he had made such exorbitant claims for it, or from events like the rebuff he received from Neagle when he tried to sell him a secret recipe.

One topic about which there is substantial information over a period of years is Peale's preoccupation with pigments and color mixtures. His sardonic (and in some cases contrarian) nature came out in his extensive annotations (on at least two different occasions) in his copy of *Practical Treatise on Painting in Oil-Colours.*[22] For instance, concerning the ignorance and dishonesty of colormen, the text of the book reads: "Many of the vendors of colours are not preparers of them"; Peale underlined "many" and wrote in the margin "*none.*"[23] On the book's claim that "to excel in colouring," a painter must understand the scientific nature of light, Peale added in the margin: "of no use to the painter!"[24] He had many comments about specific pigments, designating a number of them "not used" or "not necessary," or sometimes "bad: turns black" or "it fades."[25] Many of Peale's comments are about the confusing number of iron oxide red pigments available to artists, and he had strong but changeable opinions about which of these colors should be used for painting flesh.[26]

Both Rembrandt Peale and his father gave great importance to the experiments that Rembrandt carried out with pigment mixtures between 1815 and 1820. Charles Willson Peale believed that after his son gave him advice on pigment mixtures, his portraits were "in a better tone of Colouring than those he painted in an earlier time of Life," although he found it "necessary to guard against too brown a collouring."[27] Browner mixtures were clearly an important part of Rembrandt Peale's innovations, as is shown in another letter of about this time in which Charles Willson Peale asked his son to repeat advice on using the brown color asphaltum for glazing.[28] Charles Willson Peale also made a drawing of a palette for portrait painting recommended by Rembrandt Peale, in which the brightest white was tinged with yellow, which would tend to give a warmer tone to flesh mixtures. Another unusual feature of this palette is that mixed orange tints were placed prominently on the palette next to the white.[29] It was also at about this time (the summer of 1820) that Rembrandt Peale told Thomas Sully about the innovative flesh mixtures that he had developed for *The Court of Death*, which employed white mixed with yellow ochre as the lightest color. Peale called these mixtures "historic flesh," and they give the figures in *The Court of Death* and other paintings from these years a golden glow.[30]

A dozen years later Rembrandt Peale must have still believed in the importance of his innovations in pigment mixtures, because it was "a *certain use of pigments*" that he offered to sell to Neagle in 1832 for a fee.[31] Another motive for the Peale family's preoccupation with flesh colors—and Charles Willson Peale's willingness to change his technique—was a concern for permanence. In 1790 Charles Willson Peale noted that some of the shadows in his earlier portraits, painted with red lake pigments, had become too cold when the red lake faded.[32] However, the general sense of the family correspondence in the early nineteenth century is that Charles Willson Peale felt his cooler, eighteenth-century palette was unsophisticated compared to the up-to-date, warmer tones that his son recommended.

An unusual experimental pigment that fascinated Rembrandt Peale was a transparent brown pigment called "prussiate of copper." In a memorandum book

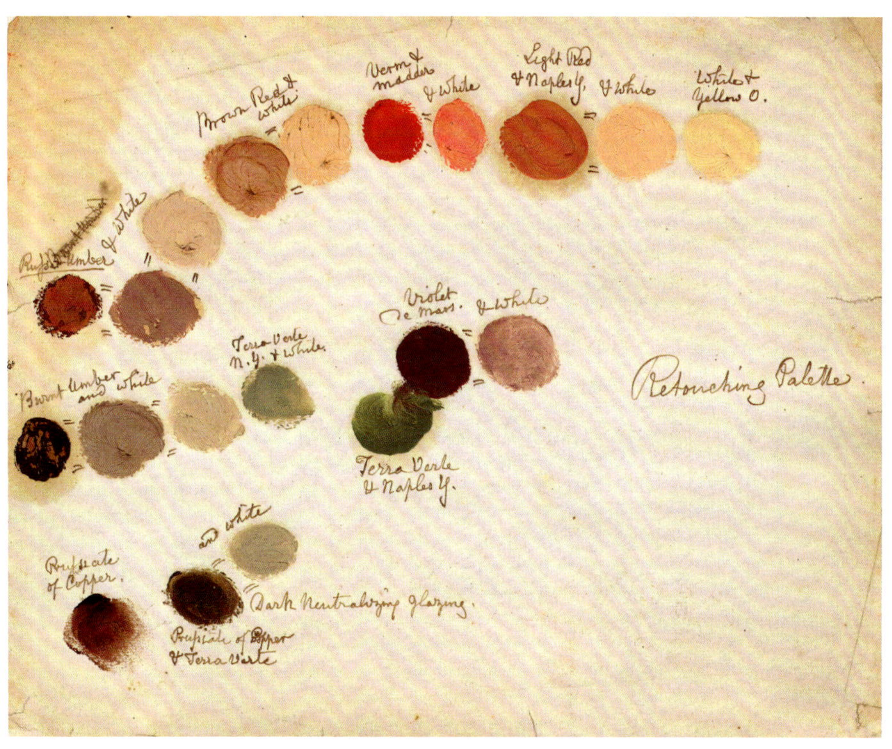

FIGURE 16

"Retouching Palette," by Rembrandt Peale, undated.

Philadelphia, American Philosophical Society, Peale Family Papers.

that Charles Willson Peale kept beginning in 1794, he called it "A beautiful & durable Brown of great richness & transparency….Rembrandt Peale says this pigment dries equally well as Prussian Blue, it is equally transparent and that it appears on tryal to stand well. Equal proportion of it with Prussian Blue makes a very deep black as a finishing color."[33]

The pigment was invented in England; it was mentioned only infrequently in nineteenth-century British and American sources,[34] but it became a favorite with Rembrandt Peale. When he compiled "Notes of the Painting Room," he recommended it for several purposes, mixing it with green or blue pigments to make a "Dark Neutralizing Glazing" for finishing flesh colors, especially for glazing around the orbit of the eye, and also mixing it with black for general toning (fig. 16). Peale wrote: "Its peculiarly harmonizing tone of Colour,—fits it to deepen any shades, or even to mark them faintly in defining the muscles in parts already painted, instead of repainting the parts—an advantage of great value."[35]

But by the time Peale finished "Notes of the Painting Room," he also knew that the permanence of prussiate of copper had been questioned by no less an authority than George Field. Peale admitted he had noticed this himself: "I have found by long exposure to the Sun, that its tints with white have become a little more gray," and he suggested combinations of more permanent pigments that might imitate it.[36] In this case experiments survive in which Peale painted out samples of dark glazing colors and exposed them to light, apparently looking for a permanent substitute for prussiate of copper.[37] Many of the samples are marked "durable," but Peale may have not found the color or the working properties of these other mixtures perfectly congenial, for he recorded that he used the fugitive—but beautiful—prussiate of copper as late as 1855 for the dark shadows in a copy of a portrait of Washington.[38]

MEGILPS AND OTHER MEDIA

Like Sully and Neagle (and William Sidney Mount as well), Rembrandt Peale made many observations about media that could be added to oil paint. Some of the notations in his copy of the *Practical Treatise* show him disagreeing with the authors on this topic. For example, under the heading "Meggellup," the text gave two different recipes for megilp, but Peale crossed out words and modified the text to show that his own preference was for neither of these two, but rather a mixture of mastic varnish and drying oil "in equal portions." In fact this is the recipe that one sees most often in America in the early nineteenth century, and it is the formula that Gilbert Stuart used.[39] Peale's annotations also show that he believed that different media might need to be added to different colors. For instance, the *Practical Treatise* said that ivory black was a bad dryer and required the admixture of sugar of lead; Peale underlined "sugar of lead" and added "especially if you add a drop or two of mastic varnish."[40] Next to the entry for asphaltum, Peale added: "Brown glaze dissolved in Sp: turp: [spirits of turpentine] used with Megellup."[41] These differing additives can help explain the varying solubilities that conservators often find in different parts of eighteenth- and nineteenth-century paintings.

"Notes of the Painting Room" shows that megilps and other added media were still an important topic for Peale in the middle of the nineteenth century. He wrote that adding megilp or varnish to certain colors, like Van Dyke brown and Cologne earth, would make a paint layer smoother and glossier.[42] But it was not only considerations of beauty or ease of handling that made Peale an advocate of adding resinous materials to oil paint—he strongly believed that adding these materials would make a painting more permanent.[43] He claimed that he had found evidence in his own practice that adding varnish to paint helped keep a paint layer from turning yellow, although he recognized that it could make it liable to damage by picture cleaners.[44] In fact conservators have found that many of Rembrandt Peale's paintings are easily soluble, presumably from varnish or other materials added to the oil paint, and many have been damaged during previous cleanings.[45]

Just as Peale's quotations from other authors in "Notes of the Painting Room" reflect the numerous written sources available at midcentury, his comments also reflect the increasing availability of ready-made art materials. He sometimes therefore took on the role of improver and perfecter rather than inventor. He told readers how to regrind and modify paint that had been ground poorly by colormen and suggested that drying oil bought in the colormen's shops would work better if the bottle was shaken slightly before use. He also told readers that the drying oil sold in colormen's shops was often not pale enough and that the painter may therefore need to make it himself.[46]

Peale did invent some things himself. Chief among these was his "magnesia vehicle," made by mixing magnesium carbonate with poppy oil (or poppy and linseed oils). Peale made great claims for this vehicle, saying it would give pigments body and keep them from running on the palette and would add transparency when needed. He recommended putting the magnesia vehicle into tubes and using it "to dilute every colour, transparent or Opaque."[47] The magnesia vehicle really does seem to be Peale's own invention; nothing like it appears in contemporary British or American sources, and it seems that Peale was still in the process of developing it as he was finishing the text of "Notes of the Painting Room" between 1850 and 1852.[48] He described painting out samples of oil mixed with various materials (including acetate of lead, calcined sulphate of zinc, and alumina) and finding that magnesium carbonate dried "the clearest and most brilliant," while some of the others discolored almost immediately.[49] Peale's magnesia vehicle is what we would nowadays call an extender—it imparts no color itself but dilutes the colors it is mixed with. The risk of using an extender might not have been apparent in Peale's tests if they lasted only a short time—the additional oil in the extender could eventually make a paint layer darken and become more yellow than a similar layer of pure paint, especially in lighter colors.[50]

Peale also invented an "improved copal vehicle." This was stimulated by J.-F.-L. Mérimée and George Field, who wrote that hard resins like copal might have been used by early painters, but that modern painters found copal difficult to use. Peale felt he had found a way to overcome these difficulties by adding a magnesia vehicle to copal, "by which it becomes attenuated, losing all viscidity, & rendered pleasant under the brush."[51] Never one to understate the advantages of his own inventions, Peale described the use of his vehicle: "The paint works in the most agreeable manner under the brush; applied without any difficulty to the previous painting, whether recent or old; and, always drying with a *lustre*, every colour remains correctly, so as to present no difficulty in the prosecution of the work from day to day."[52]

Peale also described a medium made from dammar varnish and oil that might be mixed with the copal vehicle when a more "delicate vehicle" was needed.[53] In these cases and in others, Peale sounds like a salesman. As discussed in chapter 6, he also made extravagant claims for his improvement on the atramentum of Apelles, which was made with the magnesia vehicle. Since his manuscript was never published, probably few artists were directly influenced by his ideas, although Thomas Sully thought Peale's magnesia vehicle and improved copal vehicle interesting enough that he took detailed notes about both when he read the manuscript of "Notes of the Painting Room" in 1852.[54]

OTHER OBSERVATIONS AND STUDIO TOOLS

To his credit, Rembrandt Peale was not always selling something, and he made many interesting and sensible comments on a variety of topics. For instance, he meditated on why the early Flemish painters might have wanted their paint to dry with a glossy surface.[55] He also discussed the difficult choices that artists must make between a beautiful immediate effect on the one hand and permanence on the other.[56] On whether to employ glazes, which might be ephemeral, Peale told artists to use glazes to make each painting as beautiful as possible, even if some of this beauty might be enjoyed only by the first owner.[57] Peale also made the very practical suggestion that paintings should be dried in the sun, because this was safer than adding driers to the paint, and even said he had "a Glass Room, like a Greenhouse, for the purpose."[58]

In the spirit of this inventive age, Peale also designed gadgets and other tools for painters. He invented a special roller covered with blotting paper that could be rolled across a wet ground to make the paint stand up in small points, thereby producing "a beautiful surface."[59] He designed an adjustable combination drawing desk/easel on a stand, which he said was used by students at the Pennsylvania Academy, and a palette made of zinc covered with glass, the gray color of which he described as being particularly congenial for mixing colors. He described a method for mounting a prism on a sliding rod ("as for a fire-skreen") to view a picture in reverse and thereby discover faults during the course of painting.[60]

Peale also invented a polished brass reflector he called a "Guido-Light," inspired by Guido Reni, whose paintings Peale believed showed evidence of both a primary light source and a secondary, reflected source of light (fig. 11). The curved brass surface produced "a fine *glowing* light," and it makes sense that Peale liked these golden reflections, given his interest in warm-colored pigment mixtures. He was, however, annoyed by having to keep the brass constantly polished, so he suggested making another with a silvered reflective coating.[61] He tried experiments in which he covered the window in his painting room with muslin and proposed the unorthodox theory that a south-facing window covered with muslin might provide a better light for portrait painting than the north light normally used by painters. Again, Peale's preference for warm flesh colors entered the argument: "It is said that Titian painted in such a light—his flesh tints exhibiting such a general warmth of hue."[62]

Late in his life, Peale published an article in the journal *The Crayon* in which he compared portrait painting to the new technique of photography, which some painters worried would put them out of business. Peale praised the objectivity of photography, pointing out how useful it would have been if Lewis and Clark had been able to photograph all of the new things they saw on their expedition. He also speculated on the consequences of binocular vision for a painter as opposed to the "one-eyed" view of a camera. According to Peale, certain critics claimed that photographic portraits would always be unsatisfactory because they had not passed through the medium of a sympathetic human mind. Peale, however, argued against this point and took a surprisingly objective, almost scientific view of what a portrait painter needed to do to achieve success in the era of photography (or at any time): "His success does not depend upon his *sympathy* with his sitter, but his *knowledge* of the actual *forms* which constitute expression and character, which must be represented by the learned touches of his pencil."[63]

NOTES

1   R. Peale / *Practical Treatise*. The year 1795 was a critical one for Rembrandt Peale. His father had announced his retirement from portrait painting the previous year, conceding the field to his two sons Rembrandt and Raphael, and in 1795, the seventeen-year-old Rembrandt also had the honor of painting George Washington from life.

2   Oedel 1992, 8.

3   C. W. Peale to John Isaac Hawkins, December 28, 1806 (C. W. Peale 1983–2000, vol. 2, pt. 2, p. 996); Hevner 1991, 109.

4   Ward 2004, 54–56; C. W. Peale 1983–2000, 1:494, 4:167; see also Bellion 2001.

5   C. W. Peale 1983–2000, 4:490.

6   On the interesting and convoluted history of these instruments, see R. Peale 1857b; Hindle 1982, 151–53; Benes 1995, 138; Miles 1995.

7   C. W. Peale 1983–2000, 3:457–58; Ward 2004, 55–56, 205n16; C. W. Peale 1983–2000, 4: 587.

After Gilbert Stuart's death in 1828, members of the Peale family bought his boxed set of mechanical drawing instruments from his widow (D. Evans 1999, 148n17).

8   Sully Sketchbook, leaf 12.

9   Prime 1875, 400–408.

10   Staiti 1989, 80.

11   Dunlap 1834, 2:359.

12   Westcott 1886, 1267–68.

13   Lipman 1980, 69–71.

14   Rembrandt Peale to the president of the Institute of France: "Since my early departure for America will deprive me of the advantages of the ensuing exposition at the saloon [sic] of the Louvre, I can do no more than thus give a hasty view of the subject to the Institute. If they find it worthy of their approbation it will go far to repay me the labour it has cost, before I shall be permitted to make the mode of procedure known" (R. Peale 1811, 15). Peale's convoluted syntax defies analysis, but it seems he was fishing for something more than simply the approbation of the institute.

15   Neagle "Hints" [September 1832].

16   C.W. Peale to Rembrandt Peale, January 8, 1818 (C.W. Peale 1983–2000, 3:558).

17   Dunlap 1834, 1:141.

18   C.W. Peale 1983–2000, 5:369–70. The French-born chemist was Silvain Godon. On the Peales and chrome yellow, see also chapter 11.

19   See Chapters 2, 3, and Carlyle 2001, 106.

It is somewhat surprising to see how factorylike some of the Peale family's enterprises were. Records of the artistic production of Rubens Peale and his family survive from the 1850s, showing that they assigned numbers to their still-life paintings, copying and making variations on previous designs; often several family members worked on a single painting over a period of weeks, one person "dead-coloring"(painting the underlayers) and another finishing (see Rubens Peale "Journal," 1855–57, AAA, microfilm roll D10, frames 1881–2259).

20   There are manuscripts of "Notes of the Painting Room" at the National Academy of Design and at the Historical Society of Pennsylvania. The HSP copy is clearly the final version, according to Carol Hevner (see Hevner Annotation, comparison of texts, 2).

Peale's manuscript was probably completed shortly prior to 1852, because a campaign to publish it was launched in June of that year (Miller 1992, 305n30). Peale's "Introduction and Prospectus" for the book (containing testimonials from Sully and Asher B. Durand) is published in Parker 1986. The manuscript must have been completed after the publication of Burnet 1850, which is cited. But Peale implied on one occasion that some of its content was written much earlier, saying in 1857: "Many years before the invention of Daguerre, in my 'Notes of the Painting Room,' I had written the following article" (R. Peale 1857a, 45).

21   R. Peale "Notes," 23.

22   Peale's copy of this 1795 book is held by the Winterthur Library, Joseph Downs Collection of Manuscripts and Printed Ephemera (cited here as R. Peale / *Practical Treatise*). It is impossible to date his annotations precisely, but some that seem early are done in ink and employ the old-fashioned long "s," while later notations done in pencil do not use the long "s," and some of the latter appear to mark quotations that were used in "Notes of the Painting Room."

Peale sometimes changed his mind, correcting an annotation in ink with one in pencil, confirming that the pencil annotations were done later.

23   R. Peale / *Practical Treatise*, 25–26. Of course, by the 1840s John Ridner made Peale's statement untrue (see Chapter 11).

24   Ibid., 1.

25   Ibid., 79–80 (and many comments on following pages).

26   In one place, the text reads: "Ivory-black and a little Indian red make the best general shadow-color that can be" (ibid., 78). Peale apparently changed his mind about this—in his earlier (ink) annotations he crossed out "Indian" and added "oker" after red and said in the margin "or Roman red." But in the later (pencil) annotations he crossed out "or Roman red," crossed out "oker," and underlined Ivory black and a little Indian red, as if he finally decided that the printed text was correct. On p. 80 he crossed out "Indian" and substituted "light" red, but later in pencil he underlined Indian red, as if he had reverted to a preference for that pigment.

27 C.W. Peale 1983–2000, 5:399–400 (quoting from C.W. Peale's *Autobiography*); C.W. Peale to Rembrandt Peale, January 8, 1818 (C.W. Peale 1983–2000, 3:557). On Rembrandt Peale's influence on his father, see Hevner 1991.

28 C.W. Peale to Rembrandt Peale, December 16, 1819 (C.W. Peale 1983–2000, 3:781).

29 C.W. Peale to Raphaelle Peale, June 25, 1820 (ibid., 3:828).

30 Rembrandt Peale to Thomas Sully, July 4, 1820 (ibid., 3:828). See also Mayer and Myers 1996, 11, fig. 1. The authors cleaned *The Court of Death* (1820, Detroit Institute of Arts) in 1994–95; although some discolored varnish remains because of the solubility of the paint, the flesh colors themselves have a distinctly warm tonality. Several palette settings from late in Peale's life are preserved in Philadelphia at the American Philosophical Society (R. Peale Palettes). Most of these did not have any pure white, but the one he recommended to his niece Mary Jane Peale in 1850–51 as "the most simple palette" did (see also M.J. Peale "Oil Painting").

31 Neagle "Hints" [September 1832].

32 C.W. Peale 1983–2000, 1:104n1, 592. Fading of red lakes was not noted when seven paintings by C.W. Peale painted between 1772 and 1780 were analyzed (Ashworth, Lignelli, and Butler 1989). C.W. Peale also had problems with the yellow pigment turbith mineral turning dark (Stoner, Schmiegel, and Carlson 1979).

33 C.W. Peale Memorandum Book, 46.

34 The invention was claimed by Charles Hatchett in 1802, but in 1803 a Mr. Hume wrote that he had been supplying painters with the pigment for about ten years (Hatchett 1802; Hume 1803); see also Carlyle 2001, 487; Osborn 1845, 53.

35 R. Peale "Notes," 42, 123–25.

36 Ibid., 108; Field 1835, 146; Field 1841, 261. Peale confused things slightly by saying that prussiate of copper was "sometimes called Prussian brown." Modern authorities think of these as two different pigments (see Carlyle 2001, 487–88).

37 R. Peale Miscellaneous, undated sheet beginning with "Comparative view of blacks & neutral tints…"

38 R. Peale Palettes. Several palettes describe the pigments used in some of Rembrandt Peale's paintings. Prussiate of copper was also included in the pigment mixtures he recommended to Mary Jane Peale about 1858 or shortly thereafter: "Prussiate of copper and black to darken eyelash" (Rembrandt Peale to Mary Jane Peale, recorded in M.J. Peale's "Oil Painting").

39 R. Peale/*Practical Treatise*, 46. See also chapter 4.

40 Ibid., 42.

41 Ibid., 29.

42 R. Peale "Notes," 49.

43 Ibid., 117 and 6 (where he agreed with Eastlake 1847). Rembrandt Peale disagreed with Osborn 1845, which criticized Reynolds's experiments with media. Peale replied: "Reynolds failed in his Colours, by using *Orpiment* & other fallacious pigments—not by reason of his *Vehicles*, which, on the contrary, often enabled him, as it had Titian, Corregio & Rubens, to produce the most beautiful effects—effects that could not otherwise be produced." (R. Peale "Notes," 152–53).

44 Ibid., 80.

45 This is true, for example, of *The Court of Death* (Mayer and Myers 1996).

46 R. Peale "Notes," 41, 81–82, 57.

47 Ibid., 84.

48 Ibid., 45, 84–86, 180–81. Evidence that Peale was still in the process of developing his magnesia vehicle is that on p. 83 he extolled the virtues of a hydrated alumina vehicle for exactly the same purposes, adding that magnesia also "may be employed"; as the text progressed he no longer mentioned alumina but stated that tests proved magnesia to be the best.

49 Ibid., 84–85.

50 Because Peale's magnesia vehicle was made with oil rather than varnish, at least it would not put a painting at greater risk of damage when being cleaned.

51 R. Peale "Notes," 91. Peale clearly changed his mind about copal over the course of his career. In his earlier annotations of his copy of the 1795 *Practical Treatise*, he wrote next to copal "use none" in ink, but in his later annotations in pencil (which are probably closer in date to "Notes of the Painting Room"), he crossed out the comment "use none" (R. Peale/*Practical Treatise*, 35).

52 R. Peale "Notes," 91–92.

53   Ibid., 96–97.

54   Sully "Hints," AAA, microfilm roll N18, frames 224–28 (June 22, 1852).

55   R. Peale "Notes," 168. He believed it was chiefly "that they might always see the exact state of their painting in its progress, in order correctly to adapt each new application of paint to the condition of what had previously been done, without loss of time."

56   Ibid., 168–69.

57   Ibid., 29–31, 44, 185.

58   Ibid., 175.

59   Ibid., 164.

60   Ibid., 56–57.

61   Ibid., 53–54. Around the same time, William Sidney Mount also experimented with a warm secondary light, achieved by a second window in his studio covered with an orange curtain (Mount's diary, January 25, 1847 [cited in Frankenstein 1975, 171]).

62   R. Peale "Notes," 52–53.

63   R. Peale 1857a, 44–45.

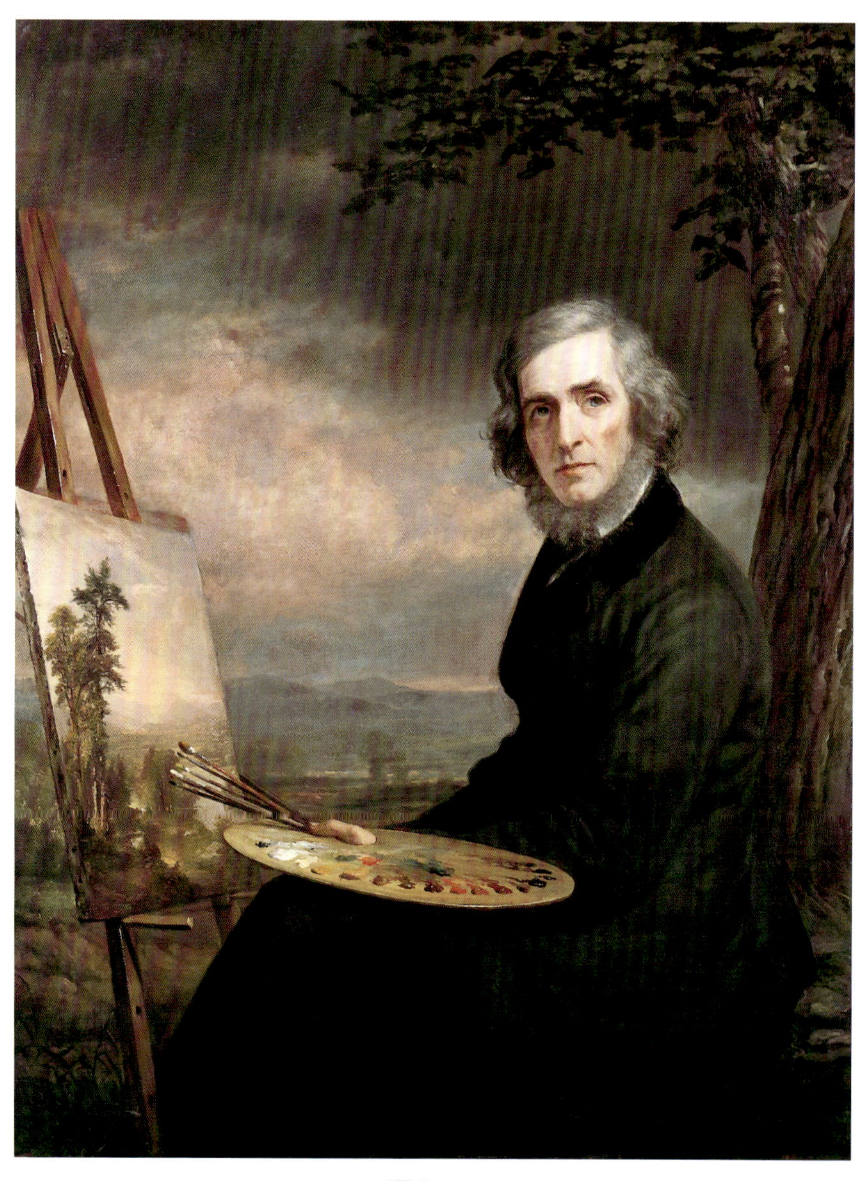

Daniel Huntington (American, 1816–1906), detail of *Portrait of Asher B. Durand*, 1857.
Oil on canvas, 142.5 × 111.8 cm (56⅛ × 44 in.). New York, The Century Association, 1864.8.

CHAPTER 11
STORE-BOUGHT SUPPLIES AND NEW MATERIALS
IN THE 1830S, 1840S, AND 1850S

ONE OF THE MOST IMPORTANT DEVELOPMENTS in the decades leading up to the middle of the nineteenth century was the growth of the trade of colorman, which would eventually permit most artists to use store-bought supplies rather than applying their own grounds and mixing up their own paint, media, and varnishes. This was also a time when many new materials, of both European and American origin, were introduced.

These developments were made possible by a noticeable growth of interest in the fine arts in America, especially in New York. The New York colorman John P. Ridner wrote in 1850 of the "unprecedented advances in a due appreciation of the arts of design within the last few years; as the number of persons now interested in them, are as a thousand to one, compared with those who but a short period before gave the subject a thought."[1] In the preface to his 1845 book on technique, Laughton Osborn despaired that there would be a time when a book like his, by an American author, would "find ten readers," bemoaning that such a day "will dawn over my unnoticed grave."[2] Osborn in fact lived to see five reprintings of his book in the 1850s and 1860s,[3] proof that more Americans than ever were seeking information about painting methods.

ART SUPPLIERS IN NEW YORK AND ELSEWHERE

The growth of New York as an art center meant that prepared canvases, varnishes, and preground paint were available there earlier than in other American cities. When John Cranch moved from New York to Cincinnati in 1840, he described how he had become accustomed to buying supplies from the New York colorman Edward Dechaux: "One thing I miss here is Dechaux's establishment—very much indeed. I have to boil my own oil, make my varnish, and I think I shall have to prepare my own canvasses. I have to grind my paints which is a great bore. I greatly miss old New York."[4]

Making paint (done by grinding pigments and oil repeatedly with a muller or other tool on a stone surface to blend them thoroughly) was such a tedious, time-consuming, and messy job that many artists were happy to purchase paint rather than make it themselves.[5] Dechaux, a French immigrant, began as a brush maker, establishing the firm of Dechaux and Parmentier in 1830, but soon he was importing and manufacturing many different artists' materials. His company was not only one of the first, but remained among the most prominent suppliers in New York from the 1830s to the 1860s. Canvases prepared and labeled by Dechaux (and by his son, after Dechaux returned to France in the 1850s) are more commonly found today than those of any other nineteenth-century American colorman.[6] Laughton Osborn gave an example of the great variety of materials that Dechaux made available to American artists (and the good use that Dechaux made of his French connections) when he wrote that four different varieties of Naples yellow, "all of French manufacture," were sold by Dechaux in 1845.[7]

The arts in New York were greatly enriched at this time by dealers, entrepreneurs, and colormen from France and Germany.[8] Goupil & Company of Paris set up a New York branch and began selling art materials in 1851,[9] and after their agent, William Schaus, left the firm in 1852, he also imported and sold—as he claimed—the finest artists' materials from London and Paris.[10] In 1853, William Sidney Mount ventured to give Schaus his opinion on the various British products: "Roberson's colors, I purchased of you, are first rate. I am delighted with them….Winsor & Newton colors I have been using. G. Rowney & Co. I believe mix Sugar of Lead with their vandyke brown & black to make them dry."[11]

In the late 1840s the following announcement appeared in a New York newspaper: "An Artists' Exchange has been established in the front part of the Art-Union building by Mr. John P. Ridner—This gentleman's knowledge of all matters connected with the Fine Arts, is of a high order, and the establishment, he has just founded, will undoubtedly be extensively patronized by the artists of the country."[12] Ridner not only sold art materials, he manufactured pigments himself and in 1850 wrote *The Artist's Chromatic Hand-book*, which gives many insights into the pigments and other painting materials available in America during this period. His book shows a deep knowledge of art materials, as well as familiarity with George Field's writings. Ridner cemented his position in the New York art establishment by serving as corresponding secretary for the Art-Union.[13]

A pattern of gradual growth can be seen in the colorman's trade outside New York as the years advanced toward midcentury. John Neagle bought supplies in Philadelphia from a variety of sources in the 1830s, only one of whom can be identified from city directories as a colorman—James W. Williams, who began as a coach, sign, and ornamental painter in the 1820s but by 1835 was advertising an "artists' emporium and repository." The others Neagle bought from may have been general merchants. A little later, in the 1840s, Neagle bought paint and canvas from Ashton & Browning, who began advertising as colormen in 1838,[14] but he continued to buy paints from another man who never advertised as a colorman but was a coach maker.[15]

Coach makers, who prided themselves on producing smooth, flawless surfaces, were as fussy about their paints and varnishes as fine artists, and there were connections between the two professions throughout the first half of the nineteenth century. (John Neagle, James Frothingham, and William Jewett all began their careers painting coaches.) Philadelphia was the home of C. Schrack & Company, which began around 1815–20 as a coach-building business, but which by the middle of the nineteenth century was manufacturing paint and varnish on a large scale and selling supplies to artists, house painters, and coach painters. The Schrack Company account books show them selling wholesale as well as retail, and an intriguing entry from 1848 documents them selling canvas to Dechaux, the New York colorman.[16] C. Schrack & Company appears to have made use of their German connections when they began to sell the new German product dammar beginning around 1849 (see below).[17]

The gradual growth of the profession of colorman in other American cities can also be followed through the 1830s, 1840s, and 1850s. In Boston, Washington Allston was a catalyst in this development: his friend Elizabeth Palmer Peabody opened a bookstore in 1835 and on Allston's recommendation carried art supplies. Peabody became New England's only importer of the products of the London colorman Thomas Brown,[18] who had a high reputation in America—Gilbert Stuart, John Trumbull, and Thomas Sully all used his products.[19] In Baltimore, the trade of colorman seems to have developed in the 1850s, when for the first time an advertiser in the Baltimore city directory, William Minifie, described himself as specifically selling artists' materials (as opposed to simply paint and oil).[20] (Colormen sometimes confused matters by selling materials made by others; about 1850, a Baltimore paint and oil dealer applied his own stamp to a canvas prepared and stamped by Edward Dechaux of New York, while for their part, New York colormen sometimes restamped canvases imported from England.[21])

In Norwich, Connecticut, the firm of Carroll & Crosby exemplifies the kind of store in a small city that did not deal in artists' supplies exclusively, but which sold many products that artists would have found useful. Records of this company survive from 1843 to 1845. Initially, it seems that the partners were setting up as druggists, buying bottles, vials, and jugs, and then castor oil, ink, spearmint oil, tooth powder, lavender, and paregoric. But soon they were carrying a wide range of pigments, turpentine, Canada balsam, sugar of lead, gilding supplies, East India copal, white rosin, and various varnishes ("cheap," coach, Japan, furniture, and mastic). Many of these supplies could have been intended for house painters, decorative painters, and other craftsmen, but their inventory of palette knives, paintbrushes as small as size 0000, and a "Portrait Painter's brush" prove that the firm counted fine artists among their clientele.[22]

In still smaller towns, itinerant painters sometimes supplied artists' materials. The portraitist Joseph Whiting Stock, who traveled across rural New England

and New York, advertised in Goshen, New York, in 1853 that in addition to painting portraits he sold artist's colors, brushes, and canvases.[23] When Stock died a year and a half later, his estate listed modest amounts of supplies in excess of what he would have needed himself: fifty-four unused tubes of paint (in addition to forty-six partly used ones), twenty-four unused brushes (plus sixty-five used ones), eleven tin boxes, twenty-seven papers containing dry pigments, and a "small roll" of canvas.[24]

By the middle of the nineteenth century one can also track the availability of artists' supplies through printed catalogues. Because artists were keeping fewer manuscript notebooks about painting materials, catalogues are (along with printed books) important tools for researchers into the methods of this period. As in the case of Sears, Roebuck & Company in later decades, catalogues made it much easier for people in the provinces to learn about and purchase products that had previously been available only in larger cities. A Dechaux catalogue of ca. 1836–40 appears to be the earliest surviving American colorman's catalogue.[25] After the middle of the century, the long reach of the London firm of Winsor & Newton became more noticeable, and in fact many post-1850 American colormen's catalogues were simply reprintings of Winsor & Newton's British catalogues with prices in dollars instead of pounds, shillings, and pence. Allowing American companies to reprint their attractive illustrated catalogues might have given Winsor & Newton a competitive advantage—in the 1850s, Schaus was importing exclusively Roberson's paints, but by the 1860s, he had switched to selling exclusively Winsor & Newton's.[26] A different approach was taken by Goupil & Company, which in the 1857 catalogue of their New York branch sold oil paints labeled with Goupil's name that were presumably imported from France.[27] Eventually, some of these firms would become more comprehensive. Tiemann & Company of New York, in a catalogue of about 1863, sold tube colors under their own name (which they said were the best), but they also sold Winsor & Newton, Rowney, Goupil & Company, and a brand of tube colors called simply "French."[28]

SUPPORTS

The first half of the nineteenth century appears to have been a transitional time in the use of wood panels in America. Gilbert Stuart often painted on wood, and believed, somewhat surprisingly, that mahogany panels lasted better than canvas in the American climate, even when used for large paintings (see chapter 4). The British author W. Sarsfield Taylor had a similar high opinion of wood as a support in 1839, when he wrote: "Panels are always preferable to canvasses, but cannot now be procured of large dimensions, and are much dearer than primed cloths."[29]

Laughton Osborn wrote in 1845 that prepared wood panels were available, with a ground already applied, "at all the colorshops."[30] But Osborn had a somewhat different view of the longevity of wood panels; he noted "the alternate giving and contracting to which by their nature they are subject" and said they were rarely used for pictures larger than "cabinet-size" (quite small). Osborn also described a preference for canvas in America at that time, and a corresponding dislike of wooden panels, saying, "You will hear an ignorant person invariably express contempt for a modern picture done on wood."[31] It is difficult to know why there would be a prejudice against wood in America in 1845 while there was none in England in 1839. It may be that American city dwellers found that wood panels had an unfortunate association with "folk" portraitists. Itinerant portrait painters had been wandering the provincial parts of America in increasing numbers during the first half of the nineteenth century, satisfying the needs of farmers and tradesmen to have themselves and their families immortalized, and these artists frequently found it easier to have a panel made by a local carpenter than to procure a stretched canvas.[32]

In spite of this alleged prejudice, Americans continued to paint on a variety of different kinds of wood panels. In 1842 William Sidney Mount described paintings done on both mahogany and "white wood";[33] the latter could mean one of several locally obtained woods having a light color and clear grain. Artists themselves may have not known exactly what type of wood they were using, as shown by John Neagle, at about this time, struggling to remember the proper name of the wood from the Boston area (basswood, baywood, or holly) used by Gilbert Stuart. In 1850–52 Rembrandt Peale enumerated the advantages and disadvantages of various kinds of wood for use in painting,[34] as Sully and Neagle had earlier in the century,[35] although there was no unanimity of opinion among the three.

An entirely new range of supports was developed at this time in response to the needs of landscape painters. The beginnings of this trend can be seen as early as 1836, when Thomas Cole (at his country house in Catskill) asked Asher B. Durand (in New York) to "learn about the new pasteboards" and thanked Durand for sending the pasteboards a month later.[36] "Pasteboard" was a general term for sheets of paper pasted together to make a stiff, lightweight board, similar to what would now be called cardboard. It is not clear whether these early pasteboards were specially prepared with a ground or not.[37] Osborn used the term in 1845, saying that pasteboards "are used by landscape-painters in studies from nature, because of their portability," although he warned that they were apt to warp and should be used only for "sketches and experiments."[38] Light, stiff boards were much easier to transport than stretched canvas (which was easily dented or punctured) when hiking in the country and sketching *en plein air*. Cole and Durand clearly used the pasteboards for outdoor sketching: in 1837 they corresponded about a painting expedition, and Cole confirmed his preparedness for the trip by itemizing his bladders of paint and other portable supplies, adding, "Pasteboards I have."[39]

Rembrandt Peale, like Osborn, warned that pasteboards were "seldom flat, & are liable to be bruised at the corners."[40] But in 1850–52 Peale noted the recent appearance of "a superior article" imported from England: "It is expensive &

heavy—yet preferable to everything else for small pictures."[41] This almost certainly refers to "Academy board"(or a slightly thicker version known as "millboard"), which was made from dense cardboard with a ground on both the front and back. As Peale implied, the British were at the forefront of this development. Winsor & Newton advertised Academy board and millboard in Britain by about 1835, but the first American references appear to date from the 1850s.[42]

Another new product was canvas board, made by gluing a piece of fabric to a stiff board. Americans seem to have taken a leading role in experimenting with canvas board during the first half of the nineteenth century. John Vanderlyn used canvas board on at least one occasion as early as the 1830s.[43] In 1850–52 Rembrandt Peale implied that he had been making his own canvas boards for many years: "For pictures of a moderate size I have used strong smooth Pasteboard, two thicknesses glued together, with fine Muslin pasted on both sides & painted in the manner of Canvas. They neither expand nor contract; and I have never found the Pictures painted on them, after the lapse of many years, to be at all cracked."[44] Peale painted a 24-by-20-inch portrait of Thomas Sully in 1859 on a similar kind of canvas board, an appropriate material for a collaboration between two of the great American experimenters.[45]

"Oil sketching paper" or "oiled paper," a strong sheet of paper sized and coated with paint, was another alternative for sketching that appeared in America by about 1836–40, somewhat earlier than Academy board or millboard.[46] William Sidney Mount, when he made a note in his diary in 1853 that he should paint outdoors more often, recalled that three years earlier "I painted landscapes in the open air—one sitting each—principally on prepared oiled paper."[47] Oil sketching paper, being less stiff than Academy board or millboard, needed to be fastened to a hard surface, such as a drawing board or the lid of a painting box, while sketching[48] and also required adroit arrangement to keep the sketches from being smeared after they were completed. Charles Lanman wrote that when painting outdoors, he "preferred oiled paper to canvass, for its convenience," adding that "my painting box is so arranged that I can carry four wet sketches at one time."[49]

Another clever development that colormen began to advertise in the 1840s and 1850s was the solid sketching block. A stack of sheets of paper (specially prepared for oil painting) was glued together at the edges, and after a sketch was completed, the top sheet could be separated from the block by running a knife around the edge.[50] This circumvented the need to pin a sheet of paper to a hard surface while painting, although the problem of transporting the wet sketches still remained.[51] Albert Bierstadt may possibly have used solid sketching blocks for some of the many oil studies on paper that he did while traveling in Europe and in the American West.[52]

Oil sketches on paper were often mounted at a later time onto boards or onto stretched canvases, which made them suitable for more formal presentation in a frame.[53] By the middle of the nineteenth century the small *plein-air* sketch had become a legitimate subject for public exhibition, especially after Asher B. Durand succeeded Samuel F. B. Morse as president of the National Academy of Design in 1845 and established a "sketch room" for displaying informal studies at Academy exhibitions.[54] The materials for sketching outdoors, which had initially been condemned as ephemeral and suitable only for experiments, therefore took on an importance far greater than they had when sketches were simply notations by artists for their own private use.

At the same time that small sketches were being displayed with increasing frequency, some artists were painting canvases that were larger than ever. In 1844, after hearing that several painters were working on large landscape paintings, William Sidney Mount wrote: "I expect there will be [a] number of ten acre pictures in the next exhibition."[55] Many of the most famous landscape paintings of the mid-nineteenth century by Frederic Church, Bierstadt, and others were "ten-footers"—ten feet wide. In 1848, in connection with a discussion of panoramas, Mount said that canvas could be bought twelve feet wide,[56] and on another occasion at about this time he wrote that canvas was available "up to 24 feet wide and 10 yards long."[57] These tremendous yardages might seem impractical, except that, as Mount noted, the panorama remained a popular art form at midcentury.[58]

Stretchers

Osborn pointed out that the old-fashioned strainer with fixed corners was "entirely out of date" by 1845, replaced by the keyable *chassis à clefs* (or stretching frame).[59] Osborn generally used the terms "stretching frame" or "frame" for a keyable stretcher, but in one case offered as a synonym the word "*stretchers*" (in italics, as if it were an unfamiliar term).[60] This may have been the first appearance of the term "stretcher" in print in English; the earliest usage of the word previously noted was in England in 1847, and in America in 1849.[61] The great advantage of a keyable stretcher was that if a canvas became slack or developed distortions in its corners, it could be tightened up again by tapping the keys at the corners of the stretcher. The device was known in France by the 1750s,[62] but nearly a century later Osborn felt he had to explain to his American audience how the keyable stretcher worked. Whether for reasons of cost or availability, many Americans, especially those working outside of major urban centers in the 1820s and 1830s, and even later, had continued to stretch their paintings on nonkeyable strainers.

An improvement over ordinary stretchers that may have been first made in America was the "panel stretcher" (or "blind stretcher," as it became known in Britain). This featured pieces of wood mortised between the stretcher-members to make a flat surface behind the stretched canvas. The solid wood behind the canvas protected it from blows from the reverse. (Modern conservators have found that paintings on such stretchers are often very well preserved, because the canvas is protected from humidity changes by the thickness of the wood.[63]) Panel stretchers required more material and skilled joinery and presumably were more expensive than ordinary stretchers, but artists must have appreciated their advantages. John Trumbull used panel stretchers by the 1830s—if not earlier—to restretch a number of his paintings that had been shipped back from England.[64] New York colormen Parker & Clover may have been the first to manufacture panel stretchers, and Thomas Cole, who was known to have purchased supplies at their shop, was probably among the first artists to use them (by 1836, and perhaps as early as 1833).[65] Cole's pupil Frederic Church also used panel stretchers by the 1850s, if not earlier, as did Asher B. Durand.[66]

GROUNDS

By the middle of the nineteenth century even Thomas Sully, John Neagle, and Rembrandt Peale, who had been applying their own grounds (with many experimental variations) for decades, can be documented to have bought prepared or "pre-primed" canvases from suppliers in New York and Philadelphia.[67] The convenience of buying a canvas that was ready to use must have been irresistible, but whether American artists chose to use prepared canvases or make their own depended greatly upon the time, the place, and the painter's ability to pay. For instance, the young Thomas Cole applied his own grounds when he was a beginning painter in Steubenville, Ohio, in 1823.[68] In 1828, two years after arriving in New York, he was still applying his own grounds, although now he was using a spatula or palette knife, rather than a brush, to produce a smooth surface.[69] But by 1831, Cole used prepared canvases when traveling in Italy.[70]

Back in America, in 1836, Cole bought prepared canvases from the New York colorman Edward Dechaux. Cole had ordered the canvases through the agency of Asher B. Durand, and Cole soon complained to Durand: "I am afraid they will not be very durable ones for it appears to me that the oil has penetrated through the cloth and you know that some sort of size is generally used to prevent that as linseed oil rots canvas in a very short time.…Will you when you see Dechaux, ask him if it is oil that is seen on the back of the canvas for I am almost afraid to work upon it."[71]

Cole must have not been satisfied with Dechaux's explanation, for he complained further to Durand: "Mr. Dechaux is a Quirkmaster. It matters little whether it is oil or not that made the canvass rotten. The piece I showed you I had just cut from a piece that you took back. I had stretched it and it was too long by an inch for the strainer and cut the superfluous piece off and by that means found out its rottenness and if he will let you try the cut piece I think you will be satisfied *though he will not*."[72]

Cole must have believed he was seeing confirmation of the widely held belief that oil would rot a canvas if it were allowed to come in contact with it.[73] For this reason a glue-size layer was often applied to the canvas to prevent oil from touching the fabric directly. Back in 1811 Rembrandt Peale had outlined other advantages and disadvantages of using a size layer, while at the same time acknowledging that a size layer was not universally used at that time: "Cloths prepared for oil-painting are heavy from the quantity of white-lead spread on them, especially when they are prepared as at present without size; besides which the oil gradually rots the linen. On the other hand when the linen is sized, although less weight of paint is employed and the linen does not rot, yet the picture is liable to crack and even to fall off in scales, especially when affected by alternate moisture and heat."[74]

Artists were aware of this dilemma. Neagle believed that oil would rot canvas,[75] and Charles Bird King and Sully thought that adding soap to a ground would "neutralize" the oil, making the use of a size layer unnecessary.[76] Neagle's and Sully's ground recipes containing nonoily materials such as starch and Venice turpentine were probably designed in part to avoid the problem of oil rotting the canvas (although the theory that the old masters used starch in their grounds may also have been an incentive).[77]

The commercial advantage for colormen to use a size layer was that size was cheaper than oil paint, and as Rembrandt Peale pointed out, less oil paint would be required. It has been suggested that Cole's problem with Dechaux may have resulted from Dechaux's cutting corners or saving time by using distemper (glue-based) paint instead of oil paint and then coating it with oil (as was recommended in a treatise by Mérimée).[78]

One consequence of Cole's dispute with Dechaux was that Cole seems to have never bought canvases from him again.[79] Another result is hinted at in a broadside found in Cole's papers announcing that one P. Caffe had opened a rival shop:

> a large establishment in the City for the purpose of manufacturing and preparing canvasses for oil paintings.…By unremitting exertions and numerous experiments, during four years that I had alone the charge of this particular branch of the business, at Mr. E. Dechaux's, of New-York, I flatter myself that I have succeeded in reducing this article, so important to the historical, portrait, and landscape painter, to a degree of perfection yet unrivalled, [h]aving discovered an entirely new process, of which I am the sole inventor, rendering thereby an equality and superiority of surface, at the same time completely divested of all pernicious ingredients (such as litharge) too frequently the cause of destroying the beauty of the artist's productions.[80]

Caffe took wholesale and retail orders from any part of the United States. Like Dechaux, Caffe appears to have been French. The broadside's appearance less than one year after the dispute with Cole hints that his dissatisfaction or that of others could have precipitated Caffe's departure, while the claim that his new process was free from "pernicious ingredients" shows that Caffe believed American artists cared a great deal about the permanence of their paintings.

Other problems plagued artists who used commercially applied grounds in the mid-nineteenth century. Water-soluble grounds, made with glue rather than oil as a binder, tended to be brittle (as well as liable to damage during subsequent conservation treatment).[81] Some commercially applied grounds consisted of mixtures of chalk (calcium carbonate) and white lead in a two-layered system, the upper layer containing a higher percentage of white lead. This would have had an economic benefit for the colorman, for although chalk was less opaque and made a less satisfactory surface, it was cheaper than white lead.[82] Artists' concerns that commercial firms were always tempted to use cheaper (or more brittle) materials may explain the protestations of Winsor & Newton in 1863 that their canvas was carefully prepared "to preclude the possibility of its peeling up or becoming detached in any way." Their further claim that their canvas was "warranted to keep any length of time, and in any climate without cracking" seems a response to artists like Neagle who worried that British prepared canvas was not suited to the American climate.[83]

An unfortunate result of defectively prepared canvases at midcentury is the phenomenon that has come to be called "variable translucency" (formerly called "ground staining"). This afflicts many American paintings, especially landscapes of the Hudson River school, including paintings by Thomas Cole, Frederic Church, Fitz Henry Lane, John Frederick Kensett, Jasper Francis Cropsey, Martin Johnson Heade, and Sanford Gifford. Dark streaks follow the lines of fabric threads, often in the vertical direction; the streaks can sometimes be quite subtle and may be most noticeable in uniformly painted areas such as skies or in thinly painted, light-colored areas.[84] The problem is connected to the chemical alteration of lead-containing components in the ground or paint.[85] The reason that variable translucency develops in some paintings and not others remains elusive, although the addition of lead acetate (sugar of lead) as a drier has been suggested.[86] Church blamed the "obnoxious" streaks that developed on his *Niagara* on a Winsor & Newton "Roman" prepared canvas.[87]

PAINT

Added Media and Unusual Media

Several new trends in media can be identified in the years leading up to the middle of the nineteenth century. By midcentury, many painters were becoming more interested in which store-bought media were best, rather than experimenting with media they could make themselves. Another trend is that some artists became dead set against megilp as an additive to oil paint. A passage from John P. Ridner in 1850 echoes Sully's comment from about the same time on the vain "delusion" of artists who sought the ideal megilp (chapter 8):

Macgilp: The use of resinous substances with oil vehicles date from the earliest history of oil painting, but was not adopted generally by the old artists, which accounts for the preservation of their works. About the end of the last century, the compound known by the above appellation got into vogue in Great Britain, and was puffed off as a great discovery; but, the premature decay of the works on which it was employed has proved its inutility, time having the effect of decomposing or separating the drying oil and mastic varnish of which it is composed, producing darkness and opacity, and disposing it to crumble off. Sir Joshua Reynolds and other contemporary artists were much addicted to the use of this nostrum, as the ruinous changes which many of their works have undergone, fully testifies. Another equally objectionable mixture called *gumtion*, composed of raw oil, mastic varnish, and sugar of lead, attained some celebrity in England about the same time.[88]

Ironically, given that megilp was being criticized by some authorities, it was easier to obtain than ever before. Osborn pointed out in 1845 that ready-made megilp "is for sale at the colorshops."[89] When paint began to be sold in collapsible tubes, the jellylike megilp was also sold in this form, and late in his career, Mount once referred to using megilp "out of the tube."[90]

But as soon as such commercially made products became available, artists began to complain about them. In the 1850s Mount criticized the megilp containing sugar of lead that was "sold by some vendors."[91] In the same decade, Jasper Francis Cropsey complained about the oil in Winsor & Newton tube paints, which he thought was too "fat," or "gummy." He also had trouble with Winsor & Newton's "copal megilp."[92]

Copal, whose qualities had been praised by both J.-F.-L. Mérimée and George Field in the 1830s, was on the upswing as a painting medium in America. The 1840s seemed to mark the peak of interest in copal on the part of both Sully and Mount (see chapters 8 and 13). Ridner followed his stinging criticism of megilp and gumtion in 1850 with the suggestion that a copal medium might make a better substitute.[93] But the media that artists used in this period remained varied in the extreme. For instance, both Sully and Mount noted that in the late 1840s and early 1850s Nathaniel Jocelyn used a mixture of drying oil, turpentine, copaiva balsam, and copal as a painting medium, and in 1859 Asher B. Durand used Canada balsam and turpentine in equal parts.[94] By the 1850s, some writers were beginning to criticize all added media, as the American John Chapman did in 1857 when he labeled the addition of media to oil paint "quackery:"

The consistency of colors, as they are generally sold, in tubes or bladders, is about as they should be employed, and the fault, so common to beginners, especially with such as have dabbled a little in watercolors—a propensity to render them more fluid, by the addition of more oil—should be avoided. This habit of quackery with the colors often arises from a disposition to seek sources of difficulty in their management anywhere rather than in our own weakness; and when they do not work, under the brush, as we desire, or imagine they should do, they are dosed with oil, spirits of turpentine, megilp, varnish, and one vehicle or another, into a deplorable state.[95]

In this period various unusual media continued to be discussed by American painters. When Sully was in London in 1838, he seemed shocked that J. M. W. Turner interlayered watercolors with his oil paints,[96] but a little later this same year Sully noticed that the British painter Pickersgill also painted a portrait in oil followed by watercolor, then more oil, and said, "It was very clear and had force."[97] In the late 1830s and first part of the 1840s Sully, Mount, and Neagle were all excited by the possibility that starch was the secret of the early Venetian painters.[98] Neagle noticed how a grain of dry rice was hard, but boiling it in water would reduce it to a soft paste, and proposed experiments to see whether he might achieve by means of rice starch the dense but bright colors of the old masters.[99] Borax as an ingredient in painting media was another fad of the 1840s that was kicked off by British writers and provoked the curiosity of Americans. Borax was used as a painting medium in India, and elaborate arguments were spun to the effect that this recipe might have been transmitted to Flanders in the fifteenth century and could have been the secret medium of the Van Eycks (or in other accounts the secret of the Venetians).[100] Neagle, Mount, and Ridner described how borax could be used to make paint, but we have seen no evidence that American painters actually tried these recipes; in fact, Mount crossed out this recipe, apparently dismissing it as a bad idea.[101] Eccentric recipes were still being passed around by some American artists in the 1850s—in this decade Mount took note of and criticized a very unusual method attributed to the French painter Horace Vernet that involved olive oil and fuller's earth.[102] In the 1850s Mount also proposed a method of making paint from a mixture of varnish and tallow,[103] while Rembrandt Peale wrote down the equally odd recipes from a Mr. Binks for paints made from glycerine and from "insoluble soaps" instead of oils.[104]

A final note on media at midcentury involves a medium that seems to have never been used, but which says something about American aspirations at the time. The British author George Field had proposed investigating cottonseed oil from the southern United States as a possible nonyellowing oil for painting. Osborn jumped on this suggestion: "Could we obtain on this side of the ocean an oil that should be unequivocally superior to any now in use for painting, America would have the satisfaction of contributing one addition to the materials of the art that would fully counterbalance all the others that she owes to Europe."[105]

Osborn's response speaks not only of how deeply painters lamented the fact that all known media had their shortcomings but also of Americans' fervent hopes that their innovations and experimentation might contribute to the general advancement of art.

Driers

Nineteenth-century American artists sometimes added materials to their paint in order to make slow-drying colors like blacks, browns, and red lakes dry more quickly. The composition of these driers changed as the nineteenth century advanced. In the first half of the century the principal driers included "drying oil" (linseed oil heated with lead compounds), Japanner's gold size (a quick-drying product of varying composition), and sugar of lead (lead acetate, which had been both praised and damned since the eighteenth century).[106] After the middle of the century, driers that could be added a drop at a time were more readily available in small bottles from art suppliers. (By the 1860s, there is evidence that Rembrandt Peale, Sully, Mount, and Frederic Church had all tried the new commercially made driers;[107] the problem with these commercial products was that since the composition was usually a trade secret, artists may not have known exactly what they were using.)

Drying oil was used in various ways. It was an important ingredient in megilp, but it was also sometimes added directly to previously ground paint. Back in 1820, when some artists were still grinding their own paints, Joshua Shaw gave complicated directions for making paint by grinding certain slow-drying pigments with "common" drying oil, while recommending the addition of a little "severe" drying oil at the time the paint was used: "Brown pink, Vandyke brown and madder lake require to be ground in drying oil. Of which there are two kinds, common and severe. When drying oil is spoken of it is the common but madder lake Vandyke brown and brown pink when used require two or three drops of the severe to be added.—Burnt sienna require to be ground, half and half, raw and drying oil. All others be ground in raw linseed except Cremnitz white, which should be ground in poppy oil."[108]

Sully, Neagle, and Peale each wrote down directions for making "homemade" drying oil,[109] although by 1845 Osborn reported that drying oil could be bought ready-made, and in fact was available "at all colorshops at a very moderate price."[110] In 1850 Peale's niece was using the commercially available product, but with troubling results. He advised her: "You complain that your Drying oil is *dark*….What you can make yourself is better than any you can buy."[111]

Peale discussed a wider variety of driers than any other American; he described Japanner's gold size and "Manganesed oil,"[112] but he disagreed strongly with Field's advice that a solution of sugar of lead in water should be sponged on a ground to make it dry.[113] Peale believed that sugar of lead would turn yellow, so it should not be used with whites, but a small quantity was safe with reds, yellows, and browns, although the dark-colored oil treated with manganese was best with blacks.[114] Peale also tried and recommended the new product Siccatif de

Harlem, which in spite of its name appears to have been a French product made by Duroziez of Paris. His use of this material in 1850–52 was much earlier than its appearance in British colormen's catalogues and perhaps owes something to the importance of colormen of French origin in the United States.[115]

The dangers of using too much drier had been long recognized. As early as the 1795 *Practical Treatise*, readers were cautioned against using too much sugar of lead.[116] It was an excess of driers that, according to Neagle, caused one of Henry Inman's paintings to crack badly in 1834 (see chapter 9). Both Peale and Mount wrote down Field's cautions about the overuse of driers,[117] and Osborn, in 1845, called driers "useful" but also "mischievous" when used "too freely."[118]

Occasionally, artists referred to varnishes as "driers," as Cole did when he told Durand to bring "some Copal varnish in a vial as a drier" on a painting expedition.[119] Sully said a similar thing when he was testing several driers in 1862 and found that "The gum damar varnish as a drier is as effective as 'severe drier.'"[120] Since varnish dries more quickly than oil paint, it could accelerate the drying of paint to a noticeable degree if a large amount were added.[121] The temptation to do this may have been irresistible if an artist was in a hurry—this seems to have been the case when Sully spoke of "painting up a picture at once," adding so much dammar varnish that his painting actually dried too quickly unless he mixed in additional oil.[122]

Pigments

American painters had many concerns about pigments in the decades leading up to the middle of the nineteenth century. As Rembrandt Peale wrote: "We suffer under no deficiency of pigments—On the contrary, we are rather perplexed by their number & variety."[123] British authors, especially George Field, gave artists plenty of reason to worry that some of these pigments might fade, darken, or be incompatible with one another, and American artists including Mount, Peale, and Cole made careful note of these warnings.

Americans generally followed the British and French in the use of pigments, although they sometimes found themselves at or near the vanguard. In 1825 Sully reported that John Trumbull had been using Indian yellow for forty years, which would have been earlier than any firmly documented European use: Field described it as a relatively new pigment in 1835.[124] The technologically innovative Peale family had a special interest in the pigment prussiate of copper, and although this pigment was invented by an Englishman, the Peales appear to have used it before its use can be documented in England.[125] The Peale family's scheme to mine chromium and manufacture the pigment chrome yellow in 1809–10 also predated the earliest known mention of the color in European artists' literature.[126] (Chrome yellow was manufactured commercially in Britain beginning about 1815, initially from American ore, and was used by such well-known London artists as Benjamin West,

Thomas Lawrence, and William Beechey.)[127] The Peales abandoned their project around 1810, when they recognized that chrome yellow was not a stable pigment—a discovery that British and French authorities did not make until the 1830s.

A noticeable change on artists' palettes by midcentury was the increasing number of pigments of American origin. Deposits of naturally occurring American earth pigments had been known since the 1790s, if not earlier.[128] It is difficult to say how soon these pigments were mined commercially or found their way onto artists' palettes, but colormen were definitely selling pigments with American names by the 1840s. "American Venetian red" and "Vermont yellow" (which might possibly be earth pigments) and "American Emerald green" (a manufactured pigment) were among the many pigments offered by Carroll & Crosby of Norwich, Connecticut, in 1843–45.[129] By about 1863, the New York colormen Tiemann & Company sold "Vermont ochre," "Baltimore ochre," "Pennsylvania ochre," and "American Siennas," in addition to European ochres and siennas.[130] Local pride in using colors made from American earth may have added to their appeal; on the practical side, it must have been much less expensive to use American earth rather than earth imported from Italy or France.

Lead had been mined in America since the eighteenth century, but it was not manufactured into the pigment white lead until 1809 by Samuel Wetherill & Son in Philadelphia. By 1819 a rival factory in Philadelphia produced one hundred tons of the pigment annually.[131] By 1836 white lead was being manufactured in other American cities as well;[132] in that year Neagle received a gift of a keg of white lead "manufactured by Avery & Ogden of Pittsburgh—I suppose he wishes me to try it & introduce it to the attention of artists. I will recommend it, if it prove good after trial."[133] The conscientious Neagle tried the pigment and recorded: "Feby 26th 1839—This is good lead."[134]

The majority of the white lead manufactured in the 1830s must have gone to house painters rather than to artists: it was the height of the Greek revival, when many American buildings had pediments and Doric pilasters and were painted to look as white as Greek temples. But by 1850 Ridner specifically targeted artists for the pigments that he manufactured, as he proudly proclaimed in an advertising supplement at the back of his book. Ridner said that he produced American cadmium yellow, lemon yellow, strontian yellow, chrome yellow, oxide of chromium, cobalt green, various mars colors, blue ochre, "&c., &c…in their greatest purity and beauty of color, which he will warrant in all cases to be fully equal in quality to any imported, and at as low a price." Ridner was also the agent, although not the manufacturer, of what he called "AMERICAN MADDER LAKES, which are fully equal—if not superior—to the best imported."[135]

Ridner's bias in favor of the pigments that he manufactured (or was agent for) is understandable; he was pleased to point out, for instance, that a lack of knowledge of pigments led to "the premature decay of many fine pictures, particularly those of the English school."[136] In his rivalry with English manufacturers, Ridner made a determined effort to keep up with the new pigments that were appearing with some regularity by the middle of the nineteenth century. In fact his reference to strontian yellow in 1850 appears to be earlier than any mention in English sources; Winsor & Newton did not offer strontian yellow for sale until about 1861.[137]

Cadmium yellow was a relatively new pigment when Ridner advertised that he manufactured it in 1850, and, in fact, Ridner's announcement is (to the authors' knowledge) the earliest datable American occurrence of this pigment. In 1845 Osborn wrote that he had heard of cadmium yellow from English sources, but he was not familiar with it himself.[138] The pigment was first advertised in England by Winsor & Newton in their 1846 catalogue, and other British makers appear to have first offered it in the late 1840s or 1850s.[139]

A more general interest in cadmium yellow on the part of American artists can be documented after 1850. Mount mentioned it as a "new color" in 1851.[140] Rembrandt Peale was familiar with cadmium yellow by the time he completed "Notes of the Painting Room" between 1850 and 1852, calling it "recently introduced." He also said, "With this pigment, Chrome Yellow may well be dispensed with,"[141] (which may refer to the Peale family's special interest in chrome yellow and their knowledge that it darkened over time).

By the late 1850s, there is evidence that still more American painters had become aware of cadmium yellow. In 1858 Jasper Francis Cropsey experimented with two types of cadmium yellow, one bought from Dechaux and the other made by Ridner.[142] An entry in a notebook kept by Mary Jane Peale, probably also from the late 1850s, included the recommendation by Edward Moran that cadmium yellow be used for painting the ocean.[143] Cadmium yellow has been identified by analysis in paintings by Martin Johnson Heade beginning in 1857.[144] Cadmium yellow's intense yellow color made it useful mostly to landscape painters, who could mix it with blue pigments to make a deep, permanent green.[145]

There was great interest in the pigment zinc white in both Europe and America around the middle of the nineteenth century. Mount mentioned it in his diary in 1847 but seems not to have actually used it, proof of Field's observation that zinc white was "more celebrated as a pigment than used."[146] In 1835 Field noted that zinc white had the advantage of being less toxic than white lead, but it also had the disadvantage of having less covering power.[147]

Americans had a special reason to be interested in zinc white because zinc ore was found in New Jersey, and this was one of the few places in the world where the pigment was manufactured.[148] Osborn, in 1845, expressed reservations about zinc white,[149] but by 1850–52 Peale discussed it in positive terms, noting especially that it retained its whiteness better than white lead. Peale wrote: "The Jersey White I have found to be better than the French."[150] A few years later a

Philadelphia importer offered a very different opinion: "The 'French Oxide of Zinc White,' is superior to White Lead, *considerably whiter than the Jersey Zinc*, and after many trials has been adopted by the French and English Governments, for all public works. It is cheaper than White Lead, from its spreading easily over a much larger surface, and unlike lead, *it is not injurious to the health of those who use it, or of those occupying newly painted rooms*."[151]

The last sentence was obviously intended for house painters, but it would have been read with interest by any painter who cared about his or her health.[152] An 1868 American book aimed at house painters told alarming stories about house painters and their customers who had been poisoned by rooms painted with toxic pigments and concluded: "All the very best and finest work in the cities is now finished with zinc," adding that zinc is "vastly whiter and more durable, and does not, like lead, turn yellow."[153]

This whiteness and durability must have appealed to fine artists as much as zinc's lack of toxicity. An article in the artists' journal *The Crayon* in 1856 claimed that zinc white kept its color so well that it could be used in place of white lead, "or in covering and protecting the more solid tints of the lead preparations from the injurious action of sulphuretted hydrogen and other gases, by final paintings or scumblings, thereby preserving the original brilliancy of the painting."[154] This may be what Church had in mind when he applied zinc white underneath the depiction of the sun in his painting *The Andes of Ecuador*.[155]

While concerns of cost and durability were undoubtedly important factors for artists who chose to use American pigments, other, more subtle reasons sometimes played a role. One of Rembrandt Peale's stories in "Notes of the Painting Room" concerned his improvement of an American pigment called "Silver's chocolate brown." Peale said that Silver's chocolate brown was normally coarsely ground and sold "for the most common purposes," such as painting houses or wagons. But Peale took the time and effort to go to the place where the pigment was mined and found that if he ground it fine and mixed it with some of his special alumina vehicle, "it becomes a Pigment of such singular Merit that I call it the *Titian shade*—producing hues, from its pure colour, & those combined with white, or other flesh tints in the rounding off into shade, of the most natural character."[156]

William Sidney Mount provides additional insights into the meaning that American pigments might have had for American artists. Beginning in the 1830s, Mount used earth pigments he dug himself from the soil of his beloved Stony Brook, Long Island, and he took considerable pride in having discovered them (see chapter 13). In 1848 he wrote a long letter to a fellow Long Islander in which he made great claims for his colors; like Peale, he claimed that "*Titian* must have used something like" one of Mount's pigments for toning flesh. Mount said that he gave some of his native umber to James Frothingham, who was "delighted" with it, and said "his old Master, Gilbert Stuart, used a native umber, and he had been a long time wishing to obtain some of it." Mount also claimed that Thomas Cole had told him that he used a native umber from the vicinity of the village of Catskill, New York.[157] Thus, Mount connected the names of Titian, Stuart, and Cole (the latter two *American* old masters) with native American pigments. When he painted a copy after a portrait by Gilbert Stuart, which Mount called "the only copy I ever made," he used a locally gathered pigment for the blue-black colors.[158] This pride in native pigments marked a subtle but significant shift in Americans' attitude toward the secrets of the old masters. At least some Americans were discovering that some secrets might be found not in Europe but here in America—in a sense, right under their own feet.

Paint in Tubes

A technological advance that changed the working habits of many painters in the nineteenth century was the development of collapsible metal tubes to hold pre-ground paint, which replaced the bladders made from animal membranes that had been used previously. Part of this story is well known: John Goffe Rand, an American painter working in London, invented the compressible tin tube sealed with a screw cap in 1841. The invention was initially marketed by the London colorman Thomas Brown, but Winsor & Newton purchased the rights to the design in 1842. The new tubes were immediately successful—Winsor & Newton advertised paint in both bladders and metal tubes in their ca. 1842 catalogue, but in their next catalogue (1846), bladders had been discontinued. Other manufacturers soon followed suit, and the design of paint tubes has changed very little ever since.[159]

Less well known is that Rand's invention was the culmination of several decades of experimentation by both Americans and Britons. Rembrandt Peale summarized some of the events in an article in *The Crayon* in 1856:

> In 1809, I made a set of thick glass tubes to hold the paint, one end stopped with a perforated cork, and the color forced out by a piston of wood. This was a clean and neat, but imperfect instrument. Mr. *C. B. King*, of Washington, improved on this, by substituting tubes of tin, with a cork piston; which we readily adopted. A sample being sent to London, Mr. *Deville*, of the Strand, still further improved by making them of brass lined with tin, and each with a top screwed on, and with a screw piston.[160]

The improvements by Charles Bird King and Mr. Deville probably occurred in the 1810s or early 1820s, because a letter from Charles Willson Peale shows the elder Peale deeply involved in the development of metal tubes in the year 1820, and describes family discussions about which metal might be best: "I bought yesterday a small pewter Syringe & converted into a paint holder by adding the Screw &c.…Some of the family supposes that the pewter is not so good as tubes made of tin. but I believe that if there is any disadvantage in one it will be equally so with others—it must be an acid in the paint that shall act on pewter or tin—Brass tubes would not answer as the oil would produce Verdegrese."[161]

In 1823 the Englishman James Harris announced the idea of a metal syringe with a screw piston. Thomas Lawrence owned a set of these syringes, and a set that once belonged to Queen Victoria is still owned by the Royal Academy.[162] In 1828 Sully referred in a letter to tin-lined brass tubes from England, but few other Americans must have known of them, for Sully felt he needed to describe them to Samuel F. B. Morse: "I have found no method of keeping ground colour, equal to putting them in Tubes, as it regards durability and convenience—But mine are made of Brass, and lined with Tin: you may easily send for a sett to London. I have a dozen assorted; which cost me twenty dollars. A young lady imported a sett, filled with colours."[163]

In 1829 Sully included refillable brass tubes in his list of the materials that he took on a painting trip; they would have been much less likely to leak than bladders when packed together with so many other items.[164] Since metal tubes had been used by at least some British and American artists since the early 1820s (or earlier), it is somewhat surprising that in 1840 Winsor & Newton introduced a glass syringe, which would have been much more fragile.[165] The high cost of the refillable brass tubes that Sully described was probably an obstacle to their wide acceptance. One of the main advantages of the collapsible tube invented by Rand was that it was so inexpensive that artists could simply throw the tube away when it was empty.

In 1845 Osborn described paint as being available in America in either bladders or in tin tubes that could be made to extrude the paint by carefully pushing a cork plunger, a device that sounds more like Charles Bird King's invention than the London-made cylinders.[166] This implies that the chronology of improvements was not so concise as in Peale's account and that several different types of primitive tubes might have been in use simultaneously. Rand's collapsible tube came to Osborn's notice just before the publication of his book, for he was able to briefly mention the new invention in a footnote and call it "a decided improvement."[167]

Both Osborn and Peale noted that some of the more expensive pigments were not available in bladders or tubes and needed to be ground in oil by the artist.[168] This may have been in part a carryover from the time when bladders, which were imperfectly sealed (punctured with a nail or pin, or cut with a knife at each use), would allow the colors to dry up fairly quickly, and no artist would want to waste expensive pigments.[169]

It has been claimed that collapsible tubes were important because they made painting outdoors possible.[170] They certainly made it more convenient, with less risk of a messy disaster from bursting bladders of paint, but some American artists had carried bladders outdoors in the first half of the nineteenth century. Cole and Durand purchased small bladders of paint when they planned a joint outdoor painting expedition in 1837,[171] and Worthington Whittredge also described packing a kit that included bladders when he painted outdoors in Kentucky in the early 1840s: "I at once made myself a knapsack and put in it my sketch box, a block of small canvasses, a dozen bladders of colors (this was before artists' colors were put up in tubes)."[172]

Peale's description of the development of tubes is full of pride in his countrymen's inventiveness. He concluded with: "It was reserved for the ingenuity of another American artist, Mr. *Rand*, to invent the present compressible tubes of pure tin, without seam, effectually preserving the colors, which are pressed out of a small nozzle, having a screw cap to prevent leakage."[173]

VARNISHING

In 1839 the itinerant portrait painter Joseph Whiting Stock was injured in a varnish-making accident. His clothing caught fire, his hands, face, and neck were badly burned, and he did not paint again for six months. Stock had been confined to a wheelchair since childhood, and his limited mobility made the consequences of his accident worse, but artists had long known that making varnishes could be dangerous—the components were often heated to dissolve them and could catch fire or explode during the heating process.[174]

The hazards of making varnishes—especially copal, which was more widely used in America by the 1830s and 1840s and could not be dissolved unless heated over an open flame—must have been yet another reason that artists were happy to find ready-made varnishes more widely available by the middle of the nineteenth century. Some ready-made varnishes were imported from Europe, but an increasing number were produced in America. For instance, the Philadelphia firm of C. Schrack & Company advertised in 1850 that they had "at considerable expense, obtained the method of making nearly all the English varnishes and Black Oil Japans now used in London."[175]

The reasons for varnishing remained the same. Osborn pointed out the protective function of a varnish, which guarded against spider droppings and other "filth."[176] But it was also recognized that a layer of varnish could greatly improve a painting's appearance. Ridner wrote in 1850 that varnish "causes the colours to bear out with their full force and beauty,"[177] while in 1846 Sully said more bluntly: "Without its aid many of the colors look dead."[178]

Copal

By the last quarter of the eighteenth century, there had been general agreement that a simple solution of mastic in spirits of turpentine was the best resin to use for a final varnish on a painting, because varnishes that contain oil, like copal, turn dark over time and can become difficult (or impossible) to remove (see chapter 3). However, copal underwent a revival of interest as a varnish in the second quarter of the nineteenth century, just as it had as a painting medium. There had been sporadic mention of copal varnish in America throughout the early nineteenth century. Since copal was a tougher varnish than mastic and survived outdoor exposure better, it was also recommended for many purposes other than varnishing oil paintings in publications with titles like *Valuable Secrets* and *Five Thousand Receipts*, which were often motley collections of recipes from earlier English books.[179]

Artists began to take greater notice of copal when it was praised in Field's *Chromatography* and in Sarsfield Taylor's translation of Mérimée, both of which appeared in the 1830s. Each author acknowledged that varnishing paintings with mastic was the prevailing practice,[180] but Field described copal's "strength, fine texture, and the greater transparency and permanence of its colour" and said that it was preferred to mastic as a final varnish for paintings that contained copal as an added medium.[181] Mérimée said that copal was "the most brilliant and the hardest of the resins" and "could be used advantageously for the first couch instead of mastic." Mérimée also said that copal was employed by early Italian masters, which may have given it extra cachet.[182]

Neagle, Peale, Sully, and Ridner all recorded Mérimée's idea of applying a thin layer of copal varnish, to be followed by a more tender varnish, such as mastic, which could be removed later if needed, leaving the harder copal layer intact.[183] Peale's account, which sounds like it was based on firsthand experience, emphasized that the layer of copal should be thin, because a thicker layer could turn brown and produce cracks.[184] By midcentury both Mount and Ridner reported that Cole had varnished his paintings with a thin layer of copal (see chapter 12). The example of Cole, who was revered by American artists both during his lifetime and after his premature death in 1848, may have given additional prestige to copal as a varnish—a little past midcentury Cropsey invoked Cole's authority for the best place to buy copal in New York.[185]

Ridner even claimed that copal varnish had helped to preserve Cole's pigments from deterioration, and while he acknowledged that mastic varnish was "more extensively used than any other varnish," said that copal varnish was "the best and most unobjectionable varnish for paintings."[186] But opinion was not unanimously in favor of copal. Ridner said that there was a prejudice against its use,[187] and Osborn revived the long-standing argument that copal was "objectionable" because it turned dark and would be difficult to remove (an opinion that modern conservators would share).[188] When Sully summed up his ideas about varnishing in 1851, he wrote: "Some recommend Copal varnish…made thin by turpentine," but said that he (without giving reasons) preferred mastic or dammar.[189]

The differing opinions about copal in the nineteenth century may have resulted in part from how thickly a varnish layer was applied, as Rembrandt Peale pointed out. Another factor is that in the nineteenth century (and in modern times) "copal" is a very loose term for resins that derive from completely different families of trees from various parts of the world.[190] Individual batches of copal, therefore, may have behaved very differently from one another.[191] An additional problem was that copal varnish was used for so many purposes other than oil painting that artists might have gotten hold of batches prepared in very different ways. Ridner referred to this in 1850, making the comment that the finer kinds of copal made for varnishing coaches could be used on paintings, but the "ordinary" copal varnish intended for furniture contained too much turpentine and "generally its dark colour would form another objection to its use."[192]

Oil Used as a Varnish

The process of "oiling out"—applying a thin layer of oil to dried paint before beginning a new painting session—had been common since the eighteenth century, although some artists criticized the practice because the oil could turn dark and yellow (see chapters 3 and 4). In the nineteenth century some painters used a layer of oil as a substitute for a final varnish as well. This practice is of interest to conservators because it could cause serious problems: unlike a mastic or dammar varnish that can be thinned or removed if it becomes dark, an oil layer will eventually become as tough and resistant as the paint below it.

Sully recorded that he sometimes applied oil on top of a varnish, as in 1837: "The portraits of Misses Andrews, altho' varnished, have become dull. I therefore passed a mixture of fat oil and turpentine over the surface—very thin."[193] Sully noted a few years later that George Field "condemned" oiling out because it "has the fault of turning brown by age."[194] But this did not keep him from occasionally applying oil mixed with turpentine as a substitute for varnish late in his career (when he was also trying out a bewildering variety of other varnishing materials and techniques).[195] Sully cited the example of West the first time he mentioned doing this: "When I last saw Mr. B. West in London, he requested me to employ a mixture of drying oil and turpentine to varnish any part of his picture painted for the hospital of 'Christ Healing in the Temple' which I might observe to require 'bringing out'—I have used the above mixture in the fancy head I have finished of a Peasant Girl."[196]

Other artists used oil as a varnish as well; on one occasion Mount considered oiling out the equivalent of a varnish (see chapter 13). Kensett also appears to have occasionally used a layer of oil in place of a conventional varnish.[197] Rubbing oil onto the surface of a painting was also recommended as a cure for the "bloom" (cloudiness) that sometimes develops on paintings varnished with mastic; Sully wrote that poppy oil could be applied for this purpose, then wiped off with a silk handkerchief.[198] The amount of oil that was applied would be very important (just as it is in the case of copal varnish). A slight amount of oil would not produce as much discoloration as a layer that was brushed on liberally.[199]

"White Lac" Varnish

In the 1835 and subsequent editions of his book *Chromatography*, Field sang the praises of a new varnish made of bleached shellac that he termed "white lac." He called white lac "by far the most perfect of varnishes" and predicted that eventually "it will probably be the principal varnish of the painter."[200] Field had a special interest in promoting white lac, for he himself had developed a process for eliminating the brown color that was normally an obstacle to using shellac as a varnish.[201] Cole, Sully, Mount, Rembrandt Peale, and Ridner all noticed and quoted or paraphrased Field's high commendations,[202] but Osborn had a slightly more jaded reaction: "We have read much in its praise, but nothing that convinces us of its necessity or advantage, either to the finished picture or the palette of the painter."[203]

As in the case of zinc white, white lac varnish may have been more talked about than used in Britain and America. To our knowledge, the only American who recorded trying it out was Rembrandt Peale, who did not have a happy experience. Peale wrote that he took great pains to prepare the varnish so as to obtain a gloss with it, but his efforts were "in vain."[204]

It is unclear where Peale obtained his white lac varnish; the authors have so far discovered only one nineteenth-century American colorman's catalogue that listed it.[205] White lac was offered sporadically in nineteenth-century British colormen's catalogues, but there are hints that even in Britain it was not easily available at midcentury, and there appears to have been gradual disillusionment on the part of British artists, who found Field's claims of the durability of white lac varnish very much exaggerated.[206]

Dammar

Around the middle of the nineteenth century a completely new varnish arrived in America. This was dammar, a resin from Asia that had made its way to Germany by about 1827 and gradually began to be used in other European countries in following decades. The first American reference to dammar that we have found is an 1849 entry in a notebook of that most inquisitive of artists, Thomas Sully.[207]

A little later (1851), Sully wrote that dammar was "much used in the United States."[208] If true, this would put Americans in advance of British artists, among whom dammar was little known in the early 1850s.[209] In fact, dammar was not generally recommended in treatises nor advertised by name for sale to painters in Britain during the nineteenth century.[210] There is circumstantial evidence that Americans' knowledge about dammar grew out of connections with German painters, which were increasing at exactly this time. Many Germans (including some artists) had immigrated to America following political upheavals in Germany in 1848, while a number of Americans had traveled to study in Düsseldorf in the 1840s. In New York, paintings by Düsseldorf artists were exhibited at the Düsseldorf

Gallery beginning in 1849, the same year that Sully first learned about dammar.[211] Further evidence of a German connection is that "Baron Schroeder" (possibly the Düsseldorf painter Adolph Schrödter) was recorded in one of Sully's notebooks as having given the varnish a high recommendation in 1851.[212] Another hint of a German-American connection is that when the Philadelphia colormen C. Schrack & Company began buying and selling dammar in 1849–50, they bought material from New York merchants Koope and Fischer, whose names (like Schrack) may be German in origin.[213]

American artists soon realized that dammar had some very good qualities. Sully wrote in 1849 that it "makes an excellent varnish, much used in Germany and called 'White varnish.'…I have tried it and am much pleased with it."[214] Rembrandt Peale also knew about and praised dammar in 1850–52, referring to it "drying & remaining lighter" than other varnishes, saying it is "nearly as clear as Water, dries quickly, with a gloss, greater than Mastic, & bears friction better, & does not bloom."[215] In 1851 Sully went even further, saying that dammar was used "almost universally in Germany" and calling it "the best varnish I have met with.…It preserves its gloss and transparency, is not given to mildew, is easily removed from the surface of a picture, and can be applied, without risk, to a freshly painted picture."[216] (The last quality would have been particularly attractive to Sully, who was at that moment carrying out experiments to try to find varnishes that would allow him to varnish a painting soon after it was painted.)

When Sully said dammar was "much used" in the United States in 1851, only two years after he had first heard about it, he may possibly have been thinking of his immediate circle, which included such experimenters as his nephew Robert Sully (from whom he probably first learned about dammar),[217] as well as Neagle and Peale, all of whom would have been eager to try a new product. John Ridner, who otherwise seems so well-informed about artists' materials, did not mention dammar in his 1850 book, implying that its new popularity was sudden indeed. But the evidence, although sparse, is that awareness of dammar continued to grow throughout America in the 1850s. For example, in a letter in 1855 Peale assumed that two other family members who were painters were familiar with dammar.[218] Word had reached Mount in Long Island by 1857, when he first mentioned dammar in his diary,[219] and in 1859 Sully recorded that at that time he was buying dammar from two different colormen.[220]

By 1860 dammar was offered for sale in Dechaux's catalogue,[221] making it still more easily available to American painters. Another sign of the easy availability of dammar at this time is that it was recommended in 1860 by colormen in a provincial part of New York state, not only as a picture varnish but for various kinds of amateur decorative painting and for painting rooms.[222] One reason that dammar was appropriate for large-scale painting, as well as used by amateurs, is that it was much less expensive than mastic.[223]

Yet in spite of the high recommendations of some artists and its low cost, dammar did not immediately replace mastic and copal. Much still remains to be learned about the exact chronology of the use of dammar. But the fact that it was used, appreciated, and written about in such detail and at such a relatively early date (compared to its use in Britain) must be due in part to the curiosity of American experimenters like Sully and Rembrandt Peale.

Other Aspects of Varnishing

Sully's experiments with a great variety of other varnishes are discussed elsewhere in this volume (see chapter 8). Rembrandt Peale also experimented with many different varnishes; he took notes on varnishes made from Venice turpentine and Venice turpentine mixed with copal or mastic;[224] he also experimented with Canada balsam as a varnish but found it "dried brittle"; to correct this he added copal and called the result "Improved Varnish," but in the end concluded that these were inferior to dammar.[225]

Peale also experimented with a new material that had been introduced from France, the quick-drying Soehnée's retouching varnish, which (like white lac) was based on a thin solution of shellac in alcohol. It was claimed to be safe to apply a thin layer soon after painting, which would allow the artist to see the design more clearly and then continue painting. Peale tried Soehnée's retouching varnish as early as 1850–52 and was pleased with the results:

> It is used, instead of oiling out colours that are sunken in, to be retouched. Experimentally I have used it successively five times on the same parts, painting on it each time, a few minutes after varnishing—the paint having been dry one or two days. The Canvas thus used was daily exposed to the sun, during many weeks, & compared with the same colours, without the Varnish, put on at the same time. There was never any sign of cracking, & the experiment was satisfactory, as showing the facility of retouching with fresh tints, working most pleasantly on a surface restored to its true colour by the Varnish.[226]

This was much earlier than Soehnée's retouching varnish appeared in British colormen's catalogues.[227] As in the case of Siccatif de Harlem (cited above), this may have been because of the importance in America of colormen of French origin, in whose catalogues Soehnée's varnish seems to have appeared first.[228] Soehnée's retouching varnish would become much more widely used in the second half of the nineteenth century.

It is difficult to generalize about the thickness of varnishes at this period. Recommended solutions of mastic and dammar in turpentine ranged from about 25 percent to 50 percent.[229] The highest percentages would make a thick and glossy varnish if brushed directly onto a picture (although no recipes that we have found from this time were as thick as the 70 percent solution that John Singleton Copley described being used by English artists in the 1770s; see chapter 3). Of course, thick solutions of varnish could be diluted by an artist prior to use, as Rembrandt Peale communicated to his niece when he sent her varnish by way of Rubens Peale in 1855: "Tell her that the Damar Varnish is thick enough to require to be *thinned* with an *equal bulk* of spirits of Turpentine, when used."[230]

Some artists applied multiple coatings of varnish. Sully, Neagle, and Peale proposed at various times brushing on two or more thin layers of varnish rather than one thick one.[231] The reasons given were that multiple coats would make a more even surface, or correct a problem when the first varnish layer did not dry properly, or reduce the risk of cracking. These accounts all seem to assume that a relatively thick varnish was the intended final result (or at least a "normal" or accepted result). As Neagle wrote: "Perhaps two or three very thin coats of varnish may prove safer than one thick one."[232] Similarly, Peale wrote about dammar varnish: "It is best to give a picture *two* coats of it, letting the first be well dry—rather than one thick one."[233]

Peale had another theory about multiple layers of varnish that would supposedly circumvent the need to wait six months or a year before varnishing. In the spirit of Mérimée's idea of a layer of copal followed by a coat of mastic, Peale wrote that an artist could apply a very thin solution of copal varnish as soon as the paint would bear it—not a distinct layer, but just enough to saturate the paint. According to Peale, it would then be safe to apply a layer of mastic or dammar "in a few days, or at most a week or two," and then, after six months or a year, another, "more effective coat" of mastic or dammar.[234]

A symbol of the difficulty of knowing exactly what an artist intended in terms of varnishing is the case of Joshua Shaw, who arrived from Britain in 1817. In 1838 he told Asher B. Durand that varnish was "the greatest curse," especially when applied to a new painting (see chapter 12).[235] But Shaw's recipe for mastic varnish, as reported by Obadiah Dickinson, was one of the thicker ones reported during this period—six ounces mastic to fourteen ounces turpentine, or almost 43 percent (weight to volume).[236] Conservators occasionally find paintings from this period that still bear their first coat of varnish, and these varnishes vary as much as the various accounts would lead one to suspect—some are quite thin, while others are thicker.

Some recipes for mastic and dammar varnish during this period consisted simply of resin dissolved in spirits of turpentine. But additives that would toughen the varnish or keep it from blooming were also mentioned with some frequency. These additives are important to conservators because, even in small proportions, they can change the way that a varnish behaves when a painting is cleaned.[237] Neagle cited the authority of Thomas Lawrence, who added "some good drying oil" to his mastic varnish.[238] An undated sheet in Neagle's papers bears variations of this, recommending the addition of "a small quantity" of Venice turpentine and "a few drops" of boiled linseed oil to a solution of mastic varnish; the reason given is that "it will dry quicker than the pure varnish."[239]

Sully seemed to vacillate about the propriety of adding oil or other materials to varnish. At some time between 1812 and 1822, he wrote out an elaborate recipe for mastic varnish in spirits of turpentine, containing no oil but small amounts of turpentine resin (colophony) and camphor (which was said to help dissolve the mastic) as well as ground glass; Neagle also copied this recipe into a notebook at a later time.[240] In 1833 or 1834 Sully wrote: "In the mastic varnish mix a small portion of drying oil; it prevents the surface from chilling."[241] Ten years later, when he took notes from Field's *Chromatography*, he recorded Field's warning: "In varnishing any addition of oil will render it liable to turn brown and it cannot be removed from a picture without difficulty,"[242] but this did not keep him from adding "a small portion" of drying oil to his mastic varnish in 1847.[243] In 1851 he added camphor to mastic varnish, and still later (in 1860), when he varnished a painting by Rembrandt Peale, he added "a few drops" of copal varnish to his dammar varnish "to prevent its blooming."[244]

NOTES

1   Ridner 1850, 7.

2   Osborn 1845, 318n.

3   There were American editions in 1852, 1854, 1856, 1860, 1869, 1872, 1879, and 1883. There was also a British edition in 1847 and a German edition in 1875 (Carlyle 2001, 318).

4   Cranch to Charles Lanman, September 10, 1840 (Lanman Papers, Library of Congress, Washington, D.C.; a copy is included in the Lanman Papers held at the Getty Research Institute, Los Angeles).

5   Dunlap 1834, 2:349, referred to a "mulatto boy who was grinding paints in another part of the room" in John Wesley Jarvis's studio around 1812, showing that this tedious job was sometimes given to the lowest on the social ladder.

6   Katlan 1987, 18–20.

7   Osborn 1845, 214, 215n.

8   In a modern compilation of New York colormen, the number of French and German names is striking (Katlan 1987, 33–270).

9   On the history of Goupil & Vibert in America, see McIntosh 2004a, 2004b, and 2006.

10   Document on the back of sheet dated 1852 (Mount Papers N-YHS); Katlan 1987, 21–23; Frankenstein 1975, 152–53.

11   Mount to William Schaus, January 4, 1853 (cited in Frankenstein 1975,165).

12   Newspaper clipping [the date 1847 added in a later hand] (Mount Papers N-YHS).

13   Mount corresponded with Ridner in this capacity and visited him several times when he came to New York; see letters from 1841 (Frankenstein 1975, 112), from 1844 (ibid., 104), and from 1847 (ibid., 118). Another example of Ridner's connections in the New York art world is the survival of an inscribed copy of his book that he presented to Asher B. Durand, president of the National Academy of Design (2001 catalogue of Charles B. Wood III Antiquarian Bookseller, Cambridge, Massachusetts).

14   Neagle Cashbook; Katlan 1992, 413, 437.

15   Torchia, Chotner, and Miles 1998, 33.

16   Schrack Daybook, October 28, 1848.

17   Many volumes of records still survive from C. Schrack & Company and remain to be studied in detail. The records are divided between the Historical Society of Pennsylvania and Eleutherian Mills Historical Library, Greenville, Delaware.

18   Allston 1993, 570. Peabody's business may have been on a relatively small scale, for she never
       advertised as an art supplier in Boston directories (Muller 1987).

19   See chapters 2, 4, 8, and 9.

20   Katlan 1992, 442–45.

21   Ibid., 447, 468, 477. For a canvas stamped by both the British colorman George Rowney and by
       Dechaux, see Zucker and Boon 2007, 37.

22   Carroll & Crosby Invoice Book.

23   Tomlinson 1976, xii–xiii.

24   Ibid., 54.

25   Katlan 1992, 318–19.

26   Ibid., 363–68.

27   A number of American artists' supplies catalogues have been transcribed in Katlan 1992,
       310–90. The collection of trade catalogues at the Winterthur Library contains many examples;
       some of these catalogues cannot be dated exactly.

28   D.F. Tiemann & Company [catalogue], New York [the date 1863 written in ink] (collection of
       Stephen Kornhauser, whom we thank for showing it to us).

29   Mérimée 1839, 346n.

30   Osborn 1845, 113–14. Mahogany panels prepared for artists (with a ground layer) were
       advertised in England by Winsor & Newton by about 1835 (Carlyle 2001, 187).

31   Osborn 1845, 113–14.

32   In 1815 Ethan Allen Greenwood recorded: "Bought two old segar boxes & had the boards of
       them planed for small portraits" (Barnhill 1993, 124).

33   Mount to Charles De la Forest, February 23, 1842 (Mount Papers N-YHS). Thomas Cole's bill
       from 1827–33 from the New York colormen Parker & Clover lists both "panels" and "mahogany
       panels." The sizes of the panels were not given, so it is difficult to compare prices and say whether
       the ones called simply "panels" were made from a cheaper kind of wood (Katlan 1992, 499–500).

34   "Panels of Mahogany are good, but heavy—Those of Basswood are light & level, but being soft
       are liable to be dented—Poplar is disposed to warp—& white Pine is dangerous by reason of
       knots, the turpentine of which strikes through & damages the Picture" (R. Peale "Notes," 19).

35   Neagle, in the account in which he praised basswood or baywood, criticized mahogany as
       "too heavy & coarse in the fibre"; the sap of yellow pine will slow the drying of the paint and
       "is inclined to change the colors of your picture"; and poplar is "apt to warp & split"(Neagle
       Commonplace Book, 74). Sully wrote in 1822 that oak and mahogany were best, but poplar was
       "treacherous" because it warps and splits, and any knothole "contains turpentine which will
       penetrate any painting you may apply to it, tho' it be covered an inch thick." Neagle had access
       to this notebook, and he added his own comment below Sully's: "(Unless sized and covered with
       silver or gold leaf. J.N.)" (Sully "Hints," AAA, microfilm roll N18, frame 96 [1822]).

36   Cole to Asher B. Durand, June 16, June 23, and July 17, 1836 (Cole Papers NYSL).

37   On pasteboard, see Katlan 1992, 262–63; and Carlyle 2001, 188, 192n3. Carlyle (p. 188) also
       reports a reference in an 1822 book to applying thin paste to a board to take away its absorbency
       (which would probably also stiffen it), which may also help explain the origin of the term
       "pasteboard."

               Since the Cole/Durand references occurred in 1836, at about the time that Academy
       board and millboard were first advertised by Winsor & Newton in England, it is possible that
       they were referring to these products and simply using a general term with which they were
       familiar.

38   Osborn 1845,113. Osborn's criticism of pasteboard closely follows Bouvier's (Bouvier 1844, 507).

39   Cole to Asher B. Durand, June 14, 1837 (Cole Papers NYSL). In their earlier (1836)
       correspondence, neither Cole nor Durand said explicitly that the pasteboards were intended for
       outdoor sketching.

40   R. Peale "Notes," 19–21.

41   Ibid., 21.

42   Katlan 1992, 264; Katlan 1999, 26–28. Alexander Katlan has studied these supports very
       thoroughly in all of their varieties. Winsor & Newton offered a much greater selection of sizes of
       millboard in their 1851–57 catalogue than in one from 1846 (Katlan 1992, 374).

43   This example was discovered by Joyce Zucker (reported in Katlan 1992, 266). It is not clear
       whether Vanderlyn made the support himself—he lived in Paris for many years, and the blue

paper that is part of the support hints at a French origin.

44   R. Peale "Notes," 18.

45   Rembrandt Peale, *Thomas Sully* (1859, National Gallery of Art, Washington, D.C.). The support on this painting differs from Peale's written description in that it is not covered overall on both sides with fabric, but the fabric overlaps slightly onto the back, and there are X-shaped strips of fabric across the reverse (Torchia, Chotner, and Miles 1998, 68, 71).

46   Katlan 1992, 270. Prior to this time, artists prepared their own paper for sketching. In 1832 Thomas Sully prepared forty-two pieces of paper by coating them with thin paste, and then with white lead oil paint (Sully "Hints," AAA, microfilm roll N18, frame 132 [August 7, 1832]). On oil sketching paper in Britain, see Carlyle 2001, 190–91.

47   Mount's diary, October 28, 1853 (cited in Frankenstein 1975, 270).

48   Normally paper would be attached with small pins or nails, but Bouvier (1844, 508) suggested that a support could be attached to the lid of a painting box with soft wax.

49   Lanman wrote about landscape painting in the 1840s and also much later; unfortunately this entry is undated ("Artistic Recollections," 8, Lanman Papers, Getty Research Institute, Los Angeles).

50   Katlan 1999, 25–26; Carlyle 2001, 191–92.

51   By the 1860s British manufacturers were selling tin frames the size of the solid block intended to protect wet sketches (Carlyle 2001, 191).

52   Katlan 1999, 26. Bierstadt sometimes sketched on paper having a ground and sometimes on paper with no ground; Bierstadt also did many paintings on Academy board and millboard prepared by Winsor & Newton and by Muller of Paris (Merrill 1992, 526; see also Carbone et al. 2006, 1: 280–81).

53   Some mounting of Bierstadt's works may have been done in his lifetime, but much was also done later (see Merrill 1992).

54   Harvey 1998, 64. Eleanor Jones Harvey's book covers many aspects of painting outdoors and the new importance of painted sketches at this time.

55   Mount to Charles Lanman, February 11, 1844 (Mount Papers N-YHS).

56   Mount's diary, January 17, 1848 (cited in Frankenstein 1975, 183).

57   Mount Diary LIMAA [1847–48].

58   For instance, the *Pilgrim's Progress* panorama of 1850 had sixty or more large scenes by numerous artists, including Frederic Church, Jasper Francis Cropsey, and Daniel Huntington (Sweeney 1994, 122–23).

59   Osborn 1845, 115.

60   Ibid., 114.

61   Katlan 1999, 23. The terms "stretching frame" and "frame" had a long life. Rembrandt Peale used only the word "frame" (R. Peale "Notes," 17–18), as did Williams 1878, 14. Patent documents from the second half of the nineteenth century continued to use both words interchangeably, or sometimes in tandem, as in "stretcher-frame" or "stretcher frame" (Katlan 1992, 125–26, 130–33).

62   The keyable stretcher was mentioned in a French book from the 1750s (Katlan 1987, 13), but it is less clear how soon it was commonly used; Watin 1772 did not mention the *chassis à clefs*, while the 1774 edition of Watin did.

63   Cole's *The Departure* and *The Return* (1837, Corcoran Gallery of Art, Washington, D.C.) are two examples of paintings that are exceptionally well preserved. For a detailed discussion of the history and use of panel stretchers, see Hartwell 2008.

64   Hartwell 2008, 184–85. Trumbull was familiar with the principle that a solid piece of wood behind a painting would protect it. For his large (12 × 18 feet) paintings for the U.S. Capitol, he specified in 1823 that they be stretched over "pannels" of "perfectly seasoned mahogany or cedar," "for the purpose of guarding against injury from careless or intentional blows of sticks, canes, &c., or from children's missiles." When the paintings suffered from high humidity, at the same time that he saturated the backs of the canvases with wax, he directed that the panels be perforated with many holes and then painted before the paintings were restretched (Trumbull 1841, 279, 284).

65   Katlan 1992, 37–41, 497. For paintings by Cole from 1838 and 1842 on panel stretchers, see Kelly et al. 1996, 81, 96. Trumbull was also familiar with Parker & Clover; in 1823 he referred to them as "young men of this town, whom I have employed for some time, and regard as excellent

workmen," and recommended them to make the frames for his paintings in the Capitol rotunda (Trumbull 1841, 280).

Beginning in the 1850s, British Pre-Raphaelite painters also favored panel stretchers, both as original stretchers and for paintings that they had lined (Townsend, Ridge, and Hackney 2004, 113, 122, 150, 190–95).

66   Merrill 1992, 527–28; Katlan 1992, 37–39. Paintings by Church from 1873 and 1877 on their original panel stretchers are described in Carbone et al. 2006, 1:376; and Kelly et al. 1996, 63.

For paintings by Durand from 1855 and 1861 on panel stretchers, see Carbone et al. 2006, 1:478; and Kelly et al. 1996, 144.

67   Sully used fabrics stamped by Dechaux and Ashton & Browning; Neagle, by Kelley and William Rogers; and Rembrandt Peale, by Dechaux (Katlan 1987, 353, 354–55, 361; Torchia, Chotner, and Miles 1998, 33).

68   Of two portraits, Cole wrote: "I had laid the grounds for both" (Cole to William A. Adams, February 8, 1823 [Cole Papers NYSL]).

69   Barry 1994, 58. The 1828 painting is *The Garden of Eden* (Amon Carter Museum of American Art, Fort Worth, Texas), and the other paintings that Barry cites as having grounds applied with a brush date from 1825 and 1826.

70   *Study for "A Wild Scene"* (1831, Florence Griswold Museum, Old Lyme, Connecticut) was treated by the authors and has a commercially applied ground.

71   Cole to Asher B. Durand, May 13 and May 24, 1836 (Cole Papers NYSL). See also Katlan 1987, 19; Katlan 1992, 493–500; Zucker 1999, 5.

72   Cole to Durand, June 7, 1836 (Cole Papers NYSL).

73   Whether oil can rot canvas remains a matter of dispute; while oil is slightly acidic and this could theoretically have an effect on the life of a fabric, conservators have observed that fabrics that are very limp (hence without a size layer) are often well preserved.

74   R. Peale 1811, 15. Mérimée's book states that in France around 1830 some fabrics were sized and some were not (Mérimée 1839, 218–20).

75   Neagle "Receipts," 71–75. Charles Willson Peale also believed that oil would rot a canvas (C. W. Peale to Rembrandt Peale, February 23, 1819 [C. W. Peale 1983–2000, 3:698–99).

76   Sully "Hints," AAA, microfilm roll N18, frame 121 (1828).

77   Neagle Commonplace Book, 39–41. See also chapter 8.

78   Zucker 1999, 6; Mérimée 1839, 220–22.

79   Katlan 1987, 19.

80   Advertisement dated May 15, 1837 (Cole Papers NYSL). Philip or Philibert Caffe advertised as a maker of artist's canvas between 1837 and 1840, after which he advertised as a merchant. Stamped canvases by P. Caffe read: "PREPARED BY / P. CAFFE / NEW YORK" in the same oval format used by Dechaux (Katlan 1987, 60–61). A painting by Alvan Clark with a canvas so labeled (*The Artist's Brother*, ca. 1840, National Gallery of Art, Washington, D.C.) has "two thin ground layers…applied after the canvas was stretched: the lower is white; the upper is warm red" (Kelly et al. 1996, 69).

81   Cases of water-soluble grounds, some of them labeled by Theodore Kelley of New York, and the resulting conservation problems are discussed by Zucker 1999, 16–18.

82   Ibid., 6; Fulton et al. 2002, 158–59. An early portrait by Martin Johnson Heade (*Portrait of a Man*, 1840, Museum of Fine Arts, Boston) has such a ground (Wright 1999, 171).

83   From a Winsor & Newton catalogue of 1863 (Katlan 1992, 375); Neagle Commonplace Book, 15. Osborn was suspicious enough of prepared canvases that he made the somewhat impractical suggestion that an artist should buy them "many months" before using them to be sure that they were completely dry and then rub the canvases with pumice and rinse them with water and alcohol before beginning painting (Osborn 1845, 114–15).

Another unusual experimental technique of this time, possibly related to fears that materials would exude from a ground layer, was painting over gold leaf applied to the ground (Sully "Hints," AAA, microfilm roll N18, frame 138 [April 14, 1835]; Sully "Memoirs" [1859 addendum], 2).

84   Zucker and Boon 2007; Zucker 1999, 11–16. For the problem in Kensett's paintings, see Dwyer 1985.

85   Noble and Boon 2007; Boon, Hoogland, and Keune 2007; Zucker and Boon 2007. For analysis of an American portrait that shows the growth of new white lead crystals on the surface of the dark

background, see Zucker and Boon 2007, 21.

86   Zucker and Boon 2007, 34–35; Zucker 1999, 13–16.

87   Zucker 1999, 11; Zucker and Boon 2007, 38–39. *Niagara* (1857, Corcoran Gallery of Art, Washington, D.C.).

88   Ridner 1850, 133–34. Osborn was not nearly so critical of megilp and gumtion, describing both in a neutral manner (Osborn 1845, 79).

89   Osborn 1845, 79.

90   Mount's diary, March 31, 1862 (cited in Frankenstein 1975, 360–61).

91   Mount to William Schaus, January 4, 1853 (cited in Frankenstein 1975, 165). Megilp made with sugar of lead would be a variety of gumtion.

92   Cropsey to Asher B. Durand, November 27, 1856 (Katlan 1992, 510, 512–14; AAA/Hart, microfilm roll D5, frames 52–53). Copal megilp in tubes had been sold by Winsor & Newton since 1846 (Carlyle 2001, 104), and since Cropsey said that he generally used Winsor & Newton products, it is likely this is the store-bought product he was talking about.

93   Ridner (1850, 134) gives a variation of a recipe from Field (1841, 375) that contains less drying oil.

94   On Jocelyn, see Mount's diary, December 12, 1852 (cited in Frankenstein 1975, 250); Sully "Hints," AAA, microfilm roll N18, frame 209 (March 25, 1849). On Durand, see Mount's diary, May 13, 1859 (cited in Frankenstein 1975, 340).

95   Chapman 1857, 213. Also, "The methods and materials of the great masters in painting were unquestionably most simple.…Many, it is true, may have indulged in experimental explorations and favorite peculiarities, of either material or process, but almost invariably has the longest and best-tested experience resulted in the adoption of the most simple" (ibid., 212–13).

96   "Turner was busily engaged in retouching his large sea piece; I think with *water* colors!! which he afterwards toned with yellow varnish"(Sully Journal, AAA, microfilm roll N18, frame 436 [February 1838]). See also chapter 6.

97   Sully "Hints," AAA, microfilm roll N18, frame 153 (February–March 1838). "Pickersgill" may have been Henry Hall Pickersgill (1812–1861) or Henry William Pickersgill (1782–1875).

98   On Sully, see chapter 8; Mount's diary, October 1844 (cited in Frankenstein 1975, 129).

99   Neagle Commonplace Book, 38.

100   Carlyle 2001, 118–21; Ridner 1850, 126.

101   Neagle Commonplace Book, 41; Mount's diary, July 4, 1858 (cited in Frankenstein 1975, 312); Ridner 1850, 126–27.
        An unusual medium of the 1840s, probably used mainly by amateur painters, was "Osborne's American Oil Colours in Cakes." These were advertised in a Philadelphia catalogue from ca. 1843 and were described as "For Landscape Sketching, Miniature Painting, and Ornamental Work"(Katlan 1992, 315–17). They may have been similar to the oil colors in cakes made by Blackman in England, having spermaceti as an ingredient, which were probably intended for amateurs (Carlyle 2001, 113–14).

102   Mount's diary, December 1, 1853 (cited in Frankenstein 1975, 270).

103   Mount's diary [1858] (cited in Frankenstein 1975, 315).

104   R. Peale Miscellaneous, undated sheet titled, "Improvements in the Composition of Paints By Mr C. Binks," citing an article from *Annals of Chemistry*, December 1854.

105   Osborn 1845, 72.

106   Sugar of lead was not mentioned in Bardwell 1756; it was mentioned as a drier in Dossie 1764, 1:162–63. The *Practical Treatise* of 1795 (which borrowed entire sections from Bardwell) added to Bardwell's account of ivory black that sugar of lead could be used with it (p. 78), but also added a caution about its overuse (pp. xii–xiin).

107   Sully used "Rowney 'Siccatif'" in the early 1860s (Sully "Hints," AAA, microfilm roll N18, frame 248 [January 29, 1860], and frame 249 [June 17, 1861]). Mount used "patent drier (liquid)" in 1864 (Mount's diary, November 24, 1864 [cited in Frankenstein 1975, 383]). Church ordered driers from Goupil in 1867 (Zucker and Boon 2007, 35).

108   Shaw Palette, ca. 1820. Sully said that "severe" drier was the same as Japanner's gold size (Sully "Memoirs," 95).

109   Sully records Rembrandt Peale's recipe in Sully "Hints," AAA, microfilm roll N18, frame 76 (April 23, 1809); he gives Chapman's recipe in frame 138 (1834 or 1835). For Neagle, see his "Reciepts," 1. Peale gives a recipe in R. Peale "Notes," 81.

110   Osborn 1845, 73. A bottle of drying oil used by Cropsey (now solidified) still exists at the Newington-Cropsey Foundation, Hastings-on-Hudson, N.Y. (Katlan 1992, 506).

111   Rembrandt Peale to Mary [Mary Jane Patterson Peale], December 18, 1850 (R. Peale Miscellaneous, APS, Peale Family Papers, B P31); also includes directions for making drying oil from linseed oil and litharge.

112   R. Peale "Notes," 97–98.

113   Ibid., 135.

114   Ibid., 136. Sully confirmed that in 1859 Rembrandt Peale still recommended sugar of lead ground in oil as a drier (Sully "Hints," AAA, microfilm roll N18, frames 246–47 [June 15, 1859]).

115   R. Peale "Notes," 181–82. Peale did not know its ingredients, but modern authorities believe that Siccatif de Harlem consisted primarily of copal with oil of spike. The earliest mention of this product found by Carlyle in British colormen's catalogues was in 1879 (Carlyle 2001, 49). On Siccatif de Harlem, see also Mayer and Myers 2010, 126n58.

116   *Practical Treatise* 1795, xii–xiin.

117   Neagle Commonplace Book, 7; R. Peale "Notes," 160; Mount's diary, June 22, 1847 (cited in Frankenstein 1975, 178). The copied passage is from Field 1841, 108.

118   Osborn 1845, 73–74.

119   Cole to Asher B. Durand, June 9, 1837 (Cole Papers NYSL).

120   Sully "Hints," AAA, microfilm roll N18, frame 249 (May 1862). Sully was comparing dammar with "severe drier" and Rowney Siccatif.

121   Of course, Siccatif de Harlem (discussed above) functioned this way as well, as opposed to having a chemical effect on the drying of oil paint.

122   Sully 1873, 26.

123   R. Peale "Notes," 99.

124   Sully Journal, AAA, microfilm roll N18, frame 290 (July 21, 1825); Harley 1982, 116–17; Townsend 1995, 184; Field 1835, 83.

125   See chapter 10.

126   C.W. Peale 1983–2000, 5:369–70; Kühn and Curran 1986, 188–89. The chemical composition of chrome yellow had been discovered in France in 1798, but a lack of ore kept the discoverer, Louis Nicolas Vauquelin, from continuing his work and publishing a detailed description of its manufacture until 1809 (Harley 1982, 100-101). See also chapter 10.

127   Harley 1982, 101–2.

128   N. Evans 2006, 158.

129   Carroll & Crosby Invoice Book.

130   D. F. Tiemann & Company [catalogue], New York [the date 1863 written in ink] (collection of Stephen Kornhauser).

131   N. Evans 2006, 158.

132   For instance, the Brooklyn White Lead Works was founded in 1825 (Carbone et al. 2006, 1:14).

133   Neagle Blotter, November 16, 1836. Thomas Sully also received a keg of white lead from the same source (Sully Journal, AAA, microfilm roll N18, frame 411 [November 14, 1836]).

134   Neagle Blotter, comment inserted in 1839 on page for November 16, 1836.

135   Ridner 1850, 145.

136   Ibid., 8.

137   Carlyle 2001, 522–23.

138   Osborn 1845, 51n. He was probably referring to Field, who mentioned cadmium yellow in the 1841 edition of *Chromatography* (pp. 152–53) but not in the 1835 edition.

139   Carlyle 2001, 524.

140   Mount's diary, April 19, 1851 (cited in Frankenstein 1975, 246). See also chapter 13.

141   R. Peale "Notes," 199.

142   Cropsey Color Book (cited in Katlan 1992, 511).

143   M. J. Peale "Oil Painting." The entry is undated but appears after comments about an exhibition in 1858.

144   Fulton et al 2002.

145   It seems somewhat surprising that Sully, who seemed to know about all the latest materials, never mentioned cadmium yellow, but as a portrait painter he might not have needed such a bright yellow.

146   Mount's diary, January 25 and June 15, 1847 (cited in Frankenstein 1975, 171, 177); Field 1835,

70; Field 1841, 131. See also Ridner 1850, 20–21.

147   Field 1835, 70. Zinc white had been suggested as a less toxic substitute for white lead as early as 1795 (*Practical Treatise* 1795, 237–43, citing a paper read by M. de Morveau in Dijon).

148   On the production of zinc white in New Jersey, see Weber 1923, 130–31.

149   Zinc white "want[s] body and consistence" (Osborn 1845, 9).

150   R. Peale "Notes," 196. The process used by the New Jersey zinc company was different from that used by French producers (Kühn 1986).

151   Advertisement for John Lucas & Company, in O'Brien's *Philadelphia Business Directory* (1853), illustrated in Katlan 1992, 425.

152   Rembrandt Peale had eccentric (and inaccurate) views on the hazards of white lead, believing that an artist was not at risk when grinding it, but that the vapors were dangerous when drying, and a painting should therefore "be placed to dry in a separate room" (R. Peale "Notes," 109).

153   *Painter's Manual* 1868, 9–18.

154   Linton 1856, 300–301.

155   Zucker 1999, 8. *The Andes of Ecuador* (1855, Reynolda House Museum of American Art, Winston-Salem, North Carolina).

156   R. Peale "Notes," 192.

157   Mount to Benjamin Franklin Thompson, December 31, 1848 (cited in Frankenstein 1975, 235–36).

158   Mount used "a piece of drift coal which I picked up on the beach for my blue black" (Mount's diary, November 1844 [cited in Frankenstein 1975, 130]). William Dunlap said that "coal-cinder makes a blue-black" when he reported the earlier use of coal-cinder as a pigment by Francis Guy (Dunlap 1834, 2:149).

159   Harley 1971; *Paint and Painting* 1982, 67–69; Carlyle 2001, 52n2; Katlan 1992, 450–51; Katlan 1999, 23–24. According to Sully, Rand was also the inventor of the practice of cleaning a painting with a raw potato before varnishing it (Sully "Incidents," 16).

160   R. Peale 1856, 102.

161   C. W. Peale to R. Peale, February 10, 14, 15, 1820 (C. W. Peale 1983-2000, 3:796). "Verdegreese" refers to verdigris, the green corrosion produced by the action of acid on copper.

162   Harley 1971; Carlyle 2001, 52n2; *Paint and Painting* 1982, 66–67 (which says that the metal syringes were first announced in 1822).

163   Sully to Samuel F. B. Morse, March 4, 1828 (HSP; AAA, microfilm roll 22, frame 476). The letter goes on to say: "I would propose to you that you should import a sett, and in the meantime let Scarlett grind you the paint you need at present, and put them up in Bladders – or if you prefer it, in tin tubes." The latter reference may be to the tin tubes invented by Charles Bird King.

164   Sully Journal, AAA, microfilm roll N18, frame 339 (September 1829).

165   *Paint and Painting* 1982, 67; Carlyle 2001, 52n2.

166   Osborn 1845, 66. Although Osborn's book was a partial translation and interpretation of an earlier book by the Swiss artist Pierre-Louis Bouvier, the observations on tubes were Osborn's, for even Bouvier's third (1844) edition referred only to bladders.

        Dechaux's ca. 1836–40 catalogue listed paint in both bladders and tubes (Katlan 1992, 318), presumably some kind of noncollapsible tube with a plunger.

167   Osborn 1845, 66n2.

168   Osborn 1845, 66; R. Peale "Notes," 131. Cole also discussed the question of which colors were available in bladders and which would need to be ground by the artist just before use (vermilion, chrome yellow, and ultramarine) (Cole to Asher B. Durand, June 9 and June 14, 1837 [Cole Papers NYSL]).

169   Another reason that some colors were not put into bladders or tubes is that they do not keep well when mixed with oil—vermilion tends to separate, and ultramarine produces a stringy texture; for this reason modern manufacturers of tube colors add stabilizers to these pigments (see R. Mayer 1970, 151–52; Wehlte 1975, 106, 140; Carlyle 2001, 511).

170   Harvey 1998, 26–27; Katlan 1999, 23–24.

171   Cole to Durand, June 9, and June 14, 1837 (Cole Papers NYSL).

172   Baur 1942, 15.

173   R. Peale 1856, 102.

174   Tomlinson 1976, 7–8. During Stock's recovery, an ulcerated hip (a result of the childhood accident that made him a paraplegic) became reinfected, and he nearly died before undergoing major

surgery, which accounts for his long convalescence—it was more than a year before he fully recovered.

Stock said specifically that he was making mastic varnish at the time of his accident; mastic, unlike copal, did not need to be heated over a fire to dissolve the resin. Perhaps Stock was in a hurry—the accident happened in winter, when varnish would take longer to dissolve in a cold room. Accounts that warn of the danger of the process include: "The operation should be performed in an open place, during the *day-light*; for, if the spirituous vapour from the heated materials should take fire, from a *lighted candle* for instance, or other ignited body, the consequences might be disastrous" (*Practical Treatise* 1795, 186). Stock's accident was caused by him violating this rule—he was making his varnish at night, and the vapors were ignited by a candle or lamp. Sully wrote about making copal varnish: "This process should be conducted in a yard, or where no damage can ensue if the flask should break" (Sully "Hints," AAA, microfilm roll N18, frame 122 [August 1828]). Sully also noted that on separate occasions Joshua Reynolds and Benjamin Robert Haydon had paid fines to the London authorities when fire engines arrived after flammable mixtures heated in a fireplace spilled and went "roaring up the chimney"(ibid., frame 232 [August 1858]).

Ready-made varnish was available by 1839, but as an itinerant working in the provinces, Stock may not have had easy access to sources for ready-made varnish or perhaps could not afford it. (Stock was selling portraits for between five and ten dollars at a time when Sully was charging two hundred dollars for a 25-by-30-inch portrait.)

175 Found on p. 4 of advertisements at end of *A. M'Elroy's Philadelphia Directory for 1850* (Historical Society of Pennsylvania, Philadelphia).

176 Osborn 1845, 295, 295n.

177 Ridner 1850, 135. Ridner also pointed out how a varnish protects a painting, "securing it from injury, and in a measure protecting it from the influences of the atmosphere."

178 Sully "Hints," AAA, microfilm roll N18, frame 207 (August 10, 1846).

179 See, for instance, *Valuable Secrets* 1795; Cutbush 1814; Porter 1826, 59; Mackenzie 1829, 23–24; and Towers 1830, 27, 28, 91. Sully said he used copal to varnish a painting in 1819, but this was a special case (an egg varnish on a two-year-old painting had become moldy, and the paint had cracked) (Sully "Hints," AAA, microfilm roll N18, frame 141 [July 2, 1836]). In 1828 he wrote down a recipe for copal varnish from "Judge T. Cooper" (ibid., frame 122 [August 1828]).

180 Field 1835, 203; Mérimée 1839, 80–81.

181 Field 1835, 203–4.

182 Mérimée 1839, 48, 66–67, 69, 82.

183 Neagle Commonplace Book, 43; R. Peale "Notes," 61–62; Sully "Hints," AAA, microfilm roll N18, frame 225 (1852); Ridner 1850, 138. Ridner also mentioned "Cowdie varnish" (presumably Kauri, a variety of copal) as a new introduction from New Zealand and Australia, saying it was said to be superior to mastic but was too new to be used until tested (Ridner 1850, 140). Rembrandt Peale also took note of Field's theory that copal varnish was the best final coating for paintings in which copal was used as a medium, while mastic was the best varnish for a painting in which mastic was added to the paint (R. Peale "Notes," 135 [citing Field 1835, 203–4]).

184 R. Peale "Notes," 62.

185 Cropsey to Asher B. Durand, November 27, 1856 (AAA/Hart, microfilm roll D5, frames 52–53; the letter is published in Katlan 1992, 512–14).

186 Ridner 1850, 26n, 136–38.

187 Ibid., 138.

188 Osborn 1845, 91.

189 Sully "Memoirs," 17.

190 Mills and White 1987, 90–92; L. Mayer 1998, 23.

191 This problem was described much later: "If, for instance, of a given resin, say copal, a package of selected was bought one day, it was quite likely to be very different in its physical properties from a package of selected copal bought from the same house six months later" (Abendschein 1909, 25).

192 Ridner 1850, 138.

193 Sully "Hints," AAA, microfilm roll N18, frame 143 (May 12, 1837).

194 Ibid., frame 197 (1843).

195 Ibid., frame 233 (September 3, 1858); frames 249–50 (January 1 and 13, 1863); frame 251

(September 1867); frame 254 (December 18, 1869, and January 17, 1870).

196   Ibid., frame 230 (June 25, 1854). The last time Sully saw West in London was 1809–10. The painting West was working on at the time, *Christ Healing the Sick* (1811, Tate Gallery, London), was sold to the British Institution, and West sent a copy to Philadelphia (*Christ Healing the Sick*, 1815, Pennsylvania Hospital, Philadelphia).

197   Dwyer 1985, 177.

198   Sully "Hints," AAA, microfilm roll N18, frame 225 (1852).

199   In fact, Sully noted that poppy oil applied to correct bloom should be wiped off with a silk handkerchief (ibid., frame 225 [1852]).

200   Field 1835, 204; Field 1841, 373–74.

201   Carlyle 2001, 87–88. On shellac as a varnish, see also Sutherland 2010 and Mayer and Myers 2010.

202   Cole Papers NYSL, undated sheet beginning with"Extracts from Fields Chromatography or Treatise on Pigments & Colours…"; Sully "Hints," AAA, microfilm roll N18, frames 196–97 (1843); Mount's diary, July 4, 1858 (cited in Frankenstein 1975, 312); R. Peale "Notes,"183–84; Ridner 1850, 139.

203   Osborn 1845, 91n.

204   R. Peale "Notes," 184.

205   *Illustrated Catalogue of Artists' Materials: Imported and for Sale by M.J. Whipple & Co. 35 Cornhill, Boston*, ca. 1855–69 (Winterthur Library, Winterthur, Delaware).

206   Carlyle 2001, 87–93. It is interesting that the only actual use of white lac varnish that Carlyle found in Britain was on a painting by Constable that was varnished by the Anglo-American artist Charles Robert Leslie in 1840.

207   Mayer and Myers 2002. Dammar is also discussed in chapter 8 in connection with the many experiments that Sully carried out with varnishes in the 1850s and 1860s.

208   Sully "Memoirs," 17.

209   A British restorer who learned about dammar on the Continent said in 1853 that "he knew nobody in England who used it, apart from himself"(cited in White and Kirby 2001, 64–65); White and Kirby also describe the slowly growing awareness of dammar in other European countries in the early 1850s. For a Dutch reference to dammar in 1855, see Townsend 2002, 48.

210   Carlyle 2001, 84–87.

211   See Mayer and Myers 2002.

212   Ibid., 134.

213   The purchase from Koope, Fischer & Company was on March 4, 1850 (Schrack Daybook beginning January 1850, p. 53). Schrack & Company sold dammar to William D. Jones on three occasions (Schrack Daybook, beginning October 21, 1848): November 21, 1849 (p. 410), November 22, 1849 (p. 482), and December 13, 1849 (p. 507).

214   Sully "Hints," AAA, microfilm roll N18, frame 210 (April 1849).

215   R. Peale "Notes," 95.

216   Sully "Memoirs,"17.

217   When he first mentioned dammar, Sully was in Richmond, Virginia, visiting Robert Sully, who was at that time engaged in experiments with painting materials, including clarifying linseed oil, making absorbent grounds, and trying out new pigment mixtures for glazing (Sully "Hints," AAA, microfilm roll N18, frame 210 [April 1849]).

218   Rembrandt Peale to Rubens Peale, July 12, 1855 (R. Peale Miscellaneous).

219   Mount's diary, June 21, 1857, and [1857] (cited in Frankenstein 1975, 308–9).

220   The two colormen were Kelly [sic] (Sully "Hints," AAA, microfilm roll N18, frame 246 [June 5, 1859]) and Earle (ibid., frame 247 [October 2, 1859]). Kelley was a colorman in Philadelphia at that time (Katlan 1987, 145). Earle could have been the Philadelphia gallery owner who may have also sold artists' materials (Katlan 1992, 415) or possibly a colorman in New York (Katlan 1987, 91–92). In 1861 Sully also bought dammar from "Gadam," who has not been identified (Sully "Hints," AAA, microfilm roll N18, frame 249 [November 23, 1861]).

221   Katlan 1992, 320.

222   Kennedy & Nichols, *Hints on Drawing and Painting, and the Use of Paints* (Auburn, N.Y., 1860), 23, 27, 31.

223   In the mid-nineteenth century dammar was about nine times cheaper than mastic (White and Kirby 2001, 65).

224   R. Peale "Notes," 176–78.

225   Ibid., 95, 178.

226   Ibid., 184. On Soehnée's varnish, see Sutherland 2010.

227   Carlyle 2001, 216.

228   *Catalogue and Price List of Artists' Materials. Goupil & Co., Print Publishers and Artists [sic]*
       Colormen, 366 Broadway, New York. Paris-London-Berlin, Baker & Godwin, Printers, New York,
       1857 (Winterthur Library, Winterthur, Delaware); and *Catalogue and Price List, Edward Dechaux*
       (Represented in New-York by P. M. Hurel,) Importer and Manufacturer of Artists' Materials,
       Brushes, Colors, Canvas, and Everything Requisite for the Fine Arts, No. 709 Broadway, Paris-
       New York, 1860 (see Kaplan 1992, 320). Goupil listed two kinds of Soehnée's varnish: number 3
       was the retouching varnish for oil paintings, and number 2 was for watercolors.

229   For example, Jacob Eichholtz gave a recipe for mastic varnish: 1 pound mastic in 3 pints spirits
       of turpentine (Eichholtz Daybook, written inside front cover). Obadiah Dickinson gives "Shaw's
       mastic Varnish for Pictures: mastic 6 oz. Turp 14 oz." (Dickinson "Remarks," 90) and "Mastic
       varnish. Gum mastic in a bottle with spirits of turpentine about ¼ pound to a pint" (ibid., 91).
       Rembrandt Peale gave the recipe of ¼ pound mastic to a pint of spirits of turpentine (R. Peale
       "Notes," 135). In 1851 Sully's recipe was 12 oz. mastic to 35 oz. turpentine, plus ½ oz. camphor
       (Sully "Memoirs," 9).
            A French source of this period (Mérimée 1839, 81–82) known to Americans gave the
       recipe of 100 parts mastic to 200 parts "oil of turpentine" [spirits of turpentine], and noted it
       could be thinned. For comparison, a somewhat later Italian source not known to Americans as
       far as we know gave: 170 g dammar in 680 g turpentine; and 170 g mastic in 510 g of turpentine
       (Forni 1866, 265).

230   Rembrandt Peale to Rubens Peale, July 12, 1855 (R. Peale Miscellaneous).

231   Neagle "Receipts," 30; Sully "Hints," AAA, microfilm roll N18, frame 246 (December 1, 1858,
       and June 5, 1859).

232   Neagle Commonplace Book, 3.

233   R. Peale "Notes," 96.

234   Ibid., 61–62.

235   Shaw to Asher B. Durand, July 28, 1838 (AAA/Hart, microfilm roll D5, frames 268–70).

236   Dickinson "Remarks," 90.

237   For instance, a high percentage of oil could make a varnish sticky under a cotton swab and make
       it difficult for a conservator to thin it evenly.

238   Neagle Commonplace Book, 3.

239   Neagle Miscellaneous, undated sheet beginning with "Varnish oil paintings with mastic…"

240   Sully "Hints," AAA, microfilm roll N18, frames 90–91 (1812–22); Neagle Commonplace Book,
       9. This recipe appears to have come from Tingry 1804 (see Carlyle 2001, 79–80). It is also almost
       exactly the recipe (only the proportions of spirits of turpentine are slightly different) that appeared
       in an American compilation of recipes (Cutbush 1814 [unpaginated]).

241   Sully "Hints," AAA, microfilm roll N18, frame 137 (1833–34). The entry is immediately after
       passages about Thomas Lawrence, so the remark may have been made by that artist, especially
       since Neagle attributed the same practice to him. "Chilling" is a whitish bloom that sometimes
       appears on a varnished painting.

242   Ibid., frames 197–98 (1843).

243   Ibid., frame 209 (September 29, 1847).

244   Sully "Memoirs," 9; Sully "Hints," AAA microfilm roll N18, frame 248 (February 13, 1860).

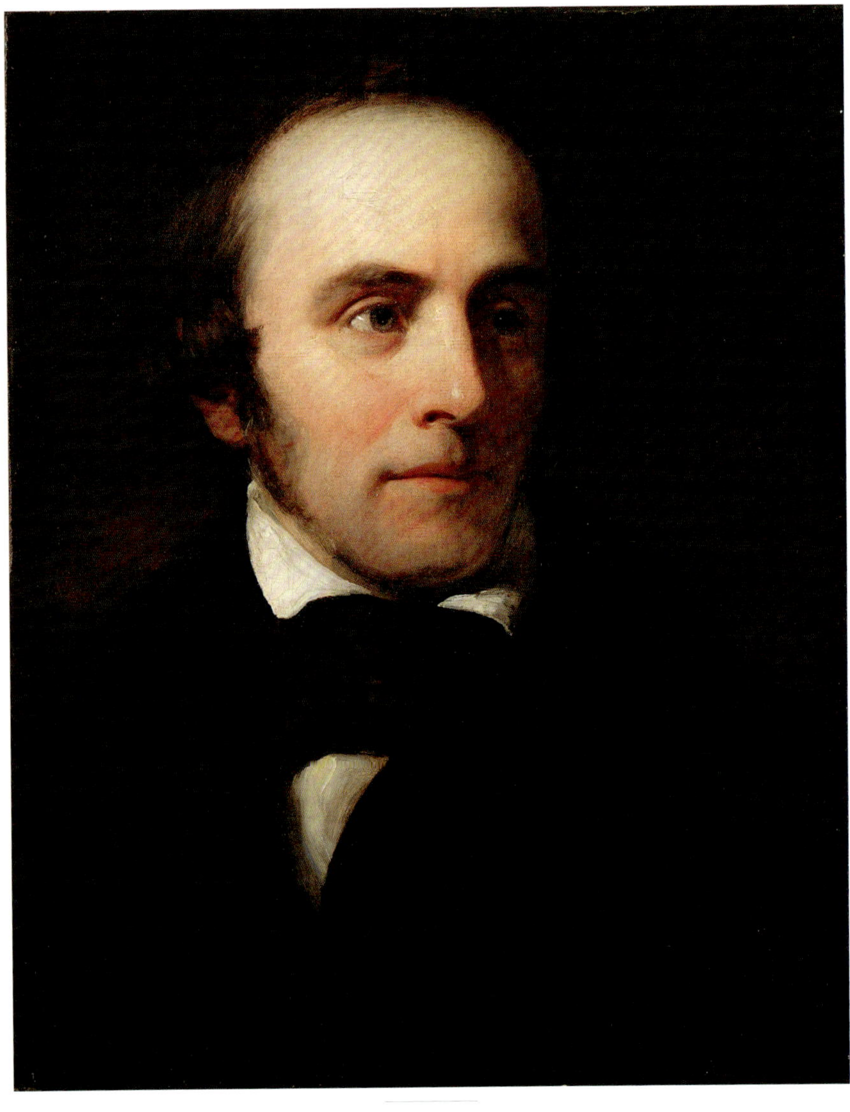

Daniel Huntington (American, 1816–1906), *Portrait of Thomas Cole*, 1843.
Oil on canvas, 50.8 × 40.6 cm (20 × 16 in.). New York, National Academy Museum, 607-P.

CHAPTER 12
THOMAS COLE: "THE BEST LANDSCAPE PAINTER IN THE WORLD"

IN THE 1830S AMERICAN CRITICS began to call Thomas Cole "the best landscape painter in the world"[1] and compared him favorably to Claude Lorrain and Domenichino.[2]

Cole's difficulties at the beginning of his career made his eventual success all the more striking. Although he had some instruction in engraving, and an itinerant portrait painter showed him the basics of oil painting, he was essentially self-taught. Dunlap gave his readers a pathetic description of the young man trudging around Ohio in the early 1820s carrying all his belongings, including a heavy stone muller for grinding paint, occasionally exchanging a portrait for food and lodging. Cole made his way to Philadelphia, where he drew at the Pennsylvania Academy, living on bread and water in an unheated room until illness required him to sell his camera obscura to obtain a stove and fuel. Finally, when he moved to New York in 1825, several of his landscapes attracted the attention of John Trumbull, William Dunlap, and Asher B. Durand, Trumbull saying, "This youth has done what I have all my life attempted in vain."[3]

COLE, THE OLD MASTERS, AND TONE

In the same conversation in which Washington Allston referred to the young Cole as "running after the old masters" (see chapter 5), the older artist gave Cole this advice: "By studying their works you will imbibe their spirit insensibly."[4] The degree to which an artist should "imbibe the spirit" of the old masters as opposed to simply observing nature looms large in any discussion of Cole's technique. The most outrageous story in this regard (as far as we know, unique among American painters) is that just prior to the time that he became known in New York, Cole "received a commission from a gentleman to paint some landscapes for his parlour. Upon these he tried an experiment of baking, which, at the time, he thought quite successful: it gave them, he fancied, finer tone and mellowness, and the air of old pictures."[5] One reason Americans may have wanted to give their works "the air of old pictures" was that in the 1820s and 1830s it remained a challenge to find collectors and critics who appreciated living American artists. For example, when Luman Reed, who had begun by collecting old European paintings and copies of earlier paintings, purchased a painting by Cole in 1833, it was his first by a living American painter.[6]

Early in his career, Cole took notes from a book on landscape painting by the British painter William Oram. Although the book was published in London in 1810, it reflected the practice of two generations earlier. Oram died in 1777, and some datable passages are attributed to British painters in Rome during the 1760s. Thus, one of Cole's earliest sources on technique originated in the world of Joshua Reynolds, Richard Wilson, and Benjamin West's early career rather than in Cole's own time. Oram's book showed the great devotion to Claude felt by British artists working in Rome. It also reflected Reynolds's practice in recommending yellow glazes over purplish underlayers and in advocating glazing with the warm brown pigments asphaltum and mummy.[7] In a passage that hints at how much old paintings were admired at that time, Oram wrote that trees should be given a warm color—not "foxy," "yet must have some appearance of brownness or redness."[8] Cole copied out passages from Oram about how to mix the colors for various parts of a landscape, and at least some modern authors have felt that the warm colors in Cole's early landscapes may be due in part to the influence of this book.[9]

Just as Thomas Sully, John Neagle, and others were holding intense discussions about "tone" in the 1820s and 1830s (see chapter 6), so the young Thomas Cole was working out for himself what the proper tone of a landscape should be. In letters exchanged with his patron Robert Gilmor in 1825–26, before he had ever been to Europe, Cole explained (perhaps somewhat defensively) the color of the sky in one of his paintings that Gilmor had purchased: "I think the colour of the sky will be much improved by varnish; but whether it will have the true saffron tint of morn I cannot say."[10] Not long after this, the landscapes of the British painter Richard Wilson, who was considered the heir of Claude, became a topic in their correspondence, and one might guess that the golden or "saffron" tone for which both those artists were famous was explicitly or implicitly a part of their discussion.[11]

When Cole began his first long sojourn in Europe (1829–32), it is perhaps significant that the first painting that he copied was one by Wilson.[12] Wilson was not only known for the Claude-like tone of his pictures but also was the artist who (in company with West) had glazed half of the pictures in a London exhibition with a warm brown glaze in the 1760s (see chapter 2). Cole may have taken too literally the example of Wilson (or the advice of Oram), because when he sent a painting back to America in 1830, a New York newspaper criticized parts of it for being "too brown and yellow, wanting the freshness and verdure of nature."[13]

While in Europe, where he could see for the first time the greatest paintings by the old masters, Cole thought a great deal about the effects of time on a painting. In London, in 1829, he wrote: "Many old pictures have pleasing qualities, which did not exist when fresh from the hand of the artist. We see in them a mellowness and lustre, a kind of inward light which is the effect of the touching of time."[14] Judging by this quotation, Cole did not think the effects of aging were a bad thing; of course, time's passage and the poignant feelings stimulated by the passage of time were favorite topics during the Romantic period (and in Cole's own writings). But somewhat later, after he had been to Italy, Cole acknowledged that admiration of the effects of time could be excessive: "Many of the Old Masters have been praised for their defects; and the blackness of age has been called tone."[15]

By the 1840s—now in a sense an old master himself—Cole observed (see chapter 5) that Allston's "great admiration for the Old Masters led him somewhat astray, for in some of his pictures he imitated the effects of time & they have often put me in mind of what Fuseli has said 'Those pictures which anticipate the beauties of time are pregnant with the seeds of decay.'"[16] Presumably Cole agreed with Fuseli that while time can put its "beauties" on a painting, these charms should not be striven for immediately or the result might be unfortunate—the "decay" could include cracking as well as having a painting turn darker than intended. There are other hints that Cole and other artists of his time may have actually welcomed the changes that time produced on a painting. Shortly after Cole's death, William Sidney Mount spoke of the effects of time on Cole's work: "His best pictures are of a cooll tone, a warmth given by glazing with warm color all over the painting, and sometimes left to time and varnish."[17] Mount himself had said on another occasion: "We know that hot pictures never improve by time, but cool pictures will,"[18] so it is difficult to know whether his observations about Cole reflect Cole's opinion or Mount's. Likewise, John Ridner wrote in 1850, two years after Cole's death: "None of [his paintings] show any perceptible change in colour; indeed, they appear in nearly every instance as perfect as when they left the easel, with the exception of the toning down which time always produces on all pictures."[19] Cole died in 1848; it would be fascinating to know what such a thoughtful artist would have felt about tone if he had lived past 1850, when so many painters and critics reevaluated their opinions about the appearance of old and modern paintings.

COLOR THEORY AND PIGMENTS

Both the practical and the romantic sides of Cole's personality came to bear in his interest in color theory.[20] The principal source of his information on color theory, George Field, also combined a scientific study of color relations with very romantic ideas about the emotional associations of each color. Cole owned a copy of Field's 1817 *Chromatics, or an Essay on the Analogy and Harmony of Colours,*[21] and in 1834 he used some of Field's ideas about color harmonies as a launching point for a scheme to make a musical instrument that would play "notes" of color: "The instrument might be played by means of keys, like those of a piano, except, that instead of their moving hammers to strike strings, they might lift when struck, dark or black screens from before coloured compartments. Transparent compartments, with either sunlight or artificial light behind, would perhaps produce the most brilliant effect."[22]

Only a month and a half later Cole wrote: "I have nearly constructed an instrument on which colour may be played[;] it is a rude one but perhaps sufficient for experimentation," but unfortunately we hear no more about Cole's color instrument after this time.[23] This experiment took place at the same time that Sully, Neagle, and Rembrandt Peale were carrying out many practical experiments with painting materials, and it is perhaps a reflection of Cole's romantic self-image that he preferred to experiment with loftier things than mere pigments and oils.[24]

Cole later took notes from a much longer and more practically oriented book by Field, *Chromatography.* Cole copied out a circular color diagram that would have reinforced his theories about color harmonies and complementary colors. *Chromatography* was first published in 1835, and it appears that Cole took notes from this first edition.[25] Cole also copied or paraphrased long passages about pigments and media from Field's text.

Two accounts, dating to 1833 and 1837, have survived in Cole's own words of the pigments he used, although the earliest list is fragmentary, containing only the primary colors and not browns or blacks.[26] William Sidney Mount also wrote a description of Cole's pigments shortly after Cole's death in 1848, although this is less reliable because it seems to incorporate secondhand accounts from others in addition to Mount's memories of having painted by Cole's side.[27]

Comparing the firsthand lists of Cole's pigments, several changes took place between 1833 and 1837. The earlier account listed Cole's three yellow pigments as Naples yellow, yellow ochre, and "sometimes" raw sienna. By 1837 Cole still listed Naples yellow and raw sienna but had substituted chrome yellow for yellow ochre, and in fact said in 1837: "Ochre I never use."[28] Chrome yellow was a topic of much discussion in the first half of the nineteenth century. The Peales had discovered that it changed color on exposure to light (see chapters 10 and 11); Cole copied out a passage from Field's *Chromatography* that said, "Crome yellow destroys Prussian & Antwerp Blues."[29] A book that we know Cole owned[30]—Sarsfield Taylor's 1839 translation of Mérimée—praised the beauty of chrome yellow but said, "It is not, however, a permanent color."[31] After Cole's death in 1848, chrome yellow must have still been controversial, for John Ridner seemed defensive when he cited Cole's usage to prove the permanence of the color:

> The late Mr. Cole—the distinguished landscape painter—it is well known, generally used this pigment [chrome yellow] for forming greens; and though many of his works have stood the test of a quarter of a century, none of them show any perceptible change in colour; indeed, they appear in nearly every instance as perfect as when they left the easel, with the exception of the toning down which time always produces

on all pictures: this is the best proof that can probably be adduced in favour of the permanency of this pigment when properly used.[32]

Artists needed to make mixed greens (by combining yellow and blue pigments) because a bright, stable green pigment was lacking at this time; a mixture of chrome yellow and Prussian blue was commonly sold in the nineteenth century as "chrome green."[33]

Blue pigments are obviously extremely important for a landscape painter in the representation of skies. Cole mentioned cobalt blue in his 1833 list, and Antwerp blue in his later (1837) list, but in both lists he also mentioned ultramarine. A critic took pains to praise Cole's use of ultramarine in 1837, in a description of his *View of Florence*: "We are strongly of the opinion that Mr. Cole has made a good and liberal use of ultramarine in his sky—a color the excellencies of which are not sufficiently appreciated by our artists."[34] Of course, the "liberal use" of ultramarine by Cole and others was made possible by the invention of the much less expensive artificial ultramarine in 1828.

Cole was also said by Mount to have used ultramarine ashes in his skies,[35] and a bill survives in which Cole ordered this pigment from the colormen Ashton & Browning of Philadelphia.[36] Ultramarine ashes is a grayish-blue color, the by-product of refining natural ultramarine. Contemporary authors differed on the usefulness and stability of ultramarine ashes. Field, in 1835, linked its use to the old masters and praised the pigment as "affording grays much more pure and tender than such as are composed of black and white, or other blues, and better suited to the pearly tints of flesh, foliage, the grays of skies, the shadows of draperies, &c. in which the old masters were wont to employ them."[37] On the other hand, the American Laughton Osborn, in 1845, said that ultramarine ashes should not be used in oil. He acknowledged Field's praise of the pigment, while cautioning, "But, observe, it is but the *refuse*, after all, of a precious color."[38]

For bright red pigments, Cole named the opaque red vermilion in both of his lists but added the bright, transparent madder lake to the later (1837) list. In terms of duller red pigments, in 1833 Cole mentioned Venetian red and burnt ochre, but by 1837 had substituted for these three different dull red pigments: Roman ochre, light red, and Indian red. It is difficult for a modern reader to understand nineteenth-century artists' preoccupation with the numerous varieties of dull red iron oxide pigments (see chapter 8). These were important for portrait painters in making dark, shadowed flesh colors, but Cole the landscape painter was apparently fascinated by them as well. Part of the explanation for artists' continual discussion of these pigments is that they are difficult to use. They have surprisingly high tinting strength: a little goes a long way, and it can be a challenge for artists to use these pigments in mixtures without making the mixture too hot, too dark, or too purplish.[39]

The transparent organic brown pigments asphaltum and mummy were recommended in the old-fashioned treatise by William Oram that Cole read in his youth. While Cole did not discuss brown or black pigments in his 1833 list of pigments, he included both mummy and Van Dyke brown in his 1837 list. Both pigments have a tarry component that gives them a transparent effect very different from opaque earth colors such as the umbers and siennas that Cole also mentioned in 1837.[40] There is a still earlier reference to Van Dyke brown in connection with Cole: in 1828 Thomas Sully sent some Van Dyke brown to Cole along with a letter praising Cole's landscapes.[41] The two artists did not appear to know each other well at that time, and the transaction hints that at this stage in his career—the year that he first met Allston, and the year before he first went to Europe—Cole had a special interest in transparent brown pigments.[42]

Rembrandt Peale wrote: "It is to be lamented that some of the most beautiful effects in the paintings of *Cole*, have suffered by the change of some pigments which he used."[43] Peale did not say which pigments had changed, but his opinion makes a great contrast with John Ridner's nearly contemporaneous view (cited above) that Cole's pigments had not changed, and his paintings were "as perfect as when they left the easel." There is evidence, in the notes that Cole took from Field's *Chromatography* about the stability of various pigments, that Cole cared deeply about the stability of his colors. In the midst of his notes from Field's book, Cole penned a poignant lament that speaks to the concern of artists of all eras that their best efforts toward permanence might in the end be frustrated: "That there is no absolute but only relative durability may be proved from the most adulated pigments—Thus the colour of *ultramarine* which under the ordinary circumstances of a picture will endure a hundred centuries, and pass through wet and fire uninjured, is presently destroyed by the *juice of a lemon* or other *acid*."[44]

MEDIA AND PAINT APPLICATION

Cole seems to have had conflicted opinions about the importance of technical processes such as adding media to paint and glazing. On the one hand, he criticized English painters for too much reliance on "the mechanism of the art—their dextrous management of glazing, scumbling, &c."[45] On the other hand, he criticized the modern Italians for not employing transparent glazes, and for treating "magilps and varnishes as though they were deadly poisons."[46]

Written sources are somewhat unclear about exactly what kind of medium Cole added to his own paint. After Cole's death, Mount said "he painted with linseed oil,"[47] which probably means he mixed additional linseed oil into paint that had already been ground in oil. (As mentioned above, Mount knew Cole, but he also appears to have relied on the accounts of others for information about Cole's techniques.) Cole took extensive notes from Field's 1835 *Chromatography* about materials that could be added to oil paint, and he wrote down more about the good qualities of copal than he did about any other paint additive; he also recorded Field's recipe for preparing copal by heating it with linseed oil.[48] It may be sheer coincidence, but in 1836, the year after *Chromatography* was published, Cole exchanged letters with Asher B. Durand about buying high-quality copal from a supplier in New York[49] (although the copal may have been intended to be used not as a paint additive but as a final varnish, as discussed below).

Nineteenth-century artists who added media to their paint believed, as Cole stated in his criticism of modern Italian painters, that such added substances produced "brilliance and transparency."[50] Another motive must have been the belief that the old masters used these sorts of materials. A description by Luigi Lanzi of the supposed methods of Correggio caught Cole's attention, and he took detailed notes from it; according to Cole's paraphrasing, the varnish that Correggio added to his paint contributed both strength and transparency: "[Correggio] painted with a strong impasto, or full body of colour, mixing it with two thirds oil and one of varnish.…Of their transparency, [Lanzi] was inclined to attribute the cause, to a varnish, more powerful than any known even to the Flemish painters whose varnishes are clear & shining but not equally strong."[51]

Glazing with transparent colors was an important part of Cole's process, which made it necessary for him to wait for his underlayers to dry before applying glazes. He once used this as an excuse when explaining to Luman Reed why *The Course of Empire* was progressing so slowly.[52] On another occasion, Cole emphasized the importance of glazing when he argued that a sketch done all at once was "never more than half true" because "the tones of Nature are too refined to be obtained without repeated painting and glazing."[53] Mount's descriptions of Cole's techniques also refer to his glazing processes, including "a warmth given by glazing with warm color all over the painting" and "in foreground he often gave strength to his palette & then glazed with transparent colors."[54] Giving "strength to his palette" must mean that in the final stages of painting Cole added different colors to his palette that produced the deep, transparent final touches in the dark foregrounds of his landscapes.

Mount described other aspects of the methods Cole used to build up the layers of his paintings. The first thing he wrote down when he recalled Cole's techniques shortly after the artist's death was: "Cole's pictures—The ground of the sky salemond [salmon] or light flesh color."[55] (Although Mount said "ground," he meant *imprimatura*, a thin layer of color applied on top of a ground.) Cole was famous for using reddish underlayers that sometimes play a role in the finished design, and, as Mount implied, the imprimatura could be a different color in different parts of a painting. In fact, this variation in color from one area to another has been found in a number of paintings by Cole. For instance, in one painting the sky and water were painted over a pink imprimatura, while the remainder of the landscape was painted directly on the white ground.[56] In the second version of

Cole's *Voyage of Life*, different parts of the design were variously underpainted in red, brown, or yellow.[57] (The teenaged Frederic Church, in a painting done while he was studying with Cole in 1845, used an imprimatura that varied from "a light buff to a deep terracotta as we move from sky to foreground."[58]) The technique of applying a warm-colored layer underneath the sky is also similar to the method that Washington Allston used on some of his paintings (see chapter 5).

Mount also described how Cole painted with bright colors and then toned them down: "Cole paints distance and retains color, but other artists in painting distance lose color in comparison. Why is it so, because he paints distance with pure (or strong) color and scumbles over with blue and white, or blue lake and white in the finishing."[59]

Scumbling is applying a thin layer of lighter-colored, opaque paint over a previously dried underlayer; it is in a sense the opposite of glazing, which is applying deeper-colored transparent paint over a lighter-colored underlayer. In this case Mount said that Cole created the effect of great distance by using a light bluish ("blue and white") or lavender ("blue[,] [red] lake and white") scumble to simulate the hazy atmosphere that comes between an observer and a distant view. In another place Mount called these scumbling colors Cole's "air tints."[60]

Mount also described Cole's method of painting skies:

> In finishing a sky, Cole would drag his brush over the fresh paint, in a strait line from the Sun, and when dry touch upon the clouds.
>
> If the Sun was on the left side, the opposite and upper part would be very blue or purple. His skys were beautifully graduated from almost pure white *naples* [Naples yellow] and *white*—naples and red inclining to the delicate purple up to a rich blue. In some of his skys he destroyed the marks of the brush, by touching gently all over the sky with the end of a large brush—one way of blending.[61]

The last practice is corroborated by Cole's own testimony: he described using a large softening brush (or "blender") to give the final touches to the sky in one of his *Course of Empire* paintings.[62]

Cole was proud of his speed as a painter, and this was noticed by others. He said of his ten-foot-wide *Mount Aetna from Taormina*: "I have finished two-thirds of it, and have only painted on it two days. I never painted so rapidly in my life." The entire painting was completed in five days.[63] Charles Lanman watched in amazement as Cole added a tree stump to the foreground of *Notch in the White Mountains* "which he painted in less than ten minutes and which turned out to be one of the finest bits in the whole production."[64]

To help him paint expeditiously, Cole sometimes used mechanical aids. As described above, Cole needed to sell his camera obscura in the early 1820s.[65] He probably purchased another instrument, for some of his drawings from subsequent years have the hesitant, "traced" quality of line that indicates they were made with some kind of optical device (see chapter 10 on optical devices used by other artists).[66] In 1840 Cole and his nephew made full-size tracings of his large *Voyage of Life* paintings, as well as detailed tracings of the human figures, "so that with them and the large tracings I can at any time paint large pictures."[67] Some of the tracings of figures have red chalk rubbed on their backs, as if Cole used them to transfer the designs to a canvas by pressing with a stylus or other sharp instrument.[68] Cole sometimes made sketches in pencil or oil for his paintings, but he also claimed a more unusual (and more romantic) approach to studying nature. He said he could study a rock or a tree until it was "as strongly impressed on my mind as possible and by looking intently on an object for twenty minutes I can go to my room and paint it with much more truth than I could if I employed several hours on the spot."[69]

COLE AND VARNISHING

Many nineteenth-century artists either did not describe varnishing at all in their writings or mentioned it only briefly in passing. However, varnishing was a relatively frequent topic in Cole's correspondence, hinting that it was particularly important to him. For instance, in 1825 he wrote that a painting "will be much improved by varnish" and in 1827 that a picture "is much sunk and will not appear to advantage until varnished." In the same year, his patron Daniel Wadsworth expressed confidence that one of Cole's paintings "will when varnished, & in its frame, be greatly improved."[70] It makes sense that paintings like Cole's, with their great contrasts between bright skies and dark foregrounds, would have these contrasts made even more dramatic by the saturation provided by a varnish layer.

Cole's correspondence also indicates he knew that a period of time should elapse before varnishing, which was one reason that he needed to discuss the topic—he had the awkward job of explaining to his patrons why their pictures did not look as good as they would eventually look after they were varnished. Ridner said Cole varnished his paintings "as soon as they became perfectly dry,"[71] which is not very specific. Mount said that Cole "did not varnish under a year,"[72] but this may have been a theoretical goal rather than his actual practice; the testimony of Cole's letters hints that he was not so dogmatic. Cole himself described working on a painting until the last minute before an exhibition,[73] and he variously told patrons that paintings recently sent to them should be left unvarnished "a short time"[74] or "one month longer."[75] Of course, once a painting was sent to a patron, varnishing was out of the hands of the artist, and the new owner was free to follow or reject the artist's advice on when to varnish, or perhaps never varnish the painting at all.

Cole's patron Luman Reed alluded to the latter possibility in 1835, when he wrote to William Sidney Mount with an unusual request. Reed asked Mount to not varnish a painting that Mount had recently painted for him, adding "I have not had my pictures by Cole varnished and the first one looks better today than the day I rec'd it. The blending of the colors gives it a richness and softness that it had not at first." Reed went on to say that he also feared cracking as a result of varnishing.[76] Some years later, in 1853, Cole's biographer Louis Legrand Noble wrote in a similar vein that a certain quality in a painting by Cole had been lost after it was varnished:

> While Prometheus was yet fresh from the easel, and without varnish, its sky was one of those marvelous approaches to nature but few times reached by the pencil. It seemed all but that dark vault itself....Previous to its exhibition, at Westminster Hall, in London, (where, by the way, it was hung in a manner that entirely destroyed its effect), it was coated with a kind of varnish that has much injured its depth and purity, and nearly taken away those subtle qualities, ethereality and moisture, for which it was really wonderful.[77]

It is difficult to know what to make of these two opinions that Cole's paintings looked better without varnish. Varnishing can give bright colors greater contrast and make dark colors deeper, but it can also sometimes surprise an artist by saturating differently colored areas in different ways (which is why artists sometimes retouch on top of varnish—to correct unanticipated problems that are visible only after varnishing). A glossy varnish can also produce distracting reflections, especially on a dark painting, and especially if a painting is hung in bad light, as Noble implied in the case of the *Prometheus*. Another document from about this time indicates the degree to which landscape painters had conflicting feelings about varnish. This is an odd letter from Joshua Shaw to Asher B. Durand in 1838, offering Durand a piece of advice: "It is on the utility of varnish, or rather its inutility—I consider it is the greatest curse which the arts have ever had cause to complain of [.] It is the foundation cause of all mischief, the mildew and kanker [worm?] which has prayed upon and destroyed two thirds, nay I may say nine tenths of all the best Pictures in exhistance. But it is still more mischievous when applied to a New Picture."[78]

Shaw went on to explain in vaguely scientific terms how varnish would blacken and destroy a painting, and that it cannot ever be safely removed. Shaw was an argumentative person with strong views on many subjects, and amid all his criticisms of varnishing he did not say specifically that varnish should never be used.[79] There is no evidence at this period of any concerted movement on the part of artists or patrons to want their paintings to remain permanently unvarnished or of their specifically seeking a matte effect (as would happen much later in the nineteenth century). The opinions of Reed, Noble, and Shaw seem rather like isolated incidents; artists generally continued to use varnish and continued to debate the merits and defects of various kinds of varnishes.

In terms of Cole's specific varnishing materials, Mount wrote that Cole varnished "with a slight coat of copal varnish with a few drops of boild oil and thinned with turpentine."[80] This sounds more like firsthand observation than some of Mount's other descriptions and is corroborated in a general way by Ridner, who wrote that Cole "always varnished his paintings with copal varnish as soon as they became perfectly dry."[81]

As described above, Cole took notes from Field's 1835 book *Chromatography* about the good qualities of copal, and he purchased copal in 1836. Field had praised the durability of copal varnish;[82] Ridner also emphasized the strength and durability of copal, saying it protected Cole's pigments from change.[83] Cole owned a copy of Taylor's 1839 translation of Mérimée, which suggested applying a thin coat of copal varnish for its strength, which could then be followed by a layer of more easily removable mastic,[84] although there is no evidence that Cole used this kind of two-layered system.

Mount said specifically that Cole used a "slight" (thin) layer of copal varnish; this might have been because copal varnish often had a brownish tinge, as Mérimée noted,[85] or because Cole feared that a thicker coat might crack or turn dark over time, as Rembrandt Peale commented.[86] But it is also perhaps significant that in 1828, before he is known to have purchased copal and before he could have read about copal in books by Field or Mérimée, Cole also gave directions that "one coat [of varnish] will be sufficient."[87] In this case, the single coating of varnish may have been an aesthetic choice, or it may be that Cole knew that the gloss on this painting was even enough that one coat of varnish would be sufficient, or that he feared a thicker varnish would be more likely to cause cracking. It is difficult to determine exactly what artists intended in terms of the thinness or thickness of their varnishes, and it seems likely that (as in earlier periods) a variety of opinions may have been shared at any given time.

NOTES

1   "Editor's Table," *Knickerbocker or New York Monthly Magazine* 5, no. 6 (June 1835): 550ff; *New York Mirror: A Weekly Journal* 13, no. 40 (April 2, 1836): 318.

2   *New York Mirror: A Weekly Journal* 12, no. 47 (May 23, 1835): 371; and no. 42 (April 18, 1835): 330. (Transcripts of many reviews of Cole's work are in the Cole Papers at the New York State Library; there are photocopies at the New-York Historical Society.)

3   Dunlap 1834, 2:351–60.

4   Henry Greenough (cited in Flagg 1892, 197).

5   Noble 1964, 27.

6   Foshay 1990, 45.

7   Oram 1810, 88–90.

8   Ibid., 30. Cole's notes from Oram are in a notebook at the Detroit Institute of Arts. Oram's observation on the color of trees connects with George Beaumont's views on brown trees in his debate with Constable (see chapter 6).

9   Wallach 1994, 28, 104n36.

10   Cole to Robert Gilmor, July 2, 1825 (cited in Noble 1964, 62).

11   The surviving correspondence is not complete, but the year after the letter about the "saffron tint," Gilmor wrote to Cole that he owned two paintings by Wilson and told him that "the coloring of

land & water is quite in the style of Claude, and entitles him to his name of the English Claude" (Gilmor to Cole, December 27, 1826 [Cole Papers NYSL]).

12   Cole to Gilmor, May 1, 1831 (cited in Noble 1964, 88).

13   *New York Evening Post*, May 1, 1830, describing *Lake Windermere*.

14   Cole's "Notes on Art," December 12, 1829 (cited in Noble 1964, 82). Cole explained this in pseudoscientific terms: "The cause of this highly valued quality…arises, evidently, from an artificial atmosphere formed by particles of opaque matter gradually deposited upon the surface. This medium through which we see the picture is dark and negative, and the light that breaks through it has greater value from the contrast" (ibid.). See also Burgard 1990, 151.

15   Cole to William Dunlap, September 1834 (Dunlap 1834, 2:365). Cole was clearly drawing on earlier notes and referred to observations made in Italy, so this opinion may date from that time.

16   Cole Journals [July–August 1843].

17   Mount's diary, April 7, 1848 (cited in Frankenstein 1975, 185).

18   Mount's diary, June 1, 1847 (ibid., 176).

19   Ridner 1850, 26.

20   Cole's practical side can be symbolized by his design for an improved steamboat (Cole Journals [spring 1837]), the romantic side by reams of flowery poetry and poetical prose in his journal.

21   Field's *Chromatics* (Field 1817) appears in an undated list of Cole's books (AAA, microfilm roll D6, frame 266).

22   Cole Journals, November 8, 1834. At this time Cole also wrote: "I made a small circular diagram of colours to-day." This may be the oil on panel referred to in Barry 1994, 66n27.

23   Cole Journals, December 21, 1834. Gilbert Stuart was also interested in correspondences between music and color (see Cogdell Diaries/Letterbooks, vol. 3, entry dated September 18, 1816), as were eighteenth-century British theorists: a color organ "that mechanically produced coordinated colors and music"was demonstrated in London in 1757 (D. Evans 1999, 26).

24   The extent of Cole's philosophizing can be gauged by a passage in his journal that immediately follows the section on his color instrument. He was apparently speculating about the center of the earth and how the earth's matter was held together, but part of this section of the journal is cut out and the rest is disfigured with large letters: "I am certain this is nonsense."

25   Cole's notes from Field's *Chromatography* are in the Cole Papers NYSL; the hand-colored diagram copied from Field is at the Art Museum, Princeton University. The date that Cole took his notes cannot be established exactly (Homer 1960, 27). However, the sequence of Cole's notes follows the first (1835) edition much more closely than the second (1841) edition. For instance, the passage about Correggio's vehicle consisting of two parts of oil and one of varnish appears in Cole's notes between discussions of oils and copal, as it does in the 1835 edition but not in the one from 1841 (where the comment about Correggio is on pp. 360–61, before any discussion of oils or copal). It is interesting that Cole had access to the first edition; our sense from the number of surviving copies is that the first edition, which was in a large (quarto) format and therefore expensive, had a small press run and was probably not widely distributed in America. Even Thomas Sully did not own a copy of the first edition, as he did the second (see chapter 8). (The second edition of Field was in 1841, not 1869, as Homer implies.)

      Chromatography does not appear in the list of books Cole owned, as *Chromatics* does. Cole's pupil Frederic Church did own a copy of *Chromatography* (Zucker and Boon 2007, 34–35).

26   The first is a copy of a letter from H. G. Morton to Cole, October 1, 1833 (Cole Papers NYSL). Morton asked what color mixtures Cole used, and Cole scribbled notes on the letter, as if preparing to write a response, but we do not know if he ever actually responded. The second is a pair of letters from Cole to Asher B. Durand, June 9 and 14, 1837 (Cole Papers NYSL). The lists were prepared for different purposes: the earlier one to help a fellow painter who sounds like a beginner, and the other to decide which paints to order for a *plein-air* expedition with Durand, and this should be taken into consideration in our interpretation of the pigments listed. For instance, in his letter to Durand, Cole clearly wanted to take paints that were available in bladders, although he himself says that he did not know which ones were available that way, so he may have listed pigments that he *thought* were available in bladders (hence perhaps the most popular ones). However, he also listed pigments that he intended to take in dry form (to be mixed with oil "in the field"), so it is our opinion that both letters probably list the colors that Cole normally used at each period.

27   An example indicating that Mount's account was cobbled together from different sources is that

he said Cole "used but five colors," but then mentioned twelve pigments that the artist supposedly used. The colors that Mount said Cole used were: ultramarine ashes, white (unspecified), vermilion, Venetian red, madder lake, terra rose, blue black, ivory black, Naples yellow, ochre (unspecified, but when unspecified usually means yellow ochre), Van Dyke brown, and umber (raw or burnt not specified) (Mount's diary, April 7, 1848 [cited in Frankenstein 1975, 185]).

28 Cole seemed to contradict himself when in 1837 he said he wanted to take "Roman ochre" (a red ochre) on the painting expedition with Durand (Cole to Durand, June 9, 1837 [Cole Papers NYSL]). Ochres come in yellow and reddish shades, but in context it is clear that when he said he never used ochre, he was referring to the yellow variety.

29 Cole Papers NYSL, undated sheet titled "Extracts from Field's Chromatography."

30 Undated list of Cole's books (AAA, microfilm roll D6, frame 266).

31 Mérimée 1839, 96.

32 Ridner 1850, 26–27. In a footnote Ridner said that the application of a thin layer of copal varnish, as was Cole's custom, helped preserve the pigment.

33 Carlyle 2001, 492.

34 Review of the National Academy exhibition in "The Editor's Table," *Knickerbocker or New York Monthly Magazine* 9, no. 6 (June 1837): 617ff. The painting might be *View of Florence* (1837, Cleveland Museum of Art).

35 Mount's diary, April 7, 1848 (cited in Frankenstein 1975, 185).

36 Bill dated July 7, 1840, with a note by Cole he paid it on July 16, 1840 (Cole Papers NYSL). Although Cole ordered ultramarine ashes, Ashton & Browning declined sending the pigment because they believed it would not meet his needs.

37 Field 1835, 170; Field 1841, 299–300.

38 Osborn 1845, 4. Osborn may have been reflecting Bouvier's bias against ultramarine ashes (Bouvier 1844, 26).

39 Mount's comments on Cole contain the observations of the painter Henry Peters Gray [Grey], who "says that he [Cole] used very little vermillion in flesh, principally venetian red and madder lake—sometimes Terra Rosa" (Mount's diary, April 1848 [cited in Frankenstein 1975, 185]).

40 In 1837 Cole also mentioned the pigment bone brown as if it were the near equivalent of mummy, although the two are quite different (Field 1835, 161; Carlyle 2001, 490–91).

41 Thomas Sully to Cole, May 27, 1828 (Cole Papers NYSL).

42 See chapter 4 on Gilbert Stuart's transition from opaque brown earth pigments to the more transparent Van Dyke brown during the first decades of the nineteenth century.

43 R. Peale "Notes," 120. Although Peale used the word "pigments," he may have been thinking as well about the problems with cracking that many of Cole's paintings exhibit. For a discussion of traction crackle in Cole's *The Garden of Eden* (1828, Amon Carter Museum of American Art, Fort Worth, Texas), see Barry 1994. It is ironic that the book by Mérimée that Cole owned has excellent advice on avoiding cracks, including not painting with fast-drying paint over slow-drying layers and not using bituminous earths in underlayers (Mérimée 1839, 92–93).

    In terms of darkening, it is interesting that a painting by Cole was thought to need cleaning as early as 1830. Thomas Sully to Daniel Wadsworth: "Scarlet thinks he can clean your picture by Cole" (AAA, Robert Graham Collection, microfilm roll D294, frames 784–85).

44 Cole Papers NYSL, undated sheet titled: "Extracts from Field's Chromatography."

45 Dunlap 1834, 2:362.

46 Ibid., 2:364–65.

47 Mount's diary, April 7, 1848 (cited in Frankenstein 1975, 185).

48 Cole Papers NYSL, undated sheet titled: "Extracts from Field's Chromatography."

49 Cole to Asher B. Durand, May 24, 1836 (Cole Papers NYSL [cited in Katlan 1987, 19]). Cole to Durand, June 7, 1836 (Cole Papers NYSL).

50 Dunlap 1834, 2:362.

51 Cole Papers NYSL, undated sheet titled: "Colouring of Correggio."

52 Cole to Luman Reed, January 13, 1836 (cited in Noble 1964, 157). The five paintings of *The Course of Empire*, 1833–36, are in the New-York Historical Society.

53 Cole to Gilmor, quoted in Stebbins 1978, 6, 48n7.

54 Mount's diary, April 7, 1848 (cited in Frankenstein 1975, 185); Mount Diary LIMAA, April 1848.

55 Mount's diary, April 7, 1848 (cited in Frankenstein 1975, 185).

56 Kelly et al. 1996, 81, 87; see also Carbone et al. 2006, 1:387, 391.

57 Kelly et al. 1996, 96. *Voyage of Life* (1842, National Gallery of Art, Washington, D.C.).

58 Zucker 1999, 7. As Joyce Zucker points out, this is very similar to the contemporaneous advice found in Laughton Osborn's treatise.

59 Mount's diary, April 11, 1848 (cited in Frankenstein 1975, 185).

60 Mount Diary LIMAA, April [?] 1848.

61 Mount's diary, May 4, 1848 (cited in Frankenstein 1975, 186).

62 Cole Journal, January 1, 1836 (cited in Noble 1964, 155–56).

63 Cole to Maria Cole, December 9, 1843 (ibid., 264). *Mount Aetna from Taormina* (1843, Wadsworth Atheneum Museum of Art, Hartford, Connecticut).

64 "Artistic Recollections," 4E (Lanman Papers, Getty Research Institute, Los Angeles). This may be *A View of the Mountain Pass Called the Notch of the White Mountains (Crawford Notch)* (1839, National Gallery of Art, Washington, D.C.).

65 Dunlap 1834, 2:359.

66 Our thanks to Elise Effmann for this observation (personal communication, 2006).

67 Schweizer 1985, 18; Kelly et al. 1996, 98–100. The tracings were a special case, for the second series was in part the result of a dispute with the heirs of the patron who had commissioned the first series. The first *Voyage of Life* has been studied using infrared reflectography, which revealed extensive pencil underdrawing, including corner-to-corner diagonal lines, outlines of contours and compositional guidelines measured out and drawn with a compass and ruler, as well as free, sketchy drawing lines (Kushel 1985; our thanks to Dan Kushel for giving us a copy of his article). For another painting by Cole showing extensive underdrawing, see Kelly et al. 1996, 87.

68 Schweizer 1985, 24–25, 27.

69 Baigell 1981, 13. For a study of drawings in twenty-one of Cole's paintings with infrared reflectography, see Alexander 1994. She describes two styles of underdrawing: "thoughtful outlining" and "squiggly lines."

70 Cole to Robert Gilmor, July 2, 1825 (cited in Noble 1964, 62); Cole to Daniel Wadsworth, November 26, 1827 (cited in McNulty 1983, 21); Wadsworth to Cole, December 4, 1827 (ibid., 22). Other references to varnishing are: Cole to Wadsworth, December 8, 1827 (ibid., 26); Cole to Gilmor, May 21, 1828 (Cole Papers NYSL).

71 Ridner 1850, 26.

72 Mount's diary, April 7, 1848 (cited in Frankenstein 1975, 185).

73 Cole to Maria Cole, no date (Cole Papers NYSL).

74 Cole to Gilmor, April 2[1? illegible], 1833 (Cole Papers NYSL).

75 Cole to Wadsworth, June 5, 1828 (cited in McNulty 1983, 42).

76 Luman Reed to Mount, November 25, 1835 (cited in Foshay 1990, 67, 205n159); also Burgard 1990, 170, 213n252.

77 Noble 1964, 289, describing *Prometheus Bound* (1847, Catskill Public Library, Catskill, N.Y.).

78 Shaw to Durand, July 28, 1838 (AAA/Hart, microfilm roll D5, frames 268–70). The letter continued: "as it locks up the [illegible] of fermentation thrown upon the surface of it while Drying and which continues to blacken and [illegible: vitiate?] the whole surface as long as it remains upon it. It never dries and is ever absorbing the dirt and dust which alight upon it and when attempted to be removed is never efected without ireparable injuring to the Painting, because it has been in some measure immalgimated with it by the salving acrid nature of the intervening vicious mucus, and the Whole Picture suffers afterwards whether it be cleaned or suffered to remain."

79 In fact, a recipe for varnish has survived that is attributed to Shaw. See chapter 11.

80 Mount's diary, April 7, 1848 (cited in Frankenstein 1975, 185).

81 Ridner 1850, 26.

82 Field 1835, 208–9.

83 Ridner 1850, 26. In a footnote to his comment that "none of [Cole's paintings] show any perceptible change in colour," Ridner wrote: "This may be owing to the fact that this artist always varnished his paintings with copal varnish as soon as they became perfectly dry, which served to protect them from change."

84 Mérimée 1839, 91–92. Ridner 1850, 138.

85 Ibid., 82.

86   R. Peale "Notes," 62.

87   Cole to Wadsworth, June 5, 1828 (cited in McNulty 1983, 42). Documents survive from this period (1827–33) that show Cole buying varnish from the New York colormen Parker & Clover, but the type of varnish was not specified (Katlan 1992, 499–500).

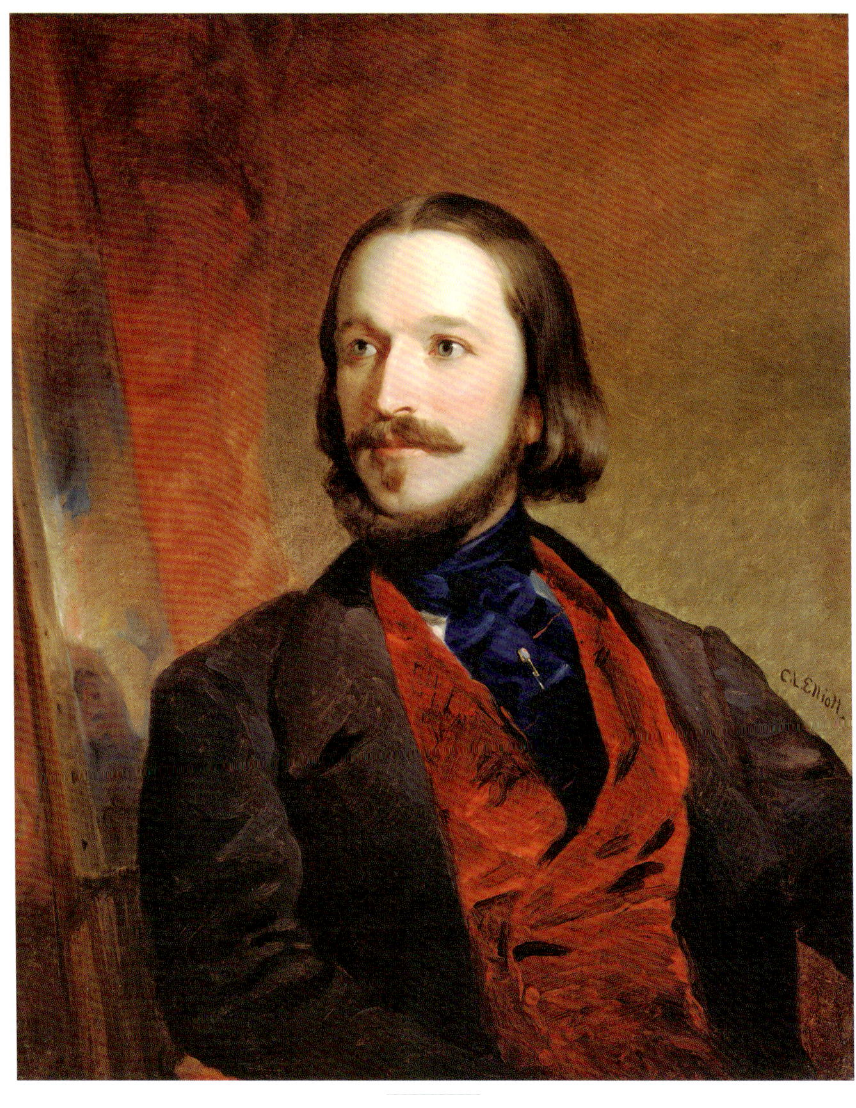

FIGURE 19

Charles Loring Elliott (American, 1812–1868), *Portrait of William Sidney Mount*, ca. 1850.
Oil on canvas, 77.2 × 64 cm (30³/₈ × 25³/₁₆ in.). Washington, D.C., National Gallery of Art,
Andrew W. Mellon Collection, 1947.17.6.

CHAPTER 13
WILLIAM SIDNEY MOUNT
"STAMPED WITH AN ENTIRELY AMERICAN CHARACTER"

WILLIAM SIDNEY MOUNT WAS APPRENTICED to his brother—a sign painter in New York—beginning in 1824, but an exhibition at the American Academy of Fine Arts in 1825 changed his life. The display included seventeenth- and eighteenth-century European paintings and two large Shakespearean scenes by Benjamin West in addition to works by modern American painters. In Mount's words: "The sight of so many pictures in rich frames, the figures the size of life looking upon me from all parts of the room—created a strange bewilderment of feeling such as I have never since known….my mind was awakened to a new life and big resolves for the future were then made."[1] Mount studied at the National Academy of Design and obtained a brief period of instruction from Henry Inman, then began to paint portraits and the genre scenes that would make him famous.[2]

Mount was a generation younger than Thomas Sully and Rembrandt Peale, and eleven years younger than John Neagle, but like them he had an insatiable appetite for information about painting techniques. His diary and correspondence document vividly many aspects of the materials and techniques that occupied the thoughts of painters between the 1830s and the 1860s. Mount spent most of his time on rural Long Island, and he never visited Europe. This isolation, combined with his personal idiosyncrasies, contributed to the uniqueness of his approach to technique—he comes across in his writings as an odd, neurotic personality who perhaps found himself his best companion. Many of his observations have a very different emphasis from those of the triumvirate of "experimentalists" from Philadelphia and Baltimore.[3]

GROUNDS AND IMPRIMATURE

Mount's thoughts on the color of grounds show how changeable his opinions could be. In the 1840s he gave what was a common opinion in the nineteenth century—that a white ground "of a brilliant whiteness" was best because it would "bare [bear] out the colours to perfection."[4] (At about this time Laughton Osborn defined the term *bear out*: "Colors are said to *bear out*, when they appear in their full vivacity."[5]) But in 1850 Mount had a different idea: "I can recommend a light grey ground. The best sketch I ever made was painted on a grey ground—more daylight—on account of the grey showing through."[6]

Somewhat later, Mount wrote that a ground could be "a coat or two of cream colored paint, or any color you desire."[7] He also proposed that an artist could "order your canvas or panel white and then you can paint it a light cream color—if you desire it, with white, yellow ochre and a little vermilion—an orange tint."[8] Late in his life, Mount was still more varied in his recommendations, telling his nephew in 1863 that a ground could be tinted slightly reddish, yellow, black, blue, or even greenish-gray, saying, "It depends very much on the subject you are going to paint—what tint you paint upon."[9]

In 1844 Mount recorded elaborate directions for painting a sunset scene, including the color of the canvas—"red or salmon colour."[10] This probably refers to an *imprimatura* (a colored layer applied on top of the ground) and may reflect the influence of Thomas Cole, for the remarks are similar to Mount's observations about Cole's techniques for using colored underlayers in skies (see chapter 12). In 1850 Mount had an idea for an unusual variation on this kind of imprimatura: "The most perfect landscape ground, I think, would be to make the center, or one third of the canvas or panel grey and the top and bottom red—the grey and red melting into each other with a perfect gradation."[11]

Still later (in 1856), Mount described, when painting his *Bone Player*, rubbing a white ground with a red imprimatura in a way that must have been experimental, for he took notes as if he were afraid he would forget the technique. "I finished the bone player this day—over white ground. I rubbed the canvas over with Venetian red—ground in oil thinned with turpentine—it should be used with drying oil. Any color can be given in the above way. When dry commence painting."[12]

In 1849 Mount wrote an elaborate account of making his own ground for canvases and panels using white lead, clay, boiled oil, Japanner's gold size, and turpentine.[13] It is not clear why he went to such trouble when commercially prepared canvases with grounds were easily available; of course, cost may have been a reason. The recipe was somewhat similar to other published recipes of the time,[14] but it appears that Mount was working out the details himself and was pleased with how his ground dried quickly to a hard, matte surface.

In a different category of observation altogether—apparently not based on his personal experience but on his fascination with unusual techniques—Mount wrote: "Some artists paint their subject at once upon the bare wood, or canvas."[15] This would appear to be an odd practice at the time, although other painters had noticed that earlier in the century Gilbert Stuart had painted on "naked" wood or on "slightly coated" panels and fabrics (see chapter 4).

MOUNT'S PIGMENTS

One of the most unusual aspects of Mount's technique was his enthusiastic use of American earth pigments that he dug himself in the 1830s and 1840s (see chapter 11). Earth pigments—ochres, umbers, and siennas—had long been imported from Europe, and it is tempting to find significance in Mount's (and others') interest in American pigments during a period in which America was beginning to feel independent of Europe in many other ways. Mount discovered brown, red, yellow, and black earth colors in Stony Brook, Long Island, but his favorite native pigment was an umber that he described as transparent and a good drier—"in the gradations of the flesh, with white it is truly delightful. It unites harmoniously with all colors."[16] He sometimes referred to this pigment as "Stony Brook umber"[17] or "Mount's umber"[18] and recorded matter-of-factly that his friend Charles Loring Elliot used Stony Brook umber when he painted Mount's portrait.[19] On one occasion, Mount even recorded a combination of store-bought pigments that could be mixed together to make a substitute for those not fortunate enough to have access to Stony Brook umber.[20]

In 1844 a critic said of Mount: "His productions are stamped with an entirely American character."[21] Mount's use of American pigments made this literally true. It is unclear exactly how many of these pigments he used on a regular basis. He himself said at one time that he had "painted several pictures"[22] with Long Island pigments, and he may have exaggerated this on occasion, for a correspondent expressed surprise that Mount had claimed to have "found most of the colours, required in your art"[23] on Long Island. One cannot help but suspect that Mount's preference for native pigments ran much deeper than simply liking their color or their cheapness.

Mount's opinions about other pigments were many and varied. In one case he may have been reacting against the complicated directions given in some published treatises for setting a palette with dozens of mixed tints before beginning painting. Mount wrote in 1847: "I do not believe in a regular sett palette. Three or four mixed tints for expidition. Fire at the heap for your tints, combine your tints with the brush."[24] "Fire at the heap" is a vivid expression for dabbing into a pile of paint with the brush to obtain mixed colors, rather than carefully mixing them up with a palette knife in separate piles beforehand.

One of Mount's peculiarities is that beginning about 1847 he seems to have arranged his palette with white pigment at the left side of his palette, which is backwards from the way that most painters had set their palettes throughout history; usually, a pile of white paint (which was used more than any other color) was placed on the right side of the palette nearest the thumbhole, which is also nearest to the hand that holds the paintbrush.[25] An earlier painting by Mount (*The Painter's Triumph*) shows white in this more typical position near the thumb.[26] Mount hinted that the motive for setting his palette backwards was to give himself a fresh approach to color mixing, writing in 1847, "For a change, place the light colours on the left of the palette, near the elbow,"[27] and he followed this reversed arrangement in all other recorded palette settings for the rest of his life.[28]

Mount had some interesting ideas about pigment mixtures, at one point (in 1859) suggesting a mixture of Prussian blue and burnt sienna as a substitute for asphaltum.[29] This must reflect the concern for permanence that runs through many of Mount's writings. Earlier in his career, he had written about the beauty and usefulness of the pigment asphaltum,[30] but by the middle of the nineteenth century many artists believed it to be unstable.[31]

Mount knew about the new pigment cadmium yellow by the year 1851, at about the same time that other American artists were first discovering it (see chapter 11). Typically, its permanence was the first thing Mount mentioned: "It is a new color. It is said to be durable," and he made a resolution to try it in place of Naples yellow.[32] By 1859 Mount had added cadmium yellow to his palette "for landscape."[33] A deep, bright yellow color like cadmium (unlike Naples yellow, which tended toward white) was particularly useful for combining with blue to make mixed greens for foliage. In 1862 and 1867 he recommended cadmium yellow to his nephew and his niece, who were beginning painters, warning his niece that chrome yellow (which was less permanent) was sometimes passed off as cadmium.[34]

Mount sought advice from others about the permanence of pigments. Around 1845 he copied out a lengthy recipe from James Jay Mapes for purifying pigments with water and honey.[35] In 1859 Mount recorded conversations with his fellow artists Joseph Vollmering and Régis Gignoux about the durability of colors and which pigments were safe to mix with others and compared their opinions with one another and with what he had read in George Field's book.[36]

PAINT APPLICATION

Mount also collected information from others about the actual process of painting. His notes included succinct, practical tips from Frederic Church: "Some paint the Horizon first. Mr. Church says he paints the distant objects first, he mixes up a set of sky tints of different gradations to facilitate his work."[37]

Mount was also one of the few painters to actually tell us the number of sittings that it took to paint some of his well-known works. "I painted the Banjo player in eight days (16 sittings), two sittings a day. The Bone player in seven days (or 14 sittings), two sittings a day forenoon and afternoon."[38]

In the 1840s Mount looked back at an earlier portrait done in one sitting and seemed to wish that he could achieve that kind of spontaneity again. He admonished himself: "I must paint on a light ground and approach as near the complection as I can the first sitting—paint daring. I must go over my work like a dare devil when it needs it."[39]

Some methods of painting struck him by their novelty, as when he took notes on the dark-toned method of Stuart's pupil James Frothingham:

> Frothingham says that he has painted a head in so low a tone that venetian red
> and madder lake were the only reds used—he glazed with madder lake and the
> highlights with raw sienna. Gold ochre is the only opaque yellow color he uses.—
> He has but few colours on his palette. His style is loose and scratchy. At a distance the
> effect of his flesh pleasing and natural, life like. Some of his portraits compare with
> any painted.[40]

Mount's curiosity also led him to record methods that might have appeared
to be of little practical use to him. In 1859 he visited the studios of two "cheap
landscape" painters who produced landscape paintings very quickly, up to sixteen
a day, painted in about half an hour each.[41] Mount drew lessons even from these
hacks. He wrote: "This rapidity of painting is worthy of attention and imitation, as
very many effects of nature are better represented by being painted quick."[42] In the
interest of speed, one painter used two palettes placed on a bench near his easel,
seldom used a maulstick, and employed a "scragly old brush" for foliage; Mount
also noted that his colors were "made very gaudy, to catch the eye."[43] More than
a month after one of these visits he recalled a tip that a "cheap landscape painter"
had given him: when painting skies, mix enough color to paint over the gradations in the sky three times.[44] Mount's account is a fascinating record of a type of
painting that is otherwise difficult to document—the ancestors of the "sofa-sized"
art and velvet paintings of recent times. The scale of production of these painters is
also a reminder that many of the art materials that we are studying were purchased
by their ilk (and by amateur painters) as well as by the more famous artists whose
works hang in museums.

BRUSHES

Mount described in more detail than any other American artist exactly how he
used brushes to achieve certain effects. In 1847 he made the following note (the
bad grammar of which leaves little doubt that this was his own thought rather
than something he copied): "Objects should be introduced in a large manner, with
large brushes—small brushes is apt to produce the small or dry manner."[45] William
Dunlap told a story in this regard: after the death of the genre painter John Krimmel, John Neagle purchased all of his brushes but found most of them too small
for his purposes, so he gave them to the painter Alexander Rider, who painted in a
"small," highly detailed manner similar to that of Krimmel.[46]

Laughton Osborn, in 1845, gave American readers a thorough account of
the various types of brushes that were then available, including which animals the
hairs came from—fitchet (polecat or stinking martin), goat, hog, badger—and confirmed the conventional wisdom that brushes made from the hair of the sable were
the best but the most expensive.[47] Mount had his own opinions about this: "Small
fitch brushes are better for some purposes than sable brushes—a small round brush

to sharpen up, light or shadow—in the finishing touches. A large round brush for rapid painting—to skim the canvas."[48]

It has always been a challenge for landscape painters to depict convincingly the effect of leaves on a tree or blades of grass in a field. In a lengthy passage, Mount suggested unusual methods, such as using old brushes with "scanty hairs" to paint leaves, or dragging a comb through a brush to make the hairs separate when portraying grasses, or even making a brush out of broom corn to paint grass.[49] At about this same time, Rembrandt Peale also believed that "for some purposes old & stiff brushes may answer to lay on & *scumble* the paint," but he also emphasized the value of a new brush on other occasions. "The vulgar saying that 'a new broom sweeps clean,' is applicable to painting. Certain finishing touches can only be made with the fine hair of a new brush, which cannot be done with the same brush when it has become worn square & harsh. A few new ones should be allotted for every Portrait."[50]

Mount, Osborn, and Rembrandt Peale all took note of the flat brushes with metal ferrules that were a new development of nineteenth-century technology.[51] Mount made a sketch of one when he bought three flat bristle brushes at Knoedler's in 1864; he also pointed out that Cole had used flat brushes.[52]

In 1859 Mount had another theory about using brushes: "An idea came into my mind to day (as I had been thinking about using brushes with longer handles), to place the end of (the handle) my brush into a port crayon—and if I wish it longer, to put a piece of brush handle in the other end."[53] Long-handled brushes were not a new idea; Charles Willson Peale had experimented with them around 1795.[54] Rembrandt Peale said that he had sometimes used brushes up to four feet long, held at arm's length, "to have the painting at an equal distance with the Sitter"; he realized that although this was a good idea in theory (or as "an occasional mode of study"), normal brushes were still necessary.[55]

In 1852 Mount applied the lessons that he had learned when painting grass and foliage to portrait painting, and meditated on the result:

> I imitated some of the flesh in the above portrait by driving the color with the end of the brush—the same as the brush is sometimes used in painting foliage and grass in landscape.
>
> In painting, "the end justifies the means." It does not matter how the color is laid on as long as the effect of nature is produced—if the painter uses his great toe in the operation.[56]

DILUENTS (THINNERS)

Mount was one of the few nineteenth-century artists who discussed in any detail the materials that artists used to thin their paints. In the 1840s he mentioned adding "a trifle turpentine" to a painting medium "to make it work free."[57] On another occasion in the 1840s Mount wrote: "A crispy touch I think is given by thinning your oils varnishes pigments with a little turpentine, for the last touches in a picture."[58]

Mount recorded contradictory opinions about the propriety of diluting paint with large amounts of turpentine. On the one hand, in 1848 a house painter told him that "turpentine freely used with oil will not crack."[59] But a decade later, in a passage that seems based on personal experience, he wrote: "To be remembered: if you paint over a panel or canvas that has been painted and thoroughly dry, with paint mixed with about two thirds turpentine when it is dry it will scale off."[60]

In 1851 Mount's curiosity led him to carry out an experiment with a diluent: "I used Megilp thined a little with Camphene. I must take notice how it stands time—if it will crack."[61] In the nineteenth century, the terms *camphene* or *camphine* meant an especially pure form of turpentine. Mount's interest in camphine was ahead of its time and shows the depth of his interest in high-quality ingredients. The only references to this material found in a study of nineteenth-century British sources date from several years after Mount's experiment (and later than mentions of camphine by Rembrandt Peale and Thomas Sully as well).[62]

ADDED MEDIA

Mount's appetite for information and his penchant for tinkering are nowhere more obvious than in his accounts of the various media he added to oil paint. He sometimes added different materials in different parts of a painting, as in the 1835 *Bargaining for a Horse*. "In the dead colouring I painted the sky with mastic varnish and turpentine mixed together. In the board fence and crib I used macguilp. In the roof of the shed I used nut oil. Fore ground and interior of the shed I painted with macguilp, the horse finished with nut oil. The farmers finished with mastic varnish and turpentine mixed together."[63]

All of these materials should be understood as having been added to oil paint. Mount might have thought that the different additives would serve different purposes in various parts of the painting—in terms of transparency or texture, for instance. Or he may have been carrying out an experiment to see if any of the materials changed color or otherwise misbehaved in the future. In fact, he second-guessed himself in this case, writing in 1847 (twelve years after he had painted the picture), "Copal and Turpentine would be better, I think"[64] in place of the mastic and turpentine he had used in the sky. (The preference for copal may possibly have reflected his reading at about that time in Field's *Chromatography* rather than any specific bad effect that he had seen on the painting.)

In an undated note that probably dates from the 1840s, Mount wrote down Field's directions on how to prepare copal for use as a painting medium by combining it with oil and turpentine (with a little wax).[65] In June 1847 he made a note that seemed to assume that copal mixed with oil and turpentine was the best medium to add to oil paint.[66] But later this same month, Mount made a surprising discovery that recalls a similar discovery by John Trumbull (see chapter 3). Mount found that the simpler methods he had used in his youth lasted better than more complicated techniques: "In my first painting when Linseed oil was used, no cracks are observed, and the colours look as fresh as the day they were laid on—nineteen years, standing."[67]

Mount concluded from this that artists should "for permanence use Linseed oil, only, and turpentine."[68] (Again, in the context of Mount's notes this almost certainly means adding linseed oil and turpentine to previously prepared oil paint.) The use of turpentine, which would evaporate, would help a painter achieve a good working consistency without adding too much oil. An excess of any medium can produce discoloration (since all oils and natural resins turn color over time), and it can produce cracking by exaggerating the movement that oil paint films undergo as they dry.[69] Mount recorded other notes about linseed oil at about this time, including how to prepare it as a drying oil[70] and who sold the best linseed oil in New York,[71] as if he had decided that linseed oil was the best medium to add to his paint.

But by 1850–52 Mount was fascinated with other media, including megilp, which his friend and mentor Charles Loring Elliott had added to glazes when he painted Mount's portrait.[72] Mount wrote: "Elliott is very particular about getting his magilp to the right consistency—using it as thin as it will stay put."[73] At this time Mount also read about Joshua Reynolds's use of wax[74] and seemed to connect this with Field's recipe for a copal megilp that contained a little wax.[75] This combination of ideas produced contradictory and sometimes alarming ideas. On the one hand, Mount made the reasonable statement that "if you must use Megilp let it be the last thing to glaze with in finishing," but in the same passage he had the reckless idea to "dissolve white wax in turpentine, then use it alone in colors while painting."[76] He noted an unusual medium used by the painter Nathaniel Jocelyn that contained copaiva balsam as well as copal,[77] and he had harsh words for color manufacturers who added sugar of lead to tubes of megilp.[78]

Mount's theories about the ideal medium continued to bounce back and forth throughout the rest of his life. In the 1850s he experimented with dammar varnish, which had only recently become available in America, using it with oil in various combinations as a paint additive and comparing it with mixtures of copal and oil.[79] In the 1850s he also noted that a picture that he had painted twenty years earlier with mastic added to his paint was in perfect condition, and at one point he made the sensible argument that "it is only when too free use of megilp is used that a painting is injured by it."[80]

Like several other artists at this period, he staked out a more conservative position toward the end of his life and seems to have reverted to his former opinion that only oil—or at least mainly oil—should be added to paint.[81] In 1862 he recommended adding only raw linseed oil in the summer and boiled oil in the winter,[82]

sometimes qualifying this opinion by permitting the addition of Japanner's gold
size or "megilp out of the tube" to colors, like black, that dried poorly.[83]

GLAZING AND TONING

Mount carried discussions of glazing and toning deeper into the nineteenth century than Sully, Neagle, and Rembrandt Peale. Mount used the terms somewhat
interchangeably, but a toning layer to him generally meant a glaze applied over an
entire painting or a large part of it. For instance, Mount wrote that he finished his
painting *Turning the Leaf* "by toning over the mass of light with yellow and a little
Madder Lake, and rubbing it off with a piece of silk—then subduing the rest of the
work with Ultramarine blue, to give value to the flesh and warm draperies. Lastly
touching in yellow and Lake on the distant skies and clouds—and blending the
whole into keeping with a large dry brush."[84]

On another occasion when he gave advice to a fellow artist, he more clearly
recommended a uniform toning of the entire painting: "When your picture is
finished and you wish to take off the effect of the paint and at the same time give
a sunny warmth, go over the whole picture with raw sienna mixed with drying oil,
use a rag in putting it on. You can use blue red and yellow, or any other compound
in the same way."[85] Sully had also used raw sienna for overall toning and believed
that the old masters had done the same thing (see chapter 6). Raw sienna is a dull
yellow color that could mimic the effect of a dark, yellowed varnish, hinting that
part of Mount's goal was to achieve something of the patina of age.

Mount took careful notes about another artist who consciously imitated the
effects of earlier painters, Joshua Reynolds, and Mount's notes make it clear that
he understood that Reynolds sometimes added red, yellow, or black pigment to his
varnish "to lower the tone of the colors."[86] Mount did something very much like
this when he painted a portrait in 1860: "I passed over sparingly vermilion with
megilp mixed with linseed oil—at every sitting from life."[87] In other paintings from
the 1860s he also glazed or toned paintings with mixtures of madder lake and raw
sienna, or madder lake alone, sometimes rubbing the glazes in with the palm of his
hand.[88] He also suggested that the pigment ivory black could be used for toning, an
echo of the opinion that was held by Rembrandt Peale.[89]

VARNISHING

Mount's views on varnishing were somewhat inconsistent. In 1846 he wrote a
note to himself to "varnish with a strong varnish."[90] This could possibly mean a
varnish that was tough (like copal) rather than brittle (like mastic), but he may
also have been thinking of a situation like the one he found himself in some years
later, when he purchased mastic varnish at a colorman's shop that was too weak
a solution and did not produce a proper gloss. "The mastic varnish sold in some
of the color shops in the City is *positively bad* for a painting.…the mastic varnish

said to be (I believe was not) mastic was too thin and dryed dead—sunk into the ground or distance."[91]

Mount said he needed to modify this thin varnish by adding linseed oil to obtain a proper gloss. He did the same thing the next year (1864), this time combining dammar, mastic, and bleached linseed oil for a final varnish.[92] Mount hedged his bets when, late in life, he took notes on how to varnish a twenty-year-old painting. He first said that mastic varnish warmed in a hot water bath should be used but then added the somewhat surprising statement that "oiling out" with linseed oil could be considered the equivalent of a varnish. "Some times the painting should be oild out with sun dryed oil—or raw oil if the varnish should dry too quick."[93] Oiling out could have unfortunate results because oil would become impossible to ever remove.

In 1850 Mount wrote: "Mr. [John Thomas] Peele varnishes his pictures with megilp varnish and touches upon it while still wet."[94] The varnish in this case functioned as a retouch varnish, and Mount once suggested that he himself should follow the unusual procedure of varnishing a painting, then applying oil on top of the varnish, then painting over the work "in parts where it is necessary."[95]

Many painters believed that a year should elapse before varnishing (although a retouch varnish was normally applied as soon as a paint layer was dry to the touch). Mount wrote at the bottom of a page in his diary: "Never varnish under a year";[96] he also knew that Cole had believed that an artist should wait a year before varnishing.[97] But according to Mount's own testimony, he varnished *Bargaining for a Horse* only five days after completing it,[98] although he was still fairly young at this time (1835) and might not have known better. In 1835 he did not varnish a painting that he sent to his patron Luman Reed, at Reed's specific request (for a fuller discussion of Cole, Reed, and varnishing, see chapter 12).

By the 1840s, Mount's diaries show that he understood the main reason for not varnishing too soon—that "thick coats of varnish, applied too rapidly, will crack."[99] (A conservator might add another reason: varnish applied too soon can penetrate into fresh paint and be impossible to remove in the future.) In 1847 Mount exchanged letters with a sitter who noticed that the portrait Mount had painted the previous year looked "rather dry" and would "appear to the advantage" if it were varnished.[100] Mount responded: "It is natural that you should desire to see your portrait to the best advantage. I sincerely feel the interest you take in it….But what can I do, when the majority of the old masters, with the sanction of the moderns, say, never varnish under a year. Many a fine picture has been injured by being varnished too soon."[101] Mount nevertheless promised to varnish the painting at the end of the following month.[102]

ADVICE ON TECHNIQUE FROM THE SPIRIT WORLD

Mount's unique approach to technique is nowhere better seen than in his belief that the old masters communicated their secrets directly to him at spiritualist séances.[103] Two long letters to Mount survive that are allegedly transcripts of letters sent by the spirit of Rembrandt, and some shorter notes include records of conversations that Mount had with the spirit of Richard Wilson.[104]

The receipt of letters written by spirits was apparently a regular occurrence in Mount's spiritualist circle. The editor of Mount's papers believed that Mount may have written the letters from Rembrandt himself and "cast them in the form of communications from the spirit world simply as a striking literary device."[105] However, Mount's accounts of his spiritualist adventures make it clear how seriously he took spiritualism and how critical he was of those who tried to debunk it, making it seem unlikely that he would write fraudulent documents.

In any case, whoever wrote the Rembrandt letters began by telling Mount exactly what he wanted to hear. Rembrandt called Mount "the best National painter of your country" and explained that he felt a special kinship with Mount because he himself had given his pictures a *Dutch* national character. Rembrandt advised Mount, among other things, that he should not base his coloring on Rembrandt's coloring, which was "too brown" for Mount's style or his American subjects. One passage that strikes a modern reader as odd is Rembrandt's statement that Richard Wilson was his greatest follower, closely imitating Rembrandt's impasto and his rich brown tints. Wilson's paintings do not seem very much like Rembrandt's, and this misunderstanding may betray the lack of sophistication of a letter writer who knew Wilson's work only through prints.[106]

Much of Rembrandt's advice was of a general nature, above all to paint confidently rather than hesitantly and to make sure that the light in a painting falls correctly. In terms of specific materials, Rembrandt said that he used no medium other than drying oil. Rembrandt introduced some anachronisms—one of these is that he said he used a flat brush—flat brushes were introduced in the nineteenth century. Rembrandt also said that for a brown glaze he used "finely powdered spanish liquorice." This is a very unusual idea for a pigment in the nineteenth century (or in any century), but it recalls the temporary glaze that Dunlap (1834) said was used by Richard Wilson and Benjamin West in the 1760s (see chapter 2), making one wonder if the letter writer had gotten the idea by reading Dunlap's book.

The spirits were somewhat confused about the chronology of the use of blue pigments. On one occasion Rembrandt said that he used blue verditer but that this was superseded in Mount's time by cobalt blue, correctly recognizing that blue verditer was used in earlier periods, while cobalt blue was a nineteenth-century invention. However, in another place Mount recorded a series of questions and answers in which an unknown spirit said that Rembrandt had used cobalt blue, which obviously could not be true. The letters from Rembrandt also contain the anachronism that Rembrandt used Prussian or Antwerp blue, both of which were not invented until after Rembrandt's death.

Rembrandt wrote that the spirit of Caravaggio would be present at Mount's spiritualist circle on the evening that Rembrandt's first letter was delivered, but no record of this potentially interesting event has survived in Mount's papers. Mount did record a conversation with Richard Wilson and some sketchy notes about the palettes of George Morland and Titian. Wilson said he did not use megilp because it "clots the colors" and painted only with turpentine and oil, specifically, poppy oil and "burnt oil" (possibly the "burnt plate oil" used in printers' ink[107]), while Morland used "very thin oil," and Titian's grounds were made of "Flour, in Water Color."[108] The oddness of some of the materials in the spirit communications tends to reinforce the theory that Mount was not their author, and, in fact, his diaries do not show that he was impressed enough by these materials to have tried them in his own practice.

Mount is a fascinating bundle of contradictions; as strange as his spiritualist views may seem, he also had a very practical side to his personality. He was proud of his innovative design for a portable studio that he had built, which was on wheels and could be pulled by a team of horses.[109] He once wrote: "I dont see why an artist should not be as particular about his studio as a Blacksmith is about his shop."[110] As in the case of Rembrandt Peale's remark cited earlier (that a knowledge of materials and techniques is as important to a painter as good materials and tools are to a mechanic in the production of watches or steam engines), this strikes a matter-of-fact, practical note that seems very American.

Some of the materials and techniques that Mount used toward the end of his life (he died in 1868) look forward to the very different artistic landscape that unfolded during and after the Civil War. His use of "recycled" wooden panels from the estate of Samuel Waldo in 1864 may be attributable to the strains of a wartime economy.[111] During the war it was difficult to obtain turpentine, which normally came from southern pine forests, so Mount (like carriage manufacturers) experimented with petroleum solvents for diluting his paint.[112] Petroleum solvents appear to have been little used by artists before this time,[113] but they would become a topic of intense discussion later in the nineteenth century. In the 1860s Mount also began to use liquid "patent drier,"[114] the kind of commercial product whose ingredients were a trade secret and which would become much more widely used in decades to come. The many and varied materials used in the post-1860 period will be the subject of the authors' forthcoming second book.

NOTES

1   Johnson 1998, 18, 92n11.

2   Frankenstein 1975; Dunlap 1834, 2:451–52.

3   Some considered Mount lazy, and he frequently chastised himself for not working harder, leading to the suspicion that one motive for Mount's continual search for new techniques was the hope

that new methods might make his job easier. George Templeton Strong's diary entry when he heard of Mount's death in 1868 read: "His few productions during the last twenty years have been extremely bad. He has been living…in eastern Long Island, that paradise of loafers, and amusing himself and his friends with his fiddle and his pencil sketches" (Strong 1952, 3:232 [November 20, 1868]).

4   Mount's diary, 1847 (cited in Frankenstein 1975, 177).

5   Osborn 1845, 328.

6   Mount's diary, October 29, 1850 (cited in Frankenstein 1975, 244).

7   Ibid., 315 (1858).

8   Ibid.

9   Mount to Samuel Seabury, October 13, 1862 (Mount Papers LIMAA); also Williams 1941. For a full discussion of Mount's advice to his nephew, see Katlan 2001; our thanks to Alex Katlan for giving us a copy of his article.

10   Mount's diary, May 23, 1844 (cited in Frankenstein 1975, 129); Mount's diary, June 1, 1847 (ibid., 176).

11   Mount's diary, October 29, 1850 (ibid., 244).

12   Mount's diary, April 3, 1856 (ibid., 307). *The Bone Player* (1856, Museum of Fine Arts, Boston).

13   Mount's diary, May 18, 1849 (ibid., 199–200). The clay was probably pipe clay or kaolin. Mount had still other ideas about grounds, including notes on the grounds of Titian (allegedly flour, white lead, and nut oil) (Mount Diary LIMAA, [1846–47?]), and hints from a decorative painter about applying grounds to pasteboard and wood panels (Mount's diary, 1852 [cited in Frankenstein 1975, 249]).

14   For example, Hundertpfund 1849, translated into English in the same year as Mount's recipe, gave a recipe for a ground that included starch paste and pipe clay but was applied in a very different manner (Carlyle 2001, 431).

15   Mount's diary, 1858 (cited in Frankenstein 1975, 315).

16   Mount to Benjamin Franklin Thompson, December 31, 1848 (cited in Frankenstein 1975, 235); see also Mount's Diary, January 1847 (ibid., 171).

17   Mount's diary, January 1847 (cited in Frankenstein 1975, 171); Mount's diary, 1859 (ibid., 342).

18   Mount's diary, October 28, 1848 (cited in Frankenstein 1975, 186); Mount Diary LIMAA, July 13, 1847.

19   Mount's diary, June 1, 1847 (cited in Frankenstein 1975, 176).

20   "Mount's umber can be made by mixing a little raw sienna, or ochre with Vandyke brown" (Mount Diary LIMAA, July 13, 1847).

21   Lanman 1845, 243.

22   Mount to Benjamin F. Thompson, December 31, 1848 (cited in Frankenstein 1975, 236).

23   Benjamin F. Thompson to Mount, December 30, 1848 (cited in Frankenstein 1975, 234).

24   Mount's diary, June 1, 1847 (cited in Frankenstein 1975, 176).

25   See the many palettes described and illustrated in Schmid 1948.

26   *The Painter's Triumph* (*The Artist Showing His Work*) (1838, Pennsylvania Academy of the Fine Arts, Philadelphia).

27   Mount's diary, January 25, 1847 (cited in Frankenstein 1975, 171).

28   Mount illustrated or described setting his palette with white on the left side in 1847 (Mount Diary LIMAA, July 13, 1847); in 1859 (Mount's diary, April 20, 1859 [cited in Frankenstein 1975, 341]); in 1860 (Mount's diary [January] 1860 [ibid., 351]); in 1862 (letter from Mount to Samuel Seabury, October 13, 1862, illustrated and discussed in Katlan 2001); and in 1867 (Mount's diary, May 7, 1867 [cited in Frankenstein 1975, 434]).

   Mount was greatly influenced by Charles Loring Elliot, and at one time he hinted that Elliot may have also set his palette this way: "his [Elliot's] colors (as they were laid on the palette, White, Naples yellow, yellow ochre" (Mount's diary, October 28, 1848 [cited in Frankenstein 1975, 186]). On Elliot's influence on Mount, see Frankenstein 1975, 15.

29   Mount copied many ideas from others, but the context of this remark hints that it was his own idea (Mount's diary [1859] [cited in Frankenstein 1975, 346]).

30   "Asphaltum can be used with black Umber, burnt sienna etc. etc. for body colour" (Mount's diary, October 13, 1844 [cited in Frankenstein 1975, 129]); also "Asphaltum can be mixed with all the transparent colours to advantage"(November 1844 [ibid., 130]).

31   George Field's book, which Mount read and took notes from, had conflicting observations about asphaltum. On the one hand, Field wrote: "Its fine brown colour and perfect transparency are lures to its free use with many artists, notwithstanding the certain destruction which awaits the work on which it is much employed"(Field 1835, 161; Field 1841, 282–83). On the other hand, Field included asphaltum in his list of "best and most permanent pigments" (Field 1835, 187; Field 1841, 327). Laughton Osborn told American artists to approach asphaltum "with caution, and even distrust, approaching it, so to speak, as one would a friend of doubtful faith"(Osborn 1845, 87). On other British views on asphaltum, see Carlyle 2001, 479–82.

32   Mount's diary, April 19, 1851 (cited in Frankenstein 1975, 246). The testimony about cadmium yellow came from Mount's fellow painter De Witt Clinton Boutelle.

33   Mount's diary, April 20, 1859 (ibid., 341).

34   Williams 1941, 35–36; Katlan 2001, 114; Mount to Emeline Mount, March 17 and 20, 1867 (Mount Papers N-YHS).

35   Mount Papers N-YHS, undated sheet [the notation ca. 1845 written in a modern hand], beginning with "To purify colours, Mr. Mapes says. . . ."

36   Mount's diary, May 13, 1859 (cited in Frankenstein 1975, 341–42).

37   Mount's diary [1858] (ibid., 316).

38   Mount's diary [May 1858] (ibid., 311). *The Banjo Player* (1856, LIMAA).

39   Mount's diary, January 1846 (ibid., 141).

40   Mount Diary LIMAA, 1847.

41   Mount's diary, February 5, 1859 (cited in Frankenstein 1975, 339–40).

42   Ibid.

43   Ibid.

44   Mount's diary, March 20, 1859 (ibid., 340).

45   Mount's diary, October 19, 1847 (ibid., 181).

46   Dunlap 1834, 2:236–37. Note that Carroll & Crosby in Norwich, Connecticut, carried brushes as small as size 0000 in 1843–45, which is very small indeed.

47   Osborn 1845, 93–95.

48   Mount's diary, December 15, 1850 (cited in Frankenstein 1975, 245).

49   Mount's diary [1858] (ibid., 315; Mount's diary [April 1865] (ibid., 385). See also a drawing of modified brushes from Mount's diary, December 21, 1865 (illustrated in Frankenstein 1975, 391). A book from later in the nineteenth century (Williams 1878, 69–70) also described using old scraggly brushes or a flat sable brush drawn over the teeth of a comb to paint foliage.

50   R. Peale "Notes,"35. Rembrandt Peale had some unusual opinions about brushes, including the notion that one can reshape a worn brush by rubbing it against sandpaper.

51   Mount's Diary, November 4, 1864 (cited in Frankenstein 1975, 382); Osborn 1845, 93–94; R. Peale "Notes," 35.

52   Mount's diary, November 4, 1864 (cited in Frankenstein 1975, 382). In 1848 he wrote: "[Cole] often used a flat brush in the foliage" (Mount's diary, May 4, 1848 [ibid., 185]).

53   Mount's diary, June 4, 1858 (cited in Frankenstein 1975, 311). A port-crayon is a double-ended metal device (usually brass) designed to hold a short piece of chalk or charcoal at each end.

54   Charles Willson Peale took brass tubes and "these he cut into pieces and sewed large wire to fit the calebure of them, and thereby he made his Pensils sticks of more than twice the usial length of such tools, for having of late accustomed himself to paint portraits with very long brushes" (C.W. Peale 1983–2000, 5: 228–29).

55   R. Peale "Notes," 124.

56   Mount's diary, October 1852 (cited in Frankenstein 1975, 257).

57   Mount's diary, June 1, 1847 (ibid., 177). By this time the word *turpentine* had generally come to mean spirits of turpentine, the liquid produced by distilling the resin from pine trees, whereas in the eighteenth and early nineteenth centuries the term had referred to the semiliquid gum that oozed from the tree.

58   Mount's diary, June 15, 1847 (cited in Frankenstein 1975, 177). Ridner wrote that spirits of turpentine "is seldom used by the artist, except to thin his oil, in cleaning his brushes and paint slab, or as a vehicle in forming varnishes" (Ridner 1850, 132).

59   Mount's diary, November 15, 1848 (cited in Frankenstein 1975, 187).

60   Mount's diary, 1858 (ibid., 315). Mount also noted that turpentine could be used to take the glossy surface from dried paint and therefore make it easier for the artist to retouch a painting

(June 1, 1847 [ibid., 177]).

61   Mount's diary, April 1, 1851 (ibid., 245).

62   Carlyle (2001, 142) found camphine mentioned in the 1856 Roberson & Company ledgers and in an 1859 book. Rembrandt Peale wrote: "When the Sp. of Turpentine is pure (camphene)" (R. Peale "Notes," 96), and this was noted by Thomas Sully: "Rembrandt Peale recommends camphine as the best and finest spirit of turpentine" (Sully "Hints," AAA, microfilm roll N18, frame 223 [April 1852]).

63   Mount Papers N-YHS, undated sheet titled: "Oils used in painting the Bargain picture"; this note was published in Williams 1939. *Bargaining for a Horse* (*Farmers Bargaining*) (1835, New-York Historical Society).

64   Mount's diary, June 15, 1847 (cited in Frankenstein 1975, 177). Mount's 1847 description of the technique he used for painting *Bargaining for a Horse* is somewhat different than in the (presumably earlier) account cited above: "In painting the sky of the Bargain picture I used Mastic varnish and turpentine mixed together. (Copal and Turpentine would be better, I think.) Also, in painting the two farmers. The roof of the shed and horse, I used nut oil; board fence, crib, foreground and interior of the shed I finished with magilp" (Mount's diary, June 15, 1847 [cited in Frankenstein 1975, 177]).

65   Mount Diary LIMAA, adjacent to notes datable to the 1840s. Mount later wrote down this same recipe (Field 1841, 376) in somewhat different form (Mount's diary, probably 1858 [cited in Frankenstein 1975, 315]).

66   "The colours and oils of the right consistency. Copal and Linseed (or nut or Poppy half and half) sometimes with a trifle turpentine mixed with it to make it work free" (Mount's diary, June 1, 1847 [cited in Frankenstein 1975, 177]). Mount's preference for copal may have been more theoretical than actual, for late in his life (probably in 1862) he wrote: "*Copal*, I have not experimented much with" (Mount's diary [April, 1862?] [cited in Frankenstein 1975, 361]).

67   Mount's diary, June 20, 1847 (ibid., 178).

68   Ibid.

69   The amount of medium that artists added or believed they should add to oil paint is difficult to measure, but Mount assumed on another occasion that his surfaces might be at least slightly glossy; see Mount's diary, June 1, 1847 (cited in Frankenstein 1975, 177).

70   Mount wrote down directions for preparing drying oil both by boiling linseed oil with litharge (Mount's diary, June 19, 1847 [cited in Frankenstein 1975, 178]) or by simply stirring in the litharge (April 7, 1848 [ibid., 185]).

71   "J. and L.K. Bridge best linseed oil—N. York. Old linseed oil is best for varnish" (Mount's diary, April 7, 1848 [cited in Frankenstein 1975, 185]).

72   Mount's diary, October 28, 1848 (ibid., 187).

73   Mount's diary, January 13, 1850 (ibid., 238).

74   Mount's diary, January 21, 1850 (ibid., 239).

75   Mount's diary, February 10, 1850 (ibid., 240).

76   Mount's diary, May 16, 1852 (ibid., 248). Wax added to paint would make the paint remain easily soluble and liable to damage during cleaning, and it could also make subsequent layers adhere poorly (see chapters 2, 3, and 8). Later, in 1858, Mount noted that Richard Wilson had added wax to his paint (Mount's diary, June 18, 1858 [cited in Frankenstein 1975, 312]). On wax, see also Mayer and Myers 2006.

77   Mount's diary, December 12, 1852 (cited in Frankenstein 1975, 250).

78   Mount to William Schaus, January 4, 1852 (cited in Frankenstein 1975, 165).

79   Mount's diary, May 31, 1857 (cited in Frankenstein 1975, 308); Mount's diary [1858] (ibid., 315); see also Carbone et al 2006, 2: 812.

80   Mount's diary, October 31, 1859 (cited in Frankenstein 1975, 345); Mount's diary, March 20, 1859 (ibid., 340). In a similar vein, he wrote: "For durability use but little vehicle with your colors after they are mixed" (Mount's diary [1858] [ibid., 315]).

81   Mount's diary, April 3, 1856 (cited in Frankenstein 1975, 307).

82   Williams 1941, 36; Katlan 2001, 115.

83   Mount's diary, March 31, 1862, and [April, 1862?] (cited in Frankenstein 1975, 360–61).

84   Mount's diary, December 8, 1848 (ibid., 197). *Turning the Leaf* (*Surprise with Admiration*) (1848, LIMAA).

85   Mount to Charles Lanman, March 11, 1844 (cited in Frankenstein 1975, 116).

86   Mount's diary, January 21, 1850 (cited in Frankenstein 1975, 239). The details of Reynolds's ledgers had been published in detail only recently (Eastlake 1847).

87   Mount's diary, January 18, 1860 (cited in Frankenstein 1975, 352).

88   "Glazed over the lower part of the 'Catching Crabs' with madder lake & raw sienna—[illegible] oil (bleached) and Demar together, added a little boild oil—glazed the sky with madder lake alone—rubbed all in with the palm of my hand. The same treatment with muzzle down and touched in some of the clouds & foliage in the glazing. Also toned "Northern sentiment" and Loitering by the way, same manner" (Mount's diary, March 19, 1865 [cited in Frankenstein 1975, 384–85]). Also, "Toned down J.R. Davis's portrait with Madder lake and raw sienna" (Mount's diary, March 10, 1866 [ibid., 422]). *Catching Crabs (Spearing Crabs)* (1865, LIMAA); *Northern Sentiment* (1865, private collection); *Loitering by the Way* (1865, LIMAA); *Portrait of John R. Davis* (1864, unlocated).

89   The passage is transcribed "For toning Ivory, Black can be added," but in context this must be a typographical error (Mount's diary, May 7, 1867 [cited in Frankenstein 1975, 434]).

90   Mount Diary LIMAA, signed and dated "WSM May 21, 1846."

91   Mount's diary, August 5, 1863 (cited in Frankenstein 1975, 367).

92   Mount's diary, November 14, 1864 (ibid., 382).

93   Mount's diary, July 28, 1866 (ibid., 426).

94   Mount's diary, April 18, 1850 (cited in Frankenstein 1975, 240). While in London, Sully noted that David Willkie varnished his paintings with weak megilp with Japanners' gold size added (the pictures having been painted with "much magilph") (Sully "Hints, AAA, microfilm roll N18, frame 146 (1837); also repeated in Neagle Commonplace Book, 61.

95   Mount's diary [April 1865] (cited in Frankenstein 1975, 385).

96   Mount Diary LIMAA, undated.

97   Mount's diary, April 7, 1848 (cited in Frankenstein 1975, 185).

98   Williams 1939, 11; Mount's diary, June 19, 1847 (cited in Frankenstein 1975, 177–78).

99   Mount's diary, June 20, 1847 (cited in Frankenstein 1975, 178).

100   Solomon T. Nicoll to Mount, February 4, 1847 (Mount Papers N-YHS). The painting, *Portrait of Solomon T. Nicoll*, 1846, is unlocated.

101   Mount to Solomon T. Nicoll, February 8, 1847 (Mount Papers N-YHS; also cited in Frankenstein 1975, 150).

102   It is not clear exactly when in 1846 Nicoll's portrait was painted, so we do not know if Mount in fact waited a full year before varnishing. His reply to Nicoll is also somewhat ambiguous, hinting that Mount's preoccupation with another painting was as much an obstacle to his varnishing Nicoll's portrait as fear of varnishing it too soon.

103   An earlier precedent was the British painter William Blake's belief that Saint Joseph appeared in a vision to tell him to use carpenter's glue as a medium in his watercolors (Gilchrist 1863, 1: 69–70, cited in Maheux 1984, 126).

104   The letters and other spiritualist writings are reproduced in Frankenstein 1975, 285–97.

105   Ibid., 285.

106   It is likely that Wilson's paintings were more brown in the first half of the nineteenth century than they are now; the decades after the artist's death in 1782 were times when the look of an old painting was admired in many quarters, and paintings by someone who was called the heir to Claude may have been even less likely to have been cleaned than paintings by other artists.

107   Mount's diary, March 25, 1855 (cited in Frankenstein 1975, 294); Mount's diary, undated (cited in Frankenstein 1975, 297). Our thanks to Mark Bockrath for the explanation of burnt oil.

108   Mount's diary, undated (cited in Frankenstein 1975, 297).

109   Mount's portable studio is described in his diary entries from 1861 and 1862, and in a letter from Mount to Samuel Putnam Avery, August 1862 (all cited in Frankenstein 1975, 262–65).

110   Mount's diary, August 29, 1846 (cited in Frankenstein 1975, 144).

111   Mount to Charles B. Wood, June 9 and 20, 1864 (cited in Frankenstein 1975, 380, 394–95).

112   Mount's diary, August 3, 1862 (cited in Frankenstein 1975, 363); Williams 1941, 36; Katlan 2001, 49; Mount's diary, November 24, 1864 (cited in Frankenstein 1975, 383).

113   Field, in the two editions of *Chromatography*, said that petroleum solvents had more disadvantages than advantages (Field 1835, 207; Field 1841, 371); Osborn did not even mention them in his 1845 book; and Ridner called them "not suited" for painting (Ridner 1850, 134).

114   Mount's diary, November 24, 1864 (cited in Frankenstein 1975, 383). See also chapter 11 on driers.

SELECTED BIBLIOGRAPHY

BOOKS, JOURNAL ARTICLES, AND THESES

Abendschein 1909

Abendschein, Albert. *The Secret of the Old Masters*. New York: D. Appleton, 1909.

Alberts 1978

Alberts, Robert C. *Benjamin West: A Biography*. Boston: Houghton Mifflin, 1978.

Alexander 1994

Alexander, Ingrid C. "Uncovering the Working Methods of Thomas Cole: An Ongoing Study." In *AIC Paintings Specialty Group Postprints: Papers Presented at the Twenty-first Annual Meeting of the American Institute for Conservation of Historic and Artistic Works, Denver, Colorado, June 5, 1993*, 6:1–5. Washington, D.C.: AIC, 1994.

Allston 1993

Allston, Washington. *The Correspondence of Washington Allston*. Edited by Nathalia Wright. Lexington: University of Kentucky Press, 1993. (Appendices by the editor include biographical notes about correspondents and a discussion of Allston's painting techniques.)

Amory 1882

Amory, Martha Babcock. *The Domestic and Artistic Life of John Singleton Copley, R.A., with Notices of His Works, and Reminiscences of His Son, Lord Lyndhurst, Lord High Chancellor of Great Britain*. Boston: Houghton Mifflin, 1882.

Anderson 1990

Anderson, Jaynie. "The First Cleaning Controversy at the National Gallery, 1846–1853." In *Appearance, Opinion, Change: Evaluating the Look of Paintings: Papers Given at a Conference Held Jointly by the United Kingdom Institute for Conservation and the Association of Art Historians, June 1990*, 3–7. London: UKIC, 1990. (Reprinted in Bomford and Leonard 2004 [see below], 441–53.)

Ashworth, Lignelli, and Butler 1989

Ashworth, Karen, Theresa Lignelli, and Marigene Butler. "An Investigation of Materials and Techniques of Seven Paintings by Charles Willson Peale." In *AIC Paintings Specialty Group Postprints: Papers Presented at the Sixteenth Annual Meeting of the American Institute for Conservation of Historic and Artistic Works, New Orleans, Louisiana, June 1–5, 1988*, 1:1–9. Washington, D.C.: AIC, 1989.

Ayres 1985

Ayres, James. *The Artist's Craft: A History of Tools, Techniques and Materials*. Oxford: Phaidon, 1985.

Baigell 1981

Baigell, Matthew. *Thomas Cole*. New York: Watson-Guptill, 1981.

Bardwell 1756

Bardwell, Thomas. *The Practice of Painting and Perspective Made Easy, in which is Contained, the Art of Painting in Oil, with the Method of Colouring… and a New, Short, and Familiar Account of the Art of Perspective.* London: S. Richardson, 1756.

Barnhill 1993

Barnhill, Georgia Brady. *Extracts from the Journal of Ethan A. Greenwood, Portrait Painter and Museum Proprietor.* Worcester, Mass.: American Antiquarian Society, 1993.

Barratt 2000a

Barratt, Carrie Rebora. "Mapping the Venues: New York City Art Exhibitions." In *Art and the Empire City, New York 1825–1861*, edited by Catherine Hoover Voorsanger and John K. Howat, 47–81. New Haven, Conn.: Yale University Press / Metropolitan Museum of Art, 2000.

Barratt 2000b

Barratt, Carrie Rebora. *Queen Victoria and Thomas Sully*. Princeton, N.J.: Princeton University Press / Metropolitan Museum of Art, 2000.

Barratt and Miles 2004

Barratt, Carrie Rebora, and Ellen G. Miles. *Gilbert Stuart*. New Haven, Conn.: Yale University Press / Metropolitan Museum of Art, 2004.

Barry 1994

Barry, Claire M. "Technical Note: 'Painting in Imagination:' The Creation of 'The Garden of Eden' by Thomas Cole." In *Thomas Cole's Paintings of Eden*, by Franklin Kelly, 55–66. Fort Worth, Tex.: Amon Carter Museum, 1994.

Baur 1942

Baur, John I. H. "The Autobiography of Worthington Whittredge." *Brooklyn Museum Journal* (1942): 4–68. (Whittredge's autobiography appears to have been written in 1905.)

Bellion 2001

Bellion, Wendy. "Likeness and Deception in Early American Art." PhD diss., Northwestern University, 2001.

Benes 1995

Benes, Peter. "Machine-Assisted Portrait and Profile Imaging in New England after 1803." In *Painting and Portrait Making in the American Northeast: Dublin Seminar for New England Folklife Annual Proceedings, 24 through 26 June 1994*, edited by Peter Benes, 138–50. Boston: Boston University, 1995.

Biddle and Fielding 1970

Biddle, Edward, and Mantle Fielding. *The Life and Works of Thomas Sully*. New York: Kennedy Graphics, 1970. (First published in 1921.)

Birkmaier, Wallert, and Rothe 1995

Birkmaier, Ulrich, Arie Wallert, and Andrea Rothe. "Technical Examinations of Titian's 'Venus and Adonis': A Note on Early Italian Painting Techniques." In *Historical Painting Techniques, Materials and Studio Practice: Preprints of a Symposium, University of Leiden, the Netherlands, 26–29 June 1995*, edited by Arie Wallert, Erma Hermens, and Marja Peek, 117–26. Los Angeles: Getty Conservation Institute, 1995.

Bjelajac 1997

Bjelajac, David. *Washington Allston, Secret Societies, and the Alchemy of Anglo-American Painting*. Cambridge: Cambridge University Press, 1997.

Bomford 1998

Bomford, David. Introduction. In *Looking through Paintings: The Study of Painting Techniques and Materials in Support of Art Historical Research*, edited by Erma Hermens, Annemiek Ouwerkerk, and Nicola Costaras, 9–12. Baarn and London: Uitgeverij de Prom/Archetype, 1998.

Bomford and Leonard 2004

Bomford, David, and Mark Leonard, eds. *Issues in the Conservation of Paintings*. Los Angeles: Getty Conservation Institute, 2004.

Boon, Hoogland, and Keune 2007

Boon, Jaap J., Frank Hoogland, and Katrien Keune. "Chemical Processes in Aged Oil Paints Affecting Metal Soap Migration and Aggregation." In *AIC Paintings Specialty Group Postprints: Papers Presented at the Thirty-fourth Annual Meeting of the American Institute for Conservation of Historic and Artistic Works, Providence, Rhode Island, June 16–19, 2006*, 19:16–23. Washington, D.C.: AIC, 2007.

Bouvier 1827

Bouvier, Pierre-Louis. *Manuel des jeunes artistes et amateurs en peinture*. Paris: F. G. Levrault, 1827.

Bouvier 1844

Bouvier, Pierre-Louis. *Manuel des jeunes artistes et amateurs en peinture*. 3rd ed. Paris: P. Bertrand, 1844.

Brandi 1949

Brandi, Cesare. "The Cleaning of Pictures in Relation to Patina, Varnish, and Glazes." *Burlington Magazine* 91, no. 556 (July 1949): 183–88.

Buckley 2008

Buckley, Barbara A. "Folding Stretchers." In *Painting Conservation Catalog. Vol. 2: Stretchers*, compiled by Barbara A. Buckley, 208–11. Washington, D.C.: Paintings Specialty Group of the American Institute for Conservation of Historic and Artistic Works, 2008.

Burgard 1990

Burgard, Timothy Anglin. "The Luman Reed Collection: Catalogue." In Foshay 1990 (see below), 121–92.

Burnet 1837

Burnet, John. *Essay on the Education of the Eye, with Reference to Painting*. London: James Carpenter, 1837.

Burnet 1850

Burnet, John. *Practical Hints on Portrait Painting: Illustrated by Examples from the Works of Vandyke and Other Masters*. London: David Bogue, 1850.

Burnt Umber 1856

Burnt Umber [pseud.]. "Letters from North Conway and Albany." *Crayon* 3, no. 9 (September 1856): 282–84.

Cadet-de-Vaux 1802

Cadet-de-Vaux, Antoine-Alexis. *A New and Cheap Composition for Painting*. New London, Conn.: J. Springer, 1802. (American edition of the 1801 English translation of French original.)

Carbone et al. 2006
Carbone, Teresa A., Barbara Dayer Gallati, and Linda S. Ferber, with Ruth E. Seidler, Kenneth Moser, Carolyn Tomkiewicz, and Richard Kowall. *American Paintings in the Brooklyn Museum: Artists Born by 1876.* 2 vols. Brooklyn: Brooklyn Museum, 2006.

Carlyle 2001
Carlyle, Leslie. *The Artist's Assistant: Oil Painting Instruction Manuals and Handbooks in Britain, 1800–1900, with Reference to Select Eighteenth-Century Sources.* London: Archetype, 2001.

Carpentier 1875
Carpentier, Paul. *Notes sur la peinture à la cire cautérisée ou procédé encaustique d'après les laborieuses recherches de Paillot de Montabert.* Paris: Librairie Renouard, 1875.

Caylus and Majault 1755
Caylus, Comte de, and M. Majault. *Mémoire sur la peinture à l'encaustique et sur la peinture à la cire.* Geneva, 1755. (Reprinted 1972.)

Chapman 1857
Chapman, John Gadsby. *Chapman's American Drawing-Book. No. IV. Sketching from Nature – Painting.* New York: J.S. Redfield, 1857.

***Compendium of Colours* 1808**
A Compendium of Colours, and Other Materials Used in the Arts Dependant on Design, with Remarks on Their Nature and Uses.... London: C. Taylor, 1808.

Cooper et al. 1982
Cooper, Helen A., with Patricia Mullan Burnham, Martin Price, Jules David Prown, Oswaldo Rodriguez Roque, Egon Verheyen, and Bryan Wolf. *John Trumbull: The Hand and Spirit of a Painter.* New Haven, Conn.: Yale University Art Gallery, 1982.

Copley 1914
Copley, John Singleton. *Letters and Papers of John Singleton Copley and Henry Pelham, 1739–1776.* Boston: Massachusetts Historical Society, 1914.

Cormack 1968–70
Cormack, Malcolm. "The Ledgers of Sir Joshua Reynolds." *Walpole Society* 42 (1968–70): 141–43, 168–69.

Craven 1990
Craven, Wayne. "Introduction: Patronage and Collecting in America, 1800–1835." In Foshay 1990 (see below), 11–18.

Cummings 1971
Cummings, Abbott Lowell. "Decorative Painting in Seventeenth-Century New England." In *American Painting to 1776: A Reappraisal,* edited by Ian Quimby, 71–125. Charlottesville, Va.: University Press of Virginia / Henry Francis du Pont Winterthur Museum, 1971.

Cunningham 1879
Cunningham, Allan. *The Lives of the Most Eminent British Painters.* Rev. ed. 3 vols. London: George Bell and Sons, 1879. (1st ed. published in 1829.)

Cutbush 1814
Cutbush, James. *The American Artist's Manual, or Dictionary of Practical Knowledge in the Application of Philosophy to the Arts and Manufactures, Selected from the Most Complete European Systems, with Original Improvements and Appropriate Engravings Adapted to the Use of the Manufacturers of the United States.* Philadelphia: Johnson & Warner, 1814.

DeMare 1954

DeMare, Marie. *G.P.A. Healy, American Artist: An Intimate Chronicle of the Nineteenth Century.* New York: David McKay, 1954.

Dossie 1758

[Dossie, Robert.] *The Handmaid to the Arts.* 2 vols. London: J. Nourse, 1758.

Dossie 1764

[Dossie, Robert.] *The Handmaid to the Arts.* 2nd ed. 2 vols. London: J. Nourse, 1764.

Dow 1927

Dow, George Francis. *The Arts and Crafts in New England, 1704–1775: Gleanings from Boston Newspapers Relating to Painting, Engraving, Silversmiths, Pewterers, Clockmakers, Furniture, Pottery, Old Houses, Costume, Trades and Occupations, and etc.* Topsfield, Mass.: Wayside Press, 1927.

Dunkerton, Foister, and Penny 1999

Dunkerton, Jill, Susan Foister, and Nicholas Penny. *Dürer to Veronese: Sixteenth-Century Paintings in the National Gallery.* New Haven, Conn.: Yale University Press, 1999.

Dunkerton, Kirby, and White 1990

Dunkerton, Jill, Jo Kirby, and Raymond White. "Varnish and Early Italian Tempera Paintings." In *Cleaning, Retouching and Coatings: Technology and Practice for Easel Paintings and Polychrome Sculpture: Preprints of the Contributions to the Brussels Congress, 3–7 September 1990,* edited by John S. Mills and Perry Smith, 63–69. London: International Institute for Conservation of Historic and Artistic Works, 1990.

Dunlap 1834

Dunlap, William. *History of the Rise and Progress of the Arts of Design in the United States.* 2 vols. New York: George P. Scott, 1834.

Dunlap 1969

Dunlap, William. *Diary of William Dunlap: The Memoirs of a Dramatist, Theatrical Manager, Painter, Critic, Novelist, and Historian.* New York: Benjamin Blom, 1969. (First published as *Collections of the New-York Historical Society,* vols. 62–64, 1930.)

Dwyer 1985

Dwyer, Diane. "John F. Kensett's Painting Technique." In *John Frederick Kensett: An American Master,* by John P. Driscoll and John K. Howat, 163–80. New York: W.W. Norton/Worcester Art Museum, 1985.

Eastlake 1847

Eastlake, Charles Lock. *Materials for a History of Oil Painting.* 2 vols. London: Longman, Brown, Green, and Longmans, 1847.

Edmonds 1981

Edmonds, Francis W. "The Leading Incidents and Dates of My Life: An Autobiographical Essay by Francis W. Edmonds." *American Art Journal* 13, no. 4 (Autumn 1981): 4–10.

Egerton 1998

Egerton, Judy. *National Gallery Catalogues: The British School.* New Haven, Conn.: Yale University Press, 1998.

***Elysium* 1806**

Elysium [pseud.]. "Art News from Rome." *Crayon* 7, part 6 (June 1860): 178. (Reprint of 1806 German article.)

England and van Zelst 1982

England, P. A., and L. van Zelst. "A Technical Investigation of Some Seventeenth-Century New England Portrait Paintings." In *Preprints of Papers Presented at the Tenth Annual Meeting of the American Institute for Conservation of Historic and Artistic Works, Milwaukee, Wisconsin, May 26–30, 1982,* 85–95. Washington, D.C.: AIC, 1982.

Erffa and Staley 1986

Erffa, Helmut von, and Allen Staley. *The Paintings of Benjamin West.* New Haven, Conn.: Yale University Press, 1986.

D. Evans 1982

Evans, Dorinda. *Mather Brown: Early American Artist in England.* Middletown, Conn.: Wesleyan University Press, 1982.

D. Evans 1999

Evans, Dorinda. *The Genius of Gilbert Stuart.* Princeton, N.J.: Princeton University Press, 1999.

N. Evans 1996

Evans, Nancy Goyne. *American Windsor Chairs.* New York: Hudson Hill Press / Henry Francis du Pont Winterthur Museum, 1996.

N. Evans 2006

Evans, Nancy Goyne. *Windsor Chair Making in America: From Craft Shop to Consumer.* Hanover, N.H.: University Press of New England, 2006.

***Exhibition of Cleaned Pictures* 1947**

An Exhibition of Cleaned Pictures, 1936–47. Rev. ed. London: National Gallery, 1947.

Fabian 1983

Fabian, Monroe H. *Mr. Sully, Portrait Painter.* Washington, D.C.: National Portrait Gallery / Smithsonian Institution Press, 1983.

Fairbanks 1982

Fairbanks, Jonathan L. "Portrait Painting in Seventeenth-Century Boston." In Fairbanks and Trent 1982 (see below), 3: 413–55.

Fairbanks and Trent 1982

Fairbanks, Jonathan L., and Robert F. Trent. *New England Begins: The Seventeenth Century.* 3 vols. Boston: Museum of Fine Arts, 1982.

Farington 1978–84

Farington, Joseph. *The Diary of Joseph Farington.* Edited by Kenneth Garlick, Angus Macintyre, and Kathryn Cave. 16 vols. New Haven, Conn.: Yale University Press, 1978–84.

Field 1817

Field, George. *Chromatics; or, an Essay on the Analogy and Harmony of Colours.* London: A. J. Valpy, 1817.

Field 1835

Field, George. *Chromatography; or, a Treatise on Colours and Pigments, and Their Powers in Painting.* London: Charles Tilt, 1835.

Field 1841

Field, George. *Chromatography; or, a Treatise on Colours and Pigments, and Their Powers in Painting.* New ed. London: Tilt and Bogue, 1841.

Fielding 1839

Fielding, Theodore Henry. *On Painting in Oil and Water Colours, for Landscape and Portraits; including the Preparation of Colours, Vehicles, Oils &c., Method of*

Painting in Wax, or Encaustic; also on the Chemical Properties and Permanency of Colours, and on the Best Methods of Cleaning and Repairing Old Paintings, &c. London: Ackermann, 1839.

Fielding 1846

Fielding, Theodore Henry. *On the Theory and Practice of Painting in Oil and Watercolours for Landscape and Portraits.* 4th ed. London: Ackermann, 1846.

Fink and Taylor 1975

Fink, Lois Marie, and Joshua C. Taylor. *Academy: The Academic Tradition in American Art: An Exhibition Organized on the Occasion of the One Hundred and Fiftieth Anniversary of the National Academy of Design, 1825–1975.* Washington, D.C.: Smithsonian Institution Press/National Collection of Fine Arts, 1975.

Fitzhugh 1997

Fitzhugh, Elisabeth West. "Orpiment and Realgar." In *Artists' Pigments: A Handbook of Their History and Characteristics, Vol. 3,* edited by Elisabeth West Fitzhugh, 47–79. New York and Oxford: Oxford University Press/National Gallery of Art, 1997.

Flagg 1892

Flagg, Jared B. *The Life and Letters of Washington Allston.* New York: Charles Scribner's Sons, 1892. (Chapter 17 presents descriptions of how Allston painted, as recorded by his friend Henry Greenough.)

Flexner 1969

Flexner, James Thomas. *First Flowers of Our Wilderness.* New York: Dover, 1969. (First published in 1947.)

Ford 1974

Ford, Brinsley. "James Byrnes: Principal Antiquarian for the English Visitors to Rome." *Apollo* 99 (June 1974): 446–61.

Forni 1866

Forni, Ulisse. *Manuale del pittore restauratore.* Florence: Successori le Monnier, 1866.

Foshay 1990

Foshay, Ella M. "Luman Reed: New York Patron and His Picture Gallery." In *Mr. Luman Reed's Picture Gallery: A Pioneer Collection of American Art* by Ella M. Foshay, with an introduction by Wayne Craven and catalogue by Timothy Anglin Burgard, 19–71. New York: Abrams/New-York Historical Society, 1990.

Frankenstein 1975

Frankenstein, Alfred. *William Sidney Mount.* New York: Abrams, 1975.

Fulton et al. 2002

Fulton, Elizabeth Leto, Richard Newman, Jean Woodward, and Jim Wright. "The Methods and Materials of Martin Johnson Heade." *Journal of the American Institute for Conservation* 41, no. 2 (Summer 2002): 155–84.

Gage 1964

Gage, John. "Magilphs and Mysteries." *Apollo* 80 (July 1964): 38–41.

Galt 1820

Galt, John. *The Life, Studies, and Works of Benjamin West, Esq., President of the Royal Academy of London.* Part 2. London: D. Cadwell and W. Davies, 1820.

Gerdts 1969

Gerdts, William H. "Washington Allston and the German Romantic Classicists in Rome." *Art Quarterly* 32, no. 2 (1969): 167–96.

Gerdts 1973a

Gerdts, William H. "Allston's 'Belshazzar's Feast.'" *Art in America* 61, no. 2 (March–April 1973): 59–66.

Gerdts 1973b

Gerdts, William H. "Allston's 'Belshazzar's Feast' II: 'That is his shroud.'" *Art in America* 61, no. 3 (May–June 1973): 58–65.

Gerdts 1979

Gerdts, William H. "The Paintings of Washington Allston." In Gerdts and Stebbins 1979 (see below), 9–174.

Gerdts and Stebbins 1979

Gerdts, William H., and Theodore E. Stebbins Jr. *"A man of genius": The Art of Washington Allston (1779–1843)*. Boston: Museum of Fine Arts, 1979.

Gettens and Stout 1966

Gettens, Rutherford J., and George L. Stout. *Painting Materials, a Short Encyclopedia.* Rev. ed. New York: Dover, 1966.

Gilchrist 1863

Gilchrist, Alexander. *The Life of William Blake.* 2 vols. London: Macmillan, 1863.

Goldberg 1993

Goldberg, Marcia. "Textured Panels in 19th-Century American Painting." *Journal of the American Institute for Conservation* 32, no. 1 (Spring 1993): 33–42.

Gombrich 1962

Gombrich, E.H. "Dark Varnishes: Variations on a Theme of Pliny." *Burlington Magazine* 104, no. 707 (February 1962): 51–55. (Reprinted in Bomford and Leonard 2004 [see above], 507–18.)

Gombrich 1963

Gombrich, E.H. "The National Gallery Cleaning Controversy. *Burlington Magazine* 105, no. 724 (July 1963): 327.

Gottesman 1970

Gottesman, Rita S., compiler. *The Arts and Crafts in New York: 1726–1776, Advertisements and News Items from New York Newspapers.* New York: Da Capo Press, 1970. (First published in 1938.)

Gullick and Timbs 1859

Gullick, Thomas John, and John Timbs. *Painting Popularly Explained; Including Fresco, Oil, Mosaic, Water-colour, Water-glass, Tempera, Encaustic, Miniature, Painting on Ivory, Vellum, Pottery, Porcelain, Enamel, Glass, &c, with Historical Sketches of the Progress of the Art.* London: Crosby Lockwood, 1859. (Excerpts of the section on tempera painting were published in *Crayon* 6, pt. 3 [March 1859]: 81–84. The 1864 edition of the book was reprinted in 2005 as *Painting Explained, a Professional Artist Reveals the Secrets of the Masters.*)

Harley 1971

Harley, Rosamond D. "Oil Colour Containers: Development Work by Artists and Colourmen in the Nineteenth Century." *Annals of Science* 27, no. 1 (March 1971): 1–12.

Harley 1975

Harley, Rosamond D. "A Nineteenth-Century Book of Color Samples." *Bulletin of the American Institute for Conservation of Historic and Artistic Works* 15, no. 2 (Summer 1975): 49–54.

Harley 1979

Harley, Rosamond D. "Field's Manuscripts: Early Nineteenth-Century Color Samples and Fading Tests." *Studies in Conservation* 24, no. 2 (May 1979): 75–84.

Harley 1982

Harley, Rosamond D. *Artists' Pigments ca. 1600–1835: A Study in English Documentary Sources.* 2nd ed. London: Butterworth Scientific, 1982.

Hartwell 2008

Hartwell, Dare Myers, with Ross Merrill. "Panel Stretchers." In *Painting Conservation Catalog, Vol. 2: Stretchers,* compiled by Barbara A. Buckley, 184–92. Washington, D.C.: Paintings Specialty Group of the American Institute for Conservation of Historic and Artistic Works, 2008.

Harvey 1998

Harvey, Eleanor Jones. *The Painted Sketch: American Impressions from Nature, 1830–1880.* New York and Dallas: Abrams/Dallas Museum of Art, 1998.

Hatchett 1802

Hatchett, Charles. "On the Utility of Prussiate of Copper as a Pigment." *Journals of the Royal Institution* 1 (1802): 306–8.

Haydon 1853

Haydon, Benjamin R. *Life of Benjamin Robert Haydon, Historical Painter, from His Autobiography and Journals,* edited by Tom Taylor. 2nd ed. 3 vols. London: Longman, Brown, Green, and Longmans, 1853.

Haydon and Hazlitt 1838

Haydon, Benjamin R., and William Hazlitt. *Painting and the Fine Arts: Being the Articles under Those Heads Contributed to the Seventh Edition of the Encyclopaedia Britannica.* Edinburgh: Adam and Charles Black, 1838.

Hevner 1991

Hevner, Carol Eaton. "Lessons from a Dutiful Son: Rembrandt Peale's Artistic Influence on His Father, Charles Willson Peale." In *New Perspectives on Charles Willson Peale: A 250th Anniversary Celebration,* edited by Lillian B. Miller and David C. Ward, 103–18. Pittsburgh: University of Pittsburgh Press/Smithsonian Institution, 1991.

Hevner 1992

Hevner, Carol Eaton. "The Paintings of Rembrandt Peale: Character and Conventions." In Miller 1992 (see below), 245–82.

Hindle 1982

Hindle, Brooke. "Charles Willson Peale's Science and Technology." In *Charles Willson Peale and His World,* by Edgar P. Richardson, Brooke Hindle, and Lillian B. Miller, 106–69. New York: Abrams, 1982.

Homer 1960

Homer, William I. "Thomas Cole and Field's 'Chromatography.'" *Record of the Art Museum, Princeton University* 19 (1960): 26–30.

Hume 1803

Hume, Joseph. "Letter to Charles Hatchett, Esq., Respecting the Prussiate of Copper." *Journals of the Royal Institution* 2, no. 1 (June 1, 1803).

Hundertpfund 1849

Hundertpfund, Libertat. *The Art of Painting Restored to Its Simplest and Surest Principles.* London: D. Bogue, 1849. (Translated from the 1847 German edition.)

Johns 1975

Johns, Elizabeth. "Washington Allston's Library." *American Art Journal* 7, no. 2 (November 1975): 32–41.

Johns 1977

Johns, Elizabeth. "Washington Allston: Method, Imagination, and Reality." *Winterthur Portfolio* 12 (1977): 1–18.

Johns 1979

Johns, Elizabeth. "Washington Allston's 'Dead Man Revived.'" *Art Bulletin* 61, no. 1 (March 1979): 78–99.

Johnson 1998

Johnson, Deborah J. *William Sidney Mount: Painter of American Life*. New York: American Federation of Arts, 1998.

Jones 1991

Jones, Rica. "Notes for Conservators on Wright of Derby's Technique and Studio Practice." *Conservator* 15 (1991): 13–24.

Jouett 1816

Jouett, Matthew Harris. "Notes Taken by M.H. Jouett While in Boston from Conve[r]sations on Painting with Gilbert Stuart Esqr." In Morgan 1939a (see below), 80–93. (Jouett's notes were taken in 1816.)

Katlan 1987

Katlan, Alexander W. *American Artists' Materials Suppliers Directory: Nineteenth Century*. Park Ridge, N.J.: Noyes Press, 1987.

Katlan 1992

Katlan, Alexander W. *American Artists' Materials: A Guide to Stretchers, Panels, Millboards, and Stencil Marks, Vol. 2*. Madison, Conn.: Sound View Press, 1992.

Katlan 1999

Katlan, Alexander W. "The American Artist's Tools and Materials for On-site Oil Sketching." *Journal of the American Institute for Conservation* 38, no. 1 (Spring 1999): 21–32.

Katlan 2001

Katlan, Alexander W. "William Sidney Mount's Palette and Pigments." *Microscope* 49 (2001): 111–18.

Kelby 1970

Kelby, William. *Notes on American Artists, 1754–1820, Copied from Advertisements Appearing in the Newspapers of the Day*. New York: New-York Historical Society, 1970. (First published in 1922.)

Kelly et al. 1996

Kelly, Franklin, with Nicolai Cikovsky Jr., Deborah Chotner, and John Davis. *American Paintings of the Nineteenth Century, Part I*. Washington, D.C.: National Gallery of Art, 1996.

Kemp 1990

Kemp, Martin. *The Science of Art: Optical Themes in Western Art from Brunelleschi to Seurat*. New Haven, Conn.: Yale University Press, 1990.

Kirsh and Levenson 2000

Kirsh, Andrea, and Rustin S. Levenson. *Seeing through Paintings: Physical Examination in Art Historical Studies*. New Haven, Conn.: Yale University Press, 2000.

Kornhauser 1991

Kornhauser, Stephen H. "Ralph Earl's Working Methods and Materials." In *Ralph Earl: The Face of the Young Republic*, by Elizabeth Mankin Kornhauser, 85–91. New Haven, Conn.: Yale University Press, 1991.

Kühn 1986

Kühn, Hermann. "Zinc White." In *Artists' Pigments: A Handbook of Their History and Characteristics, Vol. 1*, edited by Robert L. Feller, 169–86. Cambridge and Washington, D.C.: Cambridge University Press / National Gallery of Art, 1986.

Kühn and Curran 1986

Kühn, Hermann, and Mary Curran. "Chrome Yellow and Other Chromate Pigments." In *Artists' Pigments: A Handbook of Their History and Characteristics, Vol. 1*, edited by Robert L. Feller, 187–217. Cambridge and Washington, D.C.: Cambridge University Press / National Gallery of Art, 1986.

Kurz 1962

Kurz, Otto. "Varnishes, Tinted Varnishes, and Patina." *Burlington Magazine* 104, no. 707 (February 1962): 56–59.

Kurz 1963

Kurz, Otto. "Time the Painter." *Burlington Magazine* 105, no. 720 (March 1963): 94–95.

Kushel 1985

Kushel, Dan A. "Some Observations of Thomas Cole's 'Voyage of Life' Using Infrared Reflectography and X-Radiography." In Parry, Schweizer, and Kushel 1985 (see below), 54–65.

Languri and Boon 2005

Languri, Georgiana M., and Jaap J. Boon. "Between Myth and Reality: Mummy Pigment from the Hafkenscheid Collection." *Studies in Conservation* 50, no. 3 (2005): 161–78.

Lanman 1845

Lanman, Charles. *Letters from a Landscape Painter*. Boston: James Munroe, 1845.

Leslie 1845

Leslie, Charles Robert. *Memoirs of the Life of John Constable, Composed Chiefly of His Letters*. London: Phaidon, 1951. (Reprint of 2nd ed., 1845; 1st ed., 1843.)

Leslie 1855

Leslie, Charles Robert. *A Hand-book for Young Painters*. London: John Murray, 1855.

Leslie and Taylor 1860

Leslie, Charles Robert, and Tom Taylor. *Autobiographical Recollections by the Late Charles Robert Leslie, RA, Edited with a Prefatory Essay on Leslie as an Artist, and Selections from His Correspondence by Tom Taylor*. London: J. Murray, 1860. (Also Boston: Ticknor and Fields, 1860.)

Linton 1856

Linton, William. "Technical. A Summary of Modern Colors, with Their Chemical and Artistical Qualities." *Crayon* 3, no. 10 (October 1856): 300–303. (Reprinted from Linton's 1852 book *Ancient and Modern Color from the Earliest Periods to the Present Time, with Their Chemical and Artistical Properties*.)

Lipman 1980

Lipman, Jean. *Rufus Porter Rediscovered: Artist, Inventor, Journalist, 1792–1884*. 2nd ed. New York: C. N. Potter, 1980.

Lipton 1981

Lipton, Leah. "William Dunlap, Samuel F. B. Morse, John Wesley Jarvis, and Chester Harding: Their Careers as Itinerant Portrait Painters." *American Art Journal* 13, no. 3 (Summer 1981): 34–50.

Little 1947

Little, Nina Fletcher. "Winthrop Chandler." *Art in America* 35, no. 2 (April 1947): 75–168.

Mackenzie 1829

Mackenzie, Colin, *Mackenzie's Five Thousand Receipts in All the Useful and Domestic Arts*. Philadelphia: J. J. Woodward, 1829.

MacLaren and Werner 1950

MacLaren, Neil, and Anthony E. Warner. "Some Factual Observations about Varnishes and Glazes." *Burlington Magazine* 92, no. 568 (July 1950): 189–92.

Maheux 1984

Maheux, Anne. "An Analysis of the Watercolor Technique and Materials of William Blake." *Blake, An Illustrated Quarterly* (Spring 1984): 124–29.

Mahon 1962

Mahon, Denis. "Miscellanea for the Cleaning Controversy." *Burlington Magazine* 104, no. 716 (November 1962): 460–70.

Mason 1879

Mason, George C. *The Life and Works of Gilbert Stuart*. New York: Charles Scribner's Sons, 1879. (Mason uses material Jane Stuart published in *Scribner's Monthly* in 1876–77.)

L. Mayer 1998

Mayer, Lance. "Traditional Artists' Varnishes." In *Painting Conservation Catalog, Vol. 1: Varnishes and Surface Coatings*, compiled by Wendy Samet, 21–34. Washington, D.C.: Paintings Specialty Group of the American Institute for Conservation of Historic and Artistic Works, 1998.

R. Mayer 1970

Mayer, Ralph. *Handbook of Artists' Materials and Techniques*. 3rd ed. New York: Viking, 1970.

Mayer and Myers 1996

Mayer, Lance, and Gay Myers. "'The Court of Death' through Conservators' Eyes." *Bulletin of the Detroit Institute of Arts* 70, no. 1/2 (1996): 4–13.

Mayer and Myers 2002

Mayer, Lance, and Gay Myers. "A Note on the Early Use of Dammar Varnish." *Studies in Conservation* 47, no. 2 (2002): 134–38.

Mayer and Myers 2004

Mayer, Lance, and Gay Myers. "Painting in an Age of Innovation: Stubbs's Experiments in Enamel and Wax." In *Stubbs and the Horse*, by Malcolm Warner and Robin Blake, 123–39. New Haven, Conn.: Yale University Press, 2004.

Mayer and Myers 2006

Mayer, Lance, and Gay Myers. "Painting with Wax in Britain and America during the Eighteenth and Early Nineteenth Centuries." In *AIC Paintings Specialty Group Postprints: Papers Presented at the Thirty-third Annual Meeting of the American Institute for Conservation of Historic and Artistic Works, Minneapolis, Minnesota, June 8–13, 2005*, 18:53–66. Washington, D.C.: AIC, 2006.

Mayer and Myers 2010

Mayer, Lance, and Gay Myers. "American Painters and Varnishing: British, French and German Connections." *Journal of the Institute of Conservation* 33, no. 2 (2010): 117–27.

McIntosh 2004a

McIntosh, DeCourcy E. "New York's Favorite Pictures in the 1870s." *Magazine Antiques* 165, no. 4 (April 2004): 114–23.

McIntosh 2004b

McIntosh, DeCourcy E. "Merchandising America: American Views Published by the Maison Goupil." *Magazine Antiques* 166, no. 3 (September 2004): 124–33.

McIntosh 2006

McIntosh, DeCourcy E. "Fair and Square in the 1860s: A Meditation on the Worth of an Icon." *Magazine Antiques* 169, no. 2 (February 2006): 68–73.

McNulty 1983

McNulty, J. Bard. *Correspondence of Thomas Cole and Daniel Wadsworth: Letters in the Watkinson Library, Trinity College, Hartford, and in the New York State Library, Albany, New York.* Hartford, Conn.: Connecticut Historical Society, 1983.

Mérimée 1839

Mérimée, Jean-François-Léonor. *The Art of Painting in Oil and in Fresco: Being a History of the Various Processes and Materials Employed from Its Discovery, by Hubert and John Van Eyck, to the Present Time; Translated from the Original French Treatise of J. F. L. Mérimée, with Original Observations on the Rise and Progress of British Art, the French and English Chromatic Scales, and Theories of Colouring, by W. B. Sarsfield Taylor.* London: Whittaker, 1839. (Translation of the 1830 French edition.)

Merrifield 1967

Merrifield, Mary P. *Original Treatises on the Arts of Painting.* 2 vols. New York: Dover Publications, 1967. (First published in 1849 as *Original Treatises, Dating from the XIIth to XVIIIth Centuries on the Arts of Painting, in Oil, Miniature, Mosaic, and on Glass; of Gilding, Dyeing, and the Preparation of Colours and Artificial Gems.*)

Merrill 1992

Merrill, Ross. "Support Materials of Albert Bierstadt and the Hudson River Painters." In Katlan 1992 (see above), 525–28.

Merritt 1854

Merritt, Henry. *Dirt and Pictures Separated, in the Works of the Old Masters.* London: Holyoake, 1854. (Selections reprinted in Bomford and Leonard 2004 [see above], 69–72.)

Miles 1995

Miles, Ellen G. "1803—The Year of the Physiotrace." In *Painting and Portrait Making in the American Northeast: Dublin Seminar for New England Folklife Annual Proceedings, 24 through 26 June 1994,* edited by Peter Benes, 118–37. Boston: Boston University, 1995.

Miles et al. 1995

Miles, Ellen G., with Patricia Burda, Cynthia J. Mills, and Leslie K. Reinhardt. *American Paintings of the Eighteenth Century.* Washington, D.C.: National Gallery of Art, 1995.

Miller 1992

Miller, Lillian B., with an essay by Carol Eaton Hevner. *In Pursuit of Fame: Rembrandt Peale, 1778–1860*. Seattle: University of Washington Press/National Portrait Gallery, 1992.

Mills and White 1987.

Mills, John S., and Raymond White. *The Organic Chemistry of Museum Objects*. London: Butterworth, 1987.

Morgan 1939a

Morgan, John Hill. *Gilbert Stuart and His Pupils: Together with the Complete Notes on Painting by Matthew Harris Jouett from Conversations with Gilbert Stuart in 1816*. New York: New-York Historical Society, 1939.

Morgan 1939b

Morgan, John Hill. "Nathaniel Jocelyn's Record of the Palettes of Gilbert Stuart and of Washington Allston." *New-York Historical Society Quarterly Bulletin* 23 (1939): 131–34.

Morse 1914

Morse, Samuel Finley Breese. *Samuel F. B. Morse: His Letters and Journals*. Edited by Edward Lind Morse. 2 vols. Boston: Houghton Mifflin, 1914.

Muller 1987

Muller, Norman E. "Checklist of Boston Retailers in Artists' Materials: 1823–1887." In Katlan 1987 (see above), 443–60.

Müntz 1760

Müntz, Johann Heinrich. *Encaustic, or Count Caylus's Method of Painting in the Manner of the Ancients, to Which Is Added a Sure and Easy Method for Fixing of Crayons*. London: A. Webley, 1760.

Neff 1995

Neff, Emily Ballew. *John Singleton Copley in England*. Houston: Museum of Fine Arts, 1995.

Noble 1964

Noble, Louis Legrand. *The Life and Works of Thomas Cole*. Edited by Elliot S. Vessell. Cambridge, Mass.: Belknap Press of Harvard University Press, 1964. (The book was first published in 1853 by Noble as *"The Course of Empire," "Voyage of Life," and Other Pictures of Thomas Cole, N.A., with Selections from His Letters and Miscellaneous Writings, Illustrative of His Life, Character and Genius*.)

Noble and Boon 2007

Noble, Petra, and Jaap J. Boon. "Metal Soap Degradation of Oil Paintings: Aggregates, Increased Transparency and Efflorescence." In *AIC Paintings Specialty Group Postprints: Papers Presented at the Thirty-fourth Annual Meeting of the American Institute for Conservation of Historic and Artistic Works, Providence, Rhode Island, June 16–19, 2006*, 19:1–15. Washington, D.C.: AIC, 2007.

Northcote 1815

Northcote, James. *Supplement to the Memoirs of the Life, Writings, Discourses, and Professional Works of Sir Joshua Reynolds*. London: Henry Colburn, 1815.

Oedel 1992

Oedel, William T. "After Paris: Rembrandt Peale's Apollodorian Gallery." *Winterthur Portfolio* 27, no. 1 (Spring 1992): 1–27.

Oram 1810

Oram, William. *Precepts and Observations on the Art of Colouring in Landscape Painting, by the Late William Oram, Esq., of His Majesty's Board of Works; Arranged from the Author's Original MS. and Published by Charles Clarke, Esq. F.S.A.* London: Richard Taylor, 1810.

Osborn 1845

[Obsorn, Laughton.] *Handbook of Young Artists and Amateurs in Oilpainting.* New York: John Wiley and Son, 1845. (This book was reprinted without alteration many times in the second half of the nineteenth century.)

Paillot de Montabert 1829

Paillot de Montabert, Jacques-Nicholas. *Traité complet de la peinture.* 10 vols. Paris: Chez Bossange Père, 1829.

Paint and Painting 1982

Paint and Painting: An Exhibition and Working Studio Sponsored by Winsor & Newton to Celebrate Their 150th Anniversary. London: Tate Gallery, 1982.

Painter's Manual 1868

The Painter's Manual, Containing the Best Methods of, and the Latest Improvements in, House Painting, Sign Painting, Graining, Varnishing, Polishing, Staining, Gilding, Glazing…By a Practical Painter. New York: J. Haney, 1868.

Parker 1986

Parker, Peter J. "Useful Knowledge in Minute Particulars: Rembrandt Peale's 'Notes of the Painting Room.'" *Pennsylvania Magazine of History and Biography* 110, no. 1 (January 1986): 111–28.

Parry, Schweizer, and Kushel 1985

Parry, Ellwood C., III, Paul D. Schweizer, and Dan A. Kushel. *"The Voyage of Life" by Thomas Cole.* Utica, N.Y.: Munson-Williams-Proctor Institute, Museum of Art, 1985.

C. W. Peale 1983–2000

Peale, Charles Willson. *The Selected Papers of Charles Willson Peale and His Family.* Edited by Lillian B. Miller. 5 vols. New Haven, Conn.: Yale University Press, 1983–2000.

R. Peale 1810

Peale, Rembrandt. "Original Letter from Paris [to C.W. Peale and Rubens Peale]." *Port Folio* 4, no. 3 (September 1810): 275–79.

R. Peale 1811

Peale, Rembrandt. "To the President of the Institute of France." *Port Folio* 5, no. 1 (January 1811): 13–15. (Publishes a letter originally written September 3, 1810.)

R. Peale 1855a

Peale, Rembrandt. "Reminiscences. Charles Willson Peale." *Crayon* 1, no. 6 (February 7, 1855): 81–83.

R. Peale 1855b

Peale, Rembrandt. "Reminiscences. Exhibitions and Academies." *Crayon* 1, no. 19 (May 9, 1855): 290–91.

R. Peale 1855c

Peale, Rembrandt. "Reminiscences. The Stier Gallery." *Crayon* 2, no. 12 (September 19, 1855): 175.

R. Peale 1856

Peale, Rembrandt. "Reminiscences. Inventions." *Crayon* 3, pt. 3 (April 1856): 100–102.

R. Peale 1857a

Peale, Rembrandt. "Portraiture." *Crayon* 4, pt. 2 (February 1857): 44–45.

R. Peale 1857b

Peale, Rembrandt. "The Physiognotrace." *Crayon* 4, pt. 10 (October 1857): 307–8.

Plesters 1962

Plesters, Joyce. "Dark Varnishes—Some Further Comments." *Burlington Magazine* 104, no. 716 (November 1962): 452–60. (Reprinted in Bomford and Leonard 2004 [see above], 519–30.)

Porter 1826

Porter, Rufus. *A Select Collection of Valuable and Curious Arts, and Interesting Experiments, Which Are Well Explained and Warranted Genuine*. 5th ed. Concord, N.H.: William Brown, 1826.

Practical Treatise 1795

Practical Treatise on Painting in Oil-Colours. London: B. and J. White, 1795. (The copy in the Downs Collection, Winterthur Library, was owned and annotated by Rembrandt Peale; see R. Peale / *Practical Treatise* under Archival Sources below.)

Prime 1929

Prime, Alfred Coxe. *The Arts and Crafts in Philadelphia, Maryland, and South Carolina, Gleanings from Newspapers, 1721–1785*. Topsfield, Mass.: Walpole Society, 1929.

Prime 1875

Prime, Samuel Irenaeus. *The Life of Samuel F. B. Morse, LL.D., Inventor of the Electro-magnetic Recording Telegraph*. New York: D. Appleton, 1875.

Prown 1964

Prown, Jules David. "Two Manuscript Notebooks of Thomas Sully." *Yale University Library Gazette* 32 (October 1964): 73–79.

Prown 1966

Prown, Jules David. *John Singleton Copley*. 2 vols. Cambridge, Mass.: Harvard University Press, 1966.

Prown 2001a

Prown, Jules David. *Art as Evidence: Writings on Art and Material Culture*. New Haven, Conn.: Yale University Press, 2001.

Prown 2001b

Prown, Jules David. "An 'Anatomy Book' by John Singleton Copley." In Prown 2001a (see above), 12–25. (Originally published in *Art Quarterly* 26 [Spring 1963]: 31–46.)

Prown 2001c

Prown, Jules David. "Charles Willson Peale in London." In Prown 2001a (see above), 133–58. (Originally published in *New Perspectives on Charles Willson Peale: A 250th Anniversary Celebration*, edited by Lillian B. Miller and David C. Ward, 29–50.)

Prown 2001d

Prown, Jules David. "Trumbull as a History Painter." In Prown 2001a (see above), 159–85. (Originally published in Cooper et al. 1982 [see above], 22–41.)

Rather 2004

Rather, Susan. "Benjamin West, John Galt, and the Biography of 1816." *Art Bulletin* 86, no. 2 (June 2004): 323–45.

Rice 1979

Rice, Danielle. "The Fire of the Ancients: The Encaustic Painting Revival, 1755 to 1812." PhD diss., Yale University, 1979.

Richardson 1944

Richardson, Edgar Preston. "Allston and the Development of Romantic Color." *[Art] Quarterly* (Winter 1944): 33–57.

Richardson 1948

Richardson, Edgar Preston. *Washington Allston: A Study of the Romantic Artist in America.* Chicago: University of Chicago Press, 1948.

Ridner 1850

Ridner, John P. *The Artist's Chromatic Hand-Book; Being a Practical Treatise on Pigments, Their Properties and Uses in Painting, to Which Is Added, a Few Remarks on Vehicles and Varnishes; Chiefly a Compilation from the Best Authorities.* New York: George P. Putnam, 1850.

Robertson 1897

Robertson, Andrew. *Letters and Papers of Andrew Robertson, Miniature Painter to His Late Royal Highness. …* 2nd ed. N.p.: Eyre and Spottiswoode, 1897.

Saunders 1995

Saunders, Richard H. *John Smibert: Colonial America's First Portrait Painter.* New Haven, Conn.: Yale University Press, 1995.

Saunders and Miles 1987

Saunders, Richard H., and Ellen G. Miles. *American Colonial Portraits, 1700–1776.* Washington, D.C.: National Portrait Gallery, 1987.

Sawitsky 1957

Sawitsky, Susan. "Abraham Delanoy in New Haven." *New-York Historical Society Quarterly* 41 (April 1957): 193–206.

Schimmelman 1984a

Schimmelman, Janice G. "Books on Drawing and Painting Techniques Available in Eighteenth-Century American Libraries and Bookstores." *Winterthur Portfolio* 19, no. 2/3 (Summer 1984): 193–205.

Schimmelman 1984b

Schimmelman, Janice G. "A Checklist of European Treatises and Essays on Aesthetics Available in America through 1815." *Proceedings of the American Antiquarian Society* 93 (1984): 95–195.

Schimmelman 2007

Schimmelman, Janice G. *Books on Art in Early America: Books on Art, Aesthetics and Instruction Available in American Libraries and Bookstores through 1815.* New Castle, Del.: Oak Knoll Press, 2007.

Schmid 1948

Schmid, Frederic. *The Practice of Painting.* London: Faber and Faber, 1948.

Schweizer 1985

Schweizer, Paul D. "'The Voyage of Life:' A Chronology." In Parry, Schweizer, and Kushel 1985 (see above), 6–53.

Seldes et al. 2002

Seldes, Alicia, José E. Burúcua, Gabriela Siracusano, Marta S. Maier, and Gonzalo E. Abad. "Green, Yellow and Red Pigments in South American Painting, 1610–1780." *Journal of the American Institute for Conservation* 41, no. 3 (Fall/Winter 2002): 225–42.

Shank 1984

Shank, J. William. "John Singleton Copley's Portraits: A Technical Study of Three Representative Examples." *Journal of the American Institute for Conservation* 23, no. 2 (Spring 1984): 130–52.

Sheldon 1881

Sheldon, George William. *American Painters*. New York: D. Appleton, 1881.

Silberfeld 1965

Silberfeld, Kay. "The Lost Painting of Thomas Cole." *Museum News* 43, no. 7 (March 1965): 31–38.

Simon 1987

Simon, Robin. *The Portrait in Britain and America, with a Biographical Dictionary of Portrait Painters, 1680–1914*. Boston: G.K. Hall, 1987.

Sizer 1967

Sizer, Theodore. *The Works of Colonel John Trumbull, Artist of the American Revolution*. Rev. ed. New Haven, Conn.: Yale University Press, 1967.

Staiti 1989

Staiti, Paul J. *Samuel F. B. Morse*. Cambridge: Cambridge University Press, 1989.

Stebbins 1978

Stebbins, Theodore E., Jr. *Close Observation: Selected Oil Sketches by Frederic E. Church, from the Collections of the Cooper-Hewitt Museum*. Washington, D.C.: Smithsonian Institution Press, 1978.

Stemmler 1984

Stemmler, Joan K. "Cennino, Cumberland, Blake and Early Painting Techniques." *Blake, An Illustrated Quarterly* (Spring 1984): 145–49.

Stoner 1990a

Stoner, Joyce Hill. "Art Historical and Technical Evaluation of Works by Three Nineteenth-Century Artists: Allston, Whistler and Ryder." In *Appearance, Opinion, Change: Evaluating the Look of Paintings: Papers Given at a Conference Held Jointly by the United Kingdom Institute for Conservation and the Association of Art Historians, June 1990*, 36–41. London: UKIC, 1990.

Stoner 1990b

Stoner, Joyce Hill. "Washington Allston: Poems, Veils and 'Titian's dirt.'" *Journal of the American Institute for Conservation* 29, no. 1 (Spring 1990): 1–12.

Stoner, Schmiegel, and Carlson 1979

Stoner, Joyce Hill, Karol Schmiegel, and Janice H. Carlson. "A Portrait by C.W. Peale Restored by C. Volkmar: Techniques of an 18th-Century Artist and a 19th-Century Restorer." In *Preprints of Papers Presented at the Seventh Annual Meeting of the American Institute for Conservation of Historic and Artistic Works, Toronto, Canada, 30 May–1 June 1979*, 139–48. Washington, D.C.: AIC, 1979.

Strong 1952

Strong, George Templeton. *The Diary of George Templeton Strong*. Edited by Allan Nevins and Milton Halsey Thomas. 4 vols. New York: Macmillan, 1952.

Stroud 2002

Stroud, Patricia Tyson. "Point Breeze: Joseph Bonaparte's American Retreat." *Magazine Antiques* 162, no. 4 (October 2002): 130–39.

Stuart 1861

Stuart, Gilbert. "Remarks on Art, by Gilbert Stuart, 1816." *Crayon* 8, pt. 3 (March 1861): 49–50. (These remarks were edited and rearranged from Jouett 1816 [see above].)

Stuart 1877

Stuart, Jane. "Anecdotes of Gilbert Stuart by His Daughter." *Scribner's Monthly* 14 (July 1877): 376–82.

Sully 1873

Sully, Thomas. *Hints to Young Painters.* New York: Reinhold Publishing, 1965. (Reprint of original 1873 edition.)

Sutherland 2010

Sutherland, Ken. "Bleached Shellac Picture Varnishes: Characterization and Case Studies." *Journal of the Institute of Conservation* 33, no. 2 (2010): 129–45.

Sweeney 1994

Sweeney, J. Gray. "The Advantages of Genius and Virtue: Thomas Cole's Influence, 1848–58." In Truettner and Wallach 1994 (see below), 113–35.

Sweetser 1879

Sweetser, Moses Foster. *Allston.* Boston: Houghton Osgood, 1879.

Talley 1986

Talley, M. Kirby, Jr. "'All good pictures crack:' Sir Joshua Reynolds's Practice and Studio." In *Reynolds*, edited by Nicholas Penny, 55–70. London: Royal Academy of Arts, 1986.

Talley 2005

Talley, M. Kirby, Jr. "An Old Fiddle on a Green Lawn: The Perverse Infatuation with Dirty Pictures." *Metropolitan Museum Journal* 40 (2005): 37–50.

Talley and Groen 1975

Talley, M. Kirby, Jr., and Karin Groen. "Thomas Bardwell and His Practice of Painting: A Comparative Investigation between Described and Actual Painting Technique." *Studies in Conservation* 20, no. 2 (May 1975): 44–108.

Tingry 1804

Tingry, Pierre Francois. *The Painter and Varnisher's Guide; or, A Treatise, Both in Theory and Practice, on the Art of Making and Applying Varnishes; on the Different Kinds of Painting; and on the Method of Preparing Colours Both Simple and Compound: with New Observations and Experiments on Copal; on the Nature of Substances Employed in the Composition of Varnishes and of Colours; and on Various Processes Used in the Art.* London: G. Kearsley, 1804. (First published in French in Geneva in 1803.)

Tomlinson 1976

Tomlinson, Juliette. *The Paintings and the Journal of Joseph Whiting Stock.* Middletown, Conn.: Wesleyan University Press, 1976.

Torchia 1989

Torchia, Robert Wilson. *John Neagle, Philadelphia Portrait Painter.* Philadelphia: Historical Society of Pennsylvania, 1989.

Torchia, Chotner, and Miles 1998

Torchia, Robert Wilson, with Deborah Chotner and Ellen G. Miles. *American Paintings of the Nineteenth Century, Part 2.* Washington, D.C.: National Gallery of Art, 1998.

Towers 1830

Towers, William. *Every Man His Own Painter: Or a Complete Guide to Painting and Graining; Containing General Instructions in the Art of Preparing, Compounding, and Applying All Kinds of Paints, and Making Various Varnishes for House, Chair, and Furniture Paintings and Graining.* Utica, N.Y.: J. Colwell, 1830.

Townsend 1995

Townsend, Joyce H. "Painting Techniques and Materials of Turner and Other British Artists, 1775–1875." In *Historical Painting Techniques, Materials and Studio Practice: Preprints of a Symposium, University of Leiden, the Netherlands, 26–29 June 1995,* edited by Arie Wallert, Erma Hermens, and Marja Peek, 176–85. Los Angeles: Getty Conservation Institute, 1995.

Townsend 1996

Townsend, Joyce H. *Turner's Painting Techniques.* 2nd ed. London: Tate Gallery, 1996.

Townsend 2002

Townsend, Joyce H. "The Materials Used by British Oil Painters throughout the Nineteenth Century." *Reviews in Conservation* 3 (2002): 46–55.

Townsend et al. 1998

Townsend, Joyce H., Leslie Carlyle, Aviva Burnstock, Marianne Odlyha, and Jaap J. Boon. "Nineteenth-Century Paint Media: The Formulation and Properties of Megilps." In *Painting Techniques: History, Materials and Studio Practice; Contributions to the Dublin Congress, 7–11 September 1998,* edited by Ashok Roy and Perry Smith, 205–10. London: International Institute for Conservation of Historic and Artistic Works, 1998.

Townsend, Ridge, and Hackney 2004

Townsend, Joyce H., Jacqueline Ridge, and Stephen Hackney. *Pre-Raphaelite Painting Techniques: 1848–56.* London: Tate Gallery, 2004.

Truettner and Wallach 1994

Truettner, William H., and Alan Wallach, eds. *Thomas Cole, Landscape into History.* New Haven, Conn.: Yale University Press / National Museum of American Art, 1994.

Trumble and Aronson 2008

Trumble, Angus, and Mark Aronson. *Benjamin West and the Venetian Secret.* Booklet for an exhibition held September 18, 2008–January 4, 2009. New Haven, Conn.: Yale Center for British Art, 2008.

Trumbull 1841

Trumbull, John. *Autobiography of John Trumbull, from 1756 to 1841.* New York: Wiley and Putnam, 1841.

Turner 1833

Turner, Maria. *Young Ladies' Assistant in Drawing and Painting.* Cincinnati: Corey and Fairbank, 1833.

Vagts, Gerber, and Newman 1996
Vagts, Lydia, Monica Gerber, and Richard Newman. "'A very wonderfull performance:' The Paintings of John Singleton Copley in America." In *AIC Paintings Specialty Group Postprints: Papers Presented at the Twenty-fourth Annual Meeting of the American Institute for Conservation of Historic and Artistic Works, Norfolk, Virginia, June 14–15, 1996*, 9:68–75. Washington, D.C.: AIC, 1996.

Valuable Secrets 1795
Valuable Secrets Concerning Arts and Trades; or, Approved Directions, from the Best Artists. Norwich, Conn.: Thomas Hubbard, 1795.

Vanderhoof 1977
Vanderhoof, Ann Siegel. "Artists' Suppliers and Supplies in Eighteenth-Century America." MA thesis, University of Delaware, 1977.

Wallach 1994
Wallach, Alan. "Thomas Cole: Landscape and the Course of American Empire." In Truettner and Wallach 1994 (see above), 23–111.

Ward 2004
Ward, David C. *Charles Willson Peale: Art and Selfhood in the Early Republic.* Berkeley: University of California Press, 2004.

Watin 1772
Watin, Jean-Félix. *L'Art de faire et d'employer le vernis, ou l'art du vernisseur, auquel on a joint ceux du peintre & du doreur.* Paris: Chez Quillau, 1772.

Watin 1774
Watin, Jean-Félix. *L'Art du peintre, doreur, vernisseur: Ouvrage utile aux artistes & aux amateurs….* Paris: Chez Grangé, 1774.

Watin 1778
Watin, Jean-Félix. *L'Art du peintre, doreur, vernisseur: Ouvrage utile aux artistes & aux amateurs….* Liège: Chez D. de Boubers, 1778.

Weber 1923
Weber, Frederick W. *Artists' Pigments, Their Chemical and Physical Properties.* New York: D. Van Nostrand, 1923.

Webber 2001
Webber, Sandra L. "The Discovered Hand: John Singleton Copley's Underdrawing Techniques." *Porticus, Journal of the Memorial Art Gallery of the University of Rochester* 20 (2001): 48–58.

Webster 1853
Webster, Daniel. *The Great Orations and Senatorial Speech of Daniel Webster.* Rochester, N.Y.: Wilbur N. Hayward, 1853.

Wehlte 1975
Wehlte, Kurt. *The Materials and Techniques of Painting.* Translated by Ursus Dix. New York: Van Nostrand Reinhold, 1975. (Translated from 1967 German edition.)

Wescott 1886
Wescott, Thompson. *A History of Philadelphia from the Time of the First Settlements….* Philadelphia: Brinton Coxe, 1886. (A collection of newspaper clippings that originally appeared in the [Philadelphia] *Sunday Dispatch.*)

White and Kirby 2001
White, Raymond, and Jo Kirby. "A Survey of Nineteenth- and Early Twentieth-Century Varnish Compositions Found on a Selection of Paintings in the National Gallery Collection." *National Gallery Technical Bulletin* 22 (2001): 64–84.

Whitley 1928

Whitley, William T. *Artists and Their Friends in England, 1700–1799.* 2 vols. London: Medici Society, 1928.

Whitley 1932

Whitley, William T. *Gilbert Stuart.* Cambridge: Harvard University Press, 1932.

Williams 1937

Williams, Hermann W., Jr. "Romney's Palette." *Technical Studies in the Field of the Fine Arts* 6, no. 1 (July 1937): 19–23.

Williams 1939

Williams, Hermann W., Jr. "Mount's 'Bargaining for a Horse.'" *Technical Studies in the Field of the Fine Arts* 8, no. 1 (July 1939): 10–11.

Williams 1941

Williams, Hermann W., Jr. "Some Observations on Painting by William S. Mount." *Technical Studies in the Field of the Fine Arts* 10, no. 1 (July 1941): 33–36.

Williams 1878

Williams, W. *The Art of Landscape Painting in Oil Colors from the 34th London Edition.* Edited by Susan N. Carter. New York: G. P. Putnam's Sons, 1878. (Annotated American edition of a much reprinted English book published earlier by Winsor & Newton.)

Wolbers 1988

Wolbers, Richard C. "Aspects of the Examination and Cleaning of Two Portraits by Richard and William Jennys." In *Preprints of Papers Presented at the Sixteenth Annual Meeting of the American Institute for Conservation of Historic and Artistic Works, New Orleans, Louisiana, June 1–5, 1988,* 245–60. Washington, D.C.: AIC, 1988.

Woodcock 1996

Woodcock, Sally. "Body Colour: The Misuse of Mummy." *Conservator* 20 (1996): 87–94.

Wouldhuysen-Keller 1994

Wouldhuysen-Keller, Renate, and Paul Wouldhuysen-Keller. "The History of Egg White Varnishes." *Hamilton Kerr Institute Bulletin* 2 (1994): 90–141.

Wright 1999

Wright, Jim. "The Development of Martin Johnson Heade's Painting Technique." In *Martin Johnson Heade,* by Theodore E. Stebbins, Jr., 169–83. New Haven, Conn.: Yale University Press / Museum of Fine Arts, Boston, 1999.

Zucker 1980

Zucker, Joyce. "A Preliminary Pigment Analysis of Thirteen Scripture Paintings." In *A Remnant in the Wilderness: New York Dutch Scripture History Paintings of the Early Eighteenth Century,* 63–68. N.p.: Bard College Center / Albany Institute of History and Art, 1980.

Zucker 1999

Zucker, Joyce. "From the Ground Up: The Ground in Nineteenth-Century American Pictures." *Journal of the American Institute for Conservation* 38, no. 1 (Spring 1999): 3–20.

Zucker and Boon 2007

Zucker, Joyce, and Jaap J. Boon. "Opaque to Transparent: Paint Film Defects in the Work of Frederic Church and the Hudson River School." In *AIC Paintings Specialty*

Group Postprints: Papers Presented at the Thirty-fourth Annual Meeting of the American Institute for Conservation of Historic and Artistic Works, Providence, Rhode Island, June 16–19, 2006, 19:33–41. Washington, D.C.: AIC, 2007.

ARCHIVAL SOURCES*

*When Archives of American Art microfilm exists for a particular group of papers, that information has been provided to assist other researchers, even in cases where the authors consulted and cite the originals.

Birch "Life"

Birch, William Russell. "The Life and Anecdotes of William Russell Birch, Enamel Painter." Ca. 1800. Philadelphia, Historical Society of Pennsylvania, 1581. Archives of American Art, microfilm roll P20, frames 639ff.

Carroll & Crosby Invoice Book

Carroll & Crosby (Norwich, Conn.). Invoice Book. 1843–45. Winterthur, Del., Winterthur Library and Museum, Joseph Downs Collection of Manuscripts and Printed Ephemera, folio 285.

Cogdell Diaries / Letterbooks

Cogdell, John Stevens. Diaries and Letterbooks. 1808–41. 6 vols. Winterthur, Del., Winterthur Library and Museum, Joseph Downs Collection of Manuscripts and Printed Ephemera, col. 252.

Cole Journals

Cole, Thomas. Journals. 1834–38 and 1838–48. Albany, New York State Library, SC10635. Archives of American Art, microfilm rolls ALC 1–4.

Cole Papers DIA

Cole, Thomas. Papers. Detroit Institute of Arts. Archives of American Art, microfilm rolls D6, D39–40.

Cole Papers NYSL

Cole, Thomas. Papers. 1821–63. Albany, New York State Library, SC10635. Archives of American Art, microfilm rolls ALC 1–4. (Includes journals 1834–38 and 1838–48; photocopies of some of this collection are available at the New-York Historical Society.)

Dickinson "Remarks"

Dickinson, Obadiah. "Remarks on Painting." Ca. 1835–46. Winterthur, Del., Winterthur Library and Museum, Joseph Downs Collection of Manuscripts and Printed Ephemera, doc. 704.

Earl Papers

Earl, Ralph E.W. Papers. 1810–38. Worcester, Mass., American Antiquarian Society, Mss. Dept., Mss. Box E.

Eichholtz Daybook

Eichholtz, Jacob. Daybook. 1805–17. Philadelphia, Historical Society of Pennsylvania, (Phi) Am 06149. (Other volumes are in the Lancaster [Pennsylvania] Historical Society.)

Farington "Provis"

Farington, Joseph. "Provis's Process or the Venetian Secret." 1797. London, Royal Academy of Arts.

Hevner Annotation

Hevner [Soltis], Carol Eaton. Annotation, Comparison, and Appendix, Accompanying a Transcription of Rembrandt Peale's "Notes of the Painting Room." 1986. (Copies at the Historical Society of Pennsylvania and at the Library and Archives of the Philadelphia Museum of Art.)

Humphry Memorandum-Book

Humphry, Ozias. Memorandum-Book. 1772–97; 1777–95. 2 vols. London, British Library, ADMS. 22949.

Lanman Papers GRI

Lanman, Charles. Papers. 1845–1985. Los Angeles, Getty Research Institute, 930071.

Marshall Waste Book

Christopher Marshall and Son. Waste Book. 1762–68. Philadelphia, Historical Society of Pennsylvania, (Phi) Am. 916.

Martin Account Book

Martin, Nathaniel. Account Book. Ca. 1790–1810. Hartford, Conn., Connecticut Historical Society, Acct. bk. coll., microfilm roll 86862.

Mason "Recollections"

Mason, Jonathan. "Recollections of a Septuageinarian [sic]." 1866?–81. 3 vols. Winterthur, Del., Winterthur Library and Museum, Joseph Downs Collection of Manuscripts and Printed Ephemera, doc. 30.

Mount Diary LIMAA

Mount, William Sidney. Papers. 1830–74. Stony Brook, N.Y., Long Island Museum of American Art, History and Carriages, KSa13. Archives of American Art, microfilm rolls SM1–SM4. (Includes diaries, correspondence, notebooks, and other papers. Selections of the diary entries and letters have been published in Frankenstein 1975 [see above].)

Mount Papers N-YHS

Mount, William Sidney. Correspondence and Papers. 1833–68. New York, New-York Historical Society, Mss coll. Archives of American Art, microfilm roll A.

Neagle Blotter

Neagle, John. Blotter. 1825–52. Philadelphia, Historical Society of Pennsylvania, (Phi) 2112. Archives of American Art, microfilm rolls 3656–57.

Neagle Cashbook

Neagle, John. Cashbook. 1832–42. Philadelphia, Historical Society of Pennsylvania, (Phi) 2112. Archives of American Art, microfilm rolls 3656–57.

Neagle Commonplace Book

Neagle, John. Commonplace Book. 1839–. Philadelphia, Historical Society of Pennsylvania, (Phi) 448/Am. 108. Archives of American Art, microfilm roll P23, frames 453–512. (Neagle wrote that his Commonplace Book was "commenced in 1839," but it includes information copied from a memorandum book written "years before;" he used it until at least 1854.)

Neagle "Hints"

Neagle, John. "Hints for a Painter with Regard to his Method of Study &c." Undated [on paper watermarked 1818; first dated entry is signed "J. Neagle 1826"]. Philadelphia, American Philosophical Society, BN125.

Neagle Memoranda

Neagle, John. Memoranda. 1827–61. Philadelphia, Historical Society of Pennsylvania, (Phi) 2112. Archives of American Art, microfilm rolls 3656–57.

Neagle Miscellaneous

Neagle, John. Miscellaneous. Undated. Philadelphia, American Philosophical Society, B N125p box 1. (Loose sheets about a variety of topics, including pigments, varnishing, and restoring paintings, with notes on Sully's palette.)

Neagle "Receipts"

Neagle, John. "Receipts for making Megellup, Varnish and Drying oil; also for cleaning pictures, preparing grounds, restoring surfaces, setting pallates, toning pictures, tempering colours, producing tints &c. &c. &c." Inscribed 1825 [has entries from earlier and later]. Philadelphia, American Philosophical Society, BN125.

Neagle Student Notebook

Neagle, John. Student Notebook. 1824. Philadelphia, Historical Society of Pennsylvania, (Phi) 2112. Archives of American Art, microfilm rolls 3656–57.

C. W. Peale Memorandum Book

Peale, Charles Willson. Memorandum Book. 1794–. Philadelphia, American Philosophical Society, Peale-Sellers Papers, B P31. (Some pages were apparently used upside down by Rembrandt Peale.)

M. J. Peale "Oil Painting"

Peale, Mary Jane. "Oil Painting." 1851 and after. Philadelphia, American Philosophical Society, Peale Family Papers, B P31.

R. Peale Miscellaneous

Peale, Rembrandt. Miscellaneous notes, recipes, letters. Various dates, or undated. Philadelphia, American Philosophical Society, Peale Family Papers and Peale-Sellers Papers, B P31.

R. Peale "Notes"

Peale, Rembrandt. "Notes of the Painting Room, the experience of more than half a century." 1850–52. Philadelphia, Historical Society of Pennsylvania, Sartain Family Collection, 1650. Archives of American Art, microfilm roll P28. (The National Academy of Design has two earlier drafts of the manuscript. Carol Eaton Hevner [Soltis] did an annotated transcription of the HSP manuscript in 1986 [see above]. Since the pagination of the manuscript is confusing, Hevner [Soltis] used a sequential numbering system where each page reflects a page of the original manuscript; our page citations follow hers.)

R. Peale Palettes

Peale, Rembrandt. Palettes. Undated. Philadelphia, American Philosophical Society, Peale Family Papers, B P 31, no. 51.

R. Peale / *Practical Treatise*

Practical Treatise on Painting in Oil-Colours. 1795. London: B. and J. White. Winterthur, Del., Winterthur Library and Museum, Joseph Downs Collection of Manuscripts and Printed Ephemera. (This copy is signed and dated by Rembrandt Peale on the title page in ink: "REM: PEALE. 1795," and there are many annotations by Peale, done on at least two occasions.)

Rubens Peale "Journal"

Peale, Rubens. "Journal of Woodland Farm." 1855–65. Archives of American Art, microfilm roll D10.

Schrack Daybook

[C.] Schrack & Company, Philadelphia. Records. 1823–1933. Philadelphia, Historical Society of Pennsylvania, (Phi) 2080. (Records are divided between the HSP and Eleutherian Mills Historical Library, Greenville, Delaware.)

Shaw Palette

Shaw, Joshua. Palette. Ca. 1820. Philadelphia, Historical Society of Pennsylvania, (Phi) Am. 8653/1880.

Sully "Hints"

Sully, Thomas. "Hints for Pictures." 1809–71. 2 vols. New Haven, Conn., Yale University, Beinecke Library, Gen. mss. 196. Archives of American Art, microfilm roll N18. (Described in Yale's catalogue under Notebooks. The AAA microfilm is of a typescript housed at the New York Public Library; our citations use the frame numbers of the AAA microfilm.)

Sully "Incidents"

Sully, Thomas. "Incidents in the life of Thomas Sully, chiefly of painting." 1871. New York, Frick Art Reference Library. (A 1935 MA thesis by James Whitney Fosburgh, also at the Frick, discusses this manuscript.)

Sully Journal

Sully, Thomas. Journal. Vol. 1: Memoir (1792–1801) and Journal (1801–37). Vol. 2 Journal (1837–46). Philadelphia, Historical Society of Pennsylvania, 175 [Dreer] 188.1–2. Archives of American Art, microfilm roll N18. (The AAA microfilm is of a typescript in the New York Public Library; our citations use the frame numbers of the AAA microfilm. The section from September 18, 1837, to July 29, 1838, during Sully's second trip to England, is published in Barratt 2000b [see above], 75–197.)

Sully Letterbook

Sully, Thomas. Letters from England. 1837–38. 2 vols. Winterthur, Del., Winterthur Library and Museum, Joseph Downs Collection of Manuscripts and Printed Ephemera, col. 164.

Sully "Memoirs"

Sully, Thomas. "Memoirs of the Professional Life of Thomas Sully, Dedicated to his Brother Artists." 1851–59. Winterthur, Del., Winterthur Library and Museum, Joseph Downs Collection of Manuscripts and Printed Ephemera, col. 164. Archives of American Art, microfilm roll 4565 (called "Private Memorandum"). (The majority of the text was written in 1851, followed by short sections added in 1858 and 1859.)

Sully Sketchbook

Sully, Thomas. Sketchbook: Lessons in Landscape Painting. Ca. 1814–38. New Haven, Conn., Yale Center for British Art, B1981.25.2737.

Trumbull Inventories

Trumbull, John. Inventories. 1803–13. New-York Historical Society, Trumbull Papers, Mss. coll. BV Trumbull.

Trumbull Papers CHS

Trumbull, John. Papers. 1769–1838. Hartford, Conn., Connecticut Historical Society, microfilm roll 80006, reels I and II.

Trumbull Papers NYPL

Trumbull, John. Papers. 1780–1840. New York Public Library, Mss. col. 3038. Archives of American Art, microfilm roll N26.

Trumbull Papers Yale

Trumbull, John. Papers. 1750–1961. New Haven, Conn., Yale University Library, Manuscript and Archives, MS 506, microfilm HM 221.

INDEX

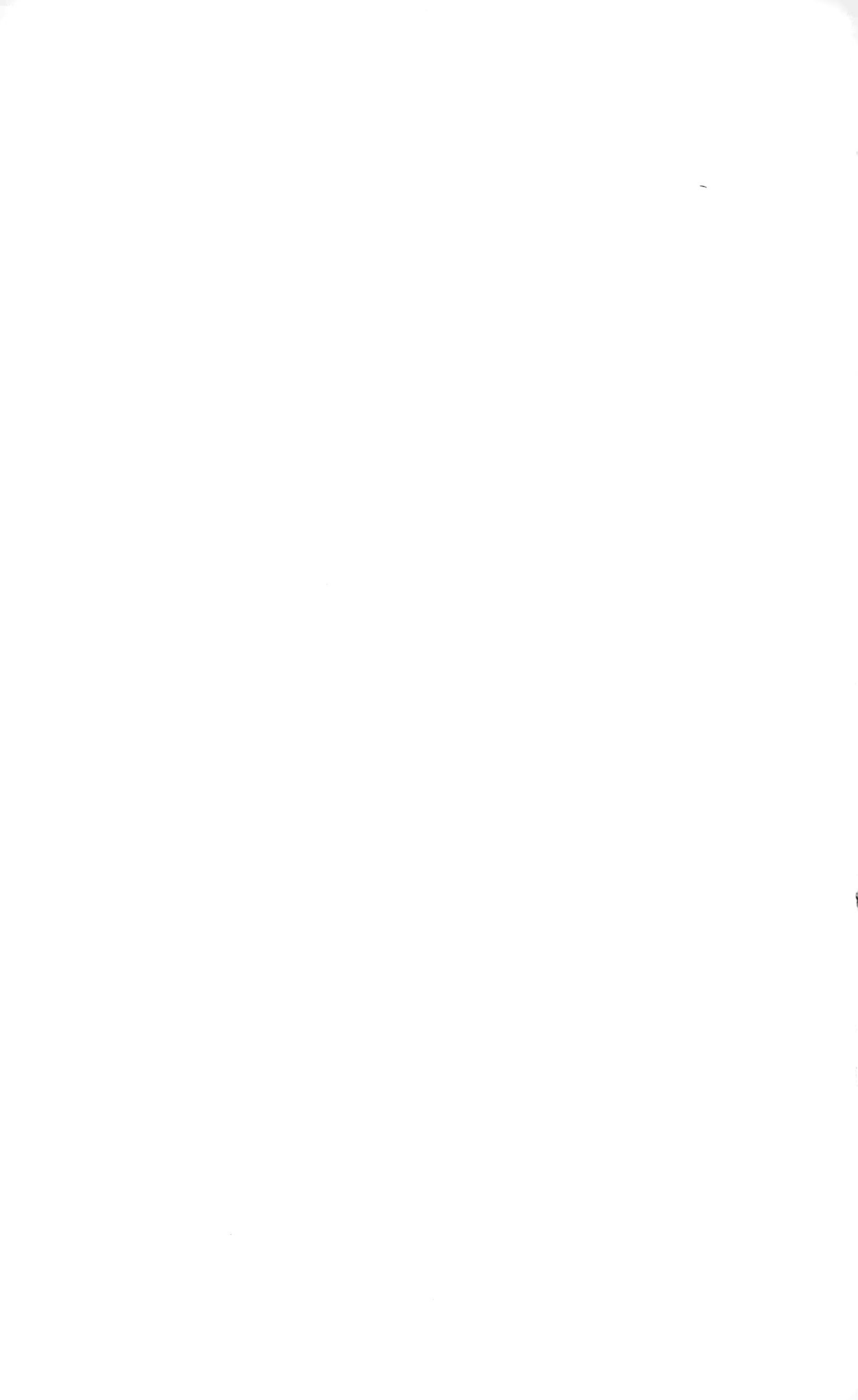